"THE
SONS
OF PIGS
AND APES"

Additional Praise for *"The Sons of Pigs and Apes"*

"Although Neil Kressel's magisterial essay is primarily addressed at those in the West who pretend that antisemitism is no more than a tragic memory, it is also of great value for those Muslims who dream of, and increasingly fight for, a free society. Kressel's message is clear: fighting anti-Jewish ideas and practices must be an integral part of any strategy for freedom in Muslim countries."

— AMIR TAHERI, AUTHOR OF *THE PERSIAN NIGHT*

"Shines new light on antisemitism in the Muslim world, and shows how hatred of the Jewish people remains a potent—even deadly—force in modern times. Kressel ably distinguishes between legitimate criticism of Israel and antisemitism and debunks the false accusation that the Jewish community wields the charge of antisemitism as a bludgeon to quash anti-Israel criticism."

— ABRAHAM H. FOXMAN, NATIONAL DIRECTOR, ANTI-DEFAMATION LEAGUE

"Many books have recently been written about Islamic antisemitism, but none is as precise, scrupulous, and well-informed as Neil Kressel's *'The Sons of Pigs and Apes,'* which is a thorough unmasking of some disgraceful attitudes, and of the widespread failure to confront them."

— IRFAN KHAWAJA, CHAIR, DEPARTMENT OF PHILOSOPHY, FELICIAN COLLEGE

"An important but disquieting book. Neil Kressel's skill as a social scientist is manifest throughout the work and his arguments persuasive. To cure a malaise one must first confront its symptoms and seek their underlying causes. In dealing with Muslim antisemitism, Kressel's work is more than helpful—it is essential."

— MICHAEL BERENBAUM, FORMER DIRECTOR OF THE UNITED STATES HOLOCAUST RESEARCH INSTITUTE AT THE U.S. HOLOCAUST MEMORIAL MUSEUM, DIRECTOR OF THE SIGI ZIERING INSTITUTE AT THE AMERICAN JEWISH UNIVERSITY, AND EDITOR OF *NOT YOUR FATHER'S ANTISEMITISM*

"A brave and important book. Kressel asks the question that few dare to pose: why are today's anti-racists and intelligentsia so silent on antisemitism?"

— RIGHT HONOURABLE DR. DENIS MACSHANE, MEMBER OF PARLIAMENT FOR ROTHERHAM, FORMER BRITISH MINISTER FOR EUROPE, FORMER CHAIR OF THE HOUSE OF COMMONS ALL-PARTY COMMITTEE OF INQUIRY INTO ANTISEMITISM IN BRITAIN

Also by Neil J. Kressel

Bad Faith: The Danger of Religious Extremism

Mass Hate: The Global Rise of Genocide and Terror

Related Titles from Potomac Books

Searching for a King: Muslim Nonviolence and the Future of Islam
—Jeffry R. Halverson

Straightening the Bell Curve: How Stereotypes about Black Masculinity Drive Research on Race and Intelligence
—Constance Hilliard

"THE SONS OF PIGS AND APES"

Muslim Antisemitism and the Conspiracy of Silence

Neil J. Kressel

Potomac Books
Washington, D.C.

Library of Congress Cataloging-in-Publication Data
Kressel, Neil J.
  "The sons of pigs and apes" : Muslim antisemitism and the conspiracy of silence / Neil J. Kressel.
     p. cm.
  Includes bibliographical references and index.
  ISBN 978-1-59797-702-9 (hardcover : alk. paper)
  ISBN 978-1-59797-811-8 (electronic)
  1. Antisemitism—Islamic countries. 2. Islam—Relations—Judaism. 3. Judaism—Relations—Islam. I. Title.
  DS146.I74K74 2012
  305.892'401767—dc23

                                                        2012018888

Printed in the United States of America on acid-free paper that meets the American National Standards Institute Z39-48 Standard.

Potomac Books
22841 Quicksilver Drive
Dulles, Virginia 20166

First Edition

10 9 8 7 6 5 4 3 2 1

Contents

Acknowledgments

It has not been my intention to preach to any choir in *"The Sons of Pigs and Apes,"* and I suspect that even generally well-intentioned and sympathetic souls may find themselves disagreeing with parts—perhaps large parts—of what I have written. The history of relations between Muslims and Jews, after all, has given rise to endless nuances of interpretation, and reasonable people may disagree. I ask only that readers try to understand and share my objective: to combat a dangerous bigotry so that Muslim-Jewish relations may develop on a firm and lasting foundation of truth and good will. While I have not focused on anti-Muslim bigotry in this volume, I hope I have made clear that it too must be opposed with vigor.

Although any errors of fact and interpretation in this book are, of course, my own, I have benefitted greatly from the assistance, counsel, and prior research of many wise people. Perhaps most significant was my affiliation with the now-shuttered Yale Initiative for the Interdisciplinary Study of Antisemitism, created and directed by Charles Small.

YIISA brought to campus many of the world's leading luminaries on today's antisemitism and related issues. In April 2008 I attended a thought-provoking YIISA conference on "Understanding the Challenge of Iran." The following year I participated in another stimulating event: the Dr. James Sacks Conference on psychological dimensions of contemporary antisemitism, which was cosponsored by the Anti-Defamation League. Most important of all was the superb August 2010 conference on "Global Antisemitism: A Crisis of Modernity." Although this conference was denounced in harsh terms by Maen Rashid Areikat, the Palestine Liberation Organization's representative in the United States, and by several members of the anti-Israel radical Left (none of whom I believe attended the event), the presenters included more than a hundred top scholars from around the world. These scholars represented a broad range of political opinion—left, center, and right—on the Arab-Israeli conflict, antisemitism, and other matters. Collectively, they had authored hundreds of books and journal articles and brought to the topic an unusually diverse set of backgrounds and methodological training. Although some of the presenters might, I think, disagree with parts of this book, I found the conference to be one of the best I had attended in recent years.

At various YIISA conferences, the YIISA lecture series, and other events, I had the opportunity to hear the views and insights of many scholars, journalists, political leaders, and human rights activists from around the world, including Hadassa Ben-Itto, David Cesarani, Phyllis Chesler, Patrick Clawson, Shoaib Choudhury, Irwin Cotler, Shalem Coulibaly, Robert Fine, András Gerö, Nora Gold, Daniel Goldhagen, Erich Goldhagen, Diana Gregor, Yossi Klein Halevi, Jeffrey Herf, Anne Herzberg, David Hirsh, Gilbert Kahn, Mehrangiz Kar, Berthe Kayitesi, Yaakov Kirschen, Jytte Klausen, Barry Kosmin, Richard Landes, Jacob Lassner, Leslie Lebl, Meir Litvak, Kenneth Marcus, David Menashri, Menahem Milson, Stephen Norwood, Orly Rahimiyan, Paul Lawrence Rose, Alvin Rosenfeld, Hannah Rosenthal, Jennifer Roskies, Barry Rubin, Michael Rubin, Thyme Siegel, Ernest Sternberg, Asher Susser, Bassam Tibi, Robert Wistrich, and Ben-Dror Yemini. In each case, I was enriched by the encounter. In addition, the YIISA video archive enabled me to benefit from many presentations that I was unable to attend in person.

YIISA also brought to New Haven a politically diverse and talented group of postdoctoral and predoctoral fellows, including, among others, Idit Shalev, Ulrike Becker, and Joshua Kaplan.

Lauren Clark, the coordinator of YIISA, was always helpful to me beyond the call of duty.

YIISA was also where I met German scholar Clemens Heni, a tireless foe of antisemitism in all its forms. Clemens, who heads the Berlin International Center for the Study of Antisemitism, read a draft of this book and gave me much useful feedback.

The recently established *Journal for the Study of Antisemitism* (*JSA*), edited by Steven K. Baum and Neal E. Rosenberg, has taken a much-needed step toward encouraging research on Jew-hatred in the past and, more importantly, in the understudied present. A 2010 conference sponsored by the journal broached the topic of Muslim antisemitism, something that many academics have been unwilling or unable to consider.

In addition, a team of social psychologists, headed by Lee Jussim and Florette Cohen, has started to address the near total absence of empirical social psychological studies on contemporary antisemitism, a gap that is curious in light of the discipline's seminal role in understanding Jew-hatred and other bigotries in the past. I hope that Jussim and Cohen's work, presented at YIISA and the *JSA* conference, will get the attention of mainstream social psychologists. I am also grateful to Jussim for presenting his work at William Paterson University, where I am a professor.

Among the people I have contacted during research for this book, scholars Irfan Khawaja and Rifat Bali were especially insightful.

I am not affiliated with the Middle East Media Research Institute in any way, and mainly I have accessed the institute's work online. However, this book could not have been written without the highly professional monitoring and translation services of MEMRI. The documentation of antisemitism is only a small part of what this organization has accomplished; it has, for example, become an essential part of the West's counterterrorism effort. It also has made inroads into the documentation of emerging moderate voices in the Islamic world. Needless to say, despite its great efforts to maintain balance and objectivity (or possibly because of these efforts), MEMRI has been repeatedly denounced in vile terms in some circles. (For example, an Egyptian presidential candidate—unhappy that some of his words had been recorded, translated, and transmitted to a Canadian journalist—referred to MEMRI as "that piece of crap.") Thankfully, the major Western media and policy elites appear to realize its worth.

Two academic institutes deserve special mention for their excellent pioneering work on contemporary antisemitism: the Vidal Sassoon International Center for the Study of Antisemitism at the Hebrew University in Jerusalem and the Stephen Roth Institute for the Study of Contemporary Antisemitism and Racism at Tel-Aviv University. More recently, the Institute for the Study of Contemporary Antisemitism at Indiana University has also become a valuable resource.

At William Paterson University, the Center for Holocaust and Genocide Studies has helped to keep past antisemitism and twentieth-century genocides in the consciousness of students, faculty, and the surrounding community. For more than a decade, I have had the opportunity to team-teach a freshman honors course on diversity and hatred with biologist Miryam Wahrman, the cofounder of the center, and other colleagues. Spirited interaction with each of these colleagues has been a pleasure. I also thank Miryam for reading early drafts of the manuscript. My longtime colleague, social psychologist Tom Heinzen, provided useful input throughout the writing of this book. Additionally, I thank my many other colleagues in the psychology department for maintaining a stimulating and intellectually open-minded atmosphere for scholarship and teaching.

Bill and Harriet Mohr, the founders of the Haiti Jewish Refugee Legacy Project, have been the source of much encouragement, and I am grateful to their organization for the Tikkun Olam Award conferred in 2011 for my work on antisemitism in the Muslim world.

Over the years, journalist Adam Brodsky has been a buddy, coauthor, critic, editor, and brother-in-law; I thank him for his superb performance in all those capacities.

Merryl Tisch has been the source of much encouragement and support. I thank her.

I further owe a debt of gratitude to Susan Ann Protter, my recently retired agent, who has played a key role in bringing all my books, including this one, to life. Hilary Claggett, my editor at Potomac Books, has been an enthusiastic champion of this book since she read the proposal. I value her levelheaded guidance throughout the process. I am also thankful to the entire team at Potomac Books for its consummate professionalism.

My greatest thanks go, as always, to my wife—and to my children who not infrequently have wondered aloud why Daddy can't write books about happier topics. I wish I could think of an answer.

1

A Litmus Test for the West

This book is about dangerous, old-fashioned Jew-hatred spreading like wildfire through large parts of the Muslim and Arab world. But, more importantly, it is about what the failure to address this exploding hostility means for everyone who cares about progressive values and the future of Western civilization.

The problem goes way beyond the Nazi-like rants of extremist clerics. And far from being a by-product of the Arab-Israeli conflict, Jew-hatred has roots in the long history and complex theology of Islam. Although the Islamic tradition might be used to sustain a liberal and tolerant mind-set, these days the upper hand in many Muslim-majority countries belongs to those who draw bigotry from their religious tradition and seek to impart such bigotry to their children. As a result of such indoctrination, Jew-hatred in many parts of the Muslim world today is far more intense and widespread than it was fifty years ago, and the Jew-hatred of tomorrow promises to be even worse.

Until this wave of hatred is addressed, understood, and reversed, efforts to forge a genuine and sustainable peace in the Middle East stand little chance of success. Moreover, Jew-hatred serves—and always has served—to deflect attention from real problems. Thus, to the extent that Muslim societies direct their energies against the Jews, they may falter in addressing many internal problems, including government repression, poverty, poor education, and mistreatment of women. It is hard to imagine a genuinely democratic reform movement thriving alongside rampant antisemitism.

Although the body count directly attributable to Muslim Jew-hatred has thus far been low, at least when judged by the bloody standards of the twentieth century, the winds of hate threaten much more violence to come. The horrible sexual assault of journalist Lara Logan in Cairo's Tahrir Square started when word spread

1

(erroneously) through a crowd that she was a Jew; more than a hundred men, presumably celebrating the downfall of a dictator, joined in the attack. *Wall Street Journal* reporter Daniel Pearl was kidnapped and beheaded in Pakistan because of his Jewish background. More recently, Dr. Warren Weinstein—an economic development expert—was kidnapped in Pakistan because of his presumed Jewish background. Jewish institutions and Jewish people—regardless of their connection to Israel—are targeted routinely for terrorism around the world. Recall, for example, the six Jews murdered at the Chabad center in Mumbai, India, by members of the Lashkar-e-Taiba group. Even in the United States, Muslim terrorists have sought to hit Jewish people and institutions many times. For example, synagogues in the Bronx, a Jewish Federation building in Seattle, an El Al ticket counter at Los Angeles International Airport, and a rabbi's house in Nashville have all been targeted.[1] In Europe, attacks on Jews and Jewish institutions have been on the rise in recent decades, and in Denmark several schools with large Muslim student bodies even report that they will not risk enrolling Jewish students because they cannot guarantee their safety.[2]

But anti-Jewish thinking also plays a central role in the mentality of many Muslim terrorists who end up selecting non-Jewish targets in the United States and elsewhere. Thus, one terrorist, Mohamad Ibrahim Shnewer, told an undercover informant his first choice was to kill Jews in Israel. As he put it, "I love to kill Jews. I tell you this, in all honesty, it is a dream of mine."[3] Instead, he settled on targeting American soldiers at the Fort Dix army base in New Jersey, where, fortunately, he and his four associates were stopped before they could do any damage. Muslim extremists who have sought to attack America and its allies have nearly always been Jew-haters, although in some cases they have spoken only of their anger toward Israel or Israeli Jews. Partly, America is hated because it is seen as a tool of the Jews or as in the hands of Jewish money. Thus, anti-Americanism can be regarded as a close cousin of antisemitism; dealing with the latter is part of dealing with the former.

There is yet another reason to pay attention to antisemitism in the Muslim world. If Holocaust-deniers and Jew-haters such as Iran's President Mahmoud Ahmadinejad succeed in efforts to develop or acquire nuclear weapons, it is not impossible that the twenty-first century might witness killing of Jews (in Israel) on a scale comparable with the European death toll of the twentieth century. This outcome may not be probable, but it is certainly possible. When Holocaust survivor and Nobel Peace Prize winner Elie Wiesel signed a petition urging the world to stop Ahmadinejad from acquiring nuclear weapons, he said:

> Remember when a leader of a nation violates all standards of morality and decency by announcing to the whole world his wish to see a nation member of the international community wiped off the map, our immediate response cannot be anything other than anger and outrage. At least he's frank in his goals and in his dreams. He really wants to see the end of the Jewish state and thus annihilating all its Jewish inhabitants. . . . They come close to a figure that will forever hound humankind's memory: six million.[4]

And yet, despite all this, much of the liberal world seems content to ignore anti-Jewish bigotry among Muslims and Arabs or, at least, to explain it away. This failure to engage the problem constitutes at the very least a blind spot in the contemporary antiracist community. At worst, it is a serious indictment.

The best way to begin understanding the extent to which Jew-hatred has infected the Muslim world is not by considering the most extreme instances of anti-Jewish terrorism or even by probing the mind-set of the most virulent haters. Every society, after all, has its lunatics. Instead, consider the life of one Muslim religious leader who had a good reputation abroad.

When Sheikh Mohammed Sayed Tantawi, arguably the most prominent religious leader in mainstream Sunni Islam, died in March 2010, most Western media honored him as the quintessential Muslim moderate.[5] As the head of Egypt's prestigious thousand-year-old Al-Azhar University, he had condemned suicide bombings, supported the American-allied government of Hosni Mubarak, and criticized the common practice of female genital cutting. Especially on religious issues concerning women, Sheikh Tantawi stood courageously against extremists who had been growing in power throughout his years at Al-Azhar.

Yet on one matter, unmentioned in most Western media and probably unknown to most Western journalists, Tantawi did not seem so liberal. He was, as it happens, a lifelong enemy of Jews, albeit, as shall be seen, a relatively moderate one. His doctoral dissertation, written in 1969, disparaged Jews with an abundance of quotations from the Quran and other religious sources. In this lengthy theological work, he detailed the Jews' supposedly evil ways and how they purportedly endeavored to entrap the Muslims during Muhammad's era. Tantawi's reading of the Quran ascribes to the Jews a slew of unflattering characteristics, including wanton envy, lasciviousness, religious fanaticism, murderousness, and a tendency toward "semantic bickering." Jews, collectively, are accused of corrupting Allah's word, consuming the people's wealth, and most ominously, murdering Allah's prophets.[6]

Even if one assumes that the Quranic text offers some basis for Tantawi's inferences, a true religious moderate might have argued that the verses in question apply only to particular Jews living in Muhammad's day. Along similar lines, a truly progressive Muslim might have tried to place Muhammad's encounter with the Jews squarely in a seventh-century context. Such reinterpretation might have required Tantawi to rethink some religious assumptions, yet the sheikh showed little desire to limit the antisocial consequences of his religious reading. Instead, he advised that the Quran speaks of two types of Jews—good ones and bad ones. The good ones, according to Tantawi, all became Muslims.

The sheikh rose rapidly to the top of Al-Azhar's leadership partly because of widespread respect for his writings, including his doctoral dissertation. In April 2002, from his august position, Tantawi turned once again to a Jewish theme, sermonizing that Jews—not just Israelis—were "the enemies of Allah, descendants of apes and pigs." A bit later, although he never rejected the sentiments behind these words, Tantawi recommended against widespread use of the "apes and pigs" epithet. The words, he decided, did not play well in the West.[7]

Still, there can be little doubt that when judged against many other prominent imams, Tantawi cannot be considered a virulent Jew-hater, and he did attempt a few steps toward building relations with the state of Israel. At some level, he accepted Egypt's treaty with the Jewish state, and importantly, he met in Cairo in 1997 with Yisrael Lau, the Ashkenazi chief rabbi of Israel at the time. This was something the previous head of Al-Azhar had been unwilling to do, and Tantawi drew criticism from more radical Islamic clerics. Criticism centered around Tantawi's supposed desire for normalization of relations with Israel, but this desire was something the sheikh vehemently denied.

Whatever his intentions, Tantawi explained publicly that he had let the rabbi know that the Quran exposes the Jews' "false claims, their atrocities, and the punishments Allah imposed on them for their oppression and their wrong-doing." So strong was the negative reaction to Tantawi's meeting with Rabbi Lau, however, that the sheikh felt further compelled to reestablish his anti-Jewish credentials by reminding people about his doctoral thesis. He declared, "I still believe everything written in that dissertation."[8]

About a decade later, Tantawi again crossed a line with the Israelis and again felt compelled by public sentiments to take back his gesture. This time, in 2008, he shook hands with Israeli president Shimon Peres but then maintained that he hadn't known whose hand he was shaking.[9]

One cannot infer with confidence that negative reactions to improvements in Egyptian-Israeli relations are driven primarily by bigotry. But one can observe in Tantawi's public pronouncements the way in which anti-Jewish sentiments, ostensibly dating back to the earliest days of Islam, provide a relevant backdrop against which relations with the Israelis can be viewed. One may also observe—partly on the basis of Tantawi's career—that in the Islamic world it is not only religious extremists and not only the most intense foes of Israel who exhibit copious amounts of what we in the West would deem anti-Jewish bigotry.

An additional message emerges from Tantawi's experience and from that of others who have tried with greater energy and enthusiasm to improve Muslim relations with Jews and Israel. Influential people in the Muslim world need not speak out against the Jews, but anyone who speaks out on their behalf ought not to expect many local allies in the ensuing fight. Moreover, while we may conclude that Tantawi should, indeed, be remembered as an anti-Jewish bigot, it is apparent that his voice on Jewish matters was very far from the worst that one encounters in Muslim-majority countries.

Transmitting Bigotry

Consider, for example, some not-so-unusual television broadcasts in the Arab world:

◆ On April 4, 2009, Hamas's Al Aqsa television network aired a drama in which a Jewish father spoke lovingly to his son. The father said, "You must drink from the blood of Muslims." The son replied, "Okay, but just one cup—because I'm full." The father agreed, saying, "Very well, my son. God will be pleased with you. Come, my son, I want you to pray. Stand next to me and pray."[10] On April 8, 2011, the same network broadcast remarks from the former minister of culture of Hamas, 'Atallah Abu Al-Subh: "The Jews are the most despicable and contemptible nation to crawl upon the face of the Earth, because they have displayed hostility to Allah. . . . Allah will kill the Jews in the hell of the world to come, just like they killed the believers in the hell of this world."[11]

◆ In Sudan, on June 5, 2009, Sheikh Abd Al-Jalil Al-Karouri told television viewers that President Hussein, his preferred name for Barack Obama, should "be fair and study the 9/11 files." The president of the United States, who—according to the sheikh's confident inference—feels a deep longing for his African and Islamic roots, would surely discover that the Twin Towers had been booby-trapped to facilitate their destruction. After all, those who flew the planes had, according to Karouri, first helped the Americans defeat the Soviets in Afghanistan in the 1980s, and in 2001 they were helping establish a pretext for the desired invasion of Afghanistan and Iraq. The whole thing, viewers learned, was "a Jewish conspiracy," a fact clearly borne out, in the sheikh's mind, by the now-famous "4,000 Jews" who were purportedly absent from work at the "World Usury Center."[12]

◆ On July 21, 2006, on Syrian television, that nation's deputy minister of religious endowment, Muhammad 'Abd Al-Sattar, posed some questions to viewers: "Who occupied the Al-Aqsa Mosque? Who attacked the prophets? Who killed the prophets?" He then provided the answers: "Even the Koran depicts the people of Israel in a very sinister and dark way. Allah did not curse any people, not even the polytheists, not even the idol worshippers. The Koran did not curse any of these. The only ones who were cursed are those murderous criminals [the Jews]."[13]

◆ On the Al-Jazeera network on January 30, 2009, Sheikh Dr. Muhammad Yusuf al-Qaradawi, an Egyptian-born Sunni religious authority, announced, "Throughout history, Allah has imposed upon the [Jews] people who would punish them for their corruption. The last punishment was carried out by Hitler. By means of all the things he did to them—even though they exaggerated this issue—he managed to put them in their place. . . . This was divine punishment for them. Allah willing, the next time will be at the hand of the believers."[14] Qaradawi is considered one of the most influential Islamic scholars living today and a very popular television figure; he is the recipient of many prizes for his scholarship.

◆ On June 6, 2010, when people everywhere were focusing on the World Cup competition in South Africa, Egyptian cleric Mus'id Anwar lamented on Al-

Rahma television network, "Some Muslim youth memorize the results of soccer matches more than they memorize the Quran." He explained, "As you know, the Jews, or Zionists, have *The Protocols of the Elders of Zion*. Over 100 years ago, they formulated a plan to rule the world, and they are implementing this plan. One of the protocols says: 'Keep the [non-Jews] preoccupied with songs, soccer, and movies.' Is it or isn't it happening? It is." After describing a soccer dispute involving Egypt and Algeria, the religious leader asked, "What has happened to the Muslims? Whose interests does this serve?" His answer: "The Jews. They had tremendous success."[15]

These examples are, to be sure, extremist voices. Arab television does not air a hatefest every night, and some of the broadcasts mentioned here did not appear on the most popular networks. Yet these broadcasts are also far from isolated occurrences. And perhaps more importantly, there is little counterbalancing positive coverage. One needs to search long and hard to discover influential, high-level leaders anywhere in the Muslim world who are willing to confront the Jew-haters directly and loudly. In contrast, on any given day, new instances of dehumanizing bigotry emanate from high and diverse places.

During the first decade of the twenty-first century, the Muslim world resurrected almost every diatribe produced in more than two millennia of European hostility toward the Jews and introduced many homegrown and novel modes of attack. Thus, the French human rights activist Morad El-Hattab El-Ibrahimi attests, "Never since the end of the Second World War has anti-Jewish 'mythology' re-emerged with such virulence and met with so little resistance in both political and intellectual circles."[16] El-Hattab is a respected writer in France, editor of a book on the genocide in Darfur, and generally a voice of reason. He considers himself a Muslim and a descendant of the fourth caliph, Ali. Yet, among many Muslims, he is scorned because of his sympathy for the plight of the Jews. His testimony is supported by abundant evidence.

Although it is impossible to determine precisely how many of the world's 1.2 billion Muslims hold anti-Jewish beliefs and how many are motivated to act because of these beliefs, one can say with confidence that much bigotry comes from the highest levels of religious and political leadership. The hatred is propagated enthusiastically by more than a few journalists and intellectuals in the most prominent and widely respected regional media. According to fairly clear social scientific evidence that I shall present, it has spread widely among the general population of several nations. That one should detest Jews is a lesson taught every day in thousands of schools in many countries.

Political expert Barry Rubin divides the contemporary Middle Eastern Arab public into three parts. He sees nationalists as the largest group (about 65 percent), followed by Islamists (20–30 percent), and liberals (about 5 percent). According to Rubin, the Islamists are overt and enthusiastic Jew-haters, whereas the liberals tend to reject the bigotry. The nationalists' attitudes toward the Jews are the most diverse and hardest to pin down; they are generally less likely to buy into overt anti-Jewish ideology than the Islamists are, but they are more likely to do so than the liberals.[17] While Rubin provides a place to begin thinking about how anti-Jewish attitudes are distributed among the Arab political public, his approach is understandably imprecise and lacking in confirmatory empirical evidence.

In Europe, the situation is far better for Jews than it is in the Muslim-majority world. Yet even there, elements in the Muslim community—in collaboration with others—have been awakening antisemitism from its apparently never-deep slumber.[18] Elsewhere, in Turkey and among Pakistan's nearly 200 million citizens—despite the many problems that originate far closer to home—hostility toward Jews is fairly intense, widespread, and growing.[19]

As noted, Iran's profoundly antisemitic regime is likely to soon possess nuclear weapons. Its leaders have publicly and repeatedly stated their desire to use whatever means necessary to end the Jewish state. While the current regime in Iran has many strong internal enemies, none have vocalized clear opposition to this policy, and the wife of Mir-Hossein Mousavi, the main opposition leader in the 2009 election, said that Israel, in any case, would remain Iran's eternal enemy.

Such statements represent more than over-the-top political rhetoric. Thus, in July 2009, Esfandiar Rahim Mashaei ran into trouble when he was appointed to be the first vice president of Iran because he had made an "offensive" remark about Israelis one year earlier. Mashaei had said Iranians were "friends of all people in the world—even Israelis." He then backed away from this boilerplate declaration as far as he could, saying that he meant only that Iranians were friends of the people in Israel who had been oppressed by the Zionists.[20] President Ahmadinejad had thought that his own anti-Jewish credentials were sufficiently strong for others to overlook this sin committed by his appointee, his son's father-in-law. But he had been wrong. The Iranian hierarchy would not hear of it; the man, they concluded, was a friend of the Jewish state, and that was the end of the story.

The image of the demonic Jew, after all, was a central founding principle of the regime. As Ayatollah Ruhollah Khomeini warned, "We must protest and make people aware that the Jews and their foreign backers are opposed to the very foundations of Islam and wish to establish Jewish domination throughout the world. Since they are a cunning and resourceful group of people, I fear that—God forbid!—they may one day achieve their goal."[21] This sort of thinking does not leave much room for reconciliation and interfaith cooperation.

Of course, few Westerners are surprised to find that Khomeini uttered hateful words of extremism. But it is perhaps more jarring to think of Palestinian Authority leader Mahmoud Abbas, a man put forth many times by the West as Israel's best hope for a negotiated settlement, suggesting in the 1980s—despite conclusive historical evidence to the contrary—that Jews for political purposes deliberately inflated the Holocaust death toll from one million to six million.[22] Or to hear now-deposed Egyptian president Hosni Mubarak—widely denounced these days by Egyptians for his "pro-Israel" policies—once saying in defense of the treaty with the Jewish state, "Against us stood the most intelligent people on earth—a people that controls the international press, the world economy, and world finances."[23] Or to recall that the powerful Saudi King Ibn Saud at the height of the Holocaust wrote, "The religious animosity between Muslims and Jews . . . dates back to the time when Islam appeared and . . . is due to the treacherous behavior of the Jews towards Muslims and their Prophet."[24] Even Egyptian president Anwar Sadat, a man who obviously rejected his early affinity for Hitler and ultimately gave his life for his sincere willingness to cooperate with the Israelis, was still telling his foreign minister in the days before he signed the historic Camp David Accords, "We are dealing with the lowest and meanest of enemies. The Jews even tormented their Prophet Moses, and exasperated their God."[25] Clearly, the pedigree of today's anti-Jewish hostility runs deep and wide. One cannot trace it so precisely, as some have attempted, to this or that extremist ideologue.

Keep in mind that Qaradawi, the cleric who called for Allah's faithful to be the next to carry out a Hitlerian genocide against the Jews, was among the first and most prominently featured religious leaders invited to address 200,000 victorious "reformers" gathered at Tahrir Square in February 2011.[26] On that day, he stated that Egypt's revolution needed to be completed. It is hard to see how this completion might include a vision of tolerant democracy should Qaradawi's Muslim Brotherhood prevail. He and his associates may yet be sent packing by liberal forces in Egypt, but there is also the chance that Egypt will abide by his declaration: "There is no dialogue between us [Muslims and Jews] except by the sword and rifle. . . . [We pray Allah] to take this oppressive, Jewish, Zionist band of people. . . . Do not spare a single one of them. . . . Count their numbers and kill them down to the very last one."[27]

The Arab Spring, thus far, has not meant an end to or even a lessening of Jew-hatred. Quite possibly, the opposite will prove true in the long run, especially as reformers' promises become more difficult to fulfill and subsequent events produce clear winners and losers. Thus far, anti-Israel stances have proved increasingly popular, and they have continued to feed into more explicit anti-Jewish bigotry.[28]

Time to Sound the Alarm

All this hatred is disheartening, but something else is even more discouraging. The world—not least, its so-called progressive and antiracist elements—does not seem to be paying much attention. On those few occasions when Western experts and leaders have addressed the matter, they have typically been dismissive and/or wrongheaded in their analyses.

Still, the logic of world affairs and the lessons of history leave little doubt that the growth of Jew-hatred always means trouble for anyone who cares about human rights, freedom, equality, democracy, constitutional government, modernity, science, civility, diversity, or world peace. Those who value such things can ignore Jew-hatred only at their own risk. There has never been an anti-Jewish regime or movement that was otherwise reasonable and progressive.

This is not a book that I ever expected to write. I came of age when antisemitism was receding everywhere. The Holocaust, according to historians and social scientists, had forever incapacitated and discredited Jew-hatred as a major force in world affairs. Moreover, Vatican Council II had deprived Catholic religious antisemites of institutional succor. Other Christian denominations took similar steps to address theological sources of hostility. What remained seemed vestigial, destined to grow weaker over time. Although some, mainly Jews, expected another Holocaust or—at least—a pogrom every time a swastika was scribbled on a synagogue or gravestone, I didn't buy it. In the seventies, eighties, and nineties, antisemitism came from its traditional home on the political fringes and from a few other spots as well. But the problem appeared manageable, not much worse than the bigotry faced by many white immigrant groups and probably less severe than that faced by blacks, other nonwhites, and gays.

During recent years, conditions have changed dramatically. Muslim antisemitism is already very dangerous and not just for the Jews. And it is likely to get far worse. It's time to sound the alarm. Perhaps some will suggest I exaggerate. The best way to address this objection is to confront the evidence—and that is what this book tries to do.

The book has several goals. Above all, it seeks to provide clear and convincing evidence that a venomous and novel antisemitism—far more dangerous than garden-variety prejudice and far more intense than anyone would have imagined possible just two decades ago—has very rapidly been enveloping much of the Muslim-majority and Arab world, and beyond. A few experts have described this hatred as genocidal. While elimination of the Jews may, indeed, be the intent of many who spew vitriolic rhetoric, and while Iranian nukes, for example, may yet produce massive body counts, one need not indulge in overstatement to grasp the severity of the problem. The book, therefore, aims to offer readers evidence so powerful as to force open the eyes even of those who press them firmly shut.

Second, and importantly, the book will document that most people in the West—owing variously to apathy, ignorance, confusion, bigotry, ideology, purported pragmatism, misguided multiculturalism, and other reasons—have largely ignored, misunderstood, or deliberately downplayed this growing epidemic of hate. As journalist Daniel Schwammenthal of the *Wall Street Journal* commented in 2009, "the depth of anti-Semitic propaganda in Palestinian and other Muslim societies is one of the most underreported facts about the Middle East."[29] What might be called a conspiracy of silence notably includes—and, arguably, is led by—human rights activists, academics, social scientists, left-leaning political leaders, liberal journalists, progressive Christian sects, United Nations officials, and others whom one might expect to stand stalwartly opposed to overt bigotry. There has been no alarm, almost no research, and precious little concern from outside the Jewish community and allied organizations.

My own field of social psychology, once a leader in the battle against segregation and antiblack racism in the United States, has failed even to begin to address problems associated with Muslim and Arab antisemitism.[30] Even many Jews have failed to see clearly the dimensions of the hatred directed against them, possibly because it is terrifying to acknowledge these dimensions. Alternatively, some Jews apparently perceive more nobility in the advocacy of universal causes than those deemed purely Jewish in scope. Even among those who agree that a new, virulent form of Jew-hatred has, indeed, taken hold in the Middle East, many maintain that, for various reasons, this bigotry should not be made a focal point of world attention.

In my view, the "justifications" for inattention and resistance to the fight against Muslim antisemitism are many and flawed; they must be refuted. To some extent, the failures of the human rights community in this regard are not a mere oversight that can be readily corrected. Instead, I think, they reflect certain contradictions and predilections that have been present in the organized quest for human rights for many years. Some of the problems came to a head in the fraudulent, UN-sponsored World Conference Against Racism in 2001 and 2009 (known as Durban I and Durban II), in which Israel and Zionism were main focal points and were attacked relentlessly often by countries with horrible human rights records.[31]

At the Durban conferences and in many other contexts, some purported opponents of racism have resisted even the classification of Arab hostility toward Jews as an instance of bigotry, preferring instead to portray it solely as an outgrowth—perhaps regrettable, perhaps understandable—of the Arab-Israeli conflict. Along similar lines, many have refused to acknowledge the religious and historical sources of Muslim Jew-hatred. This tendency comes sometimes from a flawed reading of history and other times from a desire to shield a religious and ethnic tradition from the scrutiny of scholarship. Thus, a major purpose of the book is to explain, illuminate, and clarify the broader, underlying problems in the antiracist community that render it so ineffective with regard to understanding Muslim antisemitism—much less combating it.

Why—I am sometimes asked (mainly by Jews)—should non-Jews be concerned? The question, I think, reflects an unjustified paranoia about the mind-set of the gentile world in the contemporary era. While antisemitic stereotypes are far from dead in the West—one 2009 survey found that about 40 percent of Europeans believe that Jews have too much power in business—much of the Christian world has proved sincere in its desire to root out bigotry against the Jews and other groups.[32]

In any event, current lack of concern about Muslim antisemitism is more than a matter of bigotry unanswered, moral inconsistency, and a failure to address the interests of one particular group. It is a matter of self-interest for all who value the culture and civilization of the West. Hence, a third goal of the book is to argue that Arab and Muslim antisemitism provide an acid test of the seriousness of Western liberalism, and—if this test is failed, as now seems likely—future affairs will not go well for the true proponents of democracy, constitutionalism, and human rights.

Antisemitism has very frequently been described as the "canary in the coal mine," an early sign that something very bad and more destructive is likely to occur. Noted historian Robert Wistrich has written, "Arab and Muslim antisemitism is the Trojan Horse designed to undermine the West's belief in its own values."[33] If the West fails to stand firm in defense of its core values with regard to treatment of the Jews, who or what will be next in line? For example, the 2009 plot against two Bronx synagogues provides one indicator that the consequences of virulent hatred of the Jews, if unaddressed, will not long remain outside Western borders. Along with attacking the synagogues and killing Jews, the recently converted Muslim plotters also planned to down an airliner over New York with a Stinger missile. Yet another example of the spillover of violent Muslim Jew-hatred across western borders was Mohammed Merah's March 2012 murder of a rabbi and Jewish schoolchildren in Toulouse, France. Jews were his main target, but he also saw members of the French military as enemies.[34]

Finally, this book moves beyond sounding an alarm to probe the diverse religious, political, social, and psychological forces that have created and nurtured the new hostility to Jews in the Muslim world, developing a social psychological theory of Muslim Jew-hatred. Most works on this topic are written from the perspective of the historian, political scientist, or journalist. Yet it is social psychologists who traditionally have crafted the best approaches to understanding and addressing the growth and transmission of bigotry through a population. Thus, drawing on a social psychological model, the book concludes with some ideas about what can be done to fight back against the rising epidemic of hate.

According to Brown University historian Omer Bartov,

> Hitler taught mankind an important lesson: If you see a Nazi, a fascist or an anti-Semite, then you must say what you see. If you want to justify or apologize for something, then describe exactly what you are playing down.

If a British newspaper publishes an anti-Semitic cartoon, one must call it anti-Semitic. If the attacks on the Twin Towers in New York were founded upon anti-Semitic motifs, one should say so. If a Malaysian prime minister expresses anti-Semitic opinions, one must not attempt to apologize for that which is inexcusable. If a self-proclaimed liberation organization demands the annihilation of the Jewish state, one must not pretend that it is demanding anything else. Where clarity ends, complicity begins.[35]

In this sense, many Westerners—including many of those who claim to be deeply opposed to bigotry—are complicit.

Thus, in part, this book can be viewed as a latter-day "J'Accuse . . . !" In his day, French novelist Émile Zola charged his nation's establishment with the commission of a terrible crime, convicting and sending the Jewish officer Alfred Dreyfus to Devil's Island—even though officials knew or suspected he was not guilty.[36] The military-political collusion against Dreyfus targeted a single Jew but, of course, reflected broader antisemitism in French society. The principal importance of Zola's accusations during the Dreyfus Affair, however, was that they revealed something far larger that had gone wrong in France. In the denouement of the Dreyfus Affair, the liberal intellectuals seemed to be the heroes, and history has confirmed that judgment. Now, unfortunately, the failure to face antisemitism squarely again reveals fault lines in the broader society, and this time large parts of the left-wing intelligentsia are at the core of the problem.

One might ask why and how this all happened. After all, Holocaust movies command huge audiences, and books and educational programs documenting the Nazi assault on European Jewry are still a growth industry. Social scientific studies in the United States show fairly low levels of antisemitism, at least when judged by long-term historical standards.[37] Students in many schools are taught to reject "racism and sexism" not long after they are taught the fundamentals of reading and writing—if not before. Both major political parties in the United States claim an unshakeable commitment to the state of Israel. Why then, under such circumstances, have so few observers from outside the Jewish community been willing and able to grasp the dangerous nature of revitalized antisemitism in the Middle East? This book addresses this question in depth and offers some guidance for the correction of the problem and the reclamation of the liberal soul.

Shutting Down Discussion before It Starts

Scholars who speak and write about Muslim antisemitism often encounter a dismissive wave rather than a serious refutation. Thus, philosopher Bernard Harrison wrote, "As a non-Jew, I have found, on the whole, my fellow non-Jews altogether too prone to pooh-pooh . . . Jewish attempts to sound the alarm [on the so-called new antisemitism]."[38] Charles Small, the founder of the former Yale Initiative for the Interdisciplinary Study of Anti-Semitism (YIISA), considers himself a lifelong and committed member of the intellectual Left, yet he reports that people frequently called him and the institute "neoconservative," simply because of its concern with antisemitism.[39] Cartoonist and antisemitism scholar Yaakov Kirschen observed, "The minute you say antisemitism, you are delegitimized. . . . If I say 'antisemitic,' nobody looks at that [thing I am describing]. They look at me and say, 'Oh, you're saying it's antisemitic. That means you must be right-wing.'"[40] Kirschen might have added that still others discredit those calling attention to antisemitism as paranoid Jews crying wolf, yet again.

In my own experience writing and speaking about Islamic antisemitism, I have come to expect a great deal of resistance whenever the taboo on addressing the topic is broken. This holds true even when one limits the discussion to old-fashioned bigotry—which one might presume would be less controversial than the "new antisemitism," grounded, as it is, in rejection of the Jewish state. Resistance to serious consideration of the roots and consequences of Muslim hostility to Jews comes not only from those on the left and, certainly, not only from non-Jews.

While it is a cornerstone of the search for truth that all academic works must be subjected to energetic criticism, the resistance I speak of approaches psychological denial and does not focus on particular analyses. Rather, it applies to all discussions of Muslim antisemitism even when clearly premised on evidence rather than ideology.

Indeed, most people in the West are quite ready to denounce Jew-hatred when it comes from Nazis and other long-dead antisemites. To some extent, left-leaning scholars and human rights organizations also remain eager to oppose antisemitism when it emanates from traditional, sanctioned sources, especially on the far right. Some are even open to exposing resurgent Jew-hatred in Christian Europe, for example, in contemporary Poland and Hungary. But there is deep resistance to straight-speaking, unobstructed analyses of far more dangerous hostility to

Jews—when it comes from Muslims and Arabs. Along with this resistance, one finds defensiveness, especially on the far left, when discussion turns to seemingly antisemitic utterances made by those who see themselves as merely anti-Zionists.

Yet, factual material supporting the existence of serious Muslim Jew-hatred, hatred that goes far beyond criticism of the Jewish state, can be found in many sources. Sometimes these sources disagree about the extent to which extreme denunciations of the Jewish state should be counted as antisemitism. Some analysts regard it as antisemitic when Israel is repeatedly targeted on the basis of double standards, when it is denounced as a demonic entity, or when its basic independent existence is delegitimized. But even when Israel-based hostility is excluded altogether, massive amounts of old-fashioned anti-Jewish bigotry remain.

In addition, one common objection is to the use of the word "antisemitism" to describe Jew-hatred in the Arab world. The argument seems simple enough— how can Arabs be antisemites when they are, themselves, Semites? Yet, there is more here than meets the eye.

Of the hundreds of books that have appeared with the word "antisemitism" in the title, not a single one—to my knowledge—deals with hostility toward members of some broadly defined group called Semites. Bigotry against Muslims is usually called "Islamophobia," and bigotry against Arabs is simply labeled "anti-Arab racism." As Bernard Lewis, the noted Princeton historian who has authored many volumes on Islamic history, concluded, "the term 'Semite' has no meaning as applied to groups as heterogeneous as the Arabs or the Jews, and indeed it could be argued that the use of such terms is in itself a sign of racism and certainly of either ignorance or bad faith. [Moreover] anti-Semitism has never anywhere been concerned with anyone but Jews, and is therefore available to Arabs as to other people as an option should they choose it." Nonetheless, one might ask—as some have—why not simply pick another term and get on with the discussion if this one is causing so much trouble.[41]

That this is not such a good idea becomes clear if one takes a moment to reflect on the history of the term "antisemitism" and the reasons why some people want us to abandon it. There is some uncertainty about who coined the term, but it is known that it happened in the late 1870s and that it referred to a new, racially based hostility toward Jews. Many attribute the word to Wilhelm Marr, a journalist and intellectual who in 1879 founded the League of Antisemites (Antisemiten-Liga), an organization committed specifically to combating the alleged threat to

Germany posed by the Jews. Marr himself was an odd duck. For a time, he advocated the forced removal of Jews from Germany. Yet, during his lifetime, he married several women who had been born Jewish or partly Jewish. A onetime leftist radical, an atheist, and an anti-Christian, he moved to the extreme right during his antisemitic period but retained his hostility to Christianity. Indeed, Marr needed a new term for his Jew-hatred partly to distinguish it from the older Christian variety with which he did not want to be identified. Later, toward the end of his life, he surprisingly abandoned antisemitism and apologized to the Jews.[42]

Whether originally from Marr or someone else, the word "antisemitism" rapidly gained popularity in Europe, always being used to indicate hostility to Jews. The "Semite" component of the word derived from various pseudoscientific "race" theories that had been developing in Europe over the preceding century. In 1862 the influential French scholar Ernest Renan, for example, developed a theory of Semitic peoples—including Jews, Arabs, and others—who possessed less than noble characteristics. Nowadays, the word Semitic retains meaning only as a linguistic grouping that includes modern and ancient languages such as Hebrew, Arabic, Aramaic, Amharic, Phoenician, and Ugaritic. But early political antisemites drew on the popular racial theories to provide a scientific aura for promoting hatred of Jews.

The hatred came first; the terminology of Semites and antisemites came later. More importantly, with the new racial dimension, Jews became evil by virtue of their biology and not only their theology. Thus, from its inception, the term "antisemitism" was flawed to the extent that there was no meaningful ethnic grouping that could be called Semites, and in any event members of the movement directed their hatred only against the Jews.[43]

Although, strictly speaking, the term "antisemitism" should be used only to describe racially based hatred of Jews of the sort that commenced in the late nineteenth century, many writers use it to indicate premodern, religious hostility to Jews as well. There is some historical basis for this expansion of the term, as it has rarely been the case that the bigotry against Jews has been purely religious or purely racial; usually, it is an amalgam of both.

There are no good alternatives to the time-honored word "antisemitism." "Anti-Judaism" seems to imply hostility to the religion alone and, thus, is too restrictive. "Judeophobia" parallels Islamophobia (and, to a lesser extent, homophobia); unfortunately, all these terms imply that fear of the target group is paramount—at best an arguable explanatory theory that does not belong in the descriptive term. "Jew-hatred" appears to be the best alternative, though—to many ears—it has a defamatory ring.

Most importantly, the flight from the word "antisemitism" is more political than etymological. It is a maneuver designed to avoid the traditional Western disapprobation associated with hating the Jews in the post-Nazi era. By objecting to the term, those who do not care much about hostility toward Jews can insist that what is happening in the Arab world is at its core political and not to be confused with bigotry and hatred. Avoidance of the term further enables apologists to dodge confronting the very substantial overlap between contemporary Muslim Jew-hatred and historical Christian animosity toward Jews. The use of the word "antisemitism," precisely because it has so frequently been used in other contexts, implies continuity between the old and the new, the Christian and the Islamic. This, as shall be seen, is highly appropriate—notwithstanding the desire by many to erect an insurmountable wall between the two.

One point must be made clear. There is plenty of anti-Arab and anti-Muslim bigotry in the world, and these hatreds must be addressed on their own terms. However, it is not intellectually or morally justifiable to speak—as some have—of "Zionist practices against Semitism,"[44] to subsume anti-Arab bigotry under the heading of antisemitism, or to require the avoidance of the term altogether.

Some Hope from the Thirteenth Century

Léon Poliakov, the highly regarded French historian of antisemitism, had some concerns about the endeavor to which he had dedicated his life.[45] He worried, first, that by uncovering the activities and beliefs of past antisemites he would fuel future ones. His fear was not idle, as each new generation of Jew-haters has always drawn strength from the reinforcing conviction that so many in the past have shared their obsession. For example, if one calls attention to the anti-Jewish beliefs of greatly admired Muslim religious figures from the past, particularly from the early days of the Prophet, this may have the counterproductive impact of increasing the confidence of contemporary Muslim Jew-haters. In this sense, it may, on occasion, make for good public relations to accentuate the positive and bury the negative. Yet the truth is the truth. Antisemites will in any case have little difficulty locating their own antecedents, and writers ultimately should stand by a belief in the value of telling the truth. Still, from a tactical standpoint—one that Poliakov probably considered beyond his purview—the question of how political, religious, and intellectual leaders, especially outsiders, should handle "insensitive" political, intellectual, social, and religious traditions remains challenging.

Poliakov also worried that the historian of antisemitism necessarily "becomes a denouncer, and neither the precautions he takes in the name of the rules of his art, nor the affection he comes to experience for the subject of his study, nor the justice he forces himself to render to all the protagonists discussed, can make any change in this fundamental posture."[46] As Dina Porat, a prominent Israeli scholar of antisemitism, explained Poliakov's position, "the historian is constantly calling into question the values of the non-Jewish surrounding society, pinpointing flaws and criticizing behaviours. If one bears in mind that persecution of Jews and of other minorities has always been pursued in the name of the most revered values, such as religion, the unity of a nation, uniqueness of culture and reverence for the past, then Western Christian societies must indeed be repeatedly arraigned before history's court of justice."[47] Similarly, anyone who purports to study Muslim hostility toward Jews finds himself or herself frequently in the role of denouncer, charged with the critical examination of the sacred works and deepest beliefs of many people.

It is, therefore, important to state my belief that all religions, at least all with which I am familiar, can be—and have been—a source of very good behaviors as well as very bad ones. In my last book, I tried to examine some of the social, psychological, political, and theological conditions under which religions become destructive.[48] It is my view that presently a significant portion of Islam has been infected by antisemitism and that some—though not all—of the responsibility for this hatred can be traced back to sacred sources (at least the way some Muslims have read them). The picture that I paint is generally bleak.

But the sacred sources of Judaism and Christianity also can provide, and frequently have provided, incitements to hatred—and so too have atheistic ideologies. In fact, all religious history can be viewed as the study of how believers in various eras have applied, adapted, reconstructed, and abandoned religious source precepts—via authorized and unauthorized methods—to fit the perceived needs of the day. Much of what was once gospel truth is no longer gospel truth. What Jewish law required fifteen hundred years ago is now often ignored, with the complete support of all rabbis. The Egyptian philosopher Fouad Zakariya has argued, "Islam is nothing other than what Muslims make of it."[49] Although this formula would go too far for most Muslim believers, it does force one to attend to the plasticity and diversity of belief within the Islamic world. Also, for most of the Islamic past, despite anti-Jewish religious and historical sources, Jew-hatred did not rise to the level of an obsession—as it was for many centuries in the Christian world. And therein lies some hope.

After all, even in the Christian world, things changed—and dramatically. In the 1985 edition of his important 1965 book *The Anguish of the Jews*, Father Edward Flannery suggested that it might take another 250 years for Christian antisemitism to disappear. His judgment surely must have seemed reasonable at the time, given the tremendous hostility to Jews in basic Christian sources.[50] Yet one might concur with Philip Cunningham's foreword to the 2004 edition of Flannery's volume that one might now suggest a "quicker time frame for the end of what Flannery called theologically-based 'Christian antisemitism.'"[51]

So, too, optimism might emerge from a poem by the thirteenth-century Muslim Sufi poet Muhyiddin Ibn 'Arabi:

> My heart can take on any form:
> A meadow for gazelles,
> A cloister for monks,
> For the idols, sacred ground,
> Ka'aba for the circling pilgrim,
> The tables of the Torah,
> The scrolls of the Quran.
> My creed is Love;
> Wherever its caravan turns along the way,
> That is my belief,
> My faith.[52]

Not much is heard from open-minded Sufi poets these days, but they too are part of the Islamic tradition.

And there is also hope in brave men such as Tarek Fatah, a Canadian Muslim with Pakistani roots who in 2010 authored *The Jew Is Not My Enemy: Unveiling the Myths That Fuel Muslim Anti-Semitism*.[53] Fatah cites a verse from the Quran, ignored by Islamists, that he thinks should define attitudes toward members of other faiths:

Surely those who believe,
And those who are Jews,
And the Christians and the Sabians,
Whoever believes in God and the Last Day,
And does good, they have their reward with their Lord,
And there is no fear for them,
Nor shall they Grieve.[54]

We will return to Tarek Fatah and other inspiring Muslim opponents of Jew-hatred. But first we must assess the present, as Fatah does, with open eyes.

Organization of the Book

The next chapter, "Evidence," documents two powerful strains of Muslim Jew-hatred, the first homegrown in the Islamic world and the second imported and adapted from Europe in the nineteenth and twentieth centuries. This chapter marshals evidence that Jew-hatred—not just hostility toward Israel—is widespread and virulent in many Muslim-majority countries and also among some Muslims elsewhere. Chapter 3, "The Shame of the Antiracist Community," highlights the tendency of many intellectuals, journalists, artists, political leaders, and human rights activists in the West to ignore, downplay, misunderstand, or explain away overwhelmingly corroborated Muslim anti-Jewish bigotry. Chapter 4 explores "The Flawed Logic of Antisemitism Minimization" and rebuts seven frequently heard arguments against the significance of antisemitism in the Islamic world. Chapter 5, "Ancient Roots, Modern Roots," explores why anti-Jewish bigotry has thrived in recent years, focusing on the pathways through which history becomes socially, politically, and psychologically relevant. Finally, chapter 6, "Fighting Back against Bigotry," offers some thoughts on what might be done to address the problem of Muslim antisemitism, paying particular attention to Arab and Muslim voices that have been raised against Jew-hatred.

2

EVIDENCE

In January 2009, about two weeks into Israel's attack on Gaza—which had been launched with the declared goal of protecting Israeli citizens from rocket fire—the Saudi daily newspaper *Al-Jazirah* published a bit of angry verse by S'ad Al-Bawardi:

> You were merciful, oh Hitler.
> [That is my conclusion] when I see around me
> The cruel acts
> Of the descendants of apes.
> You were wise, oh Hitler
> To rid the world
> Of some of these wild pigs.[1]

That same month, a columnist in the Kuwaiti daily newspaper *Al-Jarida* asked, Why would Israel "be so cruel and kill innocent civilians, especially children? Was it a mistake, or was it an accidental consequence of the fighting?" Neither of these answers appealed to the journalist, who, instead, opined that the conduct of the Israeli armed forces reflected "an ancient ideology [that is part of] Jewish history and comes from the book that they call the Talmud. . . . One of the psalms in the Talmud says: 'As for their children, one must focus on killing them and on dashing them against the walls. Pulverize their skulls until no trace is left of them.'" The columnist further wrote, "The occupation of Palestine is [only] the first step in a long journey [whose ultimate goal] is to take over the entire world and use its resources, according to the right granted to them by the Talmudic authority."[2] Given such beliefs, it is not surprising that the author concludes that

"Israel's talk about peace is a temporary [tactic] that is not to be trusted, because the Talmud instructs the Jews to lie, deceive and use every method that is immoral by the lights of both the ancient world and the modern."[3]

On another occasion, this time a few months after the Gaza War had ended, a young and energetic Palestinian cleric shared some hopes with a large crowd during his Friday sermon: "Allah willing, the moment will come when their property will be destroyed and their sons annihilated, until not a single Jew or Zionist is left on the face of the Earth."[4]

The poem, the newspaper column, and the sermon—which was broadcast on Al Aqsa—seemed not to focus much on distinctions among Israelis, Zionists, and other Jews. Although many Arab leaders do make such distinctions, with varying degrees of sincerity, other influential people reject any such categorizations as superficial and deceptive.

Thus, as far back as 1969, a Jordanian minister for social affairs declared, "It is our firm belief that there is no difference at all between Jews and Zionists. All Jews are Zionists and all Zionists are Jews, and anyone who thinks otherwise is not thinking logically. We consider world Jewry our adversary and enemy."[5] And in 1982, not long after the Egyptian-Israeli peace treaty was signed, Lutfi Abd al-Azim, a prominent Egyptian editor, wrote, perhaps during a moment of outrage, "A Jew is a Jew, and hasn't changed for thousands of years. He is base, contemptible, scorns all moral values, gnaws on live flesh, and sucks blood for pittance. The Jewish merchant of Venice is not different from the arch-executioners of Deir Yasin and those at the [Palestinian] refugee camps. Both are similar models of inhuman depravity."[6]

Columnists, imams, and especially poets should perhaps be granted some license to express their views. More importantly, the high volume of especially angry sentiments heard in early 2009 can certainly be understood in part as a response to Israel's military campaign in Gaza. Indeed, Hannah Rosenthal, the Obama administration special envoy who heads the State Department's Office to Monitor and Combat Anti-Semitism, has collected data on antisemitic incidents showing that 2009 was a particularly bad year; she attributes this spike in bigotry largely to the war in Gaza.[7] Although Israel claimed Operation Cast Lead, its Gaza action, was a response to thousands of Hamas rockets launched into Israel over several years, the operation was perceived by many in the Arab and Muslim world (and beyond) as an atrocity. And when one feels that one is the target of an atrocity, according to this logic, one might understandably forget the social niceties of modern intergroup relations and allow one's baser instincts to dominate.

Thus, S'ad Al-Bawardi's poem in *Al-Jazirah* went on to say:

Oh Hitler,
The descendants of apes
None are more cruel and horrifying than they are. . . .
Their wars of destruction
Are worse than the "Holocaust."
Destruction of the world is their motto,
And they are implementing it in practice
In Gaza, in the Golan and in Lebanon.
The descendants of apes are the cruelest creatures
That mankind has ever known.[8]

This poem refers to several arenas in which the Israeli government has carried out policies that are tremendously unpopular in much of the Arab world. Thus, some would argue that harsh anti-Jewish sentiments in Arab and Muslim countries are fundamentally political and not without a kernel of truth—even if the mode of their expression is excessive and boorish.

One frequently encountered theory holds that the anger behind the bigotry starts with the genuine frustrations endured by Palestinians in the Arab-Israeli conflict. Owing at least partly to Israeli insensitivity, paranoia, ethnocentricity, and/or overreliance on military methods, the Palestinians have for generations been unable to get a fair shake. After decades of mistakes made by the Israelis, the West, and the Arab states, the Palestinian situation has deteriorated to the point of extreme suffering and humiliation. And, unfortunately, some of this legitimate anger has boiled over into prejudice. Along with the Palestinians—and acting mainly out of similar motivation—many other Arabs and Muslims have indirectly experienced the suffering and pain of their brethren and joined in their hostility to Jews. But this prejudice against Jews is not like old-fashioned bigotry. Rather, it is an outgrowth of a political conflict, and its solution is at bottom political.[9]

One way to evaluate this perspective is to examine the content of anti-Jewish messages delivered in recent years. The dramatic intensification of animosity toward the Jews—not merely toward Israel or Zionists—dates back to well before the brief Gaza conflict. Indeed, Israel and the Palestinians pursued a peace process for much of the late 1990s that culminated in 2000 with Israeli prime minister Ehud Barak's offer to establish a two-state solution on terms judged by many impartial third parties to be fair. At that very time, however, Hitler's *Mein Kampf* became a favorite in the Palestinian territories.[10] Even in relatively liberal Turkey in 2005, *Mein Kampf* made it onto bestseller lists. Since 1940 the book had been published there at least forty-five times.[11] Thus, while the level of anti-Jewish hostility may indeed fluctuate in response to regional and world events, one should be cautious about reductionistic explanations that attempt to explain away antisemitism as a consequence of particular recent incidents. Consider, after all, the sources cited by the demagogues themselves.

For example, the Palestinian cleric mentioned previously—who in his sermon had hoped for the death of every Jew in the world—shared with his audience the main foundations for his judgment about the fundamental evil of the Jewish people. Like the Egyptian imam who had blamed the Jews for the invention of soccer, this cleric cited *The Protocols of the Elders of Zion*; he also claimed to derive his message as well from the holy Quran. According to the sermon, "[In *The Protocols*,] the Jews included their plan to besiege the whole world by land, by air, by sea, by ideology, by economy, and by the media, as is happening today, my brothers in the nation of the Prophet Muhammad. The Jews today are weaving their spider webs in order to encircle our nation like a bracelet encircles the wrist, and in order to spread corruption throughout the world." Then, he informed believers, "We Muslims know best the nature of the Jews, because the Koran has informed us about this, and because the pure Sunna of the Prophet Muhammad has devoted much space to informing the Muslims of the truth about the Jews and their hostility to Islam and its Prophet."[12]

It is important to note that those—like this imam—who claim to rest their hateful beliefs on sacred Islamic texts are in no sense the final arbiters of what those texts really intend or how they should be interpreted in the twenty-first century. Many Muslims are not hostile to Jews, and even when Arabs and Muslims do express unfair and extremely negative views of Israel, it might sometimes be attributable to misguided politics or misplaced nationalistic loyalty more so than to bigotry in the traditional sense. More importantly, as noted, some in Muslim and Arab communities are committed to resisting religion-based calls to antisemitism, and a few others are even dedicated to fighting it.[13]

The Arab-Israeli conflict has undoubtedly fueled and increased Muslim Jew-hatred. Still, it is possible to see anti-Jewish bigotry as a major reason why the conflict has, in the first place, lasted so long and proved so resistant to compromise. We will return to this argument later. But one thing is immediately clear: to fully understand Muslim and Arab Jew-hatred, we must examine sources—homegrown and imported from Europe—that predate the Arab-Israeli wars by some time.

Pigs and Apes

In his poem in *Al-Jazirah*, S'ad Al-Bawardi referred to Jews as "wild pigs" and "descendants of apes." These ancient designations have become quite popular in recent years. While certain Quranic verses (Sura 2.62–66; 7.163–66; 5:59–60), hadiths (sayings of the Prophet), and later commentaries clearly provide a potential source for Bawardi's ethnic slurs, it is no simple matter to assess the meaning and significance of this religious material. For example, Suhaib Webb, an American convert to Islam, suggested that the Quranic transformation of Jews into pigs and apes "does not refer to all people of the Jewish faith, but only a certain group of people from the followers of Musa [Moses]." Moreover, he argued, "It is not appropriate for one to call people of the Jewish tradition 'pigs and apes' or 'sons of pigs and apes' since, besides being extremely rude, it is not correct."[14] Similarly, Ruqaiyyah Waris Maqsood, a learned moderate British Muslim who has authored more than forty books, concluded, "None of [the Quranic] passages has any racist intent, or is racist in any way whatsoever; they all refer to a punishment that fell upon certain particular sinners, and they have nothing to do with racism."[15] If Webb and Maqsood are correct—and, in my view, they at least partly are—clearly quite a few of their coreligionists are misreading the sacred works.

A review of recent "pigs and apes" references can rapidly become tedious, but it is necessary in order to observe the epithet's acceptability in public discourse as well as the range of uses to which it has been put. As noted previously, the late—and, in many Western circles, highly regarded putative moderate—Sheikh Mohammed Sayed Tantawi of Al-Azhar University at least for a while called Jews "enemies of Allah, descendants of apes and pigs." Similarly, Dr. Muhammad 'Abd Al-Sattar, the Syrian deputy minister of religious endowment, said, "The people who were given the Torah were likened to a donkey carrying books. They were also likened to apes and pigs, and they are, indeed, the descendants of apes and pigs, as the Koran teaches us."[16]

Sheikh Abdul Rahman Al-Sudais also throws his considerable prestige behind the use of the "pigs and apes" epithet. An imam at one of the most important mosques in Mecca and the holder of a doctorate in Islamic religious law, he is renowned across the Muslim world for his beautiful recitations of Quranic verse. When he visited England to participate in the dedication of London's Islamic Cultural Centre, key British media spoke of the sheikh's message of peace and moderation.[17] Yet, about a year before this trip that played so well in the British press, Sudais had advised his flock, "Read history and you will understand that the Jews of yesterday are the evil forefathers of the even more evil Jews of today: infidels, falsifiers of words, calf worshippers, prophet murderers, deniers of prophecies . . . the scum of the human race, accursed by Allah, who turned them into apes and pigs. . . . These are the Jews—an ongoing continuum of deceit, obstinacy, licentiousness, evil, and corruption."[18]

Given the utterances of these prominent leaders, it is perhaps not surprising that many more extreme Islamic figures have taken to describing Jews consistently as pigs and apes. For example, Hassan Nasrallah, the head of Lebanon's Hezbollah organization, addressed the Jews as "the murderers of the prophets, the grandsons of apes and pigs."[19] And on Palestinian Authority television, Muslim cleric Sheikh Ibrahim Mahdi used the phrase to add vigor to his *cri de guerre* against Israel, declaring, "All weapons must be aimed at the Jews, at the enemies of Allah, the cursed nation in the Qur'an, whom the Qur'an describes as monkeys and pigs."[20]

In addition, Abdallah Bin Matruk Al-Haddal—a Saudi cleric who was sympathetic to Osama bin Laden—saw in hostility to Jews a means to divide Jews and Christians in the West. He declared on the Al-Jazeera television network:

> I am surprised that the Christian U.S. allows the 'brothers of apes and pigs' to corrupt it. [The Jews] have murdered the prophets and the messengers. [The Jews] are the most despicable people who walked the land and are the worms of the entire world. . . . The Muslims have mercy on the Christians more than they have on the Jews. Bin Laden defended the oppressed. We warn the U.S. and advise her to get rid of the Jews.[21]

A number of years earlier, before al Qaeda's declaration of war against the United States, the Egyptian Al-Jihad organization—a radical group headed by bin Laden's number two, Ayman al-Zawahiri—issued a communiqué explaining,

"The only way to recover our rights is the way of sacrifice and martyrdom, the one followed by the Jordanian *mujahid* who fired a whole round into the chests of the offspring of apes and pigs."[22] On this occasion, "offspring of apes and pigs" referred specifically to Israeli schoolchildren.

The phrase enters not infrequently into Arab discussions of Israel. In some political cartoons, Israeli leaders—for example, Benjamin Netanyahu—are portrayed with pig snouts.[23] And when Israeli troops left Lebanon in 2000 in part to forward the peace process, Salim 'Azzouz, a columnist for the Egyptian opposition newspaper *Al-Ahrar*, wrote, "They fled with only the skin on their bodies, like pigs flee. And why say 'like' when they actually are pigs and apes?" More recently, during the Gaza War, an Egyptian cleric, Safwat Higazi, described Jews as "smooth as a viper, and who lick their lips as [does] a speckled snake." He then said, "Dispatch those sons of apes and pigs to the hellfire, on the wings of the Qassam rockets."[24]

Some evidence, admittedly anecdotal, suggests that the characterization of Jews as pigs and apes has been spreading beyond the rhetoric of clerics and into the consciousness of even some very small children. In a poignant 2002 interview, one three-and-a-half-year-old girl told a pleasant, smiling hostess on *The Muslim Woman Magazine* broadcast that she did not like Jews because God in the Quran said they were "apes and pigs." The interviewer couldn't have been more pleased on this Saudi-Egyptian satellite station that purportedly aimed to highlight the "true and tolerant picture of Islam and . . . [refute] the accusations directed against Islam." A true Muslim, the interviewer explained, should know who her enemies are.[25]

In December 2005 Al-Manar, a Hezbollah television station, featured a clay animation special for small children that illustrated the transformation of some Jews into animals.[26] "Pigs and apes" language even made its way to British schoolchildren via the Saudi-funded King Fahad Academy in Acton. The textbooks were brought to the public's attention by Colin Cook, a Muslim teacher who felt he had been treated unfairly by his employer. The books noted "the repugnant characteristics of the Jews" and said they were "those whom God has cursed and with whom he is angry. . . . He has turned [them] into monkeys and pigs. They worship Satan."[27] The principal, saying that the offensive sections were not used and that the text included some good chapters, at first refused to drop the book from the curriculum. Later, facing public pressure, she relented.

One must ask how it came to pass that a few controversial—or perhaps noncontroversial—Quranic passages became the basis for so many references to Jews as "pigs and apes," "sons of pigs and apes," "descendants of pigs and apes," "brothers of pigs and apes," and "grandchildren of pigs and apes." The most common version of the ancient story of transmogrification starts with a Jewish taste for fish—although precise details vary somewhat, depending on which Quranic commentaries one chooses to follow. One frequently encountered version sets the tale at an unspecified time prior to Muhammad's era in the village of Iliya on the coast of the Red Sea.[28]

According to both Jewish and Islamic tradition, God had prohibited Jews from working on the Sabbath, and work, by common agreement, included fishing. Muhammad believed that Jews were obligated to follow the laws God had given them and that, if they did not, they would be punished. On one occasion, God wanted to test the faith of the Jews. According to the Quran, God arranged things so that "each Sabbath the fish used to appear before . . . [the Jews] floating on the water, but on week-days they never came near them." Thus, Sabbath fishing became an alluring, although deeply forbidden, activity.

The Jews sought ways to circumvent this dilemma. According to one traditional commentator, a Jew secretly caught a fish on the Sabbath, tied it to a string, threw it back, and then "caught" it again on the following day. When he got away with the deception, he repeated it. Soon some of his neighbors caught on. They began to fish openly and even sold their catch at the market.

At least, this is one version of the tale. Another has some Jews digging a tidal pool to trap the fish. There are endless stories in the commentaries about precisely what the Jews did to incur the wrath of God, some going beyond the fishing incidents. Yet, in these tales, the common theme is that the Jews were punished because they broke their own religious laws.

In the end, as Sura 7:166 in the Quran says, "when they scornfully persisted in what they had been forbidden, We changed them into detested apes." In another translation, the Quran says, "When in their insolence they transgressed [all] prohibitions, We said to them: 'Be ye apes, despised and rejected.' Two other Quranic verses make reference to the transformation, reinforcing the message and adding that some of the Jews were transformed into swine. One tradition holds that the young Jews became apes and the older ones became pigs.

The sinning Jews, some say, locked themselves into their homes, went to sleep, and awoke as apes. According to other early Islamic sources—for example,

Al-Jahiz's *The Book of Animals*—it was also believed that other animals, specifically cheetahs, lizards, eels, and mice, were originally Jews. There are also commentaries suggesting that some Christians—also "people of the book," according to Islam—had been transformed by Allah into animals, although this tradition does not garner much attention nowadays.

How is one to understand these stories? One possibility is that Muhammad was trying to win supporters. To do so, he needed to highlight the power of Allah and the superiority of the new message to those revelations that came before and to which Muhammad was obviously indebted. The transformation of humans into animals, though it sounds discordant to twenty-first-century, scientifically inclined ears, was not unprecedented or even unusual for Muhammad's day. Given how little is actually known about the Jews of the Arabian Peninsula before Muhammad, it is not implausible that the story even had roots in a local Jewish tradition—although to assert this would be pure speculation. But, clearly, Muhammad, especially in the early years, showed some respect, albeit limited, for both Judaism and Christianity.

The story, after all, tells that some Jews—the genuinely observant ones—escaped punishment. Moreover, Muslim commentators disagree among themselves about whether the transformation was literal or metaphorical; most early commentators apparently believe that the Jews actually changed physically. Classical Muslim commentators also have differing opinions about whether the transformed Jews had offspring, with most believing that they did not.

There are, however, those like Sheikh Ahmad 'Ali 'Othman, superintendent of *da'wa* (missionary) affairs at the Egyptian Ministry of Religious Endowments, who issued a 2009 fatwa declaring that all pigs in the world today are descended from Jews. According to 'Othman:

> I personally tend to believe that the pigs living today are descended from those Jews, and that is why Allah forbade us to eat them, saying, 'Forbidden unto you [for food] are carrion and blood and swineflesh [Quran 5:3].' In addition, one of the things that Jesus will do when he returns to earth on Judgment Day is kill all the pigs, and that is proof that they are descended from Jews. All the pigs on earth will be destroyed by Jesus on Judgment Day.[29]

A more progressive response to 'Othman came from Sheikh 'Ali Abu Al-Hassan, head of the Al-Azhar University Fatwa Committee. Hassan said, "When Allah punishes a group of people because they have incurred his wrath, the punishment applies only to them. When Allah was angry with the people of Moses, he turned them [and only them] into apes and pigs. It was an unusual punishment, meant to serve as a deterrent to others. But [those apes and pigs] died, and did not multiply, as Sheik Ahmad 'Ali 'Othman claims."[30] 'Othman, for his part, maintains that the Al-Azhar sheikhs secretly agree with him but that they do not want to be labeled antisemites.

If one reads the Quranic verses and commentaries in a liberal frame of mind, one can certainly see how Ruqaiyyah Waris Maqsood arrives at her ultimate judgment that the "pigs and apes" punishment "was simply used as a metaphor for supposedly believing persons (either Jews or Muslims) who had deliberately and willfully chosen to ignore commandments from God." Moreover, her notion that the transformation into animals was figurative, that no physical metamorphosis took place—while at odds with most classical commentators—is at least arguable and not altogether without classical support. Similarly, a reading of the religious sources might support the position of Dr. Muzammil H. Siddiqi, the president of the Fiqh Council of North America, who wrote, "The Qur'an does not say in any place that all Jews are apes and pigs. . . . About the Jewish people in particular it is said in the Qur'an: 'And of Moses' folk there is a community who lead with truth and establish justice therewith [7:159].'" If one accepts the line of argument advanced by Siddiqi or Maqsood, one might then infer that the Islamic religious tradition plays no role in the genesis of anti-Jewish prejudice and that bigots have misused and corrupted essentially benign source material.

In my view, this judgment absolves the religious tradition a bit too quickly. The question remains, for example, why malevolent interpretations of the Quranic tale of the metamorphosis have developed such traction in the current era. One reason is that many who do not accept the notion of a literal transformation or of a punishment that persists to the present still find justification to use the "pigs and apes" slur. Thus, Hamas leader Nizar Rayyan—who was killed in the 2009 Gaza War—told *The Atlantic* reporter Jeffrey Goldberg two years earlier that to allow a Jewish state to survive in the Muslim Middle East was an "impossibility" and "an offense against God." He had some interesting thoughts on the matter of pigs and apes. Rayyan said, "Allah changed disobedient Jews into apes and pigs, it is true, but he specifically said these apes and pigs did not have the ability to reproduce. So it is not literally true that Jews today are descended from pigs and apes, but it is true that some of the ancestors of Jews were transformed into pigs and apes, and it is true that Allah continually makes the Jews pay for their crimes in many different ways. They are a cursed people." "What were our crimes?" the Jewish reporter asked Rayyan. "'You are murderers of the prophets and you have closed your ears to the Messenger of Allah,' he said. 'Jews tried to kill the Prophet, peace be unto him. All throughout history, you have stood in opposition to the word of God.'"[31]

Some contemporary Muslim theologians would disagree with this logic, but Rayyan did not manufacture his opinions out of thin air. After all, the influential Sheikh Qaradawi also denies that the Jews of today are descendants of those who were turned into pigs and apes but nonetheless remains deeply bigoted and strongly supportive of suicide bombings against Israeli civilians.[32]

Despite Muhammad's partial respect for the Jewish and Christian faiths, some aspects of the Islamic religious tradition could plausibly be read as support for the hostile interpretation of the "pigs and apes" source material. Mostly, such potentially inflammatory elements again involve stories about particular Jews, rather than all Jews. One incident concerns Muhammad himself presiding over the massacre of hundreds of unarmed noncombatants from the Jewish Banu Qurayza tribe. According to Ibn Hisham's ninth-century version of the (now lost) earlier biography of Muhammad written by Ibn Ishaq,

> when they surrendered, the Apostle of Allah—may Allah bless him and grant him peace—had them imprisoned in Medina. . . . Then the Apostle went to the market of Medina . . . and had trenches dug. After that, he sent for them and had them decapitated into those trenches as they were brought out into groups. . . . In all, they were about six hundred or seven hundred, although some say there were as many as eight hundred or nine hundred.[33]

Later, Ibn Hisham wrote, "The Apostle of Allah—may Allah bless him and grant him peace—divided the property of the Banu Qurayza along with their wives and their children among the Muslims."[34] The impact of this precedent is hard to overstate.

Another story tells how a Jewish woman—partly motivated by anger that Muslims killed some of her family members—tries to poison the Prophet. She is unsuccessful in the short term, but according to some, her act left an illness in Muhammad that, years later, resulted in his death.[35] Numerous other stories of Jews who lack virtue and integrity show up throughout the religious literature.

Thus, when speakers nowadays describe Jews as dishonest, cunning, violators of treaties, or killers of prophets, they may—correctly or incorrectly, depending on which experts one chooses to believe—be drawing on an early religious tradition that is highly valued by Muslims across the globe. Some of these stories originate in materials whose authenticity has been questioned by various contemporary and traditional Islamic scholars, yet some come from sources consensually regarded as authentic.[36]

Stories casting Jews in a negative light and those showing anti-Jewish behavior by Muhammad need to be considered carefully in their historical and religious context—although the antisemites themselves often do not do so. One could reasonably argue that none of the negative references to Jews require that a contemporary Muslim believer possess hostility to Jews. Moreover, anti-Jewish references in the sacred sources do not explain why hostility to Jews is far more intense today than in many past eras of Islamic history. Finally, contemporary Christianity possesses at least as strong a religious foundation for Jew-hatred as Islam—in truth, much stronger—yet in the present day much of its potential for bigotry and hatred has been muted.

Religiously Based Dehumanization of the Jews

Whatever the roots of "pigs and apes" thinking, one should not minimize the significance of religiously based dehumanization of the Jews. Referring to Jews as pigs and apes is far more than mere name-calling. Indeed, nearly all scholars who study the dynamics of genocide have highlighted the role of such dehumanization in creating the preconditions for mass murder. In Rwanda, the Hutus referred to the Tutsis as *inyenzi*, or "cockroaches." Nazis spoke of the Jews as rats, tumors, or vermin.[37] As Professor Menahem Milson explained, "The belief that God once turned some Jews into apes, pigs, or other creatures [should not] be considered merely as an indication of primitive magical thinking. Repeated reference to the Jews as despised beasts dehumanizes them and provides justification for their destruction."[38] Dehumanization is often the first step to mass murder. It is much more effective when it can be plausibly attributed to an ancient and sacred source, held by believers to be infallible.

The antisemite may well conclude that an infallible God would not have described so many Jews in such unfavorable terms if, in fact, they were not evil or subhuman creatures. True, Jews (and Christians) under Islam were "dhimmis," or "protected" people. This controversial status established "peoples of the book" as second-class citizens and imposed various hardships on them, but it also afforded Jews and Christians some protection against the rhetoric of dehumanization (at least provided they played by the rules). Nonetheless, through selective reading of the sacred texts, antisemites could easily bypass this partial protection. And, solely by reading Islamic religious sources, many Muslims might well develop very negative—even if incorrectly negative—perspectives on the Jews.

Dehumanization plays a key role in the social psychology of genocide; it might be viewed as a precondition for mass killing, as something that clears, tills, and fertilizes the soil for murder. Another important ingredient in violent forms of mass hatred is fear. One usually does not kill in large numbers members of groups one dislikes unless one is afraid. Thus, Bosnian Serbs painted an image of themselves as the longtime victims of Croats and Muslims; they justified their violence against these groups as essentially defensive and preemptive. Similarly, Rwandan Hutus feared the consequences of advances by the Rwandan Patriotic Front, a Tutsi rebel army, and they looked to their own past and to the situation in Burundi for "evidence" of what might happen to them if the Tutsis became ascendant. The Turks during the First World War saw Armenians in their midst as a potential threat to the interests of their empire, and the Nazis, of course, developed a complex paranoia concerning the Jews, whom they perceived as demonically powerful. In some cases of mass hatred, the obsessive fears rest on a kernel of truth; in others, the phobic reaction rests entirely on fictitious and imagined threats.[39] A belief in immense Jewish power and secret Jewish conspiracies was long a prominent aspect of European antisemitism, and especially during the past eight decades, these beliefs have travelled down many roads to Arab and Muslim lands.

The Mentality of *The Protocols*

One cannot understand the contemporary Middle East and its many conflicts without first understanding *The Protocols of the Elders of Zion*, a collection of lectures supposedly detailing the Jews' complex, devious, and deceitful plan for defeating the gentiles and conquering the world. That this century-old forgery—ridiculous on its face and many times debunked in academia and courts of law—

keeps finding new life across the globe and that it now influences the thinking of many in the Muslim world should be deeply disturbing to all who care about the distinction between truth and falsehood.[40] New technologies have made the document and its message of Jewish conspiratorial power more immediately available to Middle Eastern publics than ever before; it can now be easily downloaded from the Web in many forms.

More importantly, a forty-one-part Egyptian television series, *Knight without a Horse* (also translated as "*Horseman without a Horse*" in various sources), based partly on *The Protocols*, was first broadcast to many speakers of Arabic in 2002. More recently, a twenty-nine-part Syrian-produced *Protocols* drama, *Al-Shatat* (The Diaspora), has aired on several stations. The Iranians also have televised in Farsi a drama and a news special (*The Secret of Armageddon*), both drawing substantially on *The Protocols*.[41] Eight years after *Knight without a Horse* first aired, its producer claimed that his series had been prophetic and that only months later the Americans had entered Iraq—bringing with them five hundred Jews. He further bragged that the main achievement of the Egyptian series had been the resulting sale of two million copies of *The Protocols* at the Cairo Book Fair.[42] In 2012 *Knight without a Horse* was rebroadcast in postrevolutionary Egypt.[43]

More and more often, the forgery is cited, usually unchallenged, as a respected historical source in Arab print and broadcast media, as well as in the media of other Islamic nations.[44] In 2007, for example, Maria Maalouf, a Lebanese television commentator on a station associated with Nabih Berri, the speaker of the Lebanese parliament, suggested that "the use that American and Israeli Zionism makes of the weapon of drugs in order to thwart *intifadas* and revolutions" is a consequence of Jews purporting "to have their own private god in the heavens, who commanded them to annihilate the nations and peoples of the world using drugs and causing anxiety, and numbing the mental, psychological, and physical capabilities of non-Jews, as written in the *Talmud* or the *Protocols of the Elders of Zion*."[45] A narrator then said, "In addition to the provoking of civil strife and to the poisoning of minds, the Jews have turned to physical poisoning. They became known in history for the poisoning of wells. They are also known for adding certain amounts of harmful substances to medicine and alcoholic beverages, as well as to flour and its products, and to other products that the Jews export, directly and indirectly, to unfriendly peoples, if not to all peoples."[46]

Under the circumstances, it's amazing how few Jews claim they know anything about *The Protocols of the Elders of Zion*. But, of course, assuming a conspiracy, if they did know, would they freely disclose this knowledge? (For that matter, it remains an open question what percentage of Jews could cite a single concept from the Talmud.)

Called "the lie that wouldn't die" and a "warrant for genocide," *The Protocols* have driven—or reinforced—virtually all of the last century's Jew-hatred.[47] The document played a role in legitimizing Russian antisemitic policies and violent pogroms in the early twentieth century. Hitler and Joseph Goebbels were true believers. So was Henry Ford, who underwrote publication of *The Protocols* in English and other languages. (Later, after doing much irreparable damage, he agreed that it was a forgery and apologized in 1927.) In the post–World War II period, antisemites on the left and right have made endless use of *The Protocols*. The Soviets distributed it when it suited propaganda purposes, disregarding the forgery's origins in the political machinations of imperial Russia. And, although there is no Hebrew translation, the document is currently available in most other major languages.

There is much variation among editions, but nearly always the reader is told that the so-called protocols themselves were fortuitously discovered and that they were never intended for gentile eyes. They are purported to be the record of a meeting of the members of a secret quasi-governmental Jewish organization. No discussion takes place at the meeting; instead, a top leader delivers the twenty-four lectures, unveiling the plan for world domination to an audience of Jewish leaders.

The meeting is sometimes said to have taken place secretly at the First Zionist Congress in Switzerland in 1897, but the plot is presented as something the Jews have long been implementing, rather than as a particular product of the Zionist movement. As might be expected, the Jews show no moral restraints and rely heavily on their control of world finances. But, beyond this, their grand plan includes appeals to class hatred; fomentation of revolutions; invention of the notion of "liberty, equality and fraternity"; secret control of the press and public officials; hypocrisy; bribery; fraud; treason; destruction of industrial prosperity; and misdirection of gentile education—in short, something for everyone.[48] The lack of specific names, places, and dates makes the document particularly portable across cultures and eras.

While it is hard to imagine someone buying the entire mélange, *The Protocols* is frequently taken as the smoking gun that establishes Jewish guilt for whatever particular crimes the reader has in mind—and also as general proof that the

Jews are evil, conspiratorial, powerful, and deceitful. One scholar of *The Protocols*, Richard S. Levy, noted that, despite its many print editions, "like that other bestseller, *Mein Kampf*, it is not the least bit clear that many have actually read the book."[49] Its power, he argued, may lie more in its general idea, passed along by opinion leaders who may have read the book or merely heard of its content. In any case, although many, perhaps most, readers would deem the document insane upon initial inspection, history shows that it can serve as a powerful indictment of the Jews for those unable or unwilling to see its inherent implausibility.[50]

Sometimes it's difficult to tell when the mentality of *The Protocols*—in some watered down form or more respectable garb—is at work. For example, is it behind the persistent survey research finding that in many Western countries large minorities of the public see Jews as possessing too much power, too much money, or too much control of the media? What is frequently observed in many Arab and Muslim countries, however, is not these diluted versions, but rather *The Protocols* thriving in its most primitive and crass form.

Consider, for example, the Hamas Charter. The founding covenant of the organization that won electoral control of Gaza in 2006 claims, "The Movement's programme is Islam. From it, it draws its ideas, ways of thinking and understanding the universe, life and man. It resorts to it for judgment in all its conduct, and it is inspired by it for guidance of its steps."[51] The charter—widely classified in the West as an extremist document because of its self-declared immutable commitment to the destruction of Israel—further holds that "Allah is its target [goal], the Prophet is its model, the Koran its constitution: Jihad is its path and death for the sake of Allah is the loftiest of its wishes." Yet, despite this explicitly religious raison d'être, the charter directly and centrally invokes the non-Islamic *Protocols*.

Thus, in describing the objectives of the enemy, the "Zionists," Article 32 states, "Today it is Palestine, tomorrow it will be one country or another. The Zionist plan is limitless. . . . Their plan is embodied in the 'Protocols of the Elders of Zion,' and their present conduct is the best proof of what we are saying." Article 22 descends even deeper into the mentality of *The Protocols*, claiming about the Jews:

> With their money, they took control of the world media, news agencies, the press, publishing houses, broadcasting stations, and others. . . . They were behind the French Revolution, the Communist revolution and most of the revolutions we heard and hear about, here and there. With their money they

formed secret societies, such as the Freemasons, Rotary Clubs, the Lions and others in different parts of the world for the purpose of sabotaging societies and achieving Zionist interests. . . . There is no war going on anywhere, without having their finger in it.

This charter was written in 1988. Sometimes, when trying to improve their standing in the West, the leaders of Hamas have attempted to cultivate a belief that the charter is no longer taken seriously. There is occasionally talk (especially in the West) about Hamas amending or dropping the document—and this may yet happen—though perhaps without abandoning the underlying sentiments. To date, however, all such hints at change have proved illusory. The charter does not permit long-term peace with Israel, but there has been mention of the permissibility of a moderately lengthy *hudna*, or "temporary truce." When asked whether he would consider amending the charter as part of a hudna deal, Khaled Meshaal, one of the organization's top leaders, was unequivocal. "Not a chance," he said.[52] And, on Al Aqsa television in April 2008, Culture Minister 'Atallah Abu Al-Subh explained, "I return to this book—*The Protocols of the Elders of Zion*—time and again. *The Protocols of the Elders of Zion* is the faith that every Jews harbors in his heart."[53]

As with "pigs and apes" defamation, references to *The Protocols* turn up in many high places. In 2002 a library was established at Alexandria, Egypt, with the goal of commemorating the great library of the ancient world that had stood not far away. The following year a display case at the library's new manuscript museum showed the holy books of the monotheistic religions. Next to the Torah was placed the first Arabic translation of *The Protocols*; on its cover was a star of David surrounded by snakes.[54]

A couple of years later, in Saudi Arabia, the daily newspaper *Al-Madina* featured a series of articles titled "The Serpent around Our Necks," allegedly confirming the authenticity of *The Protocols*. These articles alluded to the controversy concerning the origin of the document. But columnist Najah Al-Zahhar was not deterred, explaining, "The Jews all over [the world] hurried to declare that the *Protocols* had not been written by them, and that they were a forgery [created] with the intention of harming them. But their outcry was to no avail. Nobody believed them, since the match between the *Protocols* and real events is the most convincing proof of their authenticity."[55]

The widespread influence of *The Protocols* extends beyond the Arab world into other Muslim countries. In Malaysia, for example, there has been for some time a vibrant antisemitic industry, and several editions of *The Protocols* have been published. These played a significant role in spurring Jew-hatred in the late 1990s when currency speculation by George Soros, who was thought to be Jewish, may have done significant damage to the Malaysian economy (discussed in chapter 4).[56]

The Indonesian scholar Ibnu Burdah, director of the Center for Islamic and Middle Eastern Studies at the State Islamic University in Yogyakarta, reported in a carefully documented study, "*The Protocols of the Elders of Zion* is the most important source from which Indonesian Muslims define Jews." Burdah further maintained, "The absence of adequate discussion on the authenticity of *The Protocols* simply reinforces the perception of the existence of a Jewish conspiracy that threatens Muslims. It often stimulates Muslims' actions and, at certain moments, shapes Muslim reactions to the Israeli-Palestinian conflict."[57] There is nothing especially unusual about the situations in Malaysia and Indonesia; similar conditions prevail in most other Islamic countries.

Denis MacShane, a member of Parliament (MP) from the British Labour Party and an activist against global antisemitism, has noted, "Once antisemitic conspiracy theories have entered a nation's political DNA they remain for a long time."[58] While there is some clear-headed opposition to the belief in Jewish conspiratorial power in Muslim countries, one also finds those who reject belief in the veracity of *The Protocols* without rejecting hostility to Jews and/or Israel. On Egyptian television in April 2010, an Egyptian professor of Hebrew literature, Ibrahim Farid, offered a clear and principled rejection of *The Protocols*.[59] A few months earlier, however, a Saudi writer, Han Al-Naqshbandi, described belief in *The Protocols* as "self-demeaning" and "an intellectual fallacy," but he still called for revenge against Israel and for its "demise."[60]

Surprisingly, one Pakistani jihadi enthusiast linked to al Qaeda warned about attributing too much power to the Jews. He noted that Jews are often portrayed in extremist literature as the *Dajjal*—roughly a Muslim equivalent of the Antichrist. The jihadi columnist argued that although there may well be Jewish conspiracies, "in every era, the sole answer to the conspiracies of the Jews has been jihad in the path of Allah. When jihad was waged, all their conspiracies fell flat; whether Muslim[s] knew about it or not, their plots were smashed."[61] Here, oddly, even the rejection of Jewish conspiratorial power is viewed through a conspiratorial mind-set. There is a conspiracy to exaggerate the Jews' power in order to convince Muslims that there is no point to jihad.

The belief in the long arm of nefarious Jewish power often persists even among many who do not cite *The Protocols* itself and those who would be presumed to know better than to accept the authenticity of the much-debunked document. Thus, in 2003, just prior to his retirement, Mahathir Mohamad, Malaysia's longest serving prime minister, infamously told an assembly of Muslim leaders from across the globe:

> We [Muslims] are actually very strong, 1.3 billion people cannot be simply wiped out. The Nazis killed 6 million Jews out of 12 million [*sic*]. . . . But today the Jews rule the world by proxy. They get others to fight and die for them. They invented socialism, communism, human rights and democracy so that persecuting them would appear to be wrong so they may enjoy equal rights with others. With these they have now gained control of the most powerful countries.[62]

Less than twelve months before Mohamad spoke these words, an essay in the highly regarded *International Herald Tribune* declared, "The world needs to be reminded that the overwhelming majority of Muslims are peace-loving, sophisticated and keen on succeeding in the modern world. Mahathir might just be the candidate for the job."[63] The prime minister had been, on many matters, a pragmatic man. Yet, to most Western ears, his public ranting about the invention of human rights and democracy seemed like utter nonsense. Still, when viewed through the *Protocols* lens, his conclusions can be understood as merely a product of deductive reasoning. Indeed, ruling the world by proxy, gaining control of powerful countries, and getting others to fight "Jewish" wars are central tenets of the forged document.

The Ubiquity of Jewish Power

In the world of European antisemitism, it is clear that an irrational and unsubstantiated belief in Jewish power predated *The Protocols* and had many roots far back in European history.[64] Similarly, one need not argue that familiarity with the document itself is the immediate source of the demonization of the Jews in Muslim cultures in order to see that a particular body of European bigotry has hopped the cultural divide and become highly potent in many parts of the Muslim and Arab world.

As has been widely reported, many in the Muslim and Arab worlds currently see Jewish hands behind the 9/11 attacks. They blame the Israeli intelligence agency, an "Israeli art student" spy ring, and "Jewish owners" of the World Trade Center. They corroborate their theories with "evidence" of four thousand Jews who were "told to stay home on 9/11" and Israeli spies "caught" videotaping the destruction of the World Trade Center and then celebrating.[65] While one might expect some initial confused thinking in the months following such a large-scale event, it is now—more than a decade later—clear that the belief that "the Jews" caused 9/11 has entered into the worldview of at least a large minority of Arabs and Muslims. Once such lies have gained a foothold, they are exceptionally difficult to eradicate and may—if the past is any guide—persist for decades or longer.[66]

The rise of many forms of Holocaust denial in Arab and Muslim countries (and, to some extent, elsewhere in the world) can be viewed in part as another manifestation of "*Protocols* thinking." As the French scholar Pierre-André Taguieff has noted, this thinking centers around the belief that the Jews are everywhere, control everything, and will stop at nothing to achieve their aims. The facts of the real Holocaust stand powerfully as a refutation of these core antisemitic beliefs. Yet, if the Jews can be seen as the ones who crafted the "lie of Auschwitz," then surely they can accomplish anything and everything in pursuit of their ultimate aims.[67] Holocaust denial comes in many forms, sometimes subtle, sometimes not. Often, in the Muslim world, it assumes "reasonable" garb in claims that the Jews did suffer a bit but that they have grossly exaggerated the extent of their suffering. This mental callisthenic can be seen in high places; for example, in the declaration by the Libyan president of the United Nations General Assembly that Israel's siege in Gaza in 2010 created "a camp that is worse than the camps of the Nazis of the past."[68] Whether one approves or disapproves of Israel's actions in Gaza, this belief is unsustainable without a concurrent mind-set that includes Holocaust minimization.

And consider an essay on an official Iranian news website that declared that one could "never find even one single person who is an Auschwitz survivor."[69] In the summer of 2010, moreover, a "nongovernmental cultural" organization in Iran launched a new website, Holocartoons.com, featuring cartoons portraying the killing of six million Jews by the Nazis as a sheer lie; the website opened to the *Pink Panther* theme song by Henry Mancini.[70] Apparently, this was an effort to breathe new life into an old tradition. Four years earlier, the Iranian government had hosted a major ingathering of deniers from around the world, and some time before that the Iranian president had declared the Holocaust a "fairy tale." This sort of Holocaust denial coexists in antisemitic thought with two other notions: first, that Hitler did kill Jews and was therefore some sort of misunderstood hero and, second, that Hitler did kill Jews but with the complicity of the Zionists. The latter belief is entirely consistent with *Protocols* thinking in that the rich and powerful Jewish leaders are portrayed in the document as ready to sacrifice some of their brethren to achieve the higher goal of Jewish world domination.

The concept of evil Jewish power knows no limits for the true believer. Some also see hidden Zionist or Jewish conspiracies behind World War I, World War II, and the Crusades. It is widely believed that the banks and the world economy are run by Zionists or Jews. Many popular songs, movies, books, and works of art are perceived to be Jewish-inspired or Zionistic products because they are deemed to assail the moral decency of men, women, or the young. Jews or Zionists frequently are said to control the United States, including the Clinton, George W. Bush, and Obama administrations.

Without searching too hard, one can uncover an amazing array of institutions, nations, people, theories, and historical events attributed to the Jews, the Zionists, or Jewish control. For instance, in 1996 a Hamas publication included an article suggesting that Jews invented Darwin's theory of evolution. They apparently did so because they were embarrassed that some of their ancestors had been apes and consequently wanted to establish that all humans had similarly base origins.[71] Samir 'Ubeid, an Iraqi researcher living in Europe, told Al-Jazeera that the Nobel Prizes are racist, asking, "Why has the prize been awarded to 167 Jews, and to only four Arabs out of 380 million Arabs—and all four are considered traitors? . . . Democracy does not explain how it was awarded to 167 Jews, from among those 15 million scattered around the world, while abandoning 1.5 billion Chinese, a billion Indians, and 380 million Arabs. This is racism." When asked about Muhammad Yunus, who won the Nobel Peace Prize for establishing the Grameen Bank, 'Ubeid attributed the win to "the core of the *Protocols of the Elders of Zion*."[72] One can't be sure, but perhaps he was alluding to the portion of the document dealing with the Jewish support of socialism and human rights as a means of manipulating the masses.

The belief in Jewish ubiquity descends even further into fantasy, but to understand how a slight detour is necessary. Millions of people have watched Tom, the blue-gray cartoon cat, chasing Jerry, the small brown mouse. Tom rarely catches Jerry because the mouse is simply too tricky and too clever. The plot recurs endlessly as the duo takes turns inflicting pain and humiliation on each other. Despite their cruelty, both characters are lovable, but it is the diminutive Jerry who typically emerges as the winner. He may put the cat's tail in a waffle iron, slice him in half, or shut a door on his head. But, of course, the cat will always be back for more. *Tom and Jerry* cartoons have been around in many forms since 1940 and have been shown with some regularity around the world.

Yet, according to Iranian professor Hasan Bolkhari, hardly a soul knows the truth about the duo.[73] He claimed to reveal it on Iranian television in February 2006. Bolkhari holds impressive credentials, including a PhD in Islamic philosophy. He is also an adviser to the Film Council of the Islamic Republic of Iran Broadcasting and a member of the Interfaith Jury at Iran's international film festival; the Interfaith Jury, supposedly, was established with the goal of promoting interfaith communication between Christians and Muslims. A well-dressed and well-groomed academic, Dr. Bolkhari spoke in a calm and dignified manner before a large live audience that took notes.

Bolkhari first explained that *Tom and Jerry* was created by Walt Disney and that "the Jewish Walt Disney Company gained international fame with this cartoon." The cartoon was actually created by William Hanna and Joseph Barbera. It was owned by MGM and later Time Warner—not by Disney. Walt Disney was not Jewish. And curiously, his actual creation—Mickey Mouse—was not mentioned in Bolkhari's talk.

Bolkhari advised his audience to "watch *Schindler's List.* . . . The Jews were degraded and termed 'dirty mice.' *Tom and Jerry* was made in order to change the Europeans' perception of mice." According to the professor, "If you study European history, you will see who was the main power in hoarding money and wealth in the 19th century. In most cases, it is the Jews." Jewish hoarding of wealth, it seems, was at the root of the mouse-Jew equation. But the widespread detestation of mice posed a public relations problem. Hence, the Jews needed to make people think more highly of sneaky, dirty, clever mice.

Bolkhari continued:

Tom and Jerry was made in order to display the exact opposite image. If you happen to watch this cartoon tomorrow, bear in mind the points I have just raised, and watch it from this perspective. The mouse is very clever and smart. Everything he does is so cute. He kicks the poor cat's ass. Yet this cruelty does not make you despise the mouse. He looks so nice, and he is so clever. . . . This is exactly why some say it was meant to erase this image of mice from the minds of European children, and to show that the mouse is not dirty. . . . Unfortunately, we have many such cases in Hollywood shows.

In light of the professor's lecture, it is a little surprising to learn (elsewhere) that Yasser Arafat apparently loved the show. He liked that Jerry, the little guy, generally emerged victorious over the large aggressor cat.[74]

Had Bolkhari done his homework, he might also have learned that other Iranians consider Warner—the true owners of *Tom and Jerry*—to be a "Zionist" company. In March 2007 the Islamic Republic of Iran News Network (IRINN) announced that Warner's 2006 action-fantasy film *300* was part of the vast Zionist conspiracy. The film makes no claim to historical accuracy but is very loosely based on the battle between the Greeks and the Persians at Thermopylae in 480 BC. The comic-book-styled movie, replete with magic and unrealistic characters, actually follows a graphic novel written by Frank Miller, and it is hard to imagine that anyone would take it seriously as a depiction of Greeks and Persians, past or present. Still, as in better accounts of the battle (also based on limited historical evidence), the small band of heroic Greeks led by King Leonidas comes off far better than do the Persians, who vastly outnumber them. It is worth noting that to the extent that ancient Jews would have had a horse in that race, they might well have sided with the Persians, who were more tolerant of diversity than the Greeks were.

The IRINN broadcast correctly noted that the film portrayed the ancient Persians negatively and inaccurately. A voiceover then explained:

In addition to distortion of history, the Zionist Warner Company is also pursuing cultural and political objectives. . . . The Zionists and the elements affiliated [with] the U.S. have tried to launch a propaganda front against ancient and historical roots of Iranians, and the hasty production of this film is an indication of its propaganda aspect. . . . This film tries to paint a violent image of Persians, who are against peace in today's world, in order to increase the international political pressure on Iran.[75]

For others, Disney, too, serves the Zionists. A reporter on another IRINN broadcast explained, "Zionism is not restricted to the capitalistic weapons companies, such as Lockheed and the banks that support it. Cinema is considered another subtle weapon. . . . In Hollywood, Disney is the manufacturer of this weapon, and *Pirates of the Caribbean* [*Dead Man's Chest*] is its newest ammunition." Such devious programming occurs because "Disney and its productions have been associated, more than anything, with the Zionist lobby in Hollywood. In 1995, when the pro-Zionist Jews were 2.5% of America's population, they made up 7.7% of Disney's board of directors."[76] The origins of these figures are, to say the least, obscure, although the source of the belief in Jewish manipulation of culture and arts is not; it comes straight from *The Protocols*. (What's more, Walt Disney, in his grave, might be surprised to learn that having just been cleared—more or less—of charges of antisemitism, he and his company have emerged as Zionists.)[77]

No doubt, very few Muslims—and perhaps even relatively few antisemites— would believe these accusations about *Tom and Jerry*, *Pirates of the Caribbean*, Warner, and Disney. But such examples highlight the distant reach of the conspiratorial antisemitic mind-set. When the antisemite speaks of Zionists, he or she doesn't generally mean Zionists as most of the world understands the term; that is, as supporters of a Jewish homeland in Israel. And when he or she speaks of Jews, Jews may have little or no involvement in the matter at hand. Thus, the likes of Starbucks, Coca-Cola, Pepsi ("Pay Each Penny to Save Israel"), McDonald's, Tommy Hilfiger, L'Oréal, Hugo Boss, and endless others have all been labeled Zionist companies.[78] Not only Jews are implicated by conspiratorial Jew-hatred.

When one considers all the things blamed on the Jews by Muslim antisemites, it becomes clear that hostility toward Jews is—in addition to being an assault on the interests, reputation, and rights of its victims—a much broader assault on modernity, globalization, Western political values, and Western culture. Although Muslim antisemites and their fellow travelers frequently claim to support free speech and democracy, this claim is usually disingenuous. Among the antisemites, and among many of those who allow them to prosper in the Muslim world, there is no genuine support for freedom of religion, freedom of speech, or freedom of the press.

Even though the Islamic world once surpassed the Christian world in respect for minorities and tolerance for diversity, such concepts have become alien values in many Muslim and Arab countries. Real respect for women's rights and the rights of gays rarely coexist with hostility toward Jews. Sexual and familial choice frequently do not have a place in the world of the Muslim antisemite, nor is there much concern about freedom of artistic expression. Empirically, it isn't difficult to document that hostility toward Jews—in the Muslim world and elsewhere—correlates very highly with hostility toward America.[79]

Nowadays, Jew-hatred in the Middle East is most common among those who are—or claim to be—religiously observant, especially those who buy into the Islamist or Salafist agenda. While antisemitism taints many others in the Arab and Muslim world to some degree, rarely are the liberals or moderates the most hostile. Indeed, the prominence of antisemitic thinking among individuals and groups is a pretty good indicator of the extent to which more general social pathology has taken hold. Jew-hatred offers an acid test for moderation, liberality, and reality testing.

Consequently, while the ultimate outcome of the 2011 Arab rebellions will not be known for some time, the failure of so-called liberal and moderate leaders to stand firmly against Jew-hatred or in favor of a negotiated settlement with Israel counsels pessimism. Whether as a result of true beliefs or because of their reading of public sentiments, they have also decided to stay silent on Jew-hatred. And even so, liberals and moderates have been faring poorly in political contests and other measures of public sentiments. Overtly anti-Jewish comments were uttered by several prominent candidates for the Egyptian presidency.[80]

Certainly many Arabs hate Jews because Arab military defeats at the hands of the Israelis have led to devastating physical and narcissistic injuries. The Israelis are hated most of all, but so too are other Jews because they are perceived, in many cases accurately, as supporters of the Jewish state. However, this is only one part of the story. Jews, perhaps even more than Americans, are viewed as the quintessential symbol (and the main beneficiaries) of modernity, diversity, liberality, Western values, Western wealth, military effectiveness, globalization, religious liberalism, and religious tolerance. Every aspect of this symbolism can and does inflame the antisemite, regardless of whether the symbolism is accurate.

Much can be said about the sociological and psychological appeal of conspiracy theories. However, they thrive primarily because other more credible explanations of recent failures are too complex or psychologically untenable. There is sometimes something simple and calming about being able to say that the Jews did it. One need not be a Freudian to recognize that there is something safe in projecting responsibility for failure onto others and something settling about finally being able to explain how the world ticks.

How Much Evidence Is Enough?

In 2004 the European Monitoring Centre on Racism and Xenophobia (EUMC) circulated a working definition of antisemitism; the U.S. Department of State, the Organization for Security and Co-operation in Europe (OSCE), and other organizations now use the definition. According to the EUMC, "antisemitism is a certain perception of Jews, which may be expressed as hatred toward Jews. Rhetorical and physical manifestations of antisemitism are directed toward Jewish or non-Jewish individuals and/or their property, toward Jewish community institutions and religious facilities."[81] According to the explanatory text that accompanied the definition, "such manifestations [of antisemitism] could also target the state of Israel, conceived as a Jewish collectivity. Antisemitism frequently charges Jews with conspiring to harm humanity, and it is often used to blame Jews for 'why things go wrong.' It is expressed in speech, writing, visual forms and action, and employs sinister stereotypes and negative character traits." The EUMC specifically includes denial of the existence, scope, mechanisms, or intentionality of the Holocaust as potentially antisemitic acts. Furthermore, requiring Israel to adhere to standards not expected of any other democratic nation can under certain circumstances qualify as antisemitism. According to the EUMC, one must generally take into account the overall context of attitudes and behaviors in order to decide whether they are, in fact, antisemitic.

However, there remains a tremendous amount of dangerous bigotry toward Jews, even if hostility toward Israel is taken off the table.[82] To make this point, one might prefer to use the traditional definition of antisemitism still found in the Merriam-Webster dictionary: "hostility toward or discrimination against Jews as a religious, ethnic, or racial group."[83] Employing either of these definitions and considering the evidence, it is hard to avoid a judgment that Jew-hatred is widespread and virulent in many parts of the Arab and Muslim worlds—and not just among radical Islamists.

Sales figures for antisemitic classics such as *The Protocols* and *Mein Kampf* provide one type of indirect evidence concerning the extent of Jew-hatred in Muslim and Arab countries. But focused and carefully conducted empirical research would bear stronger witness. If world antisemitism were studied the way the U.S. electorate is studied during a presidential election year, we might possess detailed statistics on how many people in each of dozens of countries with substantial Muslim populations accept various antisemitic beliefs. We might also be able to calculate reasonable estimates of how these beliefs might likely impact behavior and other attitudes, such as support for terrorism, hostility toward the United States, support for freedom of religion, support for freedom of the press, and support for democratic elections. We might further possess quantitative breakdowns of Jew-hatred by education, socioeconomic status, region, age, and other relevant dimensions. But, of course, strong social pressures would likely prevent people from providing honest answers, and in any case current knowledge does not even begin to approach this level of sophistication.

As shall be seen, there are many reasons why even rudimentary studies of antisemitism in Muslim-majority nations have not been carried out. Some of these reasons are political, some ideological, some methodological, some practical. As the State Department's 2008 report to Congress on global antisemitism acknowledged, "It is important to note the challenge of collecting [relevant] information, particularly in closed societies, as we must rely on reported anti-Semitic incidents. Thus, available statistics tend to reflect anti-Semitic incidents that occur in open, democratic countries that allow transparent monitoring of societal conditions such as anti-Semitism. In contrast, information about anti-Semitic incidents in closed societies is largely unavailable, particularly because nongovernmental groups and scholars reporting from closed societies risk persecution."[84]

The problems noted here should not be construed as a mere footnote to an otherwise sound endeavor. The inability to gather data in precisely those places where Jew-hatred is most pronounced is a threat to the overall enterprise and has created misleading impressions about the global distribution of anti-Jewish beliefs. Moreover, as the State Department report noted, "since statistics focus on actual attacks against Jews and facilities used by Jews, they do not capture more generalized antisemitic attitudes or restrictions, such as those reflected in anti-Semitic

political cartoons, or anti-Semitic behavior in countries where there is not a significant Jewish population."[85] The lure of life in Israel combined with persecutory
conditions in some Arab and Muslim states has, during the past six decades, led to
a drastic reduction in the Jewish population of Arab and Muslim-majority countries. Thus, most Jew-hatred occurs in countries that are not home to many Jews.

Recent empirical studies deal mainly with Europe and the United States. Even
in these countries, however, researchers have not focused specifically on Jew-hatred
among those from Arab and Islamic backgrounds. Still, a few clear conclusions can
be drawn from this body of work:

1. Muslims in Europe tend to be substantially more hostile to Jews than are
    members of other European religious groups. One study of the British popu-
    lation, for example, found that Muslims were nearly eight times as likely as
    members of the general public to hold negative opinions of Jews. Another
    study found that more than a third of British Muslim respondents viewed
    Jews as legitimate targets in the struggle for justice in the Middle East. Yet an-
    other study in the United Kingdom found that Muslims perpetrated 30 per-
    cent of anitsemitic incidents, even though Muslims make up only 3 percent
    of the general population.[86] Disproportionate anti-Jewish sentiment is even
    found among Muslims who have come to the West from non-Arab Muslim
    countries. Christians who hail from Arab countries also tend to be more anti-
    Jewish than Christians from other countries.[87]

2. Hostility toward Jews is associated statistically with hostility toward Israel. In
    other words, if you know that somebody holds one set of beliefs, you can pre-
    dict with moderate confidence that they will hold the other. In one key study
    in Europe, five thousand people in ten countries were asked a series of ques-
    tions. Those respondents "who believed that . . . Israeli soldiers 'intentionally
    target Palestinian civilians,' and that 'Palestinian suicide bombers who target
    Israeli civilians' are justified, also believed that 'Jews don't care what happens
    to anyone but their own kind,' 'Jews have a lot of irritating faults,' and 'Jews
    are more willing than others to use shady practices to get what they want.'"[88]
    According to the authors of another study—this time using an American sam-
    ple—that appeared in the *Journal of Personality and Social Psychology*, "those
    claiming that there is no connection between anti-Semitism and hostility
    toward Israel are wrong."[89] The authors explain, "Because prejudice is itself

highly stigmatized [in the United States], many people may be reluctant to express blatant anti-Semitism. . . . Although people can condemn Israeli actions without being anti-Semitic, our research has shown that hostility toward Israel may serve as cover for anti-Semitism and, at the same time, feed back and strengthen anti-Semitism."[90]

3. The number of antisemitic incidents varies from year to year, but in most Western countries, the general trend is upward.[91]

Some fairly clear scientific data support the contention that anti-Jewish sentiments are now widely held in some Muslim populations. A 2011 poll of Palestinians in the West Bank and Gaza found that 73 percent, disturbingly, agreed with a hadith that is quoted in the Hamas Charter.[92] In translation, the quoted portion of the hadith reads, "The Day of Judgement will not come about until Moslems fight the Jews. . . . [W]hen the Jew will hide behind stones and trees[:] The stones and trees will say O Moslems, O Abdulla, there is a Jew behind me, come and kill him. Only the Gharkad tree . . . would not do that because it is one of the trees of the Jews."[93] In addition, 53 percent favored teaching songs about hating Jews in Palestinian schools.

Similarly, a 2005 report by the Pew Global Attitudes Project, a group with no readily apparent agenda with regard to the topic, found that the percentage of Jordanians and Lebanese holding favorable views of Jews was about zero, whereas 99–100 percent held unfavorable views. In Morocco, a moderate, pro-Western Arab country, 88 percent of people hold negative views of Jews. In Pakistan, 74 percent hold negative views, and in Indonesia, 76 percent. Even in Turkey, a potential member of the European Union, 60 percent of the population holds negative views of Jews. For comparison, the Pew poll found that 77 percent of Americans hold favorable views of Jews and only 7 percent hold unfavorable ones.[94] Such data are telling, and a similar 2010 study essentially corroborated the findings, although this sort of research cannot in itself be viewed as conclusive.[95] The questionnaire relied on a one-dimensional, nonspecific measure of attitudes toward Jews. One can probably better assess the extent and depth of Muslim hostility toward Jews by looking at indirect evidence.

Consider, for example, the reaction to Malaysian prime minister Mahathir Mohamad's previously discussed speech before an audience of high-level Muslim leaders from around the world. Although Mahathir is considered by many to be progressive, pragmatic, and religiously moderate, his 2003 comments could have been uttered by any of the very worst European antisemites ever. Still, according to the *New York Times*, the remarks "received a standing ovation from Muslim leaders of many nations . . . at the 57-nation Organization of the Islamic Conference, the world's largest Muslim group."[96] The ovation included the widely respected Indonesian president, Megawati Sukarnoputri; Pakistani president Pervez Musharraf; Afghan president Hamid Karzai; and Crown Prince Abdullah of Saudi Arabia.[97] In Malaysia—home at the time to the world's tallest building and a nation widely hailed for its modern outlook—the opposition leader declared that Muslims all over the world must support Dr. Mahathir's position on the Jews.[98] (Remember well this position—that Jews rule the world by proxy, that they get others to fight and die for them, that they invented democracy, socialism, and human rights as part of a plot, etc.) Iranian president Mohammad Khatami said that accusations of antisemitism in reaction to Mahathir fell under the category of well-calculated Western propaganda. Ahmad Maher, the Egyptian foreign minister (under the purportedly pro-Israel Mubarak government), called the speech very wise and said that charges of antisemitism in the speech had been blown out of proportion.[99] As for Mahathir, he found the Islamic reaction reinforcing and continues to offer hostile commentary on the Jews. Speaking in 2010, he commented that the Jews in Europe "had to be confined to ghettos and periodically massacred. . . . But still they remained, they thrived . . . held whole governments to ransom. Even their massacre by the Nazis . . . they survived to continue to be a source of even greater problems for the world."[100]

Is there a benign interpretation of the Muslim reaction to the *Protocols*-style Jew-hatred in Mahathir's speech? One might call attention to the minority response to Mahathir—those writers, imams, and lower-level political leaders who condemned his bigotry, either outright on moral grounds or in the context of forging a more effective means of dealing with the West and fighting Israel.[101] One might also argue that some of the many leaders who applauded did so not out of genuine conviction but, rather, because of peer pressure and an unwillingness to assume the unpopular role of defender of the Jews. Some may have been caught up in the moment, but few, if any, later reversed their initial positions on the speech. It is true that no data showing what percentage of the Muslim mass public supported the defamatory remarks are available, and possibly the public would have been less supportive of Mahathir than their leaders. But none of this speculation is particularly comforting or convincing.

There is much additional indirect evidence of widespread support for Jew-hatred in parts of the Muslim world. For example, in July 2009 it was headline news when King Mohammed VI of Morocco declared the Holocaust one of the most tragic chapters of modern history.[102] This declaration was newsworthy because, throughout much of the Muslim world, the Nazi assault on European Jewry is unknown, disbelieved, diminished, or viewed as yet another crime in which the Zionists participated. It took considerable fortitude for a powerful king simply to declare what every high school student in the West accepts as a basic truth.

And consider the career of Mustapha Tlass, a high-level cabinet member in Syria for more than thirty years until he left office in 2004. Tlass published a vile book in the 1980s, *The Matza of Zion*, which sought to revive medieval blood libel charges against the Jews.[103] Tlass's literary effort had no discernible negative impact on his prominent career; he spoke proudly of his anti-Jewish writing during his tenure as defense minister and in other high posts.

As has been seen, some major Arab and Muslim political and religious leaders have become free-flowing fonts of Jew-hatred, and most other key figures have gone along happily or at least quietly. Those few members of the political, cultural, and intellectual elites who have opposed overt anti-Jewish bigotry have often done so in the context of strongly expressed opposition to Israel. When that component is missing, however, as in the case of Shoaib Choudhury, expression of tolerance for Jews and Jewry can be dangerous. At a minimum, friends of the Jews become outcasts among their own people, and not infrequently they fear for their lives. In addition to Choudhury, Ayaan Hirsi Ali, Bassam Tibi, Nonie Darwish, Irshad Manji, Wafa Sultan, and others have all spoken out loudly and unequivocally against Jew-hatred in the Muslim world, and all have become targets.[104]

There are certainly anecdotes suggesting that in parts of the Islamic world hostility toward Jews penetrates deep into the populace. Ayaan Hirsi Ali, who was born in Somalia, reported of her childhood experience in Saudi Arabia:

Everything bad was the fault of the Jews. When the air conditioner broke or suddenly the tap stopped running, the Saudi women next door used to say the Jews did it. The children next door were taught to pray for the health of their parents and the destruction of the Jews. Later when we went to school, our teachers lamented at length all the evil things Jews had done and planned to do against Muslims. When they were gossiping, the women next door used to say, 'She's ugly, she's disobedient, she's a whore—she's sleeping with a Jew.' Jews were like *djinns* [evil spirits], I decided. I had never met a Jew. (Neither had these Saudis.)[105]

The extent to which Hirsi Ali's experiences reported from decades back represent an accurate description of popular sentiments in Saudi Arabia at the time—much less the degree to which similar attitudes prevail in various parts of the Islamic world today—is not known.

However, others more recently have also reported that the word "Jew" is widely employed by Islamists as a generic put-down, especially for "enlightened Muslims or simply those who dare to defend the values of equality, secularism, tolerance and freedom."[106] And the Syrian-educated psychiatrist Wafa Sultan reports that "members of the educated class, thinkers and writers—none of them are immune to this [anti-Jewish and anti-Zionist] conspiracy theory: Whenever a writer comes up with an idea that does not conform to prevailing opinion, the rumor mill accuses him of being a Zionist agent."[107] Speaking about his days as a Muslim student activist in Britain in the 1990s, Ed Husain recalled that "without question we despised the Jews."[108]

Putting all this evidence together, Muslim antisemitism seems nearly global in scope, although perhaps it is weakest among Muslims in the United States and in some other Western democracies. Large percentages of the people in many Muslim countries at least go along with elements in the antisemitic mind-set, though one cannot say for sure how many. One probably can infer that in the very large one-billion-plus Muslim world, hundreds of millions do not hold antisemitic views as central elements in their thinking and some percentage are sickened by the bigotry, yet few see for themselves a vocal role in combating it. As shall be discussed in the final chapter, only a small group at present fights energetically and publicly against the Jew-hatred in unambiguous terms.

How dangerous is all of this anti-Jewish bigotry? As I have written elsewhere,

some of the raw materials of mass hate can be found in almost every society on earth, often in plentiful supply. People everywhere tend to think in terms of 'us' and 'them,' and to prefer their own group. Across the globe, even the most tolerant people sometimes rely on simplistic stereotypes. No society has yet been able to free itself of sociopaths, extreme bigots, and aggressive personalities. And frustrating life conditions of one sort or another exist in every nation. [Moreover, f]anatics always seem to be sprouting evil schemes.[109]

Still, bigotry reaches murderous proportions in only a relatively small number of societies. To assess the danger of Muslim and Arab antisemitism, one must address how raw materials of mass hatred can combine in an explosive mixture. No simple formula can account for the many routes by which societies become destructive. Each travels down its own idiosyncratic path colored by history, politics, culture, tradition, and leadership. Yet there are certain societal characteristics that distinguish relatively normal (though, of course, undesirable) animosities from those likely to erupt into murderous hatred.

Some characteristics of potentially genocidal societies include (1) widespread and intense public anger directed against a scapegoat, (2) dissemination by leaders of dehumanizing rhetoric, (3) cultural norms and values that tolerate or encourage violence against out-groups, (4) the existence of special cadres prepared to carry out violent acts, and (5) the lack of a strong constitutionally based tradition of tolerance and checks and balances. Perhaps most importantly, there is great danger when ideologies of hatred capture large numbers of supporters, convincing them that the hated group is the source of their problems and that elimination of that group is the solution. There is even greater danger when such ideologies lack vocal domestic opponents.

No conclusive data can determine the extent to which the Muslim and Arab world exhibits these dangerous predisposing societal conditions. Yet few fair-minded analysts who attend to media reports from the Middle East would argue against the proposition that there is widespread public anger, dehumanizing rhetoric directed against the Jews, and a lack of a constitutionally based tradition of checks and balances. Whether the anger is sufficiently intense is an important question.

There are many grounds for pessimism. For one thing, hostility toward Jews is fairly common in the religious education and socialization practices that prevail in some Muslim-majority countries.[110]

And then there are demagogues such as Ahmadinejad and other Iranian leaders who will continue to promote his agenda even after he leaves the scene. Ahmadinejad and his ilk rarely cease to proclaim their hatred for Jews or their desire to destroy Israel, possibly by using the nuclear weapons that Iran seems destined to control in the near future. Opposition to Israel is not inherently antisemitic, but as former Israeli ambassador to the United Nations Dore Gold noted, "[Ahmadinejad's] talk [alone] amounts to a violation of the genocide convention."[111]

Putting all this together, it seems hard to deny that a more than garden-variety antisemitism prevails in many parts of the Muslim and Arab world—and that it has been spreading rapidly to the Muslim and Arab communities in Europe. The only reasonable matters for debate are (1) whether this bigotry is merely disconcerting or whether it has become—or may soon become—murderous in intensity and (2) whether countervailing forces, including (but not limited to) Israeli military power; Western liberal sentiments; the implicit threat of reprisals; religious and political restraints inside the Muslim world; the intrusion of other, more reality-based concerns of Muslims and Arabs; and lack of easy access to large numbers of Jews will serve to limit the damage.

We will return to these important matters, but first we must examine why it is that many in the West, particularly Jewish and non-Jewish antiracist liberals, have failed to see the dimensions of the problem we all face.

3

The Shame of the Antiracist Community

For many self-designated members of the antiracist community, Muslim antisemitism has become an unmentionable prejudice. Indeed, in some circles, mere recognition of the phenomenon can get one labeled a racist. It can also mean the end of social and political friendships.

Otherwise reliable opponents of bigotry too often duck when confronted with massive evidence of Jew-hatred in Arab and Islamic countries; they offer either dismissive interpretations or complex justifications in lieu of plainspoken opposition. More than a few "progressive" intellectuals have allowed themselves to become incapacitated by political alliances, misguided ideology, and lazy habits of mind that eschew the gathering of data. In addition, for many on the left, anti-semitism—the ultimate "dog-bites-man" story—has lost some its novelty and sex appeal. It is yesterday's news, and other concerns have taken its place.

Still, these days the overwhelming majority of politicians, scholars, religious leaders, and human rights advocates stand opposed to racism, sexism, prejudice, and bigotry, often "in every form." Countless organizations in the Western world and beyond have declared such opposition to be their raison d'être, and although one cannot readily determine which among them are sincere, these organizations do not come from any one political orientation. Antiracist groups may cite anti-semitism as a specific concern, but even when they do not, hostility toward Jews is usually understood—at least theoretically—to be subsumed under more general prohibitions against intolerance. These prohibitions have been inscribed in august official documents: the Universal Declaration of Human Rights, the resolutions of international organizations, the constitutions and laws of sovereign nations, the creeds of some religions, the mission statements of schools and universities, the policies of private corporations, and the founding covenants of numerous social justice and human rights groups.

On the basis of such paeans to tolerance, one might have expected robust and far-reaching outrage in response to well-documented anti-Jewish bigotry in many Muslim and Arab communities. Moreover, recalling the prominent role played by progressive scholars and activists in past battles against antisemitism, one might understandably have concluded that the Left possesses an especially fine-tuned ear for detecting transgressions against the Jewish people.[1]

Yet, while expressions of concern have certainly been uttered in some progressive circles, the far more prevalent reaction to Muslim anti-Jewish bigotry has been ignorance, avoidance, minimization, denial, or misinterpretation. When one moves from mainstream progressives to radical leftists—those with the greatest distaste for prejudice (if we are to accept their claims at face value)—one finds a fair number who have crossed a fateful line to aid and abet the antisemites.

A tendency to ignore, minimize, and explain away the significance of Muslim antisemitism can be found also among some political conservatives. What's more, some members of the Far Right have persisted in their ancient tradition of spewing Jew-hatred. In this pursuit, some, like members of the Far Left, have made common cause with Muslim antisemites.

However, the most disturbing and consequential current concern is the failure of mainstream antiracists, on the moderate left and on the moderate right, to grasp the depths, nature, and implications of hostility to Jews in the Muslim and Arab communities. That many gentiles often do not fully comprehend this hostility is perhaps understandable when one considers that some of those with the biggest blind spots are themselves Jews.

Writing about people in the United Kingdom, Denis MacShane, a non-Jew and committed foe of Jew-hatred across the globe, offered the judgment that most British people repudiate antisemitism but that most also hardly believe it currently exists.[2] MacShane's conclusion applies generally to much of the Center, moderate Left, and moderate Right in the United States and other parts of the West. Unfortunately, there are many reasons—logical, psychological, organizational, and political—why so many across the Western political spectrum have failed to live up to their declared commitment to fight this form of bigotry. My goal here is to document and begin to explain that failure.

The best way to start is by looking at what can happen when scholars, professors, and activists attempt to bring evidence about Muslim antisemitism into the public square.

Attacking the Messenger

Pieter Van Der Horst of Utrecht University was a well-regarded Dutch professor of theology whose main work focused on the ancient Jewish and Hellenistic context of early Christianity and the New Testament. In June 2006, after thirty-seven years of teaching, he wanted to deliver his farewell address on what he called "the myth of Jewish cannibalism."[3] In this lecture, he had planned to trace an antisemitic theme—namely, the notion that Jews eat human flesh—all the way from its Greco-Roman roots through anti-Jewish blood libels in today's Muslim world. The administration at Utrecht, one of the highest-ranked universities in Europe, had no problem with the professor's treatment of ancient Greeks, Christians, or modern Europeans.

But the rector of the university told Van Der Horst, a member of the prestigious Royal Dutch Academy of Arts and Sciences, that he had twenty-four hours to remove references to Muslim antisemitism. The rector based his decision on a report penned by some professors and himself. Three grounds for the ultimatum were provided: fear of violent reactions from "well-organized Muslim student groups," unwillingness to thwart the university's efforts at building bridges between Muslims and non-Muslims, and concern that the lecture fell far below the university's scholarly standards. "We have to protect you from yourself," he was told. At the time, Utrecht refused to provide any concrete information about specific threats of violence. The rectorate still has not provided anything indicative of danger. But inasmuch as Van Der Horst had to decide on short notice and was unable to disconfirm the rector's contentions, he reluctantly edited his address. Peeved by the unsubstantiated shots taken at his scholarly rigor, though, and also uncomfortable with the attack on academic freedom, the professor later defended himself in an opinion piece in the *Wall Street Journal*.[4]

Some of the purportedly offensive statements in Van Der Horst's proposed lecture would be regarded by most serious scholars of Muslim antisemitism as noncontroversial. For example, he called attention to (1) the World War II Palestinian leader Haj Amin al-Husseini's collaboration with Adolf Hitler,[5] (2) the contemporary demonization of Jews in many Middle Eastern countries,[6] and (3) the popularity of *Mein Kampf* in some Muslim nations.[7] These are all matters of fact rather than interpretation.

As part of his effort to defend himself, Van Der Horst assembled a group of scholars, including three professors of Islamic studies. They all agreed that his work was excellent and well-documented. Moreover, they deemed some of the professor's purportedly problematic polemical remarks about those who support antisemitism wholly appropriate in the context of the work.[8]

But the validity of Van Der Horst's arguments is, in any case, beside the point. He had the right, especially after so many decades of paying his academic dues, to make his parting points even if they were wrong. The university's subsequent attempt to portray Van Der Horst's editing of his own work as "voluntary" amounts to little more than a cover-up. As Van Der Horst said, "if something as serious as Islamic Jew-hatred cannot be the subject of public debate, it bodes ill for society at large."[9] Thankfully, however, direct and overt censorship is rare at Western universities.

However, there have been other efforts to prevent scholarly discussions about Muslim antisemitism from occurring. For example, consider the following incidents involving author Nonie Darwish, keeping in mind that Columbia University—in the academic tradition of free expression—welcomed Iranian president Mahmoud Ahmadinejad to speak his mind. "Opportunities to hear, challenge, and learn from controversial speakers of different views are central to the education and training of students for citizenship in a shrinking and dangerous world," explained Dean John Coatsworth of the School of International and Public Affairs.[10] Also recall that Princeton University not only permitted political scientist Richard Falk to speak, but also made him an honored professor emeritus for a career in which he declared (in 1979) that Ayatollah Khomeini's vision offered "a desperately-needed model of humane governance for a third-world country."[11] Falk also joined those eager to compare Israeli actions to those of the Nazis and suggested that President Bush was complicit in the 9/11 attacks.[12] Yet groups at both Princeton and Columbia found it necessary to disinvite Nonie Darwish from speaking, partly on the grounds that her views were beyond the pale of respectable debate.[13]

One might imagine that Darwish would deserve a platform by virtue of her unique personal background. As she recounted in her 2006 book *Now They Call Me Infidel*, she grew up in Egypt and Gaza as the honored daughter of an Islamic *shahid*, or martyr; her father was a high-ranking Egyptian officer who had died leading covert attacks against Israel when Nonie was eight.[14] Over decades, she gradually became disenchanted with Arab politics, with the treatment of women in her country, and with the Islamic faith. After moving to the United States, she ultimately converted to Christianity and developed politically conservative views.

Perhaps most controversially, she became an outspoken critic of the treatment of Jews in Islamic and Arab communities. She even went so far as to form a group called Arabs for Israel.[15]

Needless to say, Darwish has earned many foes in the Islamic world, where she is often denounced as a traitor. She reports that she receives death threats on a fairly regular basis. However, the criticism of Darwish that has the greatest traction in the liberal and academic world is that she is anti-Islam—and, in a sense, this charge is hard to deny. She does not limit her disapproval to the most radical versions of the faith, preferring to argue that much of mainstream Islam, especially sharia, is the source of many dysfunctional aspects of Arab and Islamic cultures. While she clearly states that the purpose of her second book, *Cruel and Unusual Punishment*, "is not to spread hatred of a people," it is easy to see how some practicing Muslims might deem unpalatable her declared goal "to tell the truth about the wickedness of Islamic Sharia law." Moreover, many of her assertions are debatable; for example, her contention that "it is naïve, at best, for the West to count on a collective Islamic repentance and reformation that would bring Muslims to appreciate peace with the West."[16]

Yet, one wonders whether debate about such matters is not precisely what intellectual honesty, religious freedom, and political necessity require. Centuries after the Enlightenment, it is surprising to hear in the West that the sensibilities of religious believers should impose any limitations on academic debate about religious doctrine and its likely impact on human behavior. Moreover, in vetting the acceptability of Arabs who have devoted their lives to exposing antisemitism and promoting the rights of Jews, one must keep in mind that there are not all that many spokespersons from which to choose. On Muslim attitudes toward Jews, Darwish speaks with clarity, integrity, and courage that are almost unbelievable given the pressures that have brought to bear against her.[17]

Her approach to Islam arguably lacks sufficient recognition of diversity within the faith, yet she never crosses the line into anti-Arab or anti-Muslim bigotry. She writes as one who has been hurt by the prevailing mores of her native religious culture and who seeks to bring a new vision to those peoples among whom she was born. Her vision further derives from a strong respect for the American culture she has adopted. Yet, as a former Muslim, an apostate, Darwish—according to some readings of Islamic law—has committed a crime whose punishment is the death

penalty. She has asked mainstream American Muslim groups to sign a pledge opposing fatwas that condemn former Muslims to death, but she reports that "not
one organization" has done so.[18]

In my view, *all* unaltered ancient systems of religious law fail by modern
moral and political standards.[19] But sharia is partly operational in some areas of
the contemporary world and has been proposed by numerous Muslims as a more
desirable form of sociopolitical organization than the one that we now have in the
West. According to one large study of Muslim opinion around the world, majorities in most Muslim countries want sharia as at least one source of legislation; in
Egypt and Jordan, the study suggested that more than half of the people supported sharia as the only desirable source of laws.[20] Under these circumstances, a
hard-hitting, comparative critique of the sharia system as it has been implemented
in some places and as it exists in theory is not needlessly mean-spirited religion
bashing. It is rather the precise sort of free expression that the theorists of constitutional democracy had in mind. One need not endorse Darwish's views to feel
outrage about the danger to Western intellectual freedom that results from death
threats against her. And one need not accept Darwish's controversial contentions
to agree that they deserve a platform.

The death threats against Nonie Darwish stand intentionally in the way of
free expression; the policies of universities may have similar impact without a clear
intention to block open debate. Darwish, for example, was able to complete a
speech at Boston University, but only after a delay caused by someone who protested her appearance by setting a fire in a nearby restroom.[21] Her autumn 2009
experiences at Princeton and Columbia were more disturbing.

At Columbia University, the local faculty chapter of Scholars for Peace in the
Middle East, a group supportive of Israel's right to exist and critical of Muslim antisemitism, invited Darwish to speak. At the last minute, the university cancelled
the event because, they said, of security risks stemming from a failure by sponsoring professors to follow proper procedures when inviting a "controversial" speaker.
Whether or not the university was capable of providing adequate security given
the notice provided, the fact remains that Darwish, who had already flown in from
the West Coast and dressed for the talk, was unable to speak on campus. "How
humiliating is that? To come all this way, to be almost out of the door of my hotel
only to be told that they had to cancel my speech because campus security felt they

could not protect me. Everyone is trying to blame someone else."[22] She ended up presenting to a small group off-campus in the private room of a local restaurant.

At Princeton, where Darwish was also scheduled to speak, it is easier to discern the motives behind the cancellation. A campus group called Tigers for Israel invited Darwish, largely because one student on the group's board knew of her work. Tigers for Israel lists among its activities conducting "political action on Israel's behalf." So this group acknowledged its support for Israel in the Arab-Israeli conflict. And given its name and stated goals, one might have expected its leadership to hang tough.

But when Princeton's Muslim chaplain, Imam Sohaib Sultan, learned that Darwish was to speak, he immediately contacted Rabbi Julie Roth, the executive director of Princeton's Center for Jewish Life. According to the rabbi, Imam Sultan e-mailed some quotations from Darwish's work that he claimed were against the Islamic religion and not just critical of extremist Islam.[23] He then claimed that Darwish's views went unacceptably beyond academic discourse—according to one account, he described her as the equivalent of a neo-Nazi.[24] Rabbi Roth claims she had, and retains, a great deal of trust in Imam Sultan, with whom she had been working to engage in "real dialogue." Thus, she agreed to bring the imam's complaint to the student leaders of Tigers for Israel, a group that was at least nominally part of the Center for Jewish Life. The leaders of the student group then decided that they had not properly vetted the speaker and that they did not wish to be seen as endorsing Darwish's perspective on Islam. So they withdrew the invitation—against the wishes of the student who had initially proposed her name. From the rabbi's perspective, this was not an attempt to prevent Darwish from speaking, but rather an effort by a student organization to exercise its right to define its own identity. Still, she acknowledged that she did agree with the Tigers' decision.

Another campus group, the Whig-Cliosophic Society, a political, literary, and debating society founded at Princeton in the eighteenth century, had previously agreed to cosponsor the event. But when they heard that the Tigers had decided to rescind the invitation, they too lost interest.

One other thing may have proved decisive. Imam Sultan had indicated that the Muslim Students Association and Princeton Committee on Palestine would be protesting the event. But Rabbi Roth claims that this was not the main reason for the decision to rescind the invitation. Additionally, following the decision by the Tigers and the Whig-Cliosophic Society, Princeton University decided to cancel security for the event—thus putting an end to efforts by the campus conservative publication, *The Tory*, to assume sponsorship of the talk.

Rabbi Roth was the critical conduit between Imam Sultan and the protesting Muslim student groups on the one hand and the Tiger sponsors on the other. She emphasizes that the students made the key decisions and that she would have abided by any choice that they made. Still, by virtue of her religious and organizational roles, she no doubt exerted considerable influence. Asked whether she thought it fair to scrutinize and analyze the religious texts of Islam, the rabbi replied that she didn't think any topic was off limits. The key questions were, What conclusions were drawn? What was the context?

Yet Rabbi Roth apparently did not consider the context of the offending quotations provided by Imam Sultan, some of which were drawn from texts penned by Muslim scholars. Moreover, she had not—at the time of her role in the Darwish affair—read either of Darwish's books. She still had not when I interviewed her in December 2010. She did, however, know that Darwish was a strong opponent of Muslim antisemitism. But she did not consider this to be of decisive importance. Asked whether she considered Muslim antisemitism a big problem in the world, she acknowledged that it did, in fact, exist. She then went on immediately to explain that, at Princeton, her encounters with Muslims had been very cordial and that she had not witnessed significant antisemitism there.

Rabbi Roth clearly has an admirable commitment to multiculturalism and especially to working with the Princeton Muslim community to build bridges.[25] These are unquestionably good objectives. Yet the rabbi may, in these enthusiasms and in her local focus of attention, have lost sight of the importance of also documenting massive injustices committed against her own people. In trying to understand Muslim attitudes toward Jews, she also seems to have assigned disproportionate importance to her own experiences at Princeton and her personal interactions with well-educated, liberal American Muslims. And, as of this writing, the Tigers have not invited any speakers on Muslim antisemitism to Princeton.

Interestingly, the same three factors that caused the rector at Utrecht to pressure Professor Van Der Horst to edit his presentation played a role in the last-minute decisions to cancel Darwish's talks at Princeton and Columbia: (1) vague security concerns, (2) an unwillingness to endanger efforts to build bridges with the Muslim community, and (3) charges of poor scholarship that appeared to be politically motivated.

Still, no one could sensibly claim that Darwish or others who want to speak about Muslim antisemitism are effectively censored in the West. Darwish, for example, did ultimately speak at Princeton in 2010 under different sponsorship (that again included the Whig-Cliosophic Society). (One of the new sponsors, *The Tory*, invited Imam Sultan to provide his reaction to her speech in its publication—which he did.)[26] And Van Der Horst eventually disseminated his unedited speech. Similarly, Matthias Kuentzel, an important German scholar of Muslim antisemitism, had his 2007 invitation to present a two-day workshop on "Hitler's Legacy: Islamic Anti-Semitism in the Middle East" revoked by the University of Leeds in England—again on grounds of security. Yet he too has managed to present his views in various other forums.[27]

Regular efforts are made to block controversial leftist-turned-rightist David Horowitz from speaking on college campuses about Muslim antisemitism. Horowitz reported that while it once was a pleasure for him to talk on campuses such as the University of Southern California (USC), "now . . . I can't set foot on [the USC campus]—or any campus—without being accompanied by a personal bodyguard and a battalion of armed campus security police to protect me and my student hosts." But, still, he was able to lecture at USC on November 4, 2009—with a bodyguard and twelve armed campus security officers—about the Muslim Student Union's posting on the official USC website of the famous hadith about the Day of Judgment coming only after Muslims fight the Jews and kill them.[28]

The real impact of withdrawn invitations and security threats is difficult to measure; it is impossible to know how many university talks might otherwise have been scheduled or how many experts might otherwise have stepped forward to speak about Muslim hostility to Jews. Understandably, most people—perhaps especially most scholars—try to avoid trouble. They don't want to expose themselves to danger. They don't want to draw protests, particularly those that passersby might interpret as impugning their integrity. They choose instead to research less controversial topics, to speak on less controversial topics, to take less controversial approaches, to invite less controversial speakers. And although each speaker or writer who raises the specter of dangerous antisemitism in the Muslim world faces particular resistance that must be answered on its own terms—and some of these critiques may occasionally have merit—it is important to realize that the underlying goal is frequently to discredit and undermine those who raise the topic in almost any form.

Pooh-Poohing Jew-Hatred

Israeli director Yoav Shamir's 2009 film *Defamation* carried an unusually chipper subtitle: *Anti-Semitism: The Movie*. With gray paint splattered by a large yellow Jewish star, the DVD jacket suggested scribbled graffiti; the jacket also featured a broadly smiling Chassidic Jew and an equally cheery image of Shamir himself. It was easy to identify the director because his face was circled and labeled with the word "me."

The film was generally received well by critics, especially those who considered themselves progressive. Michael Moore called it "an incredibly bold and brave film."[29] Writing in *Variety*, Leslie Felperin deemed it "impressively even-handed . . . even though the filmmaker never attempts to disguise his own left-leaning sympathies." She went on to describe *Defamation* as "at once intelligent, wry and—there is no way around it—quintessentially Jewish, in the best sense."[30] (What, one wonders, is the other sense?) Owen Gleiberman of *Entertainment Weekly* wrote, "This brave documentary takes on the topic of anti-Semitism in a relentlessly probing and original way."[31] The words "humorous" and "brave" kept popping up in reviews. About.com critic Jennifer Merin wrote, "Shamir's breezy personality, casual manner and deft approach . . . works brilliantly. It encourages people to speak quite candidly, and their comments are shocking—horrendous, really, but sometimes quite surprisingly funny, as well."[32] Akiva Gottlieb, writing in Los Angeles' *Jewish Journal*, called *Defamation* "the most important Jewish movie of the year."[33] Several film festivals also took favorable note of Shamir's production.[34]

In a director's statement, Shamir explained that "upon reflection" he came to realize that antisemitism (or, talk about antisemitism—he is not quite clear) "is a constant buzz, always in the background, always annoying. After a while you simply get used to it. How often are we really disturbed by the hum of an electric fixture or the drone of passing cars?"[35] Shamir called antisemitism "the ultimate 'sacred cow' for Jews," explaining that "while I did not set out to slaughter that cow, even the most sacred of cows needs to be shaken up every once in a while." He proudly declared that his approach was not going to be "academic." Instead, his guide would be his "instincts." "Any question is relevant if I believe it is. I should never be afraid to ask or challenge even the most hallowed assumptions," he said.

Shamir emphasized his desire to "learn something about the subject." Yet the methods he adopted—not to mention his lighthearted tone—made his education an unlikely prospect. He avoided knowledgeable experts, interviewed many uninformed, easily targeted Jews on the street, employed Borat-style sandbagging, failed to engage available historical and social scientific data, and heavily edited responses from just about everyone. Ambushing an unsuspecting, non-media-savvy person does not a serious argument make. Moreover, the filmmaker could exercise tight control by limiting topics under consideration and people chosen for interviews. In the end, Shamir successfully avoided the filmmaker's cardinal sin insofar as *Defamation* is not boring. But it teaches very little.

Soon after the film starts, the viewer meets a woman who utters arguably the most antisemitic remarks heard in the entire film, and she is Shamir's own grandmother. The misguided woman, who apparently trusts her grandson, doesn't require much entrapment to start making comments such as "A Jew is a crook" and "A Jew loves money. . . . That's why they [non-Israeli Jews] don't come to Israel." Such Jews earn their money by "interest . . . lending money at high rates. . . . Jews don't work." All this after she declares herself an enthusiastic Zionist.

Trying to learn whether there really is such a thing as serious antisemitism around the world, Shamir visits—of all places—New York City, possibly the most hospitable ground upon which Jews have ever lived. He finds accommodating New York Anti-Defamation League (ADL) employees in the middle of a slow week and unable to provide him with any frightening incidents of Jew-hatred for the film. On his insistence, they lead him to a minor incident where a New York woman apparently overheard a police officer say, "I'm finishing this Jewish shit." The local state assemblyman, Dov Hikind, then explains that through his intervention the woman was able to obtain an apology from the officer—and she was satisfied with this apology.

Defamation features more of the same: Jews in the West making mountains out of molehills, being treated deferentially, and showing near-pathological interest in the Holocaust. Shamir spends much time making Abraham Foxman and the ADL look foolish and implying that in addition to sharing in the collective Jewish pathology, they benefit from a good life funded by contributions. ADL leaders also appear willing to play on the guilt of well-intentioned non-Jews to achieve their objectives. There is no discussion of the organization's long history of honorable campaigns, not only against incontestably real Jew-hatred, but also on behalf of many other peoples—including Muslims—around the globe who seek greater civil and human rights. There is not one word about ADL's major efforts in support of black rights in the United States. Shamir deftly catches many of the nonprofessionals who have accompanied the ADL on one of its missions speaking freely and not always intelligently about antisemitism, partly because these well-intentioned and untrained souls thought they were engaging idle chitchat with a friendly fellow. Still, Shamir uses these interviews to show, correctly, that the Holocaust—which he informs us was seven decades ago—looms large in the collective memory and identity of many Jews.

Shamir is an equal-opportunity character slayer, and he is perfectly willing to also portray the controversial Norman Finkelstein in an unappealing light. Finkelstein is the bête noire of the ADL and others who see antisemitism as a real problem today. He authored a book titled *The Holocaust Industry*, in which he charges Jews with profiting personally, collectively, and politically from the Holocaust.[36] Numerous Holocaust scholars, for their part, consider him someone who trivializes the Holocaust and who is driven by a fanatical hatred for the state of Israel.[37] Finkelstein claims that he is not a Holocaust denier, saying that as a child of survivors, he would have to be either clinically insane or a self-hater to deny the Holocaust. (Most critics have classified him as misguided, ideologically driven, intellectually dishonest, or a Holocaust minimizer. He is not generally charged with being a Holocaust denier, and clearly he does acknowledge that the Holocaust took place.) But Finkelstein specifically challenges viewers of Shamir's film to judge his sanity.

Toward the end of the film, Shamir, who is unwilling to go as far as Finkelstein in criticizing Israel, has some fun with the controversial author. Finkelstein grows angry with Shamir's line of questioning and seems to start decompensating clinically on screen. Many viewers of *Defamation*, I think, are left with an impression of Foxman and the ADL as partly well-intentioned, partly manipulative, and partly obsessed, but in any case committed to grossly overstating the severity of antisemitism in the world. They also may leave thinking that Norman Finkelstein is psychologically a bit unbalanced and that he goes too far in attacking the "Holocaust industry." But probably they also think that he has made valid points about the Jewish obsession with antisemitism and about it being partly a consequence of Jewish collective irrationality and partly a tool self-consciously crafted for political and economic advantage.

Above all, there is one giant reason a viewer should not take Shamir's film seriously. The film does not even mention Jew-hatred in the Arab and Muslim world.

With many political and religious leaders spouting vitriol almost continuously and with this problem occupying a huge proportion of the energies of the ADL and other mainstream Jewish organizations, this omission is inexplicable in a film purporting to assess the reality of global antisemitism.

Could Shamir, an Israeli, be unaware of what is going on? Why is he talking about women in Brooklyn and nasty police officers? Why is he talking to his grandmother? Perhaps Mahathir Mohamad would not grant him an interview? Is he unaware of the huge trove of clips available from the Middle East Media Research Institute's Anti-Semitism Documentation Project?[38] And, along similar lines, where are his interviews with skinheads, neo-Nazis, and those in the West who rail constantly against ZOG—the Zionist Occupation Government of the United States? If he is unable or unwilling to obtain such interviews, where are his discussions with experts prepared to shed light on those groups?[39]

When a filmmaker uses his "instincts" as a guide, and these instincts lead him to omit completely the most important issue of all—Muslim Jew-hatred—one has to wonder. Ella Taylor defended Shamir against potential critics on National Public Radio: "No doubt Shamir will be accused of claiming that anti-Semitism is dead. He doesn't. [But] in an age of viral and often inaccurate media messaging, we have lost the capacity to distinguish between degrees of evil—between systematic racism and the minor slights that are the price we pay for living in democracies."[40] If some Jews have lost that ability, so too, it seems, has Shamir. His neglect of Islamic Jew-hatred, his failure to engage legitimate questions about the extent and significance of other strains of contemporary antisemitism, and his attempt to ridicule those in the Jewish community who do not share his perceptual limitations reflects a common breed of antisemitism denial or minimization.

In the United States, much of this antisemitism minimization comes from Jews, probably because non-Jews with similar sensibilities are more reluctant to voice their views in our sensitive political culture. Consider cartoonist Eli Valley, who is building his career on the ridicule of Jewish concern about antisemitism. Valley's work has appeared in the once neoconservative, now liberal Jewish newspaper *Forward* and on the Jewcy website, which is described as "a platform for ideas that matter to young Jews today."[41] One cartoon again targets Abraham Foxman—a favorite target for antisemitism deniers. Here Foxman is merged in an experiment gone wrong with comedian Jeff Foxworthy, and the result is a "monster more horrid than Frankenstein's"—a "Redneck who's paranoid about antisemites."[60] In another cartoon, Valley tells "the tragic tale of a liberal, socially-conscious Jew . . . who turns into a raging mass of psychopathology!" While watching PBS television news, Bruce Banner hears the newscaster make "a remark that could possibly be construed as mildly critical of Israel." In response, he turns into "a brutal, bestial mockery of a human—a creature which despises reason, living in fear and rage!" The reader then sees a familiar cartoon celebrity, the Hulk, screaming, "Hulk destroy television antisemites." By the end of the comic strip, Hulk joins the fight against abortion, supports creationism, and wants to deport homosexuals and Mexicans.[43]

Yet another Valley creation has Batman and Robin meeting Aquaman after all three have gone to work for the Jewish community. Aquaman explains that he has "finished building the world's first underwater Holocaust memorial!" Batman exclaims, "Excellent work, Aquaman! Now no Jewish child shall visit Sea World without a reminder of the horrors!"[44]

Finally, in a cartoon lauded by renowned bigot and former grand wizard of the Knights of the Ku Klux Klan David Duke, Valley tells of a rabbi, a Jewish communal leader, and an international fugitive who meet on a deserted island. The gangster has underwritten the organizational and vacation-related expenses of the other two. He explains, "No amount of racketeering, wire fraud or tax evasion gives me the same pleasure as alerting people to the dangers of anti-semitism!" The communal leader thanks him, saying, "Sir, one day, when they write the history of American Jewry, your name will top the list! You're a true prophet, one of the 36 righteous men!"[45] In Valley's view, then, the fight against antisemitism manifests either as psychopathology or corruption. Yet, to my knowledge, throughout Valley's growing opus there is not one mention of actual antisemitism, certainly not any in the Muslim or Arab world, where, incidentally, cartoonists have joined full-force in the battle against the Jews.[46]

Sometimes there is a more intellectual cast to the ridicule and denunciation of Jews who publicize their concern about antisemitism. Eli Valley might well agree with the "diagnosis" offered by the Portuguese Nobel Prize–winning novelist and journalist José Saramago. He wrote:

> Contaminated by the monstrous and rooted 'certitude' that in this cata-strophic and absurd world there exists a people chosen by God and that, consequently, all the actions of an obsessive, psychological and pathologi-

cally exclusive racism are justified; educated and trained in the idea that any suffering that has been inflicted, or that is being inflicted, or that will be inflicted on everyone else, especially the Palestinians, will always be inferior to that which they themselves suffered in the Holocaust; the Jews endlessly scratch their own wound to keep it bleeding, to make it incurable, and to show it to the world as if it were a banner.[47]

This is attack through diagnosis. Saramago would seem to give short shrift to the realistic basis for Jewish concern in a Western world tarnished by, yes, the Holocaust, but also nearly two millennia of continuous ill treatment of varying intensity. Saramago, like many others on the contemporary far left, offers a cavalier reduction of Jewish concern to pathology; he does not even bother to suggest that those Jews who disagree might simply be reading current political data incorrectly. Thus, Jews are not merely wrong; they are psychologically disturbed. This facile judgment may occur because data do not seem to matter much to Saramago and his ilk. For example, he accuses Jews, collectively, of racism without providing a shred of evidence that racist views are any more widespread among Jews than other peoples and, in fact, in the face of rather strong survey evidence to the contrary.[48] Similarly, he does not say which Jewish organizations have argued that Jewish suffering was worse than that experienced, say, by black Americans under slavery or by victims in Rwanda or Cambodia. These comparisons would indeed be counterproductive, and as far as I can tell, they are rarely made by Jewish spokespersons. Nonetheless, it is a matter of historical record that anti-Jewish bigotry has lasted longer and emerged in more diverse contexts than just about any other form of ethnic prejudice.[49] Many times, announcements of the demise of antisemitism have been premature. Most troublesome, however, is Saramago's insistence that Jews "scratch their own wound" with an eye toward perpetuating antisemitism. It requires little more than a brief perusal of daily media reports emanating from many Middle Eastern and Muslim sources to see that others are quite willing to do the scratching for them.

Saramago's argument is nonsense; most minimizers of Muslim antisemitism would not go as far as he does. But many reject the contention that antisemitism can come from anywhere other than its traditional home on the right. And even this antisemitism must be heard as the final howl of a dying beast in order to meet with the approval of progressives who, after all, like to claim credit for having already slayed—or at least for having seriously maimed—that particular demon. When writers and scholars disagree with this consensus, they are frequently suspected of reactionary motives, ethnocentrism, racism, or psychopathology.

Thus, those who take the lead in calling attention to the rise in contemporary Jew-hatred, especially its manifestation in the Muslim world, very frequently draw the scorn of a subset of self-defined progressive and anti-Israel intellectuals. Such maltreatment is particularly likely when those who raise the problem of antisemitism also empathize with Israel's predicament or support any of its actions. The problem, then, is not that Western Jews demonize all criticism of Israel; that they do not is obvious. The problem is that parts of the Western Left seek to demonize and discredit all support for Israel.

For example, the well-known Italian politician and journalist Fiamma Nirenstein reported that because of her outspoken opposition to antisemitism and her support for Israel she was widely denounced as a right-winger. She reflected, "Me? An old feminist, human rights activist, even a Communist when I was young. Only because I described the Arab-Israeli conflict as accurately as I could and because sometimes I identified with a country continuously attacked by terror, I became a right-winger?" She continued, making an important point: "In the contemporary world, the world of human rights, when you call a person a right-winger, this is the first step toward his or her delegitimization."[50]

Influential feminist Phyllis Chesler reported a similar phenomenon in her book *The New Anti-Semitism*. "I regret nothing," she explained. "I am not recanting my ideals as a civil rights worker, as a member of the antiwar movement, or as a feminist; nor have I gone over to the dark side. And yet, and yet, I must now calmly but clearly part company with many of my former friends and comrades. . . . On my left stand the internationalists (some of whom are Jews). I may remain among them as long as I am strongly anti-Zionist and anti–religious Judaism. For my part, I must also remain silent as the internationalists embrace all ethnicities and demonize only one: mine."[51] This seems to me a bit dramatic, and in any case, very large portions of the Left do not demonize Jewish identity. But it does highlight Chesler's sense that her sounding the trumpets about Muslim Jew-hatred and Muslim mistreatment of women—along with her support of the state of Israel—has led to her expulsion from many progressive circles within which she was once hailed as a heroine. Progressive feminists Nora Gold and Thyme Siegel have, to some extent, experienced the same thing.[52] The equation is opposition to Muslim antisemitism and Muslim extremism plus support for some Israeli actions equals detestable right-winger. No other variables are relevant.

Numerous progressives have reacted similarly to American writer Paul Berman, British sociologists Robert Fine and David Hirsh, French intellectuals Bernard-Henri Lévy and Pierre-André Taguieff, ADL leader Abraham Foxman, and indeed everyone else who—despite a past on the left—has attempted to face the problem of Muslim antisemitism squarely. Few of these writers have changed their fundamental values; what has changed is the way they are classified by others on the left.

In this context, it becomes less surprising that many intellectuals have been largely willing to give a pass to Muslim antisemites. The famous European Muslim scholar Tariq Ramadan—grandson of Muslim Brotherhood founder Hassan al-Banna and optimistically deemed a "moderate" by many in the West—denounced six very prominent French thinkers for speaking out against Islamic extremism and antisemitism in various ways.[53] The six—Pierre-André Taguieff, Alexandre Adler, André Glucksmann, Bernard-Henri Lévy, Alain Finkielkraut, and Bernard Kouchner—had already been targeted by some others for their positions on Islam, Islamic extremism, and the war on terrorism. But Ramadan went further by identifying them as Jews and implying that these "Jews" were up to some nefarious business. (Four of the six actually were Jewish: Taguieff was not; Kouchner was half-Jewish. These normally irrelevant facts only become relevant once one embarks upon a race-based analysis of political thought.)

American author Paul Berman tells in his detailed account that according to Ramadan, "those six distinguished people had abandoned a commitment to the universal principles of truth and justice that ought to animate anyone with a claim on the lofty office of *intellectual*."[54] The six instead were propelled by a concealed Jewish agenda to provide knee-jerk support for Israel; they had manufactured and marketed a false sense that bigotry against Jews was on the rise in France. The crime of which they were accused was, in effect, "the crime of promoting one's own little community over everyone else . . . the crime of bathing ethnic self-promotion in a light of universal rationality. The worst of all crimes, for an intellectual. A perversion of reason."[55] Of course, one might inquire whether anyone is capable of so clearly divorcing his or her own group's interests from his or her political assessments and also whether such a divorce is really desirable.

Yet the charges against these particular French intellectuals were palpably false. All had complex and different histories of involvement with many social causes. For example, Kouchner was a cofounder of Doctors Without Borders, an organization committed to the provision of medical assistance to people in troubled parts of the world. He was sufficiently far from being a knee-jerk defender of Israel to have been a serious contender for the position of United Nations High Commissioner for Refugees. Taguieff, one of the world's top scholars on antisemitism, is also generally recognized as an expert on racism. And Lévy had been one of the first in France to call for intervention in the Bosnian War to protect Muslims against atrocities being perpetrated in Serbian concentration camps.

Ramadan, for his part, did not seem to hold similarly high intellectual standards when it came to judging the works of several of his own intellectual godparents, including Muhammad Yusuf al-Qaradawi, Sayyid Qutb, and Hassan al-Banna.[56] All three are unambiguous antisemites. All three are religious extremists. And all three have played a large role in increasing the impact and deadliness of contemporary radical Islam. Ramadan occasionally parted company with them but not often. Moreover, Ramadan's own account of the religious roots of extremist behavior in the Islamic world was disingenuous at best, putting him on thin ice when he criticizes eminent French intellectuals. He had little problem misrepresenting how Jews were treated in traditional Islamic sources. But many progressive intellectuals continued to view Ramadan as a voice of moderation—partly because he had on occasion given lip service to the notion that antisemitism, at least in principle, was wrong.[57]

"It's Just about Israel, Stupid"

Yet another example of progressive thinkers dismissing and minimizing concerns about antisemitism emerges from the dispute between former Harvard president Lawrence Summers and Berkeley poststructuralist superstar professor Judith Butler. Butler's controversial scholarship has many defenders, and some credit her with launching important new ways of thinking about sexism, sexuality, gender, discrimination, and other issues. However, as a consequence of her complex mode of expression, the progressive scholar has also won dubious recognition as the winner of a 1999 bad writing contest.[58] In her dispute with President Summers, Butler's predilection toward poststructuralist theory, stylistic complexity, and ideological commitment seems to have blocked her perception of basic empirical facts about Muslim antisemitism.

One place to start this story is with Tom Paulin, an Oxford University poet of Northern Irish origin who is fairly well known in the United Kingdom. Several years ago, at the outset of the Second Intifada, Paulin published a poem in the British newspaper *The Observer* calling the Israeli army the "Zionist SS." Somewhat later, he told an Egyptian newspaper that Brooklyn-born Jews who lived in the West Bank "should be shot dead." He described these people as "Nazis" and "racists" and said he felt "nothing but hatred for them." Later, when asked how he felt about charges that he was antisemitic, Paulin answered, "I just laugh when they do that to me. It does not worry me at all. These are Hampstead liberal Zionists. I have utter contempt for them." He also told the press that he could "understand how suicide bombers feel. It is an expression of deep injustice and tragedy."[59] For Paulin, all of these comments fell into the category of legitimate and thoughtful political commentary. They were not meant to incite violence, they were not bigotry or double standards, and they did not focus disproportionately and inappropriately on Israeli misdeeds. Indeed, Paulin deemed himself a lifelong opponent of Jew-hatred; he was a self-described "philo-semite."[60]

British and other academics apparently agreed, at least, with the legitimacy of his criticism, as Paulin's remarks drew precious little condemnation from fellow British professors. Some Oxford students petitioned the university leadership objecting that "such public advocacy of violence against particular ethnic or political groups is not acceptable and the university should not pussy-foot around saying so."[61] But no reprimand was forthcoming, even though what Paulin said was arguably in violation of British laws against advocacy of terrorist violence. Thus, it was probably no surprise to any in the academic community when Harvard's English department decided to give Paulin a bully pulpit from which to pronounce, asking him to deliver the prestigious Morris Gray Lecture in Cambridge.

President Summers said privately that he was horrified by the invitation.[62] After all, it illustrated precisely what he had been talking about in a Harvard speech a few months earlier. In that speech, Summers spent some time trying to explain where he was coming from. He said, "I am Jewish, identified but hardly devout. In my lifetime, anti-Semitism has been remote from my experience."[63] He spoke of his years as a Jew in American politics and revealed his sense that there had been, in the latter part of the twentieth century, considerable "progress . . . an ascendancy of enlightenment and tolerance. A view that prejudice is increasingly put aside. A view that while the politics of the Middle East was enormously complex, and contentious, the question of the right of a Jewish state to exist had been settled in the affirmative by the world community." But he then announced that, these days, he was less complacent "because there is disturbing evidence of an upturn in anti-Semitism globally, and also because of some developments closer to home."

Summers emphasized that he was not talking about criticisms of Israeli policies, which he deemed entirely legitimate. He said, "I have always throughout my life been put off by those who heard the sound of breaking glass, in every insult or slight, and conjured up images of Hitler's Kristallnacht at any disagreement with Israel. Such views have always seemed to me alarmist if not slightly hysterical. But I have to say that while they still seem to me unwarranted, they seem rather less alarmist in the world of today than they did a year ago." Summers then mentioned synagogue burnings, attacks on Jews, swastikas on Holocaust memorials, Holocaust denial, and other recent manifestations of Jew-hatred. (He did not, incidentally, comment specifically on the intensity of Jew-hatred in the Muslim and Arab world.)

What really sparked controversy however was Summers's willingness to condemn some expressions of hostility to Israel. He never advocated the stifling of any debate, certainly not about the merits of various Israeli policies. But recent events struck him as beyond the realm of legitimate, civil academic discussion—and he hoped other academics would agree. He provided examples:

- European academics calling for an end to support for Israeli researchers, though not for an end to support for researchers from any other nation
- Israeli scholars forced off the board of an international literary journal
- university student protesters including anti-Israel hostility, even equating Israeli prime minister Ariel Sharon with Adolf Hitler, at events supposedly dedicated to questioning globalization, condemning the International Monetary Fund, and opposing capitalism
- fund-raising for organizations that support terrorism
- attempts at Harvard and elsewhere to single out Israel among all nations as the only country where universities should not be permitted to invest a portion of their endowment

Summers, the first Jewish president of Harvard, then dared to proclaim, "Where anti-Semitism and views that are profoundly anti-Israeli have traditionally been the primary preserve of poorly educated right-wing populists, profoundly anti-Israel views are increasingly finding support in progressive intellectual communities. Serious and thoughtful people are advocating and taking actions that are anti-Semitic in their effect if not their intent." He concluded by saying, "I would like nothing more than to be wrong. It is my greatest hope and prayer that the idea of a rise of anti-Semitism proves to be a self-denying prophecy—a prediction that carries the seeds of its own falsification. But this depends on all of us."

Summers could not have expected faculty minions to line up behind him. And, sure enough, many academics roundly denounced his comments as yet another attempt to defame legitimate critics of Israel by labeling them antisemites. Leading the attack on Summers was Judith Butler with her article "No, It's Not Antisemitic," published in the prestigious *London Review of Books*, known for both its literary sophistication and its anti-Israel editorial stance.[64]

Butler took some shots at straw men, claiming, "No political ethics can start from the assumption that Jews monopolise the position of victim." She further suggested that Summers classified most criticism of Israel as antisemitic, something he never said or implied. Additionally, she wrote, "A challenge to the right of Israel to exist can be construed as a challenge to the existence of the Jewish people only if one believes that Israel alone keeps the Jewish people alive or that all Jews invest their sense of perpetuity in the state of Israel in its current or traditional forms." Speaking as a Jew herself, Butler claimed that "the possibility of a substantive Jewish peace movement depends on our observing a productive and critical distance from the state of Israel (which can be coupled with a profound investment in its future course)." But Butler's core objection was that "Summers uses the 'anti-semitic' charge to quell public criticism of Israel, even as he explicitly distances himself from the overt operations of censorship. He writes, for instance, that 'the only antidote to dangerous ideas is strong alternatives vigorously advocated.' But how does one vigorously advocate the idea that the Israeli occupation is brutal and wrong, and Palestinian self-determination a necessary good, if the voicing of those views calls down the charge of anti-semitism?"

Butler wrote that a "more democratic" Israel would be better for the Jews, but she failed to define what she meant by democratic or how such a state might function, given current hostile conditions. Her argument was, at best, ahistorical.

Moreover, she took her position that Israeli policies were cruel and unjust as a given, offering no evidence or defense of this belief. She failed to specify any conditions under which critiques of Israel would be inappropriate, demonizing, disproportionate, or based on double standards. In addition, if censorship of Israel's critics was a reality, how could she explain the prevailing anti-Israel winds on the academic left?

And, as University of Washington professor Edward Alexander noted in his critique of Butler's article,

> as for the argument that nothing is antisemitic which does not explicitly target every single Jew in the world, it is Butler at her most jejune. . . . Does she really think that when Josef (later Johannes) Pfefferkorn, whose distinction between "good" and "bad" Jews became the paradigm for Jewish self-haters, urged his countrymen (in the 1520s) to "drive the old Jews out [of Germany]" he had himself in mind? When Karl Marx excoriated Jews as "the filthiest of all races," did he really mean to include himself? Do the operators of [current] Nazi websites have trouble making "exceptions" for the writings of [Noam] Chomsky or his disciple Norman Finkelstein? Indeed, Butler's requirement of total inclusiveness would have allowed Hitler himself to say (had he so wished) of his racial policy: "No, it's not antisemitic."[65]

In my view, what was most troubling about Professor Butler's article was what she omitted. She offered acknowledgment that "Summers is right to voice concern about rising anti-semitism, and every progressive person ought to challenge anti-semitism vigorously wherever it occurs." Yet, despite this purported imperative to act vigorously, she offers not one word condemning the rise of Jew-hatred in the Muslim and Arab world.

Perhaps Butler does not consider the massive dissemination by print and broadcast media of *The Protocols of the Elders of Zion* to be antisemitic. And perhaps she does not consider the regular preaching of religious-based anti-Jewish canards to be illegitimate forms of hostility either. Perhaps she has been able to interpret these utterances as critiques of Israeli policy. Perhaps Judith Butler, in all her complexity, has figured out a way to avoid classifying distribution of *The Protocols* as antisemitism or Mahathir Mohamad as an antisemite. I suspect that she would deny all this, that she instead would consider these to be examples of antisemitism.

But she can hardly be seen to be acting "vigorously" in the condemnation of any of these instances of significant bigotry. Perhaps she does not consider it a problem that one can no longer go to parts of Pakistan and proclaim oneself a Jew without putting one's life at risk.[66] She paid momentary lip service to the need to denounce "real" antisemitism, yet she has done nothing in furtherance of this objective. On the other hand, her condemnations of Israel quickly move from the theoretical to boycotts, divestiture, and other protests.

An interesting sideshow of the Butler-Summers controversy concerns literature professor Rebeca Siegel's attempt to respond to Butler using the language and ideology of the Left. Siegel, a Mexican American Jew, announced her goal: "Both in the spirit of dissent and reflection that any pluralistic society owes itself, especially from left-wing intellectuals, it is imperative that progressive academics who deplore racism or gender discrimination fight for our discursive spaces within the left by repudiating Judeophobia, the only locus where the left and the right consistently coincide."[67] She then laid out her position, disagreeing with Butler on many key points. Notably, Siegel argued that "to identify the flaws in any democracy [Germany, France, America] . . . never becomes grounds for demanding that these countries be dismantled" and that for many on the left, "the logic is that occupation allows anything." Siegel published her response not in the influential *London Review of Books*, but in a tiny progressive publication called *Bad Subjects*.

Yet, even in this obscure home, some felt the arguments voiced by Siegel did not deserve to see the light of day. In 2007, several years after her article appeared, Zack Furness, the editor who had accepted her piece, wrote a long and curious essay of his own. Furness had been feeling guilty. He explained, "I feel the need to take responsibility for what I published and what I inadvertently contributed to by doing so. At the time, I was particularly ignorant about Israel's history."[68] After talking about his teenage experiences at Jewish summer camp among other things, Furness proclaimed that he now knew something that he didn't know when he published Siegel's essay: "In looking back . . . I do not read the work of a person who is uninformed, malicious, or uncritical, and my purpose in framing this essay around my editorial decision is not to make myself look good or, subsequently, to make her look bad. Rather, it forces me to think specifically about what it means to be an editor, and more importantly, what it means to be a Leftist." And what it means to Furness is that voices like Siegel's—however informed, well-intentioned, or "critical"—should not be heard, not in the *London Review of Books* and not in *Bad Subjects*.

British writer and Oxford professor Brian Klug's attitudes toward Jew-hatred resemble those of Judith Butler. Declaring himself an unbending opponent of old-style antisemitism, Klug denounces the "new antisemitism" as a myth.[69] Rather than seeing real bigotry in the demonization and delegitimization of Israel, he, like Butler, detects partisan political tactics consciously designed to deflect criticism from Israel. In a 2004 article, Klug quoted Ludwig Wittgenstein: "Say what you choose, so long as it does not prevent you from seeing the facts."[70] Yet Klug's primary concern—anti-Israel politics—apparently hinders his ability to gauge the intensity of old-style Jew-hatred in the Muslim and Arab world. If Klug does see the facts here, he either ignores them, mentions them as an insignificant part of "the mix" of what is going on, or mischaracterizes them as equivalent in scope, intensity, religious origin, and consequence to Jewish racism against Arabs. In his reality, "there has been 'a continuum of prejudice' against Jews in the history of anti-Semitism. But this is a European, not Middle Eastern, history." Ignoring evidence of virulent antisemitism in the contemporary Muslim world as well as questionable treatment of Jews in traditional Muslim religious source material, he has written about those who call attention to global attacks on Jews (whether from Muslim or other sources): "There is no such war. It is, in fact, as much a figment of the imagination as its mirror image: a Jewish conspiracy against the world."[71] In other words, those who focus on Jew-hatred in the Muslim and Arab world are as deceived as those who believe in the core argument of *The Protocols of the Elders of Zion.*

The Silence of the Human Rights Organizations

Back in 2004 Miriam Greenspan, who declared herself a "card-carrying Leftist for the past forty years" worried that some parts of the Left had "a history of minimizing and being silent about anti-Semitism, in contrast to loudly condemning racism directed at people of color." She further suggested that leftists in the past had sometimes treated Jew-hatred as an insult rather than as something more serious. Then she verbalized something that I suspect is felt by a fair number of others on the moderate Jewish left:

> As a daughter of Holocaust survivors born in a refugee camp, I am passion-ately concerned about the fate of the Jewish people. I identify with Palestin-ians languishing in refugee camps and, at the same time, I am angry about

the rabid anti-Semitism on the streets of the West Bank and Gaza. I feel a profound sense of betrayal in relation to my Leftist brothers and sisters who obsessively condemn Israeli sins while consistently ignoring tyranny, misogyny, and anti-Semitism in the Muslim world; who excuse the murder and mutilation of Jews in Israel; who have recurrently failed to understand anti-Semitism, much less to raise their voices or rally against it. I am tired and saddened by all the polarizing accusations and pseudo-rational fact-mongering and would like to see something resembling a civil conversation on the subject of the new anti-Semitism.

"Where," she asked, "are the enlightened progressive activists who will even utter the word 'anti-Semitism' on their lists of political grievances?" Fellow leftist Jews, she suggested, "might note [whether] we are as comfortable raising the issue of anti-Semitism as we are opposing Israeli policy. [And] if not, why not?"[72]

Had Greenspan hoped to find Jewish or non-Jewish progressive voices willing to make antisemitism, much less Muslim antisemitism, a priority, she would find such hopes dashed by most human rights organizations. Groups such as NGO Monitor and UN Watch have repeatedly called to task the United Nations and the human rights community for unfair, unbalanced, disproportionate, or obsessive denunciations of Israel. But without addressing this issue, there is a more basic concern. With the exception of the ADL, the American Jewish Committee, and a few other groups, mainstream human rights organizations have utterly refused to employ their agenda-setting power to raise consciousness about serious antisemitism in the Muslim and Arab world.

Of course, lip service about the unacceptability of antisemitism in the abstract is ever present, although often this attention is paid as a defensive afterthought in the context of spine-chilling denunciations of Israel. Thus, the Unitarian Universalist program "Toward Peace and Justice in the Middle East" strongly condemns Israel in very specific terms for its "occupation" and specifically calls for various acts against the Jewish state, including divestment and withholding of weaponry key to its defense. But it also condemns "expressions and acts of anti-Semitism and acts of terror against Jews, Palestinians, or Arabs and their legitimate institutions wherever they may occur."[73] Just what this might mean remains unclear because nowhere in the vast Unitarian Universalist literature on racism, social justice, and the Middle East have I been able to find specific documentation of *Muslim* antisemitism. If such references exist, they are—in contrast to denunciations of Israel—hidden well.

It is a reasonable, if imperfect, generalization to state that while human rights organizations nearly always denounce antisemitism in general, very few see it as a priority in the contemporary world and virtually none are willing to even address the problem specifically in the context of Muslim and Arab communities. To the extent that the issue is addressed even indirectly, it is usually in the context of a denunciation of Israel or, somewhat better, in vague descriptions of "extremists on all sides" of the Arab-Israeli conflict. Yet contemporary hatred of Jews should be a specific and major concern for human rights organizations and, in the name of intellectual honesty, perhaps especially so for groups that see strong denunciations of Israel as a core part of their mission.

Robert Bernstein was one of the founders of the group Helsinki Watch, which later became Human Rights Watch, in 1978. Yale Law School described him as a "tireless champion of human rights" and a man who "devoted his life to the defense of freedom of expression and the protection of victims of injustice and abuse throughout the world."[74] Yet, at the age of eighty-six, Bernstein felt impelled to break with the organization to which he had devoted many years. Bernstein's core objection went beyond the organization's treatment of Israel and antisemitism. His concern was that the organization, as he conceived it, should be more focused on getting the principles of the Universal Declaration of Human Rights into closed societies. He explained, "The faults of democratic countries were much less of a priority not because there were no faults, obviously, but because they had so many indigenous human rights groups and other organizations criticizing them."[75] He was concerned when a Human Rights Watch board member conceded that the organization go after Israel because it was "low-hanging fruit." Yet, as he saw it, the organization's priority was to pursue "high-hanging fruit"—in other words, closed societies that were not discussing and, consequently, not addressing their own human rights problems. Israel, according to Bernstein, was a democracy that, like other democracies, committed its share of misdeeds. But it did not deserve anything like the obsessive attention it typically received in the United Nations or the human rights community.

One topic Bernstein thought deserved much more attention was genocidal hate speech directed against Israel and the Jews. He explained that Human Rights Watch and others would not "take a position on hate speech because they believe that it interferes with free speech and is a risk that must be taken." Bernstein agreed that in open societies there should be great latitude in tolerating hate speech because those with other opinions can attack the hate. However, he saw the problem differently in the Arab world and in Iran, where the hate is often government-sponsored and there is no free speech. He asked fair-minded people to consider declarations on Jews that a person might encounter in the Arab world:

> In a [Gaza] sermon, Ahmand Bahr, acting speaker of the Palestinian Legislative Council, said, "Oh Allah, vanquish the Jews and their supporters. Oh Allah, vanquish the Americans and their supporters. Oh Allah, count their numbers, and kill them all, down to the very last one." Even on the West Bank, where Salam Fayyad is improving the economic condition and security, little has been done to stop hate speech and "martyr killers" are celebrated as heroes. Saudi Arabia's publishing industry is spewing out textbooks for young children calling Jews "apes and pigs."[76]

That such bigotry goes unanswered in Arab countries and Iran—and that organizations such as Human Rights Watch have nearly nothing to say about it—is troubling for Bernstein. He notes that some hateful speech and behavior occurs in Israel but remarks, correctly, that it is contested by many domestic sources. (Consider, for example, the response when a mosque was damaged and defaced in June 2011. Immediately, and typically, the Israeli prime minister, defense minister, and other officials denounced the acts as criminal and despicable. They put the tools of the state to work to punish the perpetrators, portraying them as enemies of Israel as much as they were the enemies of Palestinian Muslims who worshipped in the mosque.)[77]

To those who would suggest that hate speech is not the concern of human rights organizations, Bernstein cogently objects: "Hezbollah and Hamas are preaching genocide, not only of Israel but of all Jews everywhere. Genocide is one of the greatest human rights violations, and the Genocide Convention states it must be acted upon when it is first threatened. I believe that Human Rights Watch's position is that their mandate to not take sides in a war takes precedence over the Genocide Convention at this time. It is fair to ask, 'Why?'" He argues that this strategy fails:

How can they [i.e., human rights organizations] protect Israeli civilians during a war when the opposition's aim is genocide and when Hamas states that there are no civilians since all Israeli Jews serve in the military? How can they protect Palestinians when their armies are not uniformed, hide their arms among the civilian population and in public buildings, and shoot from heavily populated areas? Can you ignore what might happen to the civilians after the war, depending on who wins? The whole world is talking about how to prevent Iran from getting an atomic bomb. Human Rights Watch's policy is to criticize actions, not words. One must ask, is the creation of a bomb an action, or only its firing? There is no doubt they would criticize the launch of a nuclear weapon—but of course it would be too late.[78]

Irwin Cotler, former attorney general of Canada, member of the Canadian parliament, and professor of human rights law at McGill University, has taken the lead in defining a role for the human rights community in addressing antisemitism. Like Bernstein, Cotler sees the state-sponsored and group-sponsored genocidal rhetoric of Iran, Hamas, Hezbollah, and other Islamic extremist entities as more than mere words; he sees the potential for intervention under the Convention on the Prevention and Punishment of the Crime of Genocide. More generally, he characterizes global antisemitism as "an assault on human rights" that has many dimensions and forms.[79] For example, the political rights of the Jewish people, consecrated in the International Covenant on Civil and Political Rights, are regularly denied. He quotes Martin Luther King Jr., who objected to the singling out of Jews for this sort of treatment. King said, "This is the denial to the Jews of the same right, the right to self-determination, that we accord to the African nationals and to all other peoples of the globe. In short, it is anti-Semitism."[80]

Cotler sees what he considers a global assault on the Jews manifesting in (among other things)

- physical attacks on identifiable Jews and Jewish institutions;
- dissemination of conspiracy theories, false atrocity propaganda, and *The Protocols of the Elders of Zion*;
- boycotts and divestments that target Israel alone, including boycotts of Israeli professors, Israeli Jews, and Israel supporters from universities; and
- holocaust denial and minimization and denial of the historical connection between the Jewish people and the state of Israel.

More generally, Cotler denounces the "mendacious, dehumanizing or stereo-typical allegations about Jews or the power of Jews as a collective."[81]

Yet, even without including attacks on Israel and Zionism, all this hatred adds up, especially in the Muslim and Arab world, to a mass movement aimed at hurting the Jews as individuals and as a group. There is little justification for the relative neglect of massive bigotry by organizations that have made various aspects of human rights and opposition to racism and prejudice their reason for existing. That such matters are given short shrift is particularly disconcerting in light of the ongoing assault on the state of Israel, which has been shown by many to be a preoccupation of the very same organizations.

The United Nations makes similar—sometimes egregious—errors of omission and commission. As a January 24, 2008, incident reveals, even paraphrasing Shakespeare can make trouble for the Jews when the UN Human Rights Council (HRC) is making the call.[82] David Littman, the purported culprit, is a historian, human rights activist, and United Nations delegate of the World Union of Progressive Judaism (WUPJ). This nongovernmental organization represents 1.7 million Reform, Reconstructionist, liberal, and progressive Jews. Littman was attempting to speak at a meeting devoted to the consideration of human rights abuses emanating from Israeli military incursions into the "occupied territories." Scholar Anne Bayefsky noted that this meeting "brought the total to four special sessions on Israel—compared with six sessions to address human rights in the other 191 UN member states."[83]

Judging the intentions toward Israel of Hamas—which controlled part of the occupied territories—to be relevant to the context within which Israeli military actions occurred, Littman attempted to quote Article 2 of the Hamas Charter. This article stated, "Israel will exist and continue to exist until Islam will obliterate it, just as it obliterated others before it."[84] However, Littman was interrupted before he could quote the charter, and on two other occasions that day his speech was further interrupted on the grounds that his comments were unrelated to the matter at hand. He tried to explain, "The issue is what Hamas and the government in Gaza wishes to do to Israel."[85] But his protestations were to no avail. The representatives at the highest human rights organization in the world did not reject his point of view; they did not want to hear it. Dismayed and frustrated, the British-born delegate then declared (following *Hamlet*), "There is a general malaise in the air, a feeling that something is rotten in the state of this council."[86]

The delegates were insulted by this comment, and the matter did not end there. Several months later, the United Nations committee charged with admission of nongovernmental organizations responded to pressure from the Islamic states, Cuba, and others by seeking to have the WUPJ thrown out of the United Nations after thirty-six years of observer status. The union's delegate, they explained, had made unfounded allegations against member states and sought to undermine the United Nations system. The WUPJ attempted to apologize to those 118 nations that felt offended, but few were mollified. "We are truly dissatisfied," the Cuban representative said. "We do not see this organization's intention to offer a sincere apology. We see a clear violation of [HRC rules and] believe this committee should take a stand."[87] China was upset too. Even Sudan—in the midst of perpetrating genocide in Darfur at the time—protested that the representative of the progressive Jews had violated the sprit and letter of the United Nations Charter.[88] When, during debate over the future status of the WUPJ, Qatar complained of Littman's "obscene words," it was too much for a British diplomat to bear. "Shakespeare," he explained, "is not obscene language."[89]

In the end, the Jewish group's apology sufficed, and the only consequence was a letter of reprimand for "bad behavior." However, it might be going a tad too far to say that reason prevailed. Rather, the incident provided a glimpse at the pervasiveness of hostility to Israel in the United Nations and how readily this hostility slipped into hostility toward Jews. More generally, the incident points painfully at the question of whether nations that routinely and outrageously violate human rights can ever constitute a fair and reasonable body committed to extending those rights or bringing about peace.[90]

Many reports and studies have documented the UN's preoccupation with Israel.[91] The UN-sponsored Durban I conference, ostensibly created to oppose racism, turned into a full-blown fete of Jew-hatred. According to a report by NGO Monitor, participants at this meeting of nongovernmental organizations were guilty of "violations of procedure in the preparatory and drafting processes, . . . racist treatment including violence, exclusion and intimidation against Jewish participants, and the misuse of human rights terminology in the document related to the Israeli-Palestinian conflict."[92] And at the follow-up conference in 2009, Durban II, the main speaker was Iranian president Ahmadinejad. What more needs to be said? Even Secretary-General Ban Ki-moon felt the need to put distance between himself and Ahmadinejad, but still he endorsed the tainted conference. Regardless, as Abraham Foxman noted, no amount of papering over could erase the stain of the original hate-filled event.

Hannah Rosenthal was associated with the leftist group J Street (often at odds with the mainstream Jewish community) before she became President Barack Obama's ambassador in charge of addressing antisemitism. In 2009 she counted 170 UN denunciations of Israel, compared with six for the genocidal regime in Sudan, in the six preceding years. The UN Human Rights Council directed all—100 percent—of its condemnatory resolutions toward Israel.[93] This record, of course, is noteworthy as much for whom it lets off the hook as for whom it targets.

In the United States, the belief that the United Nations is hopelessly biased against the Jewish state is fairly widespread among mainstream thinkers from the Democratic and Republican Parties. Yet the ease within which this hostility toward Israel can turn into tolerance for, or complicity with, antisemitism is less known and somewhat harder to document.

Back in the mid-1960s, former Israeli Supreme Court justice Hadassa Ben-Itto worked as part of Israel's delegation to the UN General Assembly. High on the agenda was completion of the Convention on the Elimination of All Forms of Racial Discrimination. Although no other delegation suffered similar breaches of etiquette, Ben-Itto was sometimes called "the delegate of the Zionist entity," "the lady in yellow [when she wore a yellow dress]," and even "the delegate from the Elders of Zion." At official meetings, Arab delegates made references to blood libels and the so-called Jewish conspiracy. Yet no committee chairpersons ever remarked on the lack of propriety.[94]

More recently, in 2001, at a meeting in Madrid of the UN Human Rights Commission Special Conference on Religious Discrimination, the Syrian ambassador remarked in reference to a Jewish delegate, "There are present, in this hall, representatives of an arrogant self-elected faith that defines itself as divinely chosen. They have no place here!"[95] The Jewish delegate, Shimon Samuels, was appalled. He wrote of the incident, "I turned to other human rights NGOs and appealed to them to respond to such hatred by leaving the hall with me. They refused, so I walked out—noisily and demonstratively."[96] If the goal were truly to end religious discrimination, the Syrian ambassador's comment would have been a bad omen. But perhaps one is not being too cynical to doubt whether the delegates truly had the end of prejudice in mind.

In November 2007 UN Watch issued a report charging, among other things, that Louise Arbour, the United Nations High Commissioner for Human Rights, had been virtually silent about antisemitism in the Muslim world and elsewhere. UN Watch pointed out that Arbour "holds one of the world's leading moral pulpits and her potential influence is significant. She has the power to draw public attention to the evils of anti-Semitism and should do so."[97] But it seemed unlikely that she would follow this tack with much vigor. When asked to condemn Iranian president Ahmadinejad's public denial of the Holocaust, she decided to send him private letters. A private letter was also her response when Ahmadinejad called to wipe Israel off the map (perhaps foreshadowing a war in which the United Nations uses postage stamps and the Iranians use nukes).

Worse, in 2007 Princeton professor emeritus Richard Falk—previously mentioned as a onetime fan of Ayatollah Khomeini—wrote, "Is it an irresponsible overstatement to associate the treatment of the Palestinians with [the] criminalized Nazi record of collective atrocity? I think not."[98] Yet, despite this opinion and others equally outside the American mainstream, the United Nations Human Rights Council made Falk the special rapporteur charged with investigating Israeli actions in the Palestinian territories. In response to this decision, journalist Melanie Phillips wrote, "The UN has appointed a man to investigate Israel's behaviour who is incapable of telling the difference between genocide and the attempt to defend a people from becoming its victims."[99]

The United Nations also has a special rapporteur charged with addressing religious intolerance, religious discrimination, and freedom of religious belief. As might be expected, the office of this rapporteur—a post held in recent years by Abdelfattah Amor, Asma Jahangir, and Heiner Bielefeldt—has issued many reports, mainly offering glittering generalities but also touching on a host of troubled situations around the globe. Disproportionately, the concern of these reports has been with perceived threats to the practice of Islam emanating from the West, but other matters have been addressed. A typical report, for example, discusses "violations of the principle of nondiscrimination in matters of religion or belief, namely, policies, legislation and regulations, practices and acts that discriminate against certain communities." The nations where such problems seemed particularly noteworthy, in the eyes of the special rapporteur, included Egypt, France, the Islamic Republic of Iran, and the United States of America—and Egypt and Iran were not cited specifically for antisemitism.[100]

With such a profound inability to draw meaningful distinctions, it is not surprising that except for a few general words here and there, the issue of hostility to Jews has largely fallen under the radar.[101] If a world organization devoted to religious tolerance cannot even detect a shred of Jew-hatred in the entire Muslim and Arab world, one might reasonably inquire by what right it keeps its doors open. How can the UN miss an epidemic of hatred that is sweeping through a fifth of the globe? Of course, the problem is not really lack of detection or lack of perception; it is lack of concern.

In 2005 Pedro Sanjuan, who had worked for years in a high-ranking post at the UN Secretariat, wrote an extraordinary exposé. Sanjuan reported his astonishment that, when he first assumed his position, several top officials at the secretariat, including Secretary-General Javier Pérez de Cuéllar, expressed concern that the Americans had sent them a Jew in disguise. For the non-Jewish Sanjuan, "it was the beginning of an anti-Semitic journey of ten years' duration that never ceased to amaze me, particularly after I realized that anti-Semitism was an established part of the UN way of life. It was not just a political attitude involving Israel. Anti-Semitism was a cultural mind-set, colloidally suspended or emulsified, that defined the UN 'culture.'"[102]

Sanjuan continued, "The anti-Semitic culture in the UN Secretariat did not merely reflect the anti-Semitic, anti-Israeli temper of the UN General Assembly. It reflected as well the fact that anti-Semitism has been a continuous state of mind throughout the United Nations, the Secretariat, the General Assembly, and everywhere else, particularly vividly manifested in UN agencies like UNESCO, UNIDO, WIPO, and others."[103] Sanjuan's book is an insider's memoir, and typically, many of its contentions lack corroboration. Although he strikes me as an honest man, some may choose to regard his great sensitivity to antisemitism as a bad thing. And there can be little doubt that he saw his book as an opportunity to punish many former colleagues whom he regards as scoundrels. But even if the expression and toleration of Jew-hatred in the world's most influential international organization is merely a small fraction of what Sanjuan claims, there is still a problem.

The Default of the Experts

John L. Esposito has been described as the go-to scholar for questions dealing with the Muslim world; he was editor in chief of *The Oxford Encyclopedia of the Mod-*

ern Islamic World and president of both the Middle East Studies Association of North America and the American Council for the Study of Islamic Societies. Dalia Mogahed is the executive director of the Gallup Center for Muslim Studies and was selected as an adviser on faith-based and neighborhood partnerships by President Obama. Together Esposito and Mogahed authored an influential book, *Who Speaks for Islam? What a Billion Muslims Really Think*, in 2007. The volume drew on a thirty-five-nation survey of many thousands of Muslims and had the worthy goal of rising above "contentious rhetoric." "Let the data lead the discourse," the authors advised.[104]

But from the book's first pages it became clear that they were pushing the expensive data set in surprising directions. For example, Esposito and Mogahed claimed that according to their study, only 7 percent of the world's Muslims were extremists, or to use their description, "politically radicalized." Yet, to be included in this group, a person had to indicate to an unknown interviewer that he or she thought the 9/11 attacks were "completely" justified.[105] The 7 percent figure leaves the impression that 93 percent of Muslims worldwide are not politically radicalized and, hence, may be classified as moderates. Although the authors do not present as many numbers as one might expect in an empirically based book, they do maintain that by their calculation, about nine in ten Muslims are moderates.

In 2006 Esposito and Mogahed published an article based on their multinational study in the journal *Foreign Policy*. Here they classified an additional 6.5 percent of Muslims as radicals, bringing the total to about 13.5 percent. These extra respondents were included because they agreed substantially—although not completely—that the 9/11 attacks were justified. But when preparing the book, the authors decided to go with the lower figure of 7 percent. One can make a strong argument that even the discarded higher estimate understated the prevalence of extremist views uncovered by the empirical study. As Robert Satloff, the executive director of the Washington Institute for Near East Policy, pointed out, yet another 23.1 percent of the survey respondents thought the attacks were at least a bit justified, bringing the total percentage who deemed them in some way justified above 36 percent.[106] If one were to accept this figure as the cutoff, it would mean that—in effect—Esposito and Mogahed used their method of defining Muslim radicalism to reduce the actual total by 700 million people.

Esposito and Mogahed conclude that even the 7 percent they deem politically radicalized have derived their views "from their perception of the West's politics, not its culture." Among the so-called moderates, they find substantial hostility toward the United States, support for suicide bombers, and a desire to base the legal system on Islamic religious law. Yet, all in all, the authors are not worried. Rather, they conclude:

> In contrast to expected differences, the number of commonalities we find between the Muslim world and the West shatters many myths. . . . Majorities of both groups cite the importance of religion in public life and the preservation of family values. Each group is concerned about its economic future, employment and jobs, and the ability to support its families. Each gives high priority to technology, democracy, the importance of broad political participation, and freedoms of speech and social justice. Both strongly support eradicating extremism.[107]

Reading this, one wonders whether Esposito and Mogahed's conclusions would have been the same regardless of what the data revealed. Certainly, neither author had to change previous ideas about the Middle East or Islam. They never wonder whether democracy, family values, technology, and social justice mean the same things across cultural and national borders. Satloff suggests, I think correctly, that "the not-so-hidden purpose . . . is to blur any difference between average Muslims around the globe and average Americans, and the authors rise to the occasion at every turn."[108]

To this end, Esposito and Mogahed report no survey questions and write not one word about Muslim attitudes toward Jews or Judaism. In service of their ultimate aims, the first chapter of the book provides an overview of the Islamic faith—omitting or whitewashing any controversial elements. Perhaps the authors would say that they are making the work more accessible to the public. But none of the religious texts that might support anti-Jewish attitudes, including the anti-Jewish hadiths, are even mentioned; neither are the massacre of the Banu Qurayza Jews or pigs and apes.

The authors do not consider the multinational Pew Foundation studies, discussed in chapter 2, that have uncovered in Muslim-majority countries extremely negative attitudes toward Jews. One of these studies (released in July 2005) would have been available to the authors, but it is not mentioned.[109] According to a 2010 study that Esposito and Mogahed could not have seen (but which produced similar findings to the earlier one), "more than 90% of Egyptians, Jordanians, Lebanese and Palestinians express unfavorable views toward Jews."[110] (Interestingly, among Israeli Arabs, a far lower percentage dislike the Jews—only 35 percent.) In the non-Arab Muslim countries of Turkey, Pakistan, and Indonesia, the percentage with negative views of Jews tops 70 percent, and among Muslims in Nigeria it tops 60 percent. In all these countries, the percentage of Muslims with unfavorable opinions of Jews far exceeds the percentage holding negative opinions about Christians, although these percentages are also high.

Despite this data, one could leave Esposito and Mogahed's well-regarded book on what Muslims really think with the impression that no one in the Islamic world possesses any ill will toward Jews. Yet, on the basis of the Pew data and other indexes of bigotry toward Jews, it would be hard to argue for the fundamental similarity of American and Muslim values at least on this issue. After all, polls in the United States consistently show very low levels of anti-Jewish feeling. So, rather than present uncomfortable facts, the authors omit the antisemitism issue altogether.

Esposito and Mogahed's position is especially unfortunate because—and this point is critically important—it essentially hamstrings genuine moderates in the Islamic world. Perhaps this is why Yemeni liberal Muslim Dr. Elham Mane'a panned *Who Speaks for Islam?* and sharply criticized President Obama for relying on Mogahed's counsel. According to Mane'a, "the strangest thing is that, in launching a dialogue with the Muslim world, U.S. President Obama chose an [adviser] who does not express the diversity of opinions and positions in Muslim countries. On the contrary—he chose [one] who says, 'this is Islam, and this is the way Muslim men and women are.'"[111] Thus, we are left with a purported celebration of moderation in Muslim communities that fails miserably at the first step—identifying who the moderates really are.

Logically, one might expect understanding of antisemitism in Muslim and Arab communities to be enhanced by two types of researchers: those who specialize in Middle Eastern studies and Islamic studies and those who specialize in the social scientific study of ideology, bigotry, prejudice, and race relations. Yet, for different reasons, both of these potentially vital sources of insight have largely failed to meet the challenge.

With a few notable exceptions, sociologists, psychologists, social psychologists, and other social scientists have essentially remained mum, despite their long and honorable history of combating many forms of bigotry, including antisemitism. A 2003 study examined Psychinfo, the leading online index of psychological publications. At that time, the index showed 458 publications since 1940 that addressed the topic of antisemitism, 99 of which had appeared during the previous ten years.[112] Not a single one dealt directly with hatred of Jews by Muslims or Arabs in the contemporary world. The leading index of sociological studies, *Sociological Abstracts*, told much the same story: 130 articles on antisemitism published since 1963, but not a single one centering on hatred of Jews by Arabs or Muslims.

More recently, some work has appeared, but still the topic is understudied. In the years between 2003 and the present, as the frequency and virulence of antisemitism has continued to grow in Muslim and Arab communities, a few studies on the topic were published in scientific, academic, and professional journals. A new search of Psychinfo showed about a dozen articles dealing directly with the topic and a few more touching on it peripherally. A special issue of the *International Journal of Applied Psychoanalytic Studies* focused on "Anti-Semitism in Muslim Cultures," and a special issue of *Current Psychology: A Journal for Diverse Perspectives on Diverse Psychological Issues* dealt with "Anti-Semitism the World Over in the Twenty-First Century."[113] One new journal, *Journal for the Study of Antisemitism*, launched in 2009, but it is not yet included in Psychinfo; each issue of the journal includes studies on the topic. No studies in high-impact psychology or sociology journals directly covered the topic of Muslim antisemitism, although a few studies on related topics appeared in prominent outlets.[114] An examination of existing research in social science journals has turned up no studies on attitudes toward Jews presenting data collected in Muslim-majority or Arab-majority countries. A review of recent studies cited in *Sociological Abstracts* turned up only a handful of studies that even touch tangentially on Muslim antisemitism.[115] In this tiny body of social scientific work on Jew-hatred in the Muslim world, some contributions are brief responses to others, and a few try to steer researchers away from studying the topic. And political scientists, historians, and cultural studies scholars are not, for the most part, devoting much attention to contemporary antisemitism either.

The failure of social scientists to confront this epidemic of contemporary bigotry is especially curious in light of their past prominence in studying antisemitism and, indeed, their energetic probing of many strains of prejudice. One part of the explanation has to do with what it takes to conduct a well-designed, empirical study on the topic. Those who wish to do so in Arab countries and many other parts of the Muslim world face nearly insurmountable obstacles, starting with the critical problem of access. Few countries or cultures in these regions welcome indigenous or Western interviewers—whether journalists or social scientists—who ask pesky questions (and questions about antisemitism are nearly always deemed pesky). Nondemocratic regimes in much of the Muslim world tend to place formal limits on journalists and social scientists. Moreover, many of the Westerners who frequent Muslim-majority regions tend not to cross lines or violate certain cultural taboos so as not to wear out their welcome.

Indeed, the overwhelming majority of Arabic-speaking scholars have developed greater sympathy for the Arabs than for Israel. Whether they start out with an apologetic attitude toward Islamic antisemitism or develop one over the years is not a question that is easy to answer. Moreover, Jewish social scientists, especially those suspected of sympathizing with Israel, would have a hard time carrying out their professional activities in much of the Middle East, particularly when they want to study antisemitism.

Even assuming access, funding, and successful navigation of linguistic and other cultural issues, there remains what might be called "the Daniel Pearl problem." When probing questions are directed to the wrong people, dangerous consequences may ensue. It would require uncommon bravery for Western or indigenous social scientists, especially pro-Israeli Jewish ones, not to pause once or twice before embarking on a serious, on-the-ground empirical study of Jew-hatred in the Middle East. Consider, for example, Tarek Fatah's discussion of Peshawar, Pakistan: "If there is a place on earth today where identifying oneself as a Jew means inviting serious danger to life and liberty, then the historic Pakistani city of Peshawar would easily win that honor." According to Fatah, things were not always that way. But nowadays, as one of his sources confides, "the word 'Jew' is a slur not just in the city of Peshawar but perhaps the entire Muslim world."[116] Under such conditions, Jewish researchers will be cautious—and caution does not necessarily produce abundant, high-quality research.[117]

Above and beyond the failure to conduct systematic research on Muslim antisemitism, there lies the far more serious failure to name, confront, and condemn the bigotry. Many justifications are offered for this failure, and they will be dealt with in the next chapter. There are also those who perceive Muslim antisemitism clearly enough but hold that focusing on it would be counterproductive to the war on terrorism, President Obama's outreach to the Muslims, the Arab-Israeli peace process, American-European relations, or something else. Perhaps among the well-intentioned, the biggest reason for ignoring Muslim antisemitism is, as Hebrew University professor Menahem Milson argued, the fear of being labeled "anti-Arab" or "Islamophobic." But, when all is said, the failure of social scientists and others to consider this virulent bigotry remains, in my view, scandalous.

Some of the same problems that discourage studies by sociologists and psychologists apply to academics specializing in Middle Eastern studies. Regional experts on the Middle East are likely to speak Arabic, Farsi, Urdu, Turkish, and other languages. In theory, they are better equipped to carry out studies; any deficiencies they have in research methodology could be handled through collaboration with empirically minded social scientists. Middle East experts usually feel more comfortable traveling to and from the region than would the typical sociologist or psychologist specializing in the study of prejudice. These area experts also have greater familiarity with the religious, historical, and cultural sources needed to create nuanced analyses of contemporary thinking about Jews. They are, in short, well suited by their academic training to greatly expand our understanding. And yet they have produced almost nothing on the topic.

The explanation lies in the realization that—to paraphrase Littman paraphrasing Shakespeare—these days there is something rotten in the state of Middle Eastern studies. It is beyond the scope of this book to document and explain this rot, but Professor Martin Kramer has gone far toward accomplishing this task.[118] According to Kramer, in the 1980s and 1990s Middle Eastern studies became "a field where scholarship took a backseat to advocacy, where a few biases became the highest credentials, where dissenting views became thought-crimes." Kramer attributed this transformation largely to the influence of Professor Edward Said of Columbia University and his famous 1978 book, *Orientalism*. In this book, Said argued that earlier Western scholars had mostly been writing prejudiced, imperialistic interpretations of the East. He called for a new orientation that discarded this so-called outsider approach to Arabs and Muslims.[119] Kramer wrote, "For Professor Said, no understanding of the Middle East had validity unless it was joined at the hip with political sympathy for the cause and the struggle. The cause was the empowerment of Palestinians, Arabs, and Muslims. The struggle was against an axis of evil comprised of Western orientalism, American imperialism, and Israeli Zionism."[120]

As Said's views became the orthodoxy of Middle Eastern studies, especially among a new generation of scholars, the nation's experts on the region started showing "less interest in the actual Middle East than in exposing the West's so-called 'stereotypes.'" According to Kramer, the Said-style scholars "once tenured and vested with academic power, began a systematic purge of Middle Eastern studies. . . . Under their domination, [the field] became very much like Middle Eastern regimes: full of rhetoric about liberation, but dead-set against all expressions of dissent."[121]

For example, the Student Union at the University of London's prestigious School of Oriental and African Studies banned the Jewish Society student organization following the UN's 1975 declaration that Zionism was racism; later, the Student Union withdrew funding when the Jewish Society was reestablished. Yet, the Student Union had no problem with the radical Islamic group Hizb ut Tahrir. It opposed expulsion of this organization from British campuses when the National Union of Students accused it of being anti-Hindu, antisemitic, and homophobic. In 2003 the Student Union passed a resolution condemning "any form of racism, Islamophobia, anti-Semitism, Zionism or other forms of discrimination on campus."[122] The students at the School of Oriental and African Studies saw the Israeli national movement as racism beyond the pale of acceptability; they saw Hizb ut Tahrir as deserving of a seat at the table.

Kramer continued: "By the late 1990s, the radicals could look smugly up and down their hallways and see only like-minded colleagues. . . . But while their trendy theories may have won them tenure, they also became ever more detached from the realities of the Middle East."[123] Just prior to the 9/11 attacks, the prominent new scholars were especially likely to argue against exaggerated concern about terrorism and the rise of Islamism.

And then there is the matter of money. The huge influx of wealth into Saudi Arabia and other Muslim countries since the 1970s has provided the power to shape ideas as well. Saudis, for example, have been able to increase the prominence of their Wahhabi brand of Islam across the Muslim world. Middle Eastern oil money has also had an impact on higher education in the West. The United Arab Emirates partially funded the new $4 million Edward Said Chair at Columbia University. Then, in a fairly clear conflict of interest, the occupant of this chair was named director of Columbia's Middle East Institute, which received large American government subsidies to conduct research on improving national security.[124]

In 2000 Sheikh Zayed, at the time ruler of Abu Dhabi, president of the United Arab Emirates and among the ten richest men in the world, provided $2.5 million to create a chair of Islamic studies at the Harvard Divinity School. Harvard, at first, was thrilled with the gift. But research in 2002 and 2003 by Rachel Fish—a graduate student at the divinity school—conclusively established that the sheikh was a strong supporter of antisemitism, not to mention anti-Americanism. At first, Harvard tried to refute Fish's contentions, maintaining that the United Arab Emirates was the greatest voice of moderation in the Middle East. But soon a highly regarded Jewish studies professor at Harvard, Jon Levenson, joined the fight, and the university decided to reassess whether it should keep the gift. Prior to the outcome of this reassessment, Sheikh Zayed took the matter off the table by asking Harvard to return the gift.[125]

John Esposito is the director of the Prince Alwaleed Bin Talal Center for Muslim-Christian Understanding at Georgetown University. Martin Kramer has reported that "Georgetown's endowment is a meager $680 million. Prince Alwaleed's personal worth is estimated at $23.7 billion. In other words, Georgetown's entire endowment can be tucked into the leftovers of Alwaleed's worth, to the right of the decimal point." And, in fact, Alwaleed made a $20 million donation to the Center for Muslim-Christian Understanding in 2005. Although the center at Georgetown has the declared goal of improving Muslim relations with the Christian West and helping the West to better understand Islam, it is reasonable to doubt that academic freedom plays a role in this exercise. In 2006 Kramer wrote that the Georgetown gift was

> the most dramatic visual confirmation of the deep corruption that Prince Alwaleed's buying spree is spreading through academe and Middle Eastern studies. . . . Over two years [before the 2005 donation], I predicted that Alwaleed would reduce Middle Eastern studies to a cargo cult, with university administrators vying to win the attention of the flying prince. And I wrote this passage: 'In the near future, don't be surprised to see grinning university presidents posing with Prince Alwaleed. They will say there are no strings attached. *Puris omnia pura*: To the pure all things are pure.' My prediction has come true. [126]

In theory, Georgetown's mission might include telling the truth about antisemitism in the Muslim and Arab world, but perhaps the well-endowed scholars might first ponder how such research would sit with the prince. Would he be inclined to make future gifts?

Oil money and other associated Middle Eastern wealth is having a huge impact on the way American professors think, write, and speak about the Middle East. Universities are increasingly seeking to establish branches in the region and, thus, are becoming ever more careful about saying things that might offend their hosts. For example, New York University president John Sexton gushes with excitement and pride when he speaks of the university's Abu Dhabi campus, paid for by Abu Dhabi; he hopes to use Abu Dhabi funding to provide scholarships to students from across the globe.[127] Nothing is ever said about censorship, but one wonders whether these academic leaders are truly above considering how various ideas will play in local circles. In any event, pointing out antisemitism in a region seething with anger toward Israel and the Jews is not likely to be very popular. Even in the halls of academia, he who pays the piper can sometimes call the tune.

An Acceptable Prejudice?

It does not take a subtle mind, years of specialized training, or heightened moral sensitivity to find evidence of substantial antisemitism in parts of the Muslim world. While it is somewhat harder to specify which segments of the world Muslim population exhibit venomous hatred, which are prejudiced to lesser degrees, and which are entirely free of bigotry, any fair-minded person should be able to detect a serious problem. Reasonable people may certainly disagree about the sources of this problem, including the relative importance of Israeli actions and of various Islamic texts and interpretations, but there should be consensus about the existence of widespread and undesirable antisemitism.

And yet one finds, especially in the antiracist community, many who feel strongly motivated to deny the problem, to minimize it, to excuse it, to explain it away, and to attack or ridicule those who see it as important. Some have conspired to deny a podium to those who want to publicize, explore, or combat the bigotry. Some have cried foul when highly credentialed scholars have gathered to present their research at academic conferences. Some have ridiculed and "diagnosed" those who call attention to antisemitism in the contemporary world, without showing the slightest awareness of data on Jew-hatred in countries with Muslim majorities. Poets and scholars have been deemed clever for equating Israelis with Nazis, a comparison that is at best sloppy and at most libelous. Editors have apologized for publishing the views of those whose definitions of Jew-hatred are wider than their own. An unknown few have even gone so far as to issue threats against those who speak about the unmentionable topic.

All these efforts have combined to create an environment in which many Western scholars have opted to censor themselves so as not to invite the scorn of their peers. Yet, most discouraging of all, the efforts of those who prefer silence on the matter of antisemitism in the Islamic world have been largely successful in keeping the topic off the agenda for mainstream liberals and conservatives alike.

4

THE FLAWED LOGIC OF
ANTISEMITISM MINIMIZATION

Few Westerners say openly that they are willing to tolerate or ignore Jew-hatred in the Islamic world or anywhere else. There is a simple reason. The term "antisemitism" and, to a lesser extent, its theory and practice have been discredited through association with Kristallnacht, extermination camps, and Nazi racial doctrine. Even after sixty-five years, it rarely plays well in polite society to show blatant and callous disregard for rising hostility to Jews—no matter how much doing so may square with one's ideological, strategic, political, or psychological agenda.

Instead, those who deny or minimize the significance of Muslim and Arab Jew-hatred nearly always maintain that the problem lies with the anti-antisemites—those whom they charge with misreading, misinterpreting, and misrepresenting the relevant facts. Antisemitism minimizers offer arguments that follow many tacks, but they end up concluding that despite occasional appearances to the contrary, most Muslim and Arab negativity toward Jews is not really bigotry or, even if it is, it does not merit much attention or concern.

Critics of the anti-antisemites often start by proclaiming their opposition to prejudice in all its forms, including antisemitism. Thus, a denier or minimizer of contemporary Muslim antisemitism may denounce instances of Jew-hatred drawn from Christian history, Nazism, or contemporary groups to which he or she is politically opposed (e.g., skinheads). Such declarations may be little more than ritualistic, credential-enhancing ploys, or they may be sincere. One often cannot know.

However, minimizers and deniers of Muslim antisemitism now dominate debates in the Western intellectual establishment, and their arguments are being heard with respect in the highest halls of government across Europe, America, and other democracies.

I have already mentioned the most superficial of the minimization arguments; namely, that Arabs cannot be antisemitic because they themselves are Semites. As has been seen, this argument fails historically and semantically—partly because the category of Semite is, in the main, meaningless, a half-baked fabrication of racists and pseudoscientists in the late nineteenth century. Mostly, however, the argument falls apart because there never has been a bigotry specifically targeting "Semites," whether thought of as speakers of Semitic languages or in any other way. Antisemitism always has been directed at Jews. Thus, when someone uses the "Arabs can't be antisemites" argument, they usually are not attempting to convince the unconvinced or make a sustainable argument. Rather, they are signaling their politics to their audience, demonstrating their ignorance, or trying to push opponents on to the defensive. They imply that whatever happens now in the Muslim and Arab world by definition bears no resemblance to the long and dishonorable history of Jew-hatred in the Christian world. The extent to which such resemblance exists must, of course, be assessed on the evidence, regardless of whether the word "antisemitism" is used. But by denying the appropriateness of the word "antisemitism," critics attempt to circumvent discussion through what is, in effect, a public relations maneuver. They may also attempt to derive moral standing by asserting opposition to Christian antisemitism, while at the same time contending that what we observe in the world of Islam is entirely a horse of a different color.

In truth, this discussion is necessary in the first place only because of a historical accident. Had the nineteenth-century French and German Jew-haters picked a name other than the misnomer "antisemitism" for their hatred, there would be nothing to discuss. But, unfortunately, there is no other equally appropriate term, certainly none with the same historical resonance. Reasonable people, therefore, should understand that the "Arabs can't be antisemites" argument is nothing more than an attempt to provide a particular group of people with a license to engage in bigotry with blanket immunity.

One might, however, identify seven frequently heard lines of argument that require more attention. Although the seven categories overlap, have many variations, and are often employed simultaneously, the list nonetheless helps clarify the logic of denial and minimization. This logic includes the following:

- *definitional arguments,* holding that what we say is antisemitism is not really antisemitism
- *political spillover arguments,* suggesting that whatever antisemitism does exist in the Muslim and Arab world is understandable spillover from the Arab-Israeli conflict

◆ *charges of bad history,* arguing that Muslims and Islam have always treated the
   Jews well so what we are now witnessing cannot reflect deep-seated animosity

◆ *disagreements about commonness and intensity,* claiming that only a tiny handful of Muslims and Arabs actually exhibit anti-Jewish bigotry and that this
   unfortunate prejudice is not really dangerous for Jews or the West

◆ *arguments from civility,* counseling that nice people do not criticize other ethnic groups or their religious beliefs

◆ *charges of Islamophobia,* maintaining that bigotry against Muslims and Arabs
   is the most significant bigotry of our day and that accusations of Muslim antisemitism actually constitute part of that bigotry

◆ *arguments based on benign neglect,* acknowledging the reality of Muslim and
   Arab antisemitism but contending that it is unwise to call attention to the
   problem

I will assess each of these arguments.

Definitional Arguments

One frequently hears that the hostility observed in the Muslim and Arab world
is not really antisemitism. Usually this argument assumes one of the following
forms: (1) "Muslims and Arabs don't hate Jews; they just hate Israelis," (2) "Muslims and Arabs don't hate Jews; they just hate Zionists," (3) "all criticism of Israel
isn't antisemitic," or (4) "the 'new antisemitism' is a myth." The first two contentions are empirically incorrect, the third irrelevant, and the fourth at bottom a
matter of semantics.

"MUSLIMS AND ARABS DON'T HATE JEWS; THEY JUST HATE ISRAELIS AND/OR ZIONISTS"

As Canadian human rights lawyer David Matas has pointed out, "Taking a racial
slur or stereotype directed against someone who is Jewish and replacing the word
Jew with the word Zionist does not change the slur into acceptable discourse."[1]
One must search far and wide to locate Islamists who maintain a clear and credible distinction among Jews, Zionists, and Israelis. Aside from overtly anti-Jewish
declarations—of which there are tons—one finds in various Middle Eastern and
Muslim media many instances in which "Zionists" commit offenses well before
the start of the Zionist movement. Moreover, Zionists and Israelis are frequently

seen by Islamists to act from motivation that is religiously Jewish rather than political. For example, in one article in the Saudi daily *Al-Watan*, journalist Ashraf
Al-Faqi claims (offering no specifics) that undesirable Israeli policies in 2009
derive from "the Jewish interpretation of the Torah."[2] And writing in the Saudi edition of the daily *Al-Hayat*, Islamic researcher 'Abd Al-Rahman Al-Khatib
describes the Jews as religious fanatics and claims that their ideology, which is
reflected in *The Protocols of the Elders of Zion*, stems from the Torah and the Talmud and is currently being implemented in Gaza. He further explains that "Jewish ideology has only two sources: the *Torah* and the *Talmud*. This ideology has
spawned many secondary texts, including *The Protocols of the Elders of Zion* by
Matvei Golovinski, *The Jewish State* by [Theodor] Herzl and [oddly] *The Prince*
by [Niccolo] Machiavelli."[3] Those rare occasions when Islamists do articulate distinctions among Jews, Israelis, and Zionists generally occur in response to queries
from Western journalists and leaders.

It is hard, in any case, to take much comfort in the "they just hate Zionists"
defense, if only because—these days, especially—Zionism has no generally understood definition and may, for some, though clearly not for all, be a politically
correct code word for Jews or Israelis. Probably most people in the West simply
think "enthusiastic Israel-supporter" when they hear the term "Zionist." Few have
much sense of the many ways the diverse proponents of Zionism used the word in
the pre-1948 era.[4] And today a great many Israelis would not describe themselves
as Zionists even though they support the state. People sometimes think that Zionism implies support for an ingathering of Jews from other countries to Israel,
although this plan is decidedly unpopular among many of Israel's strongest Jewish
supporters in the Diaspora.

In addition to all this confusion, there are disingenuous, far-fetched, and libelous uses of the term "Zionist." Recall that the frequently referenced antisemitic
classic is titled *The Protocols of the Elders of Zion*, not "the Elders of Judaism,"
and the fictitious meetings described in *The Protocols*, according to some antisemitic accounts, took place at the First Zionist Congress in Switzerland. Thus, the
distinction between antisemitism and anti-Zionism has been a muddy one for
many years. The former Soviet Union contributed to this confusion by packaging
its antisemitic policies under the label of anti-Zionism.[5] Many people must also
have been influenced by the now-revoked but oft-repeated 1975 United Nations
resolution equating Zionism with racism and similar allegations equating Zionism

with support for apartheid. Nowadays, not infrequently, conspiratorially minded souls on the left and right ascribe American actions on the international scene to a Zionist cabal in Washington; some on the lunatic right go so far as to speak of "ZOG" in Washington. Indeed, the term "Zionist" has been so confused in common usage and so widely discredited in some circles that it is hardly surprising that many Muslims, Arabs, and others would describe themselves as anti-Zionist— and feel good about doing so. What they mean by this—aside from opposition to something evil perpetrated by Jews or Israelis—is anybody's guess. When one scratches the surface of anti-Zionism, one finds many things in many people. Antisemitism is often one of these things.

It is hard to determine how many non-Islamist Muslims and other Arabs draw clear distinctions among Jews, Zionists, and Israelis. Certainly, specifically anti-Jewish rhetoric is less common in these groups than it is among the Islamists. However, the previously cited data from the Pew studies do not counsel optimism; they show nearly consensual unfavorable attitudes toward "Jews."

Perhaps it is necessary to point out that hatred directed against all or most of the people in a country, even Israel, is still bigotry.[6] In addition, while Israelis are the primary targets of the prejudice, Jews outside Israel usually come under fire because they are perceived to be among Israel's strongest supporters—unless they publicly distance themselves. Thus, from the perspective of the ardent anti-Israeli, a criterion for Jewish rights and the acceptability of being Jewish becomes public rejection of the Jewish state. No other people faces this sort of conditional acceptance. Another aspect of this issue concerns whether anti-Israeli prejudice extends to non-Jewish Israelis or whether it applies exclusively to Israeli Jews. If the prejudice does not apply, say, to Muslim Israelis, then the Jewishness of the targets would appear to be centrally important.

A few previously cited scientific studies have assessed the degree of statistical association between anti-Jewish and anti-Israel attitudes in various populations, although not in Muslim-majority countries.[7] These correlational studies cannot permit us to determine which came first, hostility toward Israel or hostility toward Jews, or, for that matter, which was cause and which effect. Indeed, to the extent that both attitudes may be associated with additional beliefs, including hostility toward the United States, attitudes toward sharia law, and attitudes toward Palestinians, a third belief may be the cause of both antisemitism and anti-Israel sentiment. Even though they are limited, the empirical studies do strongly suggest a fairly substantial correlation between the two types of beliefs in the populations studied. This means that, in many cases, the same people are both anti-Israel and anti-Jewish, although there are certainly a fair number of exceptions to the rule. The studies are, from a scientific standpoint, more preliminary and suggestive than confirmatory. It is reasonable to conclude, however, that a person may like Jews and hate Israel, or hate Jews and like Israel, but that such cases are not especially common.

"All Criticism of Israeli Policies Is Not Antisemitic"

When American currency speculator George Soros was a boy, his father reportedly changed the family name from Schwartz in an effort to avoid growing prewar Jew-hatred in his native country of Hungary. Currently, Soros styles himself an atheist, but his many political interests include the politics of the Arab-Israeli conflict and antisemitism. He once expressed some possibly justified concern that his own role as a powerful financial player had reinforced antisemitic stereotypes across the globe. Indeed, in the 1990s Soros's manipulation of the Malaysian currency market may have fed the rise of anti-Jewish sentiment in that country. Nowadays, Soros blames "the pro-Israel lobby's success in suppressing divergent views" for negative attitudes toward the Jewish community.[8] The lobby, in his view, lends credence to the false belief that there is an all-powerful Zionist conspiracy.

Many critics charge that the lobby and other Jewish groups purportedly control debate about the Arab-Israeli conflict through misuse of the antisemitism label and other tactics. For example, Canadian university professors Judy Rebick and Alan Sears speak of "the deployment of anti-semitism as an accusation to silence criticism of Israel." Peter Beaumont, the foreign affairs editor of London's *Observer*, accuses proponents of the "new antisemitism" of devastating simplicity in their position: "Criticise Israel, and you are an anti-Semite just as surely as if you were throwing paint at a synagogue in Paris." It is easy to find dozens more examples of such charges.[9] The core contention is always that "all criticism of Israeli policies is not antisemitic."

The best response to this contention comes from British scholar David Hirsh who said, "No, of course not, but who says that it is? There are very few Jewish communal spokespeople or Israeli politicians who are prepared to make such an evidently false claim. The contention that criticism of Israel is necessarily anti-Semitic nearly always functions as a straw-man argument."[10] Even among the most outspoken critics of anti-Zionism, none simplistically equate criticism of Israeli policies with antisemitism.

Consider, for example, Phyllis Chesler, who is as aware of Muslim antisemitism as anyone around and who clearly distances herself from numerous Israeli policies in her book *The New Anti-Semitism*. She is tough on Israeli treatment of Arab citizens, the theocratic aspects of the Israeli state, and what she considers a sacralized misogyny caused by the disproportionate influence of Orthodox Jews.[11] Denis MacShane, another prominent opponent of antisemitism and anti-Zionism, starts his treatise by explaining that the politics of "Israel, right or wrong" has never made any sense to him.

Those parts of the American Jewish community that strongly support the existence of the state of Israel, despite accusations to the contrary, have never marched in lockstep. Intellectual and political diversity is a hallmark of Jewish politics, including its pro-Israel wing. The notion that Jews stand together to control debate, suppress criticism of Israeli policies, enforce uniformity of perspective, and denounce as antisemites all who disagree at best is an attack on a straw man and at worst bears some resemblance to the canard of Jews as a supremely powerful controlling entity.

Certainly, with Middle Eastern studies departments in universities overwhelmingly sympathetic to the Arab position, the suppression has not been working very well. It is hard to find a newspaper in the United States, including in the Jewish community, that has not devoted a tremendous amount of ink to criticizing Israeli policies.

So it is hard to grasp just what Soros means when speaks of the "success" of the Jewish lobby in suppressing debate. Surely, if such an effort exists, it has been spectacularly unsuccessful. Harvard Professor Alan Dershowitz has challenged those who claim that "mere criticism" of Israel is often denounced as antisemitism to document the charge. He wants actual quotations, in context, with sources identified. He explained, "I am not talking about the occasional kook who writes an anonymous postcard or email. I am talking about mainstream supporters of Israel." To date, no one has taken up his challenge, and he has concluded that the charge that Jews misuse antisemitism to suppress criticism of Israel is a big lie, "a fabrication of Israel's enemies who seek to play the victim card."[12]

It makes sense to reframe the issue. Should criticism of Israel ever lose legitimacy because it contains antisemitism? What, for example, is one to make of "criticisms" of Israel that justify or explain away suicide bombings directed against civilians in Israel? And consider the following:

◆ Desmond Tutu told the Cape Town Opera not to perform in Israel because it is unconscionable to bring *Porgy and Bess*'s message of nondiscrimination to that country.[13]

◆ Political cartoons have criticized Israel by portraying its leaders with inaccurate and stereotypically Jewish physical features or insinuating blood libel charges.

◆ The Jewish lobby—in contrast to all other lobbies—has been described in terms strongly reminiscent of *The Protocols of the Elders of Zion*.

◆ Current Israeli "misdeeds" have been linked to the way Jews supposedly behaved toward Muhammad and seventh-century Muslims.

◆ Israeli academics—in contrast to academics from all other countries—have been denied academic privileges on European campuses because of the way Israel has allegedly behaved.

◆ Israelis have been accused—without a shred of evidence—of perpetrating the 9/11 attacks and of illegally harvesting organs for sale.

◆ Israelis have been denounced as Nazis.

Surely, few reasonable people would hold these examples to be merely vigorous criticism of Israeli policy, unless the policy opposed is Israel's policy of existing. Some criticism of Israel is legitimate, some is illegitimate but not antisemitic, and some is illegitimate and antisemitic. But it is not so simple to assign particular speech and action to the appropriate category.

"The 'New Antisemitism' Is a Myth"

This book is primarily about "old-style" antisemitism and not about intense criticism of Israel that may or may not have underlying anti-Jewish motivation. Thus, for my argument, there is no need for new definitions or for expansion of old ones. What I have been talking about is straightforward bigotry. The portrait of the Jew that too often appears in the contemporary Middle East includes heinous character traits, unappealing physical features, malignant motives, insinuations of inappropriate power, calls for discrimination, and even exterminationist sentiment—all of which have turned up notoriously in other cultures and times. The religious sources of anti-Jewish bigotry in Islam, of course, differ from those in the Christian tradition (although, even here, some parallels are evident).

I have tried to remove from my central argument as much as possible references to the new "antisemitism."[14] Defined in various ways, this phenomenon involves extreme criticism of Israel that some contend has crossed the line into prejudice. As one human rights lawyer put it,

> one form of antisemitism denies Jews access to goods and services because they are Jewish. Another form of antisemitism denies the right of the Jewish people to exist as a people because they are Jewish. Anti-Zionists distinguish between the two, claiming that the first is antisemitism, but the second is not. To the anti-Zionist, the Jew can exist as an individual as long as Jews do not exist as a people. To anyone grounded in human rights, that distinction has to be nonsense. The full realization of human rights requires respect for both individual and collective rights. Respect for the dignity and worth of the human person requires respect for every person's right to full membership in a people that freely pursues its own economic, social, and cultural development.[15]

All definitions of the new antisemitism rest on some variation of what has been called the 3-D test, a means of separating legitimate and illegitimate criticism of Israel proposed by Israeli politician and former Soviet refusenik Natan Sharansky.

Sharansky, who originally went by the first name of Anatoly, was a victim of Soviet-style anti-Zionism. In 1973 the Soviet Union turned down his request for an exit visa to Israel. Sharansky soon became one of the leading dissidents in the USSR; he monitored a broad range of Soviet human rights abuses and courageously spoke out against them. One of his regular activities in those days, he wrote, was monitoring antisemitism in the Soviet Union and smuggling out evidence about it. For his activities as a leading refusenik, Sharansky was charged with spying for the United States, and he languished for nine years in the Siberian Gulag, where he was subjected to torture. He would have spent more years there had Ronald Reagan not pressured Mikhail Gorbachev to release him in 1986.

Sharansky ultimately made it to Israel, and by 2004 he was a minister in the Israeli government, charged once again with monitoring Jew-hatred. He reports that during his years in the Soviet Union he had believed "that the free world, particularly after the Holocaust, would always be a staunch ally in the struggle against anti-Semitism." However, during his years in Israel, he came to believe that this assumption had been incorrect. In part, his disillusionment stemmed from a conviction that the new antisemitism—aimed at the Jewish state, rather than the Jewish people or the Jewish religion—was very real. He explained, "Since this anti-Semitism can hide behind the veneer of legitimate criticism of Israel, it is more difficult to expose. Making the task even harder is that this hatred is advanced in the name of values most of us would consider unimpeachable, such as human rights."[16]

Concerned about his inability to hammer home to foreign officials the seriousness of antisemitism, new and old, Sharansky developed his 3-D test. Criticism of Israel, whether he agreed with it or not, was legitimate unless it fell into any of three categories: demonization, double standards, or delegitimization. According to Sharansky,

◆ criticism falls into the category of demonization when "the Jewish state is being demonized; when Israel's actions are blown out of all sensible proportion; when comparisons are made between Israelis and Nazis and between Palestinian refugee camps and Auschwitz;"

◆ it can be categorized as a double standard "when Israel is singled out by the United Nations for human rights abuses while the behavior of known and major abusers, such as China, Iran, Cuba, and Syria, is ignored; when Israel's Magen David Adom, alone among the world's ambulance services, is denied admission to the International Red Cross;" and

◆ it can be considered delegitimization "when Israel's fundamental right to exist is denied—alone among all peoples in the world."

Thus, portraying Israel as the embodiment of evil, turning it into a pariah state, and judging it by different criteria than those used for other states under similar circumstances are all defining features of the new antisemitism.

Sharansky made no claim to originality for his test, and indeed its principles have been embodied to a greater or lesser extent in every conceptualization of the new antisemitism. Back in 1979 the French poet, political theorist, and World War II resistance fighter Jacques Givet suggested, "The anti-Zionist becomes an overt anti-Semite as soon as he goes beyond criticism of the policies of the Jerusa-lem government (a favourite activity of the Israelis themselves) and challenges the very existence of the State of Israel. For to refuse the Jews their right to nation-hood is to perpetuate their bondage. To 'de-Zionize' Israel would be like trying to 'de-Helvetize' Switzerland."[17] Critics often delegitimize Israel by emphasizing its reemergence during the colonial era. Givet, however, noted that many countries are "artificial" creations tied to the European colonial era—for example, many Af-rican states and Lebanon—yet nobody questions their legitimacy. To the contrary, Western powers usually speak of the importance of maintaining their "territorial integrity."

In 1997 Bard College president Leon Botstein argued:

> Zionism, even as a code word, is the litmus test with respect to anti-Semitism throughout the world, even in America. The facile rhetorical linkage of Zionism with imperialism and racism is little more than an admission that Jews are uniquely not entitled to be like everyone else and live as citizens as part of a majority in a nation, for better or for worse. Zionism, as mirrored in the State of Israel, has proven the point that Jews are in fact just human. Israel has displayed a full range of human achievement and weakness and of decency and its absence common to all nations. Comparatively speaking, one can make the case that Israel has behaved better, given its circumstances. The anti-Zionist, like the anti-Semite a century ago, does not allow the Jew the privilege of normalcy.[18]

Similarly, in 2004 former Swedish deputy prime minister Per Ahlmark sug-gested, "Anti-Zionists accept the right of other peoples to national feelings and a defensible state. . . . They are not judging Israel with the values used to judge other countries. Such discrimination against Jews is called antisemitism."[19]

To some extent, the tests for new antisemitism are reflected in the previously mentioned EUMC working definition of antisemitism, now used—at least some-times—by the U.S. Department of State and other important bodies. Specifically, the EUMC draft notes:

> Examples of the ways in which antisemitism manifests itself with regard to the State of Israel *taking into account the overall context could include* [my italics]:

Denying the Jewish people their right to self-determination, e.g., by claiming that the existence of a State of Israel is a racist endeavor.

Applying double standards by requiring of it a behavior not expected or demanded of any other democratic nation.

Drawing comparisons of contemporary Israeli policy to that of the Nazis.

However, criticism of Israel similar to that leveled against any other country cannot be regarded as antisemitic.[20]

Note the EUMC use of the word "could" in the definition. One must, according to the draft, judge the context in which deeds and statements occur in order to determine whether they qualify as antisemitic. Thus, the criteria may leave too much to the eye of the beholder.

Although Sharansky's 3-D test has won many supporters, it has drawn criticism as well—not least because it does not require antisemites to have anti-Jewish motives. Philosopher Bernard Harrison, who for the most part accepts new antisemitism theory, has written:

Serious anti-Semites [in the past], after all, have never been backward in openly avowing that *Jews*, and the harm they supposedly do, are hateful *in themselves*. Someone who claimed that Jews, *in themselves*, enjoyed his warmest sympathy, and that his objections were merely to the activities of certain organizations that happened to be run by Jews, would hardly have been welcomed with open arms, for example, in the German National Socialist Party in 1933, though he might, of course, have been treated as a useful pawn.[21]

So even though the new antisemitism may not, in the long run, be better than the old, something about it is very different—at least, in its public expression. Sharansky's 3-D test does not assess whether someone dislikes Jews or holds stereotypical views about them. And there is no requirement, at least for Sharansky, that demonization, delegitimization, or double standards stem from hatred of Jews as such.

Nonetheless, some analysts of the new antisemitism controversially suggest that latent traditional antisemitism, driven underground by the dictates of political correctness, does indeed provide motivation for the unjust treatment of Israel. In response, some point to reasons other than antisemitism for "singling out" Israel. For example, one critic suggested:

global interest in the Israel/Palestine conflict for religious, strategic, and journalistic reasons contributes to the ongoing focus; comparative ease of access for journalists and for human rights fieldworkers is another factor. Nor should we discount the considerable amount of criticism of Israel put forward by Jews, including Israeli Jews. These factors at least partly explain the amount of criticism directed against Israel, though this does not exclude the possibility that genuine hostility or hatred of Jews as Jews might be driving some of it.[22]

Still, it is not clear that the motive to hate must be definitively established in all or most cases of bigotry. It would seem unfair, for example, to subject the highly qualified applications of Asian engineering students to extra scrutiny in order to find reasons to reject them, even if one's motive were to open up opportunities for other groups.

To those who contend that delegitimization and calls for the destruction of Israel stem from antisemitic motivation, social scientist Josh Kaplan and others have responded that this would depend on the place that Jews are afforded in the new reality. There is much controversy about what those who propose to do away with Israel have in mind as a replacement. Supporters of Israel, for example, often see the end of Israel spelling death, exile, or subjugation for its current Jewish inhabitants. But some Palestinian supporters of a one-state solution contend that it would be far more hospitable for Jews. One may argue, Kaplan suggests, that such predictions of a benevolent non-Israeli state are incorrect, but a person who believes in such a future could not be justly deemed an antisemite. Similarly, the recently deceased Israeli writer and activist Ami Isseroff acknowledged the existence of Muslim antisemitism, but he too did not see extreme anti-Zionism as necessarily antisemitic. Isseroff wrote, "It is not 'anti-Semitism' for a Palestinian to say, 'I want to destroy Israel to get my land back.' This may be an odious view, but it is not racist. It is the position of someone who has been done an injury and seeks redress for himself first, whether justifiable or wise or not."[23]

Sharansky's demonization criterion has also come under some attack. Critics have suggested that it is wrong to rule out all Nazi allusions, especially because—despite the apparent lack of racist ideology and death camps—there may sometimes be appropriate parallels, especially with prewar Nazism and perhaps regarding contemporary Jewish extremists. These critics assert that some of Israel's deeds may in fact be demonic, and even if they are not, speakers and writers may be excused for engaging in hyperbolic speech to make their points. Yet, this criticism ignores the fact that every comparison of Israel and Nazis is a misrepresentation of Nazism, whether before or after 1933. Years before Hitler came to power, Goebbels, in his book "*The Nazi-Sozi*," was already speaking about Jews as fleas and issuing calls to put them "out of commission."[24] Where is the basis for any comparison between even this mind-set, let alone full-blown Nazism, and Israeli behavior? Clearly, the motivation for such comparisons lies somewhere other than in a desire for accurate analysis.

Moreover, it is hard to deny that the demonization of Israel contributes to an environment in which antisemitism can thrive, especially when the demonizers do not publicly and conscientiously take on the overt antisemites in their midst. Yet, as in the case of double standards, one might agree that the practice of invoking the Nazis and the devil—symbols rich with meaning from the history of anti-semitism—may be detestable. But is this practice antisemitic? One might, after all, make the case that Israel's enemies are deliberately choosing the most hurtful approach and, possibly, the one most likely to have impact on key audiences. Thus, again, the remarks might be inappropriate and ideologically driven without being antisemitic per se.

Some such as Irfan Khawaja, a philosophy professor who has spoken out boldly against Jew-hatred in the Islamic world, object to the treatment of anti-Zionism as ipso facto antisemitic. Khawaja asks his readers to "suppose the anti-Zionist case was false. To infer from its falsity to the moral corruption of its proponents is to assume that there is no honest way of being an anti-Zionist." Yet Khawaja speaks with obvious integrity: "The point is not that the charge of 'anti-Semitism' should never be made: some people deserve it. Nor must it always be made with trepidation: some people obviously deserve it. Nor must anti-Zionists be thought immune to the charge: too many of them are guilty." But Khawaja worries that to equate anti-Zionism with antisemitism would result in huge, seemingly inappropriate lists of antisemites who just don't seem antisemitic.[25]

Josh Kaplan claims to offer tactical advice to the new antisemitism theorists. He thinks that by expanding the definition of antisemitism to include Sharansky's new forms, Jewish leaders have fed cynicism about more traditional Jew-hatred and led human rights organizations to define real antisemitism as a nonproblem.[26] He objects especially when leaders like Abraham Foxman condemn antisemitism in the same breath that they defend Israeli actions. But, to follow Kaplan's implied advice, Jewish leaders would have to abandon their perceived political interests and their position on the Arab-Israeli conflict in order to gain traction on the antisemitism issue.

Another perspective comes from Earl Raab, a renowned student of Jewish affairs for more than a half century who is fully aware of the dangers of both anti-Israelism and antisemitism. He noted in 2002 that it is tempting to merge the two pathologies: "One prejudice is directed against the supposed negative character-istics of an entire ethnic/religious group; the other is directed against the presup-posed negative policies and proclivities of a nation-state, which, in this case, is largely peopled by that ethnic/religious group. One can easily be suspicious." For Raab, anti-Israelism can be identified by what he calls the "four horsemen" of all prejudice: prejudgment, stereotype, double standard, and scapegoat. Nonetheless, he counsels against merging the two types of prejudice and prefers to maintain separate categories for antisemitism and anti-Israelism because there is "a particu-lar set of ideological worldviews that create[s] prejudice against Israel as a nation-state and must be dealt with independently."[27]

All in all, it seems fair to conclude that (1) there is a tremendous amount of traditional antisemitism in the Muslim and Arab world, (2) there is tremendous amount of fairly obvious antisemitism that simply uses the word "Zionist" as a synonym for Jew, (3) there is much legitimate criticism of Israel, and (4) much criticism of Israel is extreme, unfair, and illegitimate—along the lines outlined by Sharansky. This final category of criticism assumes the characteristics of a preju-dice. However, whether or not it makes sense to expand the traditional meaning of antisemitism to include it is a complex matter about which reasonable people may disagree—although everyone should understand that this is more a matter of nomenclature than substance.

Political Spillover Arguments

Some minimizers attribute Muslim and Arab anti-Jewish hostility to the politics of international conflict and, thereby, seek to diminish its significance as prejudice. Two frequently encountered arguments include (1) "The real issue is not hostility toward Jews, but sometimes there is a little unavoidable spillover from the Arab-Israeli conflict," and (2) "How else would we expect people to react to all those Israeli transgressions against human rights and morality?"

"The Real Issue Is Not Hostility toward Jews, but Sometimes There Is a Little Unavoidable Spillover from the Arab-Israeli Conflict"

In March 2004 I argued in the *Chronicle of Higher Education* that students of prejudice needed to pay more attention to Arab and Islamic antisemitism.[28] A call for more research under other circumstances might have been taken as relatively noncontroversial. But this was not the case in the context of American academic thinking on the Middle East. All the published letters to the editor in response to the article expressed disapproval. For example, Stanley Morse, a professor of psychology and sociology at the Kuwait campus of the University of Maryland, contended, "anti-Semitism in the Middle East is the result of Zionist activities that culminated in the establishment of Israel. It has nothing to do with primordial, group-based hatred." He went on to write that my essay could "be seen only as an example of historical and cultural ignorance, if not also Jewish paranoia. It is a not-so-subtle attempt to dismiss—by pathologizing them—the entirely rational concerns of the vast majority of people in the Middle East." Morse even asserted that better educated people may show more rather than less antisemitism as a reflection of "their presumably better knowledge and understanding of existing realities."[29]

Three years later, Nadia Ramzy, a self-described Egyptian-Coptic-American psychoanalyst and coeditor of the *International Journal of Applied Psychoanalytic Studies*, saw Muslim hostility toward Jews as "horrifying and deeply disturbing" enough to devote an issue of her journal to the topic. She published an essay I wrote and commissioned several responses because the topic was deemed controversial. In her own commentary, Ramzy averred that the "prejudice is a political one—it is the prejudice that people feel toward their enemies in war—not a prejudice embedded in a racist ideology directed toward an entire ethnic group."[30]

Like Ramzy and Morse, other commentators have completely or partially explained away Muslim and Arab antisemitism with its presumed connection to the Middle East conflict. This argument is frequently buttressed by a contention that the Jews were treated well in the Muslim world until Israel arrived on the scene. As Ramzy put it, "To claim that '. . . the roots of contemporary Jew-hatred are deep and, as in the case of Christian antisemitism, part of the blame belongs to the religious tradition' is simply not correct when applied to Islamic culture."[31] In the next section, we will consider the historical validity of this contention.

But, first, we must acknowledge the immense impact that the rise of Zionism, the birth of Israel, and the Arab-Israeli conflict have obviously had on the growth of Muslim Jew-hatred. Every time the conflict flares up—regardless of the reason—fuel is tossed onto the bonfire of the antisemites. It is no simple matter to speculate about how Muslim-Jewish relations might have progressed had there never been a state of Israel or had the majority of Arabs followed the few in the early years of Zionism who welcomed the Jews back into the neighborhood. But those who see the politics of conflict as a contributing factor in the growth of anti-Jewish bigotry are certainly right.

The problem lies in the next step: concluding from this that such bigotry is *just* politics. To do so would require us to implicitly validate a great deal of past and present prejudice and discrimination around the world. Some would have us believe, especially with regard to Muslim antisemitism, that when history, politics, and economics have something to do with anger and hate, then it's not "classic" bigotry.

But what exactly is classic bigotry? Politics, economics, real and perceived competition for scarce resources (like land), real and perceived past grievances, manipulation by unsavory leaders—all of these have played a key role in many types of prejudice. For example

- traditional interethnic and interracial prejudice in the United States has been fed by competition in labor markets,
- black slavery in the South proved resistant to change partly because of perceived economic dependency on a system of involuntary servitude,
- Turks perpetrated the Armenian genocide in part because they perceived a threat to the state from Armenians,
- longstanding Hutu resentment of Tutsis had roots in the system of Tutsi overlordship that prevailed in Rwanda prior to the arrival of the European colonialists and that persisted under colonial rule,
- antisemitism in late-nineteenth-century France had something to do with the old guard fearing that its status had been diminishing in the post-Enlightenment era,
- fears of dropping real estate values contributed to white racism in the housing market, and
- high crime rates in the American black community feed stereotypes about blacks.

There probably is no such thing as pure, classic prejudice. Nearly all instances of prejudice have something to do with the political, economic, and psychological needs and desires of the perpetrators. And there has never been a requirement that victims of prejudice establish their absolute innocence.

"How Else Would We Expect People to React to All Those Israeli Transgressions?"

Israeli journalist Yossi Klein Halevi disapproves when Israel's supporters boast that the Israeli army is "the most moral in the world." In April 2009 he presented a paper to an audience at Yale University. Following the presentation, in answer to a question from the group, he asserted that the Israeli army was good but that "an army is an army" and Israel's army makes mistakes. Yet Halevi also sensibly insisted that Israel need not be the best in order to free it from the attacks of those who see it as the worst.[32] This point is important.

Along with Israel, the United States, Britain, and perhaps a few other nations are carefully watched and held to high standards of conduct. But most nations in the world do not appear to be judged at all in international forums. Freedom House, an organization that carefully collects data on a variety of human rights abuses, has rated China, Kazakhstan, Syria, Angola, Congo, Burma, Vietnam, Cambodia, Belarus, Saudi Arabia, Zimbabwe, Cuba, Pakistan, and many other countries "not free." Tanzania, Malaysia, Bangladesh, Thailand, Bolivia, Colombia, and many more have been rated "partially free." Israel is rated "free," as is the United States, Western Europe, Canada, Australia, and Japan.[33] Yet nearly all the relatively unscrutinized and unfree nations join enthusiastically in the chorus of condemnation of Israel.

To the extent that any nation is judged, it should in principle be by the totality of its record and against standards that are universally applied. Some have argued that life is by nature unfair, and the lack of perfect justice for Israel does not equal antisemitism. This may be true. Nonetheless, it would be hard to argue that the Jewish state has been treated equitably. Israel is routinely accused by anti-Zionist academics and activists—sometimes with the imprimatur of the United Nations or other international organizations—of just about every conceivable crime. Thus one hears accusations of genocide, colonialism, terrorism, war crimes, crimes against humanity, apartheid, ethnic cleansing, racism, organ sales, and disease invention. Sometimes these charges come from the same people who argue that Jews have greatly exaggerated their suffering during the Second World War. But more often they are made by critics whose credentials are not so obviously tarnished. Many evidence no signs of old-style antisemitism.

For any open-minded person, anyone not blinded by ideology, it ultimately becomes apparent that the worst charges against Israel are nearly always baseless. Those accusations with a kernel of substance generally show Israel to be behaving imperfectly but in line with expectations for a functioning democracy facing long-term existential conflict. Several human rights lawyers have assembled evidence that on nearly any human rights measure, Israel's record—while leaving significant room for improvement—is better than the record of both the nations with whom it has been struggling and many of those that criticize it regularly.[34]

Canadian attorney David Matas, senior legal counsel for B'nai Brith Canada and 2010 nominee for the Nobel Peace Prize for his investigation of organ-harvesting crimes against Falun Gong practitioners in China, has painstakingly reviewed the many charges hurled against Israel and found them to be deeply flawed. It is beyond the scope of this book to review his arguments, but some of Matas's general thoughts on the process of demonizing and delegitimizing Israel are worth mention. In 2005 he wrote, "Anti-Zionist propaganda has been so widespread and sustained that it has assumed a life of its own. Inattentive observers must think that with this much smoke there must be a whale of a fire." Some of the grist for the anti-Zionist mill comes from the healthy and frank internal Israeli debate about right and wrong, which helps correct errors and is largely absent from the Arab world. Mainly, Matas contended, "anti-Zionist condemnations of Israel work backwards. Anti-Zionists move from opposition to Israel to charges against Israel rather than from wrongdoings by Israel to anti-Zionism. Their starting point is the vocabulary of condemnation rather than the practices of Israel. Any unsavoury verbal weapon that comes to hand is used to club Israel and its supporters. The reality of what happens in Israel is ignored. . . . The more repugnant the accusation . . . the better." So, for example, Israel stands accused of genocide, although there is "no external reality on which this accusation hangs."[35] There is quite simply no case for genocide to be made here. The purpose of the accusation is to instill hatred, not to further objective analysis.

The charge that Israel is an outpost of Western colonialism also makes little sense. Most Israelis came not long ago from other Middle Eastern countries or are the descendants of those who came from such countries. Hebrew is a Middle Eastern language. Israeli culture, like other Middle Eastern cultures, blends the indigenous with the imported. The Jews have historic roots in the land dating back millennia, and despite expulsions some Jews have always lived there. Aside from imperial rulers and crusader kingdoms, the last independent state in the region before Israel was also Jewish. Notwithstanding the Balfour Declaration of 1917, which established ambiguous support for a Jewish homeland in the region, the British took many steps to fight against the formation of a Jewish state. So it is hard to see what exactly adds up to a colonialist venture.

Moreover, those who accuse Israel of being an apartheid state must either know little about South African apartheid, know little about Israeli treatment of Arab citizens, or be consciously obfuscating the truth about one, the other, or both. In South Africa, blacks constituted an overwhelming majority. In Israel, Arabs are not close to being a majority. Also, a state of war with some surrounding Arab nations has existed since Israel's founding. And there are other obvious problems with the analogy. Consider the following:

- Rana Raslan, a Muslim Arab, was selected as Miss Israel in 1999.
- Singer and songwriter Mira Awad, an Arab, represented Israel at the 2009 Eurovision Song Contest.
- Salim Joubran, a Christian Arab, serves on the Israeli Supreme Court.
- Many Arabs serve (and have served) in the Knesset; two Druze and one other Arab have served as deputy speaker in the Knesset.
- Walid Badir, an Arab, is an Israeli soccer star and captain of the Hapoel Tel Aviv team.
- Omar Barghouti, a fierce critic of Israel and a leading advocate of the cultural and academic boycott of the state, is currently studying for his graduate degree at Tel Aviv University.
- Polls repeatedly show that in the event that a Palestinian state is created, most Israeli Arabs would prefer to remain in Israel.[36]

None of this seems consistent with the notion that Israel practices apartheid or anything close.

As Matas noted, "Israel has not since its inception taken away vested Israeli citizenship of even one Palestinian for the sole reason that the person is ethnic Palestinian. Israel has not created designated territories within its borders to which it has forcibly removed its own citizens who are ethnic Palestinian."[37] The situation of the Arabs living in the territories acquired in the defensive 1967 war is not the same as the situation of Israel's Arab citizens. One might object to the treatment of Palestinians living in the territories or view such treatment as necessary in light of continued hostility and the failure of Palestinian leaders to take advantage of opportunities that might have led to an independent state. But the proper context for this discussion is treatment of civilians in territories acquired after a war. There is no parallel to South African apartheid.

Sociologist David Hirsh sharply criticizes Israel's policy in the West Bank, which he sees as unfairly favoring Jewish settlers over Palestinians. Yet, in 2008, writing in a South African newspaper, he too rejected the apartheid charge as groundless. Hirsh wrote:

The Israel-Palestine conflict is a small but nasty confrontation between two communities, not a fight between good and evil. Israel does not profit from Palestinians and its oppressive policies neither stem from self-interest nor bad faith; they are products of successive failures, including by Palestinian leaders, to make peace; it is fear, not evil or greed which fuels the violence. . . . The Apartheid analogy . . . tries to position Israel at the centre of all that is threatening by building a global movement for its destruction.[38]

In Lebanon, Gaza, and elsewhere, Israeli actions have resulted in a substantial number of unintentional civilian deaths. But in an Arab world in which Israel and Jews are routinely demonized, one could hardly expect populations to fairly consider the possibility that Arab leadership contributed to creating the circumstances under which these deaths occurred.

Despite their apparent vacuity, the most extreme charges hurled against Israel are making headway in the West as well as in the Middle East by repetition and the power of the big lie.[39] The constant drumbeat of accusations against Israel is being received unthinkingly in well-regarded places, even after charges are exposed as groundless. The international community has many Muslim states and one Jewish one, so on the basis of numbers alone, Israel loses all votes. Human rights organizations seem naturally to prefer losers over winners and to reject military force, regardless of its justification. And these are only a few of the reasons why the focus on Israeli transgressions in the world media has been out of proportion to the dimensions of these transgressions.

At a minimum, the Far Left's propensity for extreme opposition to Zionism and Israel creates fertile ground for antisemitism. Hirsh, speaking in the language of the academic Left, noted, "Antiracist anti-Zionism is creating commonsense discourses which construct antisemitism as thinkable and possible. There are some people who are prepared to experiment openly with antisemitic ways of expressing themselves and are nonetheless accepted as legitimate by some antiracist organizations and individuals."[40] The actual deeds of Israel (and the United States) may themselves fertilize Jew-hatred, but more often it is not the deeds themselves but rather the view people take of them that feeds the bigotry. Thus, Hirsh cited leftist scholar Moishe Postone, who argues, "It is a serious mistake to view [the] surge of antisemitism only as a response to the United States and Israel. This empiricistic reduction would be akin to explaining Nazi antisemitism simply as a reaction to the Treaty of Versailles. While American and Israeli policies have doubtlessly contributed to the rise of this new wave of antisemitism, the United States and Israel occupy subject positions in the ideology that go far beyond their actual empirical roles."[41]

Along similar lines, nobody questions that Palestinians—and for that matter, many other Arabs and Muslims—have suffered for decades. Moreover, people often respond to suffering, misfortune, and humiliation with anger and hate. Such social psychological processes are the subject of the next chapter, but for now it is important to note that a problem arises when political scientists, psychologists, and others use the frustration-aggression link to excuse bigotry.

Consider the point made by Joseph Montville, a former American diplomat to Muslim countries and the former director of the Center for the Study of Islam and Democracy. In his critique of my 2007 article on antisemitism in the Muslim and Arab world, Montville accused me of being "disrespectful." He argued, "Any identity group that has been beaten militarily and politically and has suffered traumatic loss of life and homes and the existential faith in the idea of justice is enraged. They have suffered unbearable blows to their sense of collective self-worth. And this sense of narcissistic wounding and justice denied becomes a key component of the group identity that is passed on from generation to generation."[42] There is at least a kernel of merit in this explanation.[43]

But what Montville suggests need not occur and does not have to persist for decades. Jewish Holocaust victims and their descendants don't hate Germans to-day—or, if they do, they keep their hostility to themselves. Many nations have lost wars, and their people have moved on to make the best lives they can for themselves and their children. It is not a requirement that resentment burn eternally. More importantly, Montville and others deem irrational processes of scapegoating irrelevant to Arab and Muslim anti-Jewish psychology. I disagree.

For many, Israel has become a central element in a collective obsessional delusion. With no shortage of injustices close to home in countries such as Pakistan, Indonesia, Sudan, Libya, and Saudi Arabia, one wonders how so many people find so much energy to devote to a far-away conflict. Even if Israel were conducting itself as unjustly as its detractors maintain, it remains to be explained why these particular infractions should loom so large in Muslim and Arab public consciousness.

Moreover, anger is not necessarily directed at the true sources of one's problems. The many misfortunes, injustices, and "narcissistic wounds" experienced by large numbers of people in the many parts of the Arab world have a plethora of causes. Most (but not all) of the time, blaming Israel has been little more than a form of irrational scapegoating rather than an accurate direction of anger toward the source of the troubles.

It is hard to imagine how a more accurate diagnosis of the reasons for Palestinian suffering might have emerged in the Middle East. Try to envision a Muslim journalist or professor who stood up to advance the argument that Israel had, for the most part, acted reasonably. In Israel not only have speakers advancing strongly dissenting perspectives on the Arab-Israeli conflict been tolerated, but more than few have also ended up in the Knesset, led departments at major universities, or headed human rights organizations dedicated to helping Israeli Arabs and Palestinians in the territories. Yet, in much of the Arab world, the person who publicly announces that "Israel hasn't been so bad" is likely to lose his or her platform quickly.

Finally, even if Israel were guilty of major transgressions, that would not seem to justify antisemitism.

Charges of Bad History

"Every honest Jew who knows the history of his people cannot but feel a deep sense of gratitude to Islam, which has protected the Jews for fifty generations, while the Christian world persecuted the Jews and tried many times 'by the sword' to get them to abandon their faith."[44] So concludes controversial left-wing Israeli writer Uri Avnery. On this point some more moderate Jewish writers would agree with him. Thus, critics not infrequently respond to those who express concern about contemporary Muslim antisemitism by alluding to a benign history of Muslim-Jewish relations. Such thinking in turn supports antisemitism minimization via two arguments: (1) "Muslims have always treated Jews well, so how can we say that what we are now witnessing is a serious instance of dangerous bigotry?" and (2) "It is historically inaccurate to say that Islam contains the seeds of contemporary antisemitism." There are also those who contend for historical reasons that Christians are the deeper enemies of the Jews.

"Muslims Have Always Treated Jews Well, so How Can We Say That What We Are Now Witnessing Is a Serious Instance of Dangerous Bigotry?" and "It Is Historically Inaccurate to Say That Islam Contains the Seeds of Antisemitic Belief"

The first answer to both of these arguments is, even if the roots of Muslim and Arab antisemitism were all recent, it would not negate, or even much reduce, the danger of the current manifestation of hatred. The second, more important answer is, the "rosy past" scenario greatly overstates Islam's historic open-mindedness about Jews.

At present, a heated debate is raging among the small cadre of informed experts on contemporary Muslim antisemitism. One side in this debate, which might be labeled the received wisdom, sees Jew-hatred as essentially alien to Islamic history and culture. Here, experts may acknowledge a variety of negative references to Jews in the Islamic religious literature and occasional antisemitic incidents through the years, but they portray Islamic political and social traditions as fundamentally tolerant, at least when judged by the standards of their day.[45] They call attention to religious verses that they interpret as respectful of Jews and supportive of peaceful coexistence. They see antisemitism mainly as a European import, brought to the Muslim world by manipulative European antisemites and fueled by the Arab-Israeli conflict. Historian Mark R. Cohen suggests, for example, "it is precisely because classical Islamic sources have so little that can be construed as anti-Semitic that the *Protocols of the Elders of Zion* are so popular in the Muslim world today."[46]

Historian Jeffrey Herf focuses on the importance of documents he has unearthed that detail conscious Nazi efforts to spread antisemitism through the Middle East as a means of mobilizing Muslims in the war effort.[47] Bernard Lewis also focuses on modern European colonialist contributions to Muslim antisemitism.[48] Some say the magnanimity of the essentially tolerant Islamic faith begin to crack in the twentieth century, when Zionism, European colonialism, globalization, or other modern movements disrupted the natural course of Islamic history. Present-day hostility toward Jews, these experts maintain, is consequently without deep indigenous roots.

On the other side of the debate, the challengers of the received wisdom acknowledge that Jews at times fared tolerably well under Muslim rule in some places; however, they emphasize that Islamic environments were, as a rule, difficult places for Jews. The challengers of the received wisdom include Norman Stillman, Martin Gilbert, Bat Ye'or, and Andrew Bostom, each of whom has his or her own specific take on the matter.[49] These scholars assign more weight to hostile statements and incidents concerning Jews in the Quran, hadiths, and other religious documents of Islam. Moreover, they reject as historically untrue the notion that Islam has been a fundamentally tolerant culture, calling attention to burdensome, discriminatory, and degrading rules Jews and Christians had to abide by in order to survive. The dhimmi—the protected Jew or Christian under Muslim rule—was often subject to special taxes, clothing requirements, rules about riding horses and bearing arms, and limitations on religious observance.

Writers in this tradition sometimes argue that the vision of a tolerant Islam is, despite a few prominent exceptions, mainly (or to some extent) an idyllic fairy tale created partly by poorly informed European Jewish historians (for example, Heinrich Graetz) who were dismayed by conditions in the West and seeking—for various political, ideological, and psychological reasons—greener grass on the other side. Scholars such as Stillman, Bostom, and Gilbert argue that a considerable body of anti-Jewish material, significant anti-Jewish discrimination, and substantial violence preceded the modern Israeli state and Zionism for centuries and sprouted from seeds planted at the very inception of Islam.

Indeed, against Uri Avnery's debt of gratitude, one might cite Leon Cohen's conclusion to his review of several recent books on Muslim-Jewish relations: "The state of Israel exists every bit as much in response to Muslim civilization's prejudices and crimes against the Jewish people and Judaism as because of anything that happened in Christian Europe."[50] This judgment may be overstated and incorrect to the extent that, historically, it was Jews fleeing from Europe who felt the urgency to launch the state. However, an honest review of Muslim history shows sufficient evidence of institutionalized and noninstitutionalized discrimination to establish at least some moral responsibility.

Those who see Islamic Jew-hatred as largely indigenous sometimes complain that present-day advocates of the opposing viewpoint are attempting to whitewash Islam in the interest of political correctness or other misguided and, perhaps, naive political motives. Those who argue against the Islamic roots of Jew-hatred sometimes accuse the other group of poor scholarship or anti-Islamic prejudice. I am not a historian of Jews under Islam, and a resolution of this disagreement lies beyond my competence. However, the whole debate might benefit from being toned down a bit. Islamic history, after all, covers a great many people, many years, and many places. The story is complex and doesn't fit either perspective perfectly. Polemics aside, there is considerable basis for agreement among reasonable people on both sides of the debate.

The best summary, I think, is that Jews, under Islam, were treated considerably better much of the time than Jews in Christian Europe—but also that such a conclusion is unfortunately not saying all that much.[51] Until recent times Christianity set a very low standard for treatment of Jews, varying from bad to worse to intolerable to genocidal. Islam, by contrast, created a political and religious world that despite some violent episodes, did sometimes provide a degree of tolerance for Christians and Jews. This tolerance was based on second-class citizenship and often—but not always—came at a high price.

As is the case in many religions that believe they possess the one true faith for everyone, Islamic theology—or, more accurately, parts of Islamic theology—show significant disdain toward those with a different perspective. Muhammad initially had high hopes for converting the Jews and considerable respect for their traditions. Like Martin Luther, however, his initial favorability turned into anger when Jews did not flock to convert. The implications of this anger and its permanent imprinting on sacred Muslim sources will be discussed later. For now I will cover two other parts of Muhammad's legacy: his rejection of forced conversion and his message that Jews and Christians, at least in theory, worshipped the same god and were to be, at some level, tolerated.

Not inconsistent with Muhammad's message, later Muslim leaders believed that Islam had been ordained to dominate the world, and 100 percent acceptance of this domination was generally the cost of survival for Jews. Within that limitation—a big one—Jews could sometimes carve out a decent lifestyle of sorts. For example, under Muslim rule in the eighth, ninth, tenth, and eleventh centuries, the great and ancient Jewish academies of Sura and Pumbedita in present-day Iraq were thriving, productive centers of learning, and many Jews, to the best of our knowledge, were able to make reasonable lives for themselves. Compared with conditions in the Christian world at the time, Jewish civilization was faring well. However, the flourishing religious culture surrounding the Pumbedita Academy ended when the Muslim caliph tortured the Jewish political and religious leader (i.e., the exilarch and gaon) Hezekiah ben David to death. As further evidence that even during this relatively good era all was not roses, the caliph had already imprisoned Hezekiah ben David's two predecessors and confiscated their property.

Under both Christianity and Islam, the Jews' fate usually depended on the needs and whims of particular leaders. But, much of the time, Islam lacked the obsessive preoccupation with the Jews that one generally observed in Christianity from the very beginning, or at least from several decades after the very beginning. After the seventh-century tribal struggles described in the Quran concluded with the victory of Islam and the expulsion of the Jews from Arabia, the Muslim obsession with the Jews died down for many centuries because Jews were no longer occupying the role prescribed for them by Islam and Muslims could no longer force them to do so.

Even taking all this into account, the distant religious and historic tradition is only one source of contemporary Jew-hatred in Muslim and Arab countries. Those who focus primarily on ancient religious traditions are omitting an important part of the story. One need not probe very deeply before the substantial overlap between antisemitism in the Christian and Muslim worlds becomes apparent, and part of this was attributable to the importation of the European antisemitic culture. Almost every major theme from Christian and secular European antisemitism makes an appearance in the contemporary Islamic world, none more prominently than the dangerous idea that rich, powerful, ubiquitous, immoral, lying Jews are conspiring to control the world.[52]

A few more conclusions about the debate concerning the historical origins of Muslim antisemitism are in order:

◆ It does not make one a bigot to argue that the Islamic religious and historical tradition bears some—even much—responsibility for contemporary anti-
Jewish prejudice in Muslim and Arab countries. Similarly, it does not make
one an apologist for antisemitism to argue that today's Jew-hatred is largely
an import from the West. However, the most sensible conclusion is that both
indigenous and borrowed (or implanted) sources are important.

◆ Those who argue that recent Jew-hatred comes from Europe should not necessarily conclude that contemporary Muslim antisemitism has shallow roots.
The depth and intensity of a belief are not immediately determined by what
happened in the past; they are instead a function of the extent to which the
belief is currently embedded in a society. This, in turn, has to do with modes
of indoctrination as well as the degree to which that belief currently meets the
social and psychological needs of its adherents. A belief that was brought to
the Islamic world fifty years ago can be every bit as powerful and difficult to
eradicate as one that has roots going back many centuries.

◆ The argument that Jew-hatred came to the Islamic world via Europe is not
really an argument that the hatred has "recent" roots. The process of import-
ing European antisemitism dates back at least to the nineteenth century, and
even Sayyid Qutb's highly influential and notorious work of religious and
political antisemitism, *Our Struggle with the Jews*, is now six decades old.[53]
Moreover, top Nazis had warm relationships with the influential and popular
grand mufti of Jerusalem in the 1940s; he was especially close with Heinrich
Himmler.[54] They shared a mind-set with regard to the Jews, which was recognized by Hitler when he made the grand mufti one of the first non-Germans
to be told about the Final Solution. Antisemitism was already so tolerated in
the Arab world that the relationship with the Fuehrer did not cost the grand
mufti (who might well have been tried as a war criminal) any points with his
constituency and may have helped him reassert his authority in the postwar
period. Moreover, the grand mufti had no trouble assembling Muslim troops
for the Handzar Division to fight on behalf of National Socialism. So, even if
one argues that the roots of Muslim antisemitism don't go back to the inception of the faith or many centuries, they surely go back many decades.

◆ If, as some historians contend, Islam did not make much use of its potentially
anti-Jewish religious source material until the twentieth century, this does

not mean that current uses of such material will not endure or have serious consequences.

◆ Whatever tolerance did exist in Muslim history was predicated on Jews accepting second-class status; there is no prominent model in Muslim history—distant or recent—for treating Jews as equals. (In fairness, traditional Jewish religious law does not provide a firm basis for political equality either. Such notions emerge mainly from modern political theory.)

The argument concerning the extent and depth of anti-Jewish discrimination under Islam is partly an argument over which sources to trust and partly a glass-half-full-or-half-empty problem. About the status of Jews under Islam in the distant past, there is, however, room for reasonable people to debate. About the prevalence of Jew-hatred in the contemporary Muslim world, there is no such room.

"The Real Propagators of Antisemitism Are Christians"

Some argue that extremist Christians are the deeper enemies of the Jews. Based on an overall quantitative assessment over two thousand years of history, I'd agree. Also, based on the centrality of pernicious anti-Jewish imagery in the traditional theology, I'd also agree. However, Christianity has taken many constructive steps during the past half century to limit and control its antisemitic potential. In 2011, for example, Pope Benedict XVI clearly reiterated the Catholic Church's complete exoneration of the Jewish people for the death of Jesus on the cross.[55] His position built on the 1965 Vatican Council II statement *Nostra Aetate*. Such declarations—along with similar ones from other Christian denominations—have in effect removed much of the theological basis that sustained mainstream Christian religious antisemitism over the years. Thus, as Christopher Hitchens noted in reference to the Muslim nations of the Middle East, "in point of fact, there is only one area of the world where pure, old-fashioned undiluted Jew-hatred is preached from the pulpit, broadcast on the official airwaves, given high-level state sanction and taught in the schools."[56]

A related objection is that Jews, Christians, and Muslims should get together and fight the right-wingers and neo-Nazis who are the real enemies of both the Jews and the Muslims. It is true that no one knows where the next wave of anti-semitism might originate. And there has long been a disturbing amount of hatred coming from the extreme Right and neo-Nazis. In the United States, some evidence from opinion polls suggests that a subset of the American population, fairly small in size, holds both Jews and Muslims in low regard.[57] So one need not be dismissive about right-wing Christian extremism, and certainly the dangers of one type of extremism should not be used as grounds to deflect interest in the other. But in my view, though circumstances can always change rapidly, Islamic Jew-hatred is the more pressing current concern.

Disagreements about Commonality and Intensity

When confronted by apparent examples of traditional Jew-hatred in the Muslim and Arab worlds, many respond by acknowledging that specific instances of bigotry do exist. However, they object that those who call attention to Islamic and Arab antisemitism are painting with too broad a brush. On the basis of a few bad eggs, they say, we are announcing to the world that the entire basket is rotten.

"THOSE WHO CALL ATTENTION TO ISLAMIC AND ARAB ANTISEMITISM ARE PAINTING WITH TOO BROAD A BRUSH"

Some people may think charges of antisemitism in the Muslim world imply that all or nearly all Muslims are antisemitic or that Muslims are necessarily antisemitic. Such a conclusion would be unjust, unwarranted, and insulting to millions of Muslims who do not harbor any such hatred. Moreover, it would reflect ignorance insofar as some Muslim theologians have found in Muhammad's message the basis for positive relations with Jews.

It is, therefore, logically, morally, and strategically important to establish in some detail an accurate topography of antisemitism in the Muslim world. Where is antisemitism more prevalent and why? Where has it not taken hold? Those who object to talk about the Islamic world as monolithic are certainly right. Hostility toward Jews is strong in some Islamic countries and among some Islamic populations, probably—for example, in Egypt, Syria, Iran, Jordan, and Saudi Arabia. It is likely weaker and less central to the mind-set of many Muslims living, for example, in Southeast Asia and India and, possibly, weakest in the United States. Still, high levels have been reported in Pakistan, Bangladesh, and Malaysia and among Muslims living in some parts of the West. It is important to learn how anti-Jewish attitudes break down by class, religiosity, age, distance from Israel, access to Western-language media, and other dimensions. A key question concerns the prevalence of anti-Jewish attitudes among non-Muslim residents of Muslim-majority countries. This book does not provide adequate answers to questions such as these. Only carefully designed and well-funded studies could provide definitive data. And, while possible, these studies would—as previously noted—be difficult to execute for political and methodological reasons. Still, serious instances of virulent Jew-hatred can be observed in many parts of the Muslim and Arab world. And we do not have the luxury—especially for such a tremendously under-researched topic—to await well-developed, systematic, and comprehensive studies before speaking out against the hate.

Many have suggested that only a handful of Muslims endorse antisemitism. In a sense, of course, virtually every sociological generalization about a group is painting with too broad a brush. Generalizations rarely apply to everyone. For example, when people speak about the racist South in the United States during the late nineteenth and early twentieth centuries, they do an injustice to progressive-minded Southerners from that era. But the inability or unwillingness to speak of dysfunctional tendencies in social, political, ethnic, or national groups means the end of useful sociology. Although one cannot yet precisely quantify the diffusion of antisemitic hatred into various Muslim populations, enough evidence to say that the "handful" theorists are dead wrong is already available.

Let us review this evidence:

◆ Pew Global Attitudes Project surveys show extremely high percentages of Muslim populations expressing a negative view of Jews. In Lebanon, Jordan, and Egypt, 95 percent or more had negative views of Jews in 2009. In Pakistan, Turkey, and Indonesia, 70 percent or more expressed negative views. Among Nigerian Muslims, 60 percent had unfavorable views.[58] The expression of unfavorable views to a survey researcher does not prove that respondents are prejudiced; such responses may reflect both legitimate and illegitimate judgments as well as confusion about the meaning of the question. But clearly the data hint—if they do not prove—that overwhelming majorities of Muslims in some countries do not like Jews.

◆ By contrast, Hamas, an organization that cites *The Protocols of the Elders of Zion* in its charter, openly expresses antisemitism, and considers the destruction of Israel to be its raison d'être, receives favorable ratings from 60 percent of Muslims in Jordan, 39 percent in Indonesia, 49 percent in Nigeria, 49 percent in Lebanon, and 49 percent in Egypt.[59] If the people who provide these ratings are not antisemitic, they certainly do not regard Jew-hatred as a disqualifier in the political arena.

◆ Esposito and Mogahed's survey study doesn't mention Jew-hatred, but it establishes that Islamism, which has been shown to be associated with prejudiced attitudes toward Jews, is widespread.[60]

◆ Research suggests that anti-Israel attitudes are somewhat predictive of antisemitic ones, and no one questions that hostility toward Israel is widespread among Muslim and Arab populations.[61]

◆ Many influential political and religious leaders have voiced virulent, overt, even murderous antisemitic opinions in some Muslim countries without doing detectable damage to their careers.

◆ Survey studies in Europe have shown that antisemitic attitudes are associated with the Muslim religion and Middle Eastern origin.[62]

◆ World Islamic leaders—almost without exception—responded favorably to Malaysian prime minister Mahathir Mohamad's overtly antisemitic speech.[63] No Muslim or Arab heads of state felt the need to publicly and unambiguously distance themselves from his bigotry.

◆ Classic antisemitic tracts such as Hitler's *Mein Kampf* and *The Protocols of the Elders of Zion* have shown up on several bestseller lists in Muslim countries.

◆ Numerous progressive Muslims, ex-Muslims, and others with personal experience in various parts of the Muslim world have testified to the prevalence of anti-Jewish bigotry. Representing a broad array of backgrounds and outlooks, they include Bassam Tibi, Tarek Fatah, Khaleel Mohammed, Haras Rafiq, Morad El-Hattab El-Ibrahimi, Rachid Kaci, Irshad Manji, Ed Husain, Amir Taheri, Nonie Darwish, Ayaan Hirsi Ali, Irfan Khawaja, and Mark Gabriel.[64]

Indeed, if the "handful" designation applies to any subgroup of the Muslim population, it applies to those who speak out loudly and clearly in denunciation of antisemitism. Recognizing the reality of widespread hatred in a culture does not make one a hater. It might make one Islamophobic but only in the sense that that term implies fear. And fear of venomous hatred is not a form of bigotry.

Arguments from Civility

One lesson I learned while writing my last book, *Bad Faith: The Danger of Religious Extremism*, is that nobody is offended by the study of religious extremism—

provided one speaks in general terms. After all, no one considers himself or herself an extremist, and all are happy to acknowledge that other people fit the bill. As Congressman Peter King found out when he convened his hearings on Muslim extremism in the United States, public relations problems develop when one moves from the general to the specific and especially when one talks about the religion of other people using terms that are, to any degree and for any reason, unflattering. In part, this taboo, having emerged from the historical lesson that frankness in confessional matters can lead to endless destructive conflict, is constructive. Thus, many people—some well intentioned—counsel that nice people don't criticize other people's religious beliefs. But that advice hinders clearheaded analysis of antisemitism in the Muslim world.

"Nice People Don't Criticize Other People's Religious Beliefs"

The problem is that terrible things have been done throughout history under the banner of religion, and it is intellectually dishonest to say that religion has been causally irrelevant. Although many people like to assert that the source of evil behavior is never religion but rather the corrupters of religion, this semantic trick doesn't hold water. And to maintain that criticism of religion is out of bounds is to offer a screen behind which evil-doers may operate with impunity.[65]

The reluctance to listen to those who criticize religion, especially Islam, is part of a trend that extends beyond reactions to charges of Muslim antisemitism. According to philosopher Austin Dacey, who has spoken before the UN Human Rights Council in Geneva as a representative of the International Humanist and Ethical Union, "the Inquisition is back, and this time it has set up shop at the United Nations." The UN has passed a series of resolutions that, in Dacey's words, "decry a 'campaign of defamation of religions,' intensifying since 2001, in which 'the media' and 'extremist organizations' are 'perpetuating stereotypes about certain religions' (read Islam) and 'sacred persons' (read Muhammad)." Dacey argues that the attitude that underlies these resolutions "conflates peaceful criticism of Islam with anti-Muslim bigotry and seeks to stifle free speech in the name of 'respect for religions and beliefs.'" This approach is problematic because, as Dacey pointed out to the Human Rights Council, "every religion begins with a prophet or teacher who speaks the truth as his or her conscience dictates it, no matter who may disagree. The advance of religious truth hangs, in the end, on the right to doubt, to dissent, to discover. To combat the so-called defamation of religions is, then, in the end, to combat religion."[66]

When religious sources can plausibly be used to justify hatred or discrimination against a particular racial, ethnic, gender, or religious group, it is hard to see how one can be antibigotry without sometimes criticizing aspects of a religion. It is, of course, far better if criticisms come from within the faith, but if such voices are insufficiently loud, they must be supplemented by those from outside. And, certainly, it is not right to bar the victims of bigotry from speaking directly about the sources of their victimization.

Reinforcing the taboo against criticizing aspects of a religion is yet another taboo against denouncing anything associated with "diversity," especially diversity provided by non-Western groups who were once victims of Western colonialism. Perhaps especially since the publication in 1978 of Edward Said's *Orientalism*, Western scholars have felt that it was not their place to pass judgment on the ways of the East.[67] Sometimes this perspective is acknowledged proudly; other times one needs to read between the lines. A recent call for papers for an international conference on diversity explained, "The conference examines the concept of diversity as a positive aspect of a global world and globalized society. Diversity is in many ways reflective of our present world order, but there are ways of taking this further without necessarily engendering its alternatives: racism, conflict, discrimination and inequity. . . . The conference will seek to explore the full range of what diversity means and explore modes of diversity in real-life situations of living together in community."[68] Thus, the call for papers, on the one hand, says its wants studies on the "full range of what diversity means." Yet, on the other hand, it implies in several places that research should arrive at the conclusion that encouraging "diversity" will lead to positive outcomes and not to bigotry, discrimination, and inequity. Clearly, the conference organizers are reluctant to focus on negative aspects of diversity; for example, indigenous prejudice against out-groups. One would not expect much coverage of Muslim antisemitism, here, although certainly the topic has much to do intercultural differences and intergroup relations.

Even among people who seem to clearly perceive the problems of extremist Islam, there is sometimes a sense that it is more constructive to focus on the positive. For example, in 2008 Sumbul Ali-Karamali wrote a book, *The Muslim Next Door*, that sought to correct misimpressions about Islam.[69] Yet Ali-Karamali, who credibly asserts that she is not antisemitic and has many Jewish friends, is disturbed that people identify significant antisemitism in the Muslim world. In a 2009 essay, she cited a wide variety of Islamic rules and traditions that she perceives as sympathetic to the Jews, noting, for example a time in the seventh century when the prophet Muhammad urged believers to fast on the Jewish holiday of Yom Kippur "in solidarity with the Jews." She explained, "Antisemitism has no place in Islam, just as Islamophobia has no place in Judaism. For their time, these two religions sought to decrease violence and bigotry in the world. The weight of history, if we can but remember it, is on the side of pluralism. Islam accepts Judaism, as well as Christianity, as part of the Islamic tradition." Moreover, she argued, "because Islam is part of the Judeo-Christian tradition, the Qur'an grants Jews and Christians an exalted status."

Then she explained her perspective on Muslim-Jewish relations: "I'm not saying that any of our histories are perfect. My local bookstore prominently featured a book on how some Muslim preacher allied himself with the Nazis to spread antisemitism. Well, I find that disgusting. But where's the balance?"

Karamali then alluded to instances where Muslims, including the King of Morocco as well as some Albanians, helped Jews during the Holocaust. She further called attention to the home provided in the Muslim world to many Jews fleeing the Spanish persecutions of the fifteenth century. In Karamali's view, it makes more sense to downplay intergroup conflict and to accentuate "the countless cooperative, cross-religious acts of generosity instead, using those to drive forward our vision of the future."[70]

Karamali's 2009 essay highlights several barriers faced by those seeking to explain contemporary Islamic antisemitism to well-intentioned liberals and Islamic moderates. The first is that those seeking constructive encounters often prefer not to focus on conflict, especially when such conflict has its roots in religion or tribal identity. There is a strong tendency to assume benign relations even when none exist. Second, without questioning the admirable exceptions she cites, Karamali invokes a rosy image of the past that, quite simply, is not supported by the facts. Third, she tells a one-sided story about the treatment of Jews in Islamic sacred writings, yet to correct this misimpression requires one to venture into politically incorrect waters. Fourth, Karamali speaks about "a preacher" who sided with the Nazis; she is apparently referring to the grand mufti of Jerusalem, the official head of Palestinian Muslims during World War II and a prominent leader in the Arab Islamic world of his day. Fifth, she misleadingly implies that Islamophobia is just as prevalent in contemporary Judaism as antisemitism is in contemporary Islam. All of Karamali's misconceptions can be corrected, but one might ask in a world where so many Muslims hate Jews passionately, what is the point of engaging in this unpleasant discussion with someone whose heart seems to be in the right place? The answer is that although Karamali seems to be trying hard to bring about the right kind of world, she can't succeed by simply assuming it is already here. Nor, as a general principle, will focusing on the positives do much to eliminate the negatives in the world. Not by accident, recognizing a problem is widely acknowledged as the first step to solving it.

Charges of Islamophobia

Some argue that the far greater problem in the world today is bigotry directed against Muslims and that this somehow cancels out or minimizes the importance of Muslim Jew-hatred. They suggest that what we should be talking about is Islamophobia.

"What We Should Be Talking about Is Islamophobia"

Why should attending to one prejudice lessen the importance of attending to another? We should, indeed, be talking about Islamophobia. Although the purpose of this book is to address the neglect of Muslim and Arab antisemitism, prejudice against Muslims and Arabs is also a real problem that deserves serious attention. The two bigotries do not cancel each other out; both merit concern. Beyond moral considerations, prejudice against Muslims and Arabs constitutes a problem for those who believe—as I do—that the long-term struggle against religious extremist violence turns largely on retaining the loyalty and cooperation of moderate Muslims in Western nations.

Western attitudes toward Muslims have been heavily studied. A body of poll data that has grown significantly since 9/11 suggests that many in Western nations have unfavorable impressions of Islam and Muslims; a subset of these people show significant signs of intolerance and prejudice. Following are a few examples of data from polls conducted in the United States:

◆   In a January 2010 study, Gallup interviewers asked a sample of Americans, "Thinking honestly about your feelings, how much prejudice, if any, do you feel towards each of the following groups?" They then presented a list. Nine percent of Americans said they felt "a great deal of prejudice toward Muslims," and 43 percent said they felt at least "a little" prejudice toward them. To compare, only 18 percent said they felt at least a little prejudice toward Christians, 15 percent toward Jews, and 14 percent toward Buddhists. Very few said they felt a great deal of prejudice toward these groups.[71]

◆ An August 2009 Pew Forum poll showed 58 percent of Americans judging that "there is a lot of discrimination" against Muslims; 64 percent judged similarly for gays and lesbians, 52 percent for Hispanics, 49 percent for blacks, 37 percent for women, 35 percent for Jews, 27 percent for evangelical Christians, 26 percent for atheists, and 24 percent for Mormons.[72]

◆ An April 2009 ABC News/*Washington Post* poll showed 48 percent of the American respondents saying they had "favorable" views of Islam and 41 percent saying their views were "unfavorable." Though there had been short-term fluctuations in results, these numbers were about the same as they were in October 2001.[73] For comparison, 42 percent of Americans have favorable views of the Mormon religion, and 46 percent have an unfavorable view. Scientology is also viewed less favorably than Islam. But Judaism, Protestant Christianity, Catholicism, and Buddhism are viewed much more favorably.[74]

◆ Some measures deal more directly with traditional markers of prejudice. In July 2006, 22 percent of Americans said they would not want Muslims as neighbors. The percentages for others groups were 92 percent for drug addicts, 72 percent for heavy drinkers, 27 percent for homosexuals, 14 percent for Hindus, and 4 percent for Jews.[75]

Americans appear split in their response to pollsters; some see Islam and Muslims positively, some negatively, and some do not have clear feelings either way. Some of the negative views derive from bigotry.

But American attitudes toward Islam are complex. There is reason to believe that a substantial component of the negativity derives from fear—whether justifiable or not—and thus the term "Islamophobia" makes sense. Differences in perceptions of reality are also important. Consider the following findings:

◆ Perspectives on Islam—positive and negative—appear to be based on low levels of knowledge about the faith. By their own admission, 63 percent of Americans say they have very little or no knowledge about the religion. Greater knowledge does not appear to be associated consistently with more or less favorable impressions of Islam.[76]

◆ When pollsters ask non-Muslim Americans how much various religions resemble their own, only 16 percent see Islam as "very similar" or "somewhat similar." Thus, nonadherents typically rate Islam less similar to their own religion than Catholicism and Protestantism (both 43 percent) and Judaism (35 percent), about the same as Buddhism (15 percent), and slightly more similar than Hinduism (12 percent).[77]

◆ Twenty-three percent of Americans do not think that American Muslims cooperate in the war on terrorism.[78]

◆ About six months after 9/11, about one quarter of Americans thought Islam was more likely than other faiths to encourage violence. Over the next year, that group grew larger, and by July 2003, 44 percent of Americans thought so. Since then, the percentages have remained near the 40 percent mark. Those Americans who describe themselves as Democrats and liberals are considerably less likely to associate Islam with encouraging violence.[79]

◆ Thirty-five percent of Americans judged Muslims as "respectful of women," but 52 percent said they were not.[80]

◆ Twenty-six percent of Americans agreed that Muslims teach their children to hate.[81]

◆ A 2006 poll showed that 44 percent of Americans agree that Muslims are "too extreme in their religious beliefs."[82]

◆ While 37 percent of respondents in a March 2006 poll had "somewhat unfavorable" or "very unfavorable" opinions of Muslim countries, 82 percent of these respondents thought that Muslim countries had "somewhat unfavorable" or "very unfavorable" views of the United States.[83]

◆ In April 2009, 81 percent of Americans thought it important for President Obama to try to improve relations with Muslim countries.[84]

The evidence from these public opinion polls is tricky to interpret. When pollsters ask people—many of whom are not even able to identify the Quran or Allah—brief structured questions, they may not get a clear image of what the people are thinking. Indeed, the poll respondents themselves may not have a clear image of what they are thinking. For example, when respondents agree with the statement "Muslims teach their children to hate," they may interpret "Muslims" to mean some Muslims, many Muslims, most Muslims, or all Muslims. They may also wonder, Teach their children to hate what? When some Americans disagree with the statement "American Muslims cooperate in the war on terrorism," they may think they are being asked whether there should be more cooperation, or they may think the question could be rephrased as "Is there any cooperation?" The question is extremely vague. With whom should Muslim-Americans cooperate, and how? Also, who knows what pollsters are measuring when they ask people to think honestly and then say whether they themselves are prejudiced against a group? Possibly the more prejudiced people may not admit it. If people confess to prejudice in today's politically correct environment, they may be defining it as a measure of how favorably they feel about a set of religious practices rather than as a measure of whether they engage in thought processes and behaviors typically defined as bigotry. Otherwise, they might well try to conceal their hatred.

Additionally, many of the questions gauge perceptions of reality. And, to assess responses, poll interpreters need a consensual understanding of the nature of that reality. Thus, in theory, all religious faiths might be equally capable of inspiring religiously based violence, or maybe there are differences among the faiths. Without having knowledge, or at least consensus, about the nexus between Islamic doctrine (or some readings of Islamic doctrine) and violent acts, it does not seem fair to classify a person as a bigot on the basis of an instantaneous survey response. Similarly, it does not seem right to classify someone as a bigot if his or her notion of appropriate gender relations leads to a conclusion that Islam does not respect women. Others may disagree, and they may have the stronger argument, but the contrary opinion should not count as prima facie evidence of prejudice. Thus, Gallup's January 2010 headline, "In U.S., Religious Prejudice Stronger against Muslims," may not be wrong, but it certainly goes beyond the data.[85]

In my view, a substantial portion of what the pollsters observe is bigotry against Muslims. America, at present, is not sufficiently true to its creed in its treatment of Muslim-Americans, and fear is not a good excuse for this prejudice. While there is still residual bigotry in the United States toward many groups, I suspect the bias against Muslims is greater than that directed against any group except perhaps homosexuals, atheists, and maybe Mormons. Jews, blacks, and Hispanics are all less likely to be subjected to discrimination. What's more, anti-Muslim prejudice in the United States targets one of the most moderate and pro-democratic Muslim communities in the world.

There are, however, several key differences between the anti-Muslim prejudice in the United States and the antisemitism that pervades the Muslim and Arab world. Political leaders in the West, after all, end their careers by openly catering to haters; in the Middle East, hatred has been a foundation for building many careers. The sort of widespread, venomous hatred that has been directed against and approved by high-level political and religious leaders is nowhere evident against Muslims in the United States at present, nor does it seem likely to emerge in the foreseeable future. Leaders in Muslim countries denounce the Jews with impunity; there is never a local backlash. U.S. political figures cannot attack the Muslims without repercussions. No one publicly uses murderous language here, and were one to do so, he or she would likely be denounced even by those who express negative views of Islam. And few in the antiracist community in the United States or elsewhere doubt that anti-Muslim prejudice exists.

Consider the Juan Williams case. Williams had blue-chip credentials as a journalist and writer on civil rights matters. But in 2010 he announced on television, "You know the kind of books I've written about the civil rights movement in this country. But when I get on the plane, I got to tell you, if I see people who are in Muslim garb and I think, you know, they're identifying themselves first and foremost as Muslims, I get worried. I get nervous."[86] He said this in the context of comments that such feelings should not be used as a basis to deny anyone their rights and that Muslims in general should not be blamed for the acts of terrorists. In short, he was expressing his fears but counseling that such fears be controlled. A July 2006 national survey showed that 31 percent of Americans felt more nervous when a Muslim was taking the same flight.[87] Yet, for expressing fears that nearly a third of Americans acknowledge, Williams was summarily dismissed from his job as a commentator on National Public Radio. Whether one considers the firing just or not, it certainly attests to the strong wall of propriety and fairness that protects Muslim Americans against potential ill will and prejudice.

Most Jews fled (or were chased out of) the Arab world in the middle of the last century; Muslims and Arabs flee to the West despite anti-Muslim prejudice. While the situation for Jews who remain in some Arab and Muslim countries is nightmarish, Muslim Americans report good lives in the United States despite the prejudice—although their reported contentment may be diminished somewhat by prejudice.[88] In one of the most tolerant societies in the history of the world, there certainly remain all sorts of prejudices against gays, blacks, Hispanics, Asians, women, Jews, immigrants, and others. To some extent, stereotypical and ethnocentric thinking may well be part of human nature. Yet, among the various groups subjected to such thinking, Muslims emerge as one that elicits the most negative feelings and cognitions from Americans. Whether this is the result of bigotry, fear, differing judgments about the nature of Islam and world affairs, or some combination of all these, the Muslim in the United States—whatever his or her religious sensibilities—faces a tough situation. Fortunately, America provides the most advanced system of protections ever developed to counter prejudices and unsupportive public feeling and to ensure fair treatment in the public arena.

Nonetheless, non-Muslim Americans must work to create a more hospitable home for Muslim Americans. As to which is worse in Western countries, antisemitism or anti-Muslim feeling, Jewish historian Deborah Lipstadt offers the reasonable opinion, "This is too broad a question to answer easily. It depends where— what country—and what situation. I think there is more overt anti-Muslim feeling in the U.S. today and a far greater fear of Muslims than Jews. I think the situation in France or the United Kingdom is quite different."[89] But, no matter how you slice it, there is too much bigotry against Muslims in the West.

"Aren't Jews Just as Bigoted against Muslims?"

Imagine a Jew in the midst of long centuries of massive Christian antisemitism. The popes are bigots. The priests are bigots. The neighbors are bigots. Would the Jewish person who complains that there is a great deal of Christian antisemitism in the world become a bigot on the basis of the complaint?

The "aren't Jews just as bigoted" question is really several questions. Do Jews hold unfavorable views of Muslims? Do Jews hold more negative views of Muslims than do others in the West? Does the Jewish religion provide a foundation for anti-Muslim bigotry, and if so, does this tradition constitute part of contemporary Jewish attitudes toward Muslims? Do Jews hold bigoted or otherwise unfair prejudicial views concerning Muslims, and do they act on these views? In other words, are many Jews anti-Muslim bigots in the same sense that many Muslims are anti-Jewish?

To answer this last question first, of course some Jews are—but hardly any of these racists have political, social, or religious clout. And there is little reason to believe that Jews are any more prejudiced than members of any other Western group against Muslims and possibly some reason to suspect that Jews (or Jewish Americans) might be less prejudiced. Consider the following evidence:

◆ Research establishes that Jews in Western nations—historically and now—frequently show lower levels of prejudice than other white ethnic groups against blacks and others.[90]

◆ In opinion polls, Jews seem more tolerant generally (on racial and other matters) than other, mainly Christian, religious groups—although there is some variance in level of tolerance among the denominations. Atheists have been shown to be the most tolerant group of all, and that group includes many ethnic Jews.[91]

◆ When looking closely at the groups with the most unfavorable attitudes toward Muslims, one finds groups in which Jews are typically underrepresented.[92]

◆ One American study of self-declared bigotry against Arabs concluded that the best predictor of such bigotry was hostility toward Jews. Although there is relatively little antisemitism in the United States, those few antisemites apparently are quite likely to dislike Muslims also.[93]

◆ Muslim Americans and Jews were the most enthusiastic supporters (by religious affiliation) of President Obama, followed by those with no religious affiliation.[94]

However, Jews are often targeted by Muslim extremists and to a lesser extent by others in Muslim and Arab countries. So, insofar as fear seems to be a component in negative ratings of Islam, one might expect Jews to form less favorable impressions of the religion.

To explore this issue scientifically, one would need a sophisticated multidimensional approach. Yet one simple study of New York City voters did find Jews somewhat more likely than other voters to disagree that Islam is a peaceful religion; Jews were also less likely than other New Yorkers to express a favorable opinion of the Muslim religion. These questions do not deal directly with prejudice, and the liberal New York City voting public is hardly typical of America. But the poll does reveal some greater negativity toward Islam in at least one sample of Jews.[95]

Although most American Jews feel connected to Israel—far more so than the nonevangelical American public—they hardly seem extreme in their views on the

Arab-Israeli conflict. According to a 2009 survey, 49 percent of American Jews favor the establishment of a Palestinian state, whereas 41 percent oppose it.[96] Sixty percent think Israel should be willing to dismantle all or some Jewish settlements in the West Bank as part of a permanent settlement. They hold these views even though 75 percent believe that the goal of the Arabs is the destruction of Israel and 99 percent believe that antisemitism around the world is either a very serious or somewhat serious problem.

Another question concerns whether elements in the Jewish religious and historical tradition might have a negative impact on contemporary Jewish attitudes toward Muslims and Islam. Looking back into the distant past, one will find many debates about the validity of Islam and Christianity, as well as many rules for how Jews should interact with the larger surrounding religions that generally possessed tremendous power over them. This is not the place to review this history. But most of the debates about the nature of Islam concerned whether the religion was merely untrue or was idolatry. The great Jewish scholar Maimonides concluded that Islam was not idolatry, and this view has generally prevailed. There were also debates about whether it was better to become a martyr or convert to Islam.[97] Beyond this, many scholars attempted to craft rules for dealing with Muslims; these rules reflected survival demands, theology, and tribal affinities. In the various deliberations, the Jewish scholars at times showed their lack of knowledge about the specifics of beliefs and practices associated with Islam. As a result of the power imbalance, however, Jews never had any power to harm Muslims with their religious decisions. And, in any case, the Jewish religious tradition—with its enlightened and unenlightened components—does not constitute a meaningful source of the contemporary attitudes of Jews toward Muslims.

Evidence may yet emerge showing Jews to be more prejudiced against Muslims than other Westerners, or it may turn out that Jews, with their prevailing tradition of tolerance, turn out be less anti-Muslim than Western populations as a whole. In any case, it is incumbent upon Jewish leaders to continue to fight the anti-Muslim bigotry that exists in their group, just as it is incumbent upon non-Jewish leaders to do the same. But opposing bigotry against Muslims does not require closing one's eyes to the murderous Jew-hatred that is being perpetrated by many Muslim religious leaders and large portions of their flocks in the name of the faith.

Arguments Based on Benign Neglect

Sometimes minimizers acknowledge the existence of antisemitism in the Muslim world and then explain why we should deliberately ignore it. Some say that ignoring or downplaying Jew-hatred in the Muslim and Arab world is, for one reason or another, the best way to combat it in the long run. More often, minimizers say that fighting antisemitism must take a backseat to higher goals, such as resolving the Arab-Israeli conflict, pursuing better relations with the billion-strong Muslim world, or pursuing the West's interests in the war on terrorism. The arguments for "benign" neglect can be complex.

No one is arguing that foreign policy must be one-dimensional or monomaniacal with regard to antisemitism. There are, indeed, times when prudence dictates that the issue not be raised. However, the quiet strategy can be too quiet, and neglect of such venomous and potentially dangerous intergroup hostility can be anything but benign. Simple truth sometimes beats out wily sophistication in the pursuit of reasonable policy. And truth, maligned as it is by policy sophisticates, can prevent a less valid moral calculus from taking root.

"FOCUSING ON ANTISEMITISM IS NOT IN THE INTEREST OF THE ARAB-ISRAELI PEACE PROCESS; PURSUING THAT PROCESS ARDENTLY IS THE BEST WAY TO REDUCE ARAB AND MUSLIM ANTISEMITISM"

The basic argument here is that if only we could solve the Arab-Israeli conflict, Arab antisemitism would begin to dissipate, and antisemitism in the non-Arab Muslim world would rapidly disappear. However, this approach underestimates the continuing impact of decades of massive antisemitic socialization in many parts of the Middle East and elsewhere in the Muslim world. Plus, the argument calls to mind the old story about landing on a desert island with only an economist for companionship and several crates of canned food for sustenance. "How," you ask the economist, "can we open the cans?" He replies, "First, assume a can opener."

How can the Arab-Israeli conflict be resolved when an irrational hostility to Jews who possess power and partial control over their destiny forms a key barrier to the resolution of that conflict? Shall we first assume a solution? Absent anti-Jewish irrationality and bigotry, the Arab-Israeli conflict would certainly have ended with the Israeli offer for a two-state solution in 2000, and probably much earlier.

"Focusing on Antisemitism Is Not a Good Idea If We Hope to Encourage Muslim Moderates; It Does Not Advance Plans to Reach Out to the Muslim World" and "Focusing on Antisemitism Is Not in the Interests of America's War on Terrorism"

The underlying assumption here is that in the strategic pursuit of America's goals, the less said about Jews and antisemitism, the better. America, after all, has many interests throughout the vast and diverse Muslim world, and these interests may not be advanced by keeping Israel and the Jews on the agenda. Precisely because delusional thinking about the Jews prevails, some argue that it would be best to make progress on other issues. Then, perhaps, there would be a cooperative foundation on which the matter of antisemitism might be addressed. If, for example, the Americans made progress with the Iranians, the Iraqis, the Libyans, the Egyptians, the Pakistanis, the Syrians, the Turks, or others, then America would be in a better position to discourage Jew-hatred. Similarly, if Europe could arrive at understandings with ever-so-slightly antisemitic—but otherwise moderate—Muslims at home and abroad, then such Muslims might be more willing and able to abandon their antisemitic ways.

In principle, this approach seems pragmatic, and in moderate doses it might sometimes work. But there remains the possibility that delusional thinking also exists in the West. Putting aside the oxymoronic nature of the "antisemitic moderate," Europe and America may be misleading themselves about the extent to which such "moderates" will become partners on antisemitism or other matters. The proposed benign neglect may be turn out to be destructive and even fraudulent. As noted in chapter one, Robert Wistrich has written, "Arab and Muslim antisemitism is the Trojan Horse designed to undermine the West's belief in its own values." So-called pragmatic Westerners who claim to be pursuing national interests may be sowing the seeds of future trouble. Wistrich suggested that "Islam is at present winning [its struggle with the West] because Europe is cooperating—because of its lust for oil, because of electoral considerations with the increased Muslim populations in their countries, because of past colonialist sins and because of the naive belief that the weak is always right. But the West must not sacrifice Israel on any altar of appeasement. Europe is liable to find itself once more entrapped in a complex of partners in destructive crime." Perhaps Wistrich worries too much—but perhaps not—when he claims, "The annihilation of Israel is the precursor to a successful Jihad, as was Hitler's war against the Jews, which is also viewed as the opening salvo in gaining world domination. The Nazis, like Stalin in the final years of his rule, accused World Jewry of having the same ambitions they themselves fostered."[98]

Wistrich's point deserves some thought. A realistic foreign policy is important, but too much realism can lead to deals with the devil, and for well-functioning democracies like America's and others in the West, such deals are never "pragmatic" for very long.

Understanding Denial and Minimization

While it never suffices to explain away or dismiss a critic without first addressing his or her criticism, it is also true that the expressed reasons for adopting a position are not necessarily the same as the real reasons. Politics sometimes starts in the gut and only later acquires an intellectual carapace. Thus, one may legitimately wonder what really motivates those who deny or minimize the significance of Muslim antisemitism. Given the dearth of empirical research and an inability to put subjects on the couch, answers to this question cannot be definitive.

The most controversial explanation is that many deniers and minimizers across the globe are themselves at least mildly antisemitic. It has been suggested that although these observers may reject the most extreme bigotry, they secretly believe there is truth to at least some Muslim and Arab Jew-hatred. According to this line of argument, they are unwilling to risk respectability by openly acknowledging their prejudices, but they will show solidarity with overt Jew-haters by averting their gaze or excusing the hatred in one way or another. In a sense, then, the refusal to focus on Muslim and Arab antisemitism can be viewed as an act of jury nullification. It is not altogether unlike the situation of the secret drug user on the jury who refuses to convict a drug dealer despite the prosecution's airtight case.

One cannot readily refute the contention that closet bigots exist among the deniers and minimizers. But in the absence of credible information about their relative numbers, this approach does not seem useful or convincing. In any event, there are better explanations.

Lack of familiarity with the evidence can explain a lot. Many people in the West have arrived at their judgments about antisemitism in the Muslim world through various types of extrapolation. In the United States, for example, people reasonably infer from their observations and experiences that the local Jewish pre-dicament is not all that bad, especially when compared with the situation of Jews in the past and other minorities nowadays. People further base their assessments on interactions with Muslims in the United States, most of whom are moder-ates. Extrapolations from observations of Muslims participating in interfaith initiatives—again, a disproportionately liberal, moderate, and well-intentioned bunch—can be even more misleading.

Some observers may minimize in their minds the threat of Muslim antisemi-tism primarily because they perceive—in some instances, accurately—a Jewish tendency to cry wolf. Thus, they overcorrect, presuming that complaints about Muslim and Arab antisemitism are yet another manifestation of the "overly defen-sive" Jewish psychology.

These extrapolations are critically flawed, not least because circumstances in the Middle East, in Muslim-majority countries, and even in Europe are substan-tially different from those in the United States. Equally important, extremists and antisemites only rarely peddle their poison in English to the Western media, and for reasons addressed later in this chapter, these media outlets may be less than eager to report the antisemitism that they do detect.

More generally, intuitions and instincts that come from observations and studies of other forms of bigotry—say, anti-black and anti-Hispanic racism in the United States—do not serve well as guides to Jew-hatred. Antisemitism in many ways does not fit the model of other prejudices; for example, it frequently rests on imagined fears of great power and deep envy of Jewish success. One cannot, therefore, assess the potential for destructive antisemitism on the basis of how well Jews are faring economically or politically.[99]

Wishful Thinking and the Desire to Get Along

Most Westerners in America, Europe, and Israel—left, right, and center—strongly desire improved relations with the Muslim and Arab world. Poll data confirm this, and so does a daily perusal of major Western newspapers. Politicians frequently elevate the desire for better relations to a first-order goal of international policy, as when—shortly after taking office in 2009—President Obama declared his inten-tion to seek closer ties with Muslim nations.[100] Clergy who try to improve inter-faith relations are seen by many as heroes of our time.[101] It is not only those on the left who hope to achieve a "just, peaceful, humane and sustainable world" by encouraging leading Islamic religious figures to broadcast statements of moderation. The objective in all of this is to keep the West from ending up in a conflict with Islam, Muslims, and Islamic states. It is a worthy goal, but it has a problem.

Gaining the cooperation of many Muslim religious and political leaders has proved far more difficult than expected, and hostility toward the United States appears more broad-based than initially believed in the days following 9/11. In this context, some see focusing attention on widespread bigotry emanating from large segments of the Muslim and Arab world as fanning the flames of conflict by identifying negative characteristics of the community with which the West wants to get along. There is a strong impulse to leave this one stone unturned in the battle against bigotry.[102]

Foreign policy realists, those who understand foreign affairs in terms of the coldhearted pursuit of national interests, routinely downplay the ideological underpinnings of Hamas and Hezbollah and call on America to treat these nonstate actors as normal participants in international politics.[103] Left-leaning Middle East studies professors end up in a similar place, although for different reasons; they have repeatedly pushed for negotiation with and, consequently, legitimation of Hamas.[104] How then should one expect them to address the presence of murderously antisemitic hadiths and straight-faced citations of *The Protocols of the Elders of Zion* in the Hamas Charter? And how should one expect them to deal with evidence suggesting that hostility toward Jews may be common even among some so-called moderates in the world of Islam?

In his 2006 book *The Resurgence of Anti-Semitism,* philosophy professor Bernard Harrison commented, "A central plank of one current left-liberal belief system [is] that all human conflict without exception can be resolved by negotiation; with the further proviso that where negotiation fails it is invariably because one has not gone far enough in viewing matters from the standpoint of those with whom one is negotiating."[105] Renowned liberal political theorist Michael Walzer similarly noted a tendency among liberals to be accommodationist and conciliatory; those on the left look for means of coexistence even with groups not prepared to coexist. Walzer thinks the liberal West is engaged in an ideological struggle against radical forms of Islam but worries that "too many of us are not prepared to accept the burdens of that struggle. [One] burden involves engaging at every moment the false claims of religious zealots."[106] French philosopher and political scientist Pierre-André Taguieff detected a "Munich-style quest for peace at any price, involving agreement to negotiate with the Islamists and then bow to their conditions."[107] Paradoxically, those who advocate most strongly for conciliation with the Muslim world may also sense that hostility toward Jews and Israel is so deeply ingrained that the West best not press the issue, for it will be unsuccessful. Dialogue rises above principle, and the West must give way. And because Israel does not give way sufficiently, because it does not yield to the essentially eliminationist demands of Hamas, Hezbollah, Ahmadinejad, and other extremists, it is widely perceived—especially in Europe—as a dangerous threat to world peace.[108]

Another problem is that if the West faces the existence of venomous Jew-hatred in Iran squarely, then it need also face what will happen when this bigotry becomes armed with nuclear weapons. This problem may lie at the heart of former ambassador Joseph Montville's attempt to deflect attention from antisemitism. In 2007 he wrote, "Muslim-Jewish antagonism in its political form is nuclear armed. ... The situation is serious. To understand the genesis and underlying dynamics of Arab and Muslim expressed public hatred of Israel in particular and by extension Jews in general requires the most profound—and respectful—scholarship so that the enormity of the nuclear threat and ways to transform it can be discovered."[109] Lurking beneath this opinion, perhaps, is the conscious or unconscious sentiment that Western analyses must yield certain conclusions—true or not—because the alternative is nuclear war. Though understandable, it is an unusual and defeatist way to think.

The prospect of nuclear-armed Jew-haters is indeed frightening, not only because such a weapon might be used on Israel. The presence of such extreme hatred in such high places leads one to doubt the mental stability of the leaders who would control such weapons and to suspect that they might use newly acquired power to foment all sorts of trouble in the region. That such fear might beget denial of the threat—something some psychoanalysts might predict—is a possibility. In any case, many on the left regard the use of military force by Israel in conjunction with Western powers as anathema, no matter what the reason—and they are afraid of thinking about the implications of confrontation with an almost-nuclear-armed, genocidal antisemitic power.

What's Wrong with the Progressive World?

Many on the moderate and mainstream left see antisemitism as yesterday's news—a malady of the European past, a disease of nationalism and fascism, that has, for most part, withered away in the new Europe. Such liberals are not necessarily naive; they may acknowledge the long tradition of antisemitism that stained the works of many socialist and leftist thinkers as well. They may retain some concern about the possibility of a resurgence of Jew-hatred. But, against the prospect of revitalized antisemitism, they counsel careful monitoring of right-wing groups in the West. To the extent that moderate liberals misread Muslim hostility to Jews, it is largely because they have not been exposed to the evidence or because they are blinded by a desire to avoid conflict with Muslims and Arabs at all costs.[110]

For elements of the radical Left, the situation is different. Most are skeptical about Europe's antiracist declarations. The conservative writer Richard Baehr distinguished between liberals and leftists on basis of a test: "If you tend to regard America as a primarily flawed, evil, unjust racist country (or at least when Republicans are running it), and most importantly, believe that the US is the primary threat to world peace internationally, then you are a leftist, and not a liberal."[111] In any case, the radical Left sees racism running rampant in Europe and the United States, especially racism against Muslims. But, for many, a new ideology has taken hold, with elements that undermine any attempt to perceive Muslim and Arab antisemitism clearly.

Terrorism expert Ernest Sternberg journeyed into the ideological politics of the radical Left. He noted that by the 1990s "the fall of communism and the revelations of the tens of millions killed under Stalin and Mao—who had only Hitler as their competitor in the magnitude of their crimes—temporarily disgraced the radical Left."[112] But many on the left built a vision that "misery in the world is caused by a global capitalist Empire, led by America. This Empire dominates national governments. It exploits the world economy through multinational corporations. It manufactures popular consent through media manipulation. And it uses American soldiers, along with international mercenaries, as its enforcers." Sternberg continued, "The new revolutionary vanguard is made up . . . of transnational social movements. The poor, the failed, the ignored, the oppressed, the humiliated, the alienated, and the angry can all qualify, since their miseries flow from the depredations of Empire."[113]

But, having decided this, the radical Left faced what Sternberg called a "ticklish problem." The various discontents in the new revolutionary vanguard were too diverse and included too many groups that would not get along: jihadists, human rights groups, neocommunist atheists, pacifists, gays, and others. A common enemy was needed. Logically, America and its empire might be ideal, but according to Sternberg, it would be better to have "a scapegoat manageable enough in size and devilish enough in popular imagination that it will elicit the requisite loathing. Enter Israel, the only Western nation under long enough threat that it has had to fight ongoing wars to survive."[114] He explained, "Stripped of all context, Israel's actions can be made to fit the needed image of aggressor, and its being Jewish is all the better." If Israel didn't fit, anti-Zionist propaganda would make it fit.

Whether or not Sternberg's speculations are correct, the ideology of the radical Left clearly sketches both America and Israel as supremely destructive participants in world affairs. Sometimes hatred for Israel is a convenient way to express hatred for America.[115] Sociologist Robert Fine explained, "In recent years the European radical intelligentsia has become increasingly inclined to treat Israel as its primary enemy. Israel is represented as a racist state, a pariah people, an imperial power, the tail that wags the American dog, the extension of colonial Europe into the Middle East and so forth."[116] According to David Hirsh and Jane Ashworth, Israel became "a symbol for all that is wrong with a world dominated by U.S. imperialism." There are no shades of gray in the radical Left's worldview. Instead, "it is Manichaeism: the world is a great struggle between heroes and villains, only to be resolved by a great revelation and a final undoing. Conversely, the Palestinians have come to symbolise all victims, and their struggle has become the defining struggle against imperialism. Symbolic Zionists and victims replace real Jews and Palestinians in the left anti-Zionists' imagination."[117]

Such hostility, for most radical leftists, is not antisemitism, but it is obsessive— going far beyond a demand that Palestinians be treated fairly.[118] Hirsh and Ashworth suggest "anti-Zionism is not motivated by anti-semitism. It is motivated by concern for the oppressed. But it nevertheless creates a movement and a worldview that singles out Jews as being the central force for evil and imperialism in the world. Naturally, such movements are beginning to spawn people who are indeed motivated by anti-semitism."[119] Hirsh and Ashworth may be naive in accepting that most anti-Zionism stems from concern for the oppressed; there is much more to the psychology of hostility to toward the Jewish state. But they are certainly correct that there has been much seepage of Jew-hatred into the anti-Zionist community.

It is hardly surprising that ideologically obsessed Israel-haters would fail to detect and denounce Jew-hatred in their ranks or in the Muslim and Arab world. It would require a tightrope walker to maintain the levels of anti-Israel hostility that are a central defining feature for much of the radical Left and at the same time keep up sensitive antennae to those who cross over into overt antisemitism. But several other factors reinforce antisemitism denial and minimization among radical leftists and sometimes others—liberals and conservatives—as well:

- a reluctance to incriminate those who are themselves the victims of racism and discrimination[120]
- the lack of a politically acceptable language with which one can speak accurately about a race, religion, or people
- an unwillingness to judge the deeds of non-Western people by Western values because of the doctrine of moral relativism
- a decline in sympathy for Jews as they lost the victim and underdog status that won support in the past[121]
- a reluctance, especially in Europe, to alienate large blocks on Muslim voters important to political coalitions

Jews who are part of the Left, especially the radical Left, may feel particular pressures to conform their views on the Arab-Israeli conflict and antisemitism to the prevailing ideology. Because such issues hit close to home, they become part of a test on which Jewish leftists must prove good faith and sincerity. Failure to pass the test may have implications for career advancement and reputation. Yet, since most radical Jews often do not maintain their primary social ties to the mainstream Jewish community, they do not face strong countervailing pressures.[122]

It is always dangerous to venture into the realm of psychoanalysis, yet some features in non-Jewish Europe's anti-Israel anger—coming only a half century after the Holocaust—seem to demand such a detour. For the past half century, not only Germans but most Europeans have expressed public regrets repeatedly for the antisemitic crimes of the Second World War and for the bigotry perpetrated during nearly two millennia of history. These recitations of guilt have been burdensome, and nobody likes to feel guilty. By portraying the Jews as guilty of human rights violations or, better still, Nazi-like crimes, Germans in particular, but also other Europeans, can relieve some of the guilt. After all, they can reason, everyone does it—even those too-good Jews who keep throwing the Holocaust in our face. Similarly, the Christian churches can "escape lingering guilt about the Holocaust, turning Israel into a villain."[123] As Robert Fine put it, Israel is demonized "as the Other of an idealised new Europe." It is represented as "the incarnation of all the negative properties postnational Europe has allegedly thrown off: a racially defined state that denies human rights to those who do not belong to the nation and inclines itself toward ethnic cleansing or even genocide." He further noted, "The irony of this fake reconstruction of European self-belief is that it presents the European perpetrator as having learned the universal lessons of the Holocaust, whilst it presents the Jewish victim as having learnt only to reinstate the very malpractices the new Europe has overcome."[124]

All in all, when one looks at the psychological and political implications, hostility toward Israel and insensitivity to antisemitism make a neat package, especially for Europeans. Liberal Europe proves its superiority to America; shows that its own Jewish victims, by extension, couldn't have been all that blameless; rescues its religious tradition; and proves that it is now more moral than ever by helping the Palestinian victims who suffer the onslaught of U.S.-Israeli power. It also has the benefit of keeping Muslim voters happy, keeping the oil flowing, and possibly deflecting and deterring terrorist strikes. If facts about antisemitism get in the way, the facts be damned.

In 2007 former UNESCO official Michael Fineberg noted, "For two thousand years people have been persecuted and killed for being Jews and, while on occasion a minority of non-Jews have gone so far as to raise their voices in protest or, indeed, more rarely to defend the victims, this tradition of persecution has been paralleled by a tradition of ignoring, condoning or justifying its perpetrators."[125] In the twenty-first-century West, that latter tradition remains alive and well.

5

ANCIENT ROOTS, MODERN ROOTS

The origins of contemporary Muslim antisemitism lie partly in the long history of Islam and the peoples who practice it. But the Islamic past is not an engine propelling the present along roads drawn on an ancient map. After all, recent political realities, social conditions, and educational practices determine which historical events matter and which are consigned to the ash heap of the past. Thus, the most important question is how the numerous and ambiguous elements of theology, history, and politics become psychologically relevant sources of present-day bigotry.

Every manifestation of Jew-hatred stems from an amalgam of past and present sources. Consider, for example, the antisemitism of Abd Al-Wahhab 'Adas, an editor of the Egyptian government-sponsored daily newspaper *Al-Gumhouriyya*. Back in 2004 'Adas charged:

> If you want to know the real perpetrator of every disaster or every act of terrorism, look for the Zionist Jews. They are behind all the violent and terror operations that have occurred everywhere in the world. [They do this] first of all in order to slap [the label of attacker] on the Arabs and Muslims, and second to harm them, distort their image, and represent them to the world as terrorists who endanger innocents. What is even more dangerous is that after every terror operation they perpetrate, they leave a sign, clue, or traces meant to show that the perpetrators are Arab Muslims.[1]

'Adas went on to discuss the then recent terrorist bombing of the Madrid transit system in which 190 people died and approximately two thousand were wounded. Immediately following this attack, an al Qaeda affiliate claimed credit, but other theories of responsibility, one involving the Basque Euskadi Ta Askatasu-na (ETA), soon surfaced. Controversy still surrounds the question of who planned and conducted the bombings. At present, the most widely accepted theory is that a small group of Islamic extremists—the ones convicted at a trial in Spain in 2007—were in fact responsible, although they were probably not under direct al Qaeda control. No serious analysts have found any evidence at all of Israeli or other Jewish involvement. But days after the bombing, 'Adas, a respected journalist in Egypt, had complete certainty about the culprits. He wrote, "It is obvious that the Jews are the ones who placed these things, in order to prove to the entire world that the Arabs and Muslims are behind the bombings."

'Adas did not require specific evidence to buttress his conclusion. Rather he derived Jewish guilt from Jewish character, explaining, "It is the Jews, with their hidden filthy hands, who play their part with expertise in order to harm the Arabs and Muslims and to intensify hatred towards them. They have experience in this area. All precedents attest to this. Their black history is the best possible proof that hatred toward the Arabs and the Muslims fills their hearts and blinds their eyes."

'Adas finally declared, "Actually, it is they [the Jews] who are behind the events of September 11." Here, he cites as proof the much-touted "fact" that "4,000 Jews of American origin who worked at the World Trade Center received instructions from the Mossad not to go to work that day." He thinks that America knows well that the Jews and the Mossad were responsible for 9/11 but that American leaders want to "evade the evil of these Jews and of the Zionist lobby that infiltrates and rules the decision-makers in America."

Although 'Adas offers his remarks as analysis, few fair-minded people would dispute that they reflect bigotry. But is this bigotry a product of Arab or Muslim history? The answer is not so simple, as there are many plausible sources. For example, his comments do not focus directly on the Arab-Israeli conflict, yet he writes, "Israel is not settling for its barbaric massacres of the Palestinian people or the ongoing annihilation of everything Palestinian. . . . Its crimes are spreading outward so that its hand will reach other innocent peoples." His bigotry against Jews, then, has some roots in his perception of Israel's interactions with Palestinians as demonic. His charge of "ongoing annihilation of everything Palestinian" is, of course, impossible to sustain, but this does not seem to trouble him. He writes in an environment in which such perceptions are widely shared. And that such hyperbolic charges can be cited as unchallenged assumptions is something that, in itself, must be explained.

Even so, the existence of a nexus between 'Adas's views of Israel and his views of Jews is obvious. In an alternate universe, absent the Arab-Israeli conflict, 'Adas probably never would have fixated to the same extent on the Jews. His bigotry also serves to defend the Islamic public image and his own Islamic identity from the ego-threatening tarnish of association with terrorist attacks, regardless of what he really believes about the Spanish case.

'Adas readily accepts the notion of ubiquitous Jewish power, possibly because he has absorbed directly or indirectly cultural beliefs that developed in response to the importation of the Russian-forged *The Protocols of the Elders of Zion*. On the other hand, his spotlight on so-called Jewish trickery may derive from themes found in the age-old commentaries on Muhammad's interactions with the Jews of Medina. His belief in the "black" history of Judaism may be an indirect consequence of imported European antisemitism; for example, versions of Jewish history reflected in Édouard Drumont's *La France Juive* and other nineteenth- and twentieth-century European works of racism. His belief in Jews as the roots of evil throughout the ages might also be reinforced by stories from early Islamic history; for example, those portraying Jews as having falsified their religious heritage and abandoned their god.

However, these themes were hardly obsessions through much of Islamic history and, therefore, cannot in themselves account for 'Adas's worldview. One might ask why Islamic values regarding tolerance for Jews and Christians do not come into play. The answer perhaps lies in theological limitation of protections to Jews, which are rendered operative only when Jews act in a subservient role as dhimmis. Some modern-minded Islamic clerics have attempted to extend the traditional notion of tolerance, but 'Adas apparently has not come under their influence.

As a successful journalist, 'Adas must also be mindful of the situational demands of his job. No doubt he knows what someone in his position can and cannot say. Journalistic and governmental norms in Egypt when he wrote (and still today) must have included some toleration of the sort of bigotry found in his work. In addition, his uncritical acceptance of "the 4,000 absent Jews" theory of 9/11 reflects his willingness to abandon journalistic curiosity and professionalism, perhaps because of personal bigotries, perceptual biases, or a sense that anti-Jewish bigotry may be an aid to his career.

'Adas's remarks alone do not indicate what he thinks about influential Islamist Sayyid Qutb, but 'Adas's views appear to have been influenced by Qutb's outlook as expressed in his anti-Jewish writings in the middle of the twentieth century. Perhaps other Islamist and non-Islamist antisemitic writers were more important influences for 'Adas personally. The specifics remain uncertain. But somehow the journalist is the product of his education—acquired via his family, his schooling, his mosque, his reading, and his personal experiences.

Finally, 'Adas's remarks may have deeper psychological sources. Perhaps he possesses an unconscious need to see himself as a defender of the faith and an attacker of its enemies. Such needs may have roots in some complex intrapsychic mechanism or even in acts of blasphemy or apostasy for which he feels a need to repent. This, of course, is mere speculation. But it is not implausible that these or similar motives may be at work.

One also might suspect a Freudian defense mechanism in which 'Adas is ascribing his own feelings to others. Hence, when he speaks of hatred of Arabs and Muslims filling Jews' hearts and blinding their eyes, he may really be speaking about himself and his attitude toward Jews. At a minimum, 'Adas's cognitive abilities appear diminished by blinding, psychologically based hatred. So it is no simple matter to understand where even a single antisemitic utterance originates.

The renowned social psychologist Gordon Allport noted in his 1954 classic, *The Nature of Prejudice*, that when people read the works of enthusiastic proponents of any theory of prejudice, they "sometimes gain the impression that the author feels that he has buttoned up the subject completely. Yet as a rule most 'theories' are advanced by their authors to call attention to some one important causal factor, without implying that no other factors are operating."[2] Allport's judgment may be a bit too charitable with regard to some theorizing about Muslim antisemitism in which scholars are all too ready to purposely exclude entire classes of explanatory factors. For example, some scholars say that none of the core elements of Jew-hatred are rooted in the early history, texts, and theological writings of Islam. Others deny that antisemitism is fed by norms currently prevailing in some Muslim countries. Still others ignore the key role of the Arab-Israeli conflict in intensifying Muslim anti-Jewish attitudes.

In truth, all these forces play a part. Allport explained:

> A person acts with prejudice in the first instance because he perceives the object of prejudice in a certain way. But he perceives it in a certain way partly

because his personality is what it is. And his personality is what it is chiefly because of the way he was socialized (training in family, school, neighborhood). The existing social situation is also a factor in his socialization and may also be a determinant of his perceptions. Behind these forces lie other valid but more remote causal influences. They involve the structure of society in which one lives, long-standing economic and cultural traditions, as well as national and historical influences of long duration. While these factors seem so remote as to be alien to the immediate psychological analysis of prejudiced acts, they are, nonetheless, important causal influences.[3]

To elaborate on all the elements in Allport's comprehensive model would be a huge task, but the remainder of this chapter calls attention to some ways historical and contemporary forces have interacted to produce anti-Jewish prejudice in the Muslim world. One critical linkage of past and present happens via mass media representations of the past, and it would be hard to describe these representations as educational.

Real and Imagined History: How the Past Becomes Present

Hala Sarhan was clearly proud of her influential work, the forty-one-part Egyptian miniseries *Knight without a Horse*. She is a personable woman with a doctorate who has hosted a popular Egyptian television talk show.[4] A decade ago, as senior production executive, she played a key role in televising the *Knight* miniseries, which told a story of Jewish conspiracy based largely on *The Protocols of the Elders of Zion*. In one typical scene, a Jewish leader from a bygone era discussed how to convince the world to submit to Jewish laws; he concluded, "Money and bullets lead to the same result."[5]

The highly promoted 2002 production is famous in some circles and infamous in others. It reached millions of homes in the Middle East, North Africa, and even parts of Europe and was broadcast repeatedly in the years that followed. *Knight without a Horse*, in Sarhan's eyes, was a huge success. Although nearly all mainstream Western commentators on the show—left, right, and center—have condemned it for spreading slanderous lies and perpetuating a notorious forgery, Sarhan was not troubled.

Asked about the antisemitic content of the broadcast, she answered (in English), "This is a lie that the American media created. This is a big lie. It's not antisemitic. It's not anti-Jewish. Nothing from that sort. . . . It was a historical show and some of the characters were [pause] Jewish people and they were together planning . . . writing . . . their new rules or . . . it's part of a dramatic historical show. It's imagination. It's imaginary drama."[6]

Hassan Hamed, the graying and soft-spoken executive director of Egyptian state television at the time of the original broadcast agreed, explaining, "That was talking about something of the past and it has nothing to do with the situation with the Jews."[7] He later added, "You know, my point is—was there something called *Protocols* or not? We were not propagating the *Protocols*. We were saying some people in that series stole this manuscript which is the *Protocols*. It was nothing." These comments remain difficult to decipher, but in any case, Hamed's subtlety was probably lost on a large segment of the audience who doubtlessly perceived the broadcast as a fairly accurate historical rendering.

It is important to realize that *Knight without a Horse* was not one dissenting far-out voice on Jewish history. While the show did not entirely escape criticism in the Arab world, to my knowledge there have been no major broadcasts in the region portraying Jewish history objectively, much less sympathetically. And many other shows have parroted the weltanschauung evident in *Knight without a Horse*.[8]

The broadcasting of hateful lies under the cover of artistic license is only one way fabricated histories take root in the public mind. Insofar as the percentage of the public that reads carefully documented objective histories is as tiny in the Muslim world as it is in the West, the only historical awareness most people possess is one that has been filtered many times by teachers, clergy, writers, mass media executives, and other opinion leaders.

In the contemporary West, however, a multitude of diverse perspectives and norms against bigotry provide at least some protection, admittedly imperfect, against the widespread acceptance of hateful and distorted history. For example, Jewish and Arab historians in Israel have questioned many aspects of the mainstream Israeli perspectives on the past. Indeed, what is deemed mainstream in Israel regularly changes in response to new research and writing. Further, Muslims and Arabs in the West have produced at least some writing that has portrayed aspects of Jewish and Israeli history with some sympathy. But in many parts of the Muslim-majority world, tolerant writings regarding Jews and Israelis are either absent or marginalized.

Lies about the past have been hammered home without the slightest nod toward evidence or logic. Thus, for some years, Iran has been sponsoring conferences, contests, and other events designed to raise questions about whether the Holocaust occurred and whether it truly had devastating consequences for the Jewish people. Needless to say, the Holocaust is so well documented that questioning its occurrence is roughly equivalent to questioning the very possibility of historical inquiry.[9] Yet the Iranians present their Holocaust denial in the context of an open and idealistic academic exploration that they say has been thwarted in the West.

But sometimes they abandon this guise. Holocartoons.com, the relatively new Iranian website mentioned in chapter 2, for example, includes English, Spanish, Arabic, and Farsi material. An e-book featured on the site claims to "denounce the conspicuous lie of the 'plan[n]ed murder of 6 million Jews during the Second World War' allegedly called 'Holocaust.'" According to the book, this lie "is so obvious that there is no need for any further explanation."[10]

The e-book includes an absurd "questions and answers" section about the Holocaust, replete with cartoons. A typical question is, "How did the German discharge the gas from the ceiling while there was not any hole to do so?" An accompanying illustration shows a speaker standing at a podium; a roll of toilet paper (or paper towels) covers his mouth to prevent speech. The paper holder has a Jewish star on it, and the answer (or nonanswer) reads, "Shut up! You criminal [sic] and anti-Jews! How did you dare to ask such a question? You the beast, wicked, criminal, foul, murderer!" In other words, the Jews have kept reasonable people from examining evidence of fraud in their theory of the so-called Holocaust. (The true answer, that there were holes in the ceiling, is not mentioned.)[11]

It is easy to imagine an uninformed person coming away from the Iranian website believing that the Holocaust was a fraud perpetrated by the Jews or at least a matter of dispute among scholars in which one side (the deniers) has not been permitted to speak. Although even the most superficial grounding in history as taught in Western universities would be enough to refute much of Holocartoons.com's content, many people—particularly if they lack such grounding—could be taken in.

Misinformation about more recent historical events also circulates widely. Thus, polls show that many in Muslim countries believe that no Jews numbered among the victims of the World Trade Center attack. And the notion that the Jews killed Yasser Arafat is taking root. Some evidence of the spread of this false history comes from a 2009 broadcast on Palestinian television in which young children, perhaps ten or eleven years old, offered their thoughts and feelings about Arafat. Here are three of their comments (none of which were corrected or refuted by the producers of the broadcast):

> From one girl: "[Arafat] was our former president. He was under siege in Ramallah, and when he was under siege we were very upset. The Jews poisoned him and I hate them very much. Allah will repay them what they deserve."
>
> From a boy: "[Arafat] died from poisoning by the Jews. Well, I don't know what he died from, but I know it was by the Jews."
>
> From another boy: "They destroyed his whole house and he was left in one room and in the end the Jews poisoned him and blamed someone else."[12]

So, recent history, as it exists in the minds of many old and young, is a fabrication—the result of lies broadcast and circulated through media and by word of mouth. When one speaks of the distant history of Jews and Muslims, the line between historical and theological messages becomes blurred. Regarding events further back in the past, even highly educated and well-informed Muslims may believe and promote inaccurate messages about the Jews.

Thus, a Saudi-born Massachusetts endocrinologist and former board member of the Islamic Society of Boston, Walid Fitaihi, wrote a series of Arabic-language articles in which he argued that the Jews were the "murderers of prophets."[13] He also wrote that Jews will be "scourged" because of their "oppression, murder, and rape of the worshipers of Allah." Moreover, he said that Jews "have perpetrated the worst of evils and they have brought the worst corruption to the earth, and what we see of them these days is glad tidings for the Muslim heralding the fulfillment of Allah's promise of victory after the second transgression." These remarks appeared in the Arabic-language London daily newspaper *Al Sharq al-Awsat* on October 18, 2000.[14]

Hazem Sallah Abu Isma'il, once considered one of the frontrunners for the Egyptian presidency, also sees continuity between Jewish behavior in ancient and modern times. Isma'il, a lawyer and radical Islamist who spent some time lecturing about Islam in Los Angeles, explains:

As I've told you, following the great victory at the Battle of Badr, the Muslims felt joy and enjoyed stability, but the Jews, the hypocrites, and the infidels felt boiling rage and fury towards Islam. For instance, if they encountered a Muslim woman in the market, they would harass her. As you know, things like that have also happened recently, following 9/11. Muslims were harassed in the markets of America and Europe. There were some incidents, although not many, in which a man would strip a Muslim woman of her veil in the market.[15]

The harassment Isma'il mentions involved exposing the private parts of a Muslim woman. Some Jews, according to the story, joked about the woman not wanting to expose her face and then clapped and laughed as one Jewish man stripped her of her clothing. According to Isma'il, a Muslim man who witnessed the incident became angry and killed the Jewish abuser. Next, some of the Jews who were present killed the Muslim. Then Muhammad, according to Isma'il, did not kill the Jews; instead, he issued a decree expelling them from Medina. Not bothering to reflect on the matter of collective punishment, Isma'il concludes, "How wonderful are the judgments and wisdom of Islam." And so, according to the Islamist politician, Muslims came to rightfully oppose the Jews because of a supposed Jewish misdeed more than a millennium in the past.

The attempts of Isma'il and Fitaihi to ground their hatred in references to the early days of Islam are not at all unusual among Muslim antisemites. Some may interpret such efforts as evidence that ancient events have played a direct and important causal role in creating twenty-first-century hostility toward the Jews. But this is an example of the ancient animosities error, and to make any such direct link from the seventh century to the twenty-first would be incorrect.[16] One might, after all, quite reasonably interpret negative judgments against Jews in ancient Arabia as applying only to those particular Jews who carried out or supported specific misdeeds in that era. And, for some liberal Islamic believers today, the early anti-Jewish comments in the Quran are no more relevant than, say, the biblical injunctions for Jews to kill Amalekites wherever they may find them. In this sense, antisemitism is not an inherent feature of Islam.

To understand why fabrications about the past have taken hold, one can look to real history—in particular, to nine major historical sources of anti-Jewish trends in Islam. Too often, historians, journalists, polemicists, and partisans have chosen to attribute contemporary Muslim hostility to Jews to one or two sources of the nine, while the truth is more complex. One needs to consider all of the following:

♦ *Events in the seventh century.* All surviving accounts of Muhammad's conflicts with the Jews come from the religious sources of one side. Thus, there is no definitive historical evidence about what actually transpired in the seventh century. For example, did any Jews actually break treaties with Muhammad? Did the sexual harassment of a Muslim woman by a Jew in the marketplace really happen? Historical truth, by now, has become largely irrelevant. Tales of Jews as deceivers, treaty violators, falsifiers of sacred books, Sabbath violators who were transformed into pigs and apes, and more have roots that can be traced back to the Quran and other early religious sources.[17] Along with this negative imagery, there coexists some notion of tolerance for Jews and Christians and even a modicum of respect—at least when judged against other contemporaneous standards for treatment of people with different outlooks.

♦ *Early attempts to put spin on Muhammad's conflict with the Jews.* Tarek Fatah has made a reasonable case that certain parties in the early centuries after Muhammad's death, notably the then-powerful descendants of the Meccans who had rejected Muhammad, had reason to portray the Jews as the greatest enemies of the prophet.[18] Thus, some unreliable hadiths may have greatly reinforced the anti-Jewish aspects of Muhammad's era, even creating for him a role that he may never have played in presiding over the massacre of the unarmed Banu Qurayza Jews. According to Fatah, the worst antisemitism in the early Islamic tradition may have been fabricated. But it should be pointed out that Fatah's fascinating arguments notwithstanding, most observant Muslims regard Muhammad's murder/punishment of the Banu Qurayza Jews as a historical event. It is hard to know whether Fatah's argument is correct or merely wishful thinking, but his heart is in the right place.

♦ *The long Muslim political and religious tradition of discrimination and prejudice.* The Islamic religious tradition, like other religious traditions, has an element of contempt for nonbelievers. In the past, however, negative sentiment toward Jews usually did not rise to the level of hate or obsession observed in the Christian world. Still, institutionalized discrimination, a sense of superiority, and various restrictions on free religious practice were rarely missing over many centuries. It remains a matter of debate just how widespread, intolerable, and injurious various anti-Jewish measures were.[19] It also remains a matter of historical debate whether the Christian experience of life under Islam was better, worse, or the same as the Jewish experience.

♦ *Importation of European antisemitism.* European colonialists brought a more intense and obsessive Jew-hatred with them as they reached into various parts of the Muslim world. Christian missionaries and later secular antisemites added stories of blood libels and notions of Jewish conspiratorial plots to the mix. Under the Nazis, especially from 1937 to 1945, a large-scale effort to make common cause with Arabs and Muslims and to spread Nazi-style Jew-hatred to the Middle East was somewhat successful.[20]

♦ *The impact of Zionism.* Zionism was initially conceived as a cure for antisemitism, but it quite obviously has not had that impact. Although in the early days of Zionism, prior to the growth of Arab nationalism—much less Palestinian nationalism—it may have seemed possible for large numbers of Jews to return to their ancestral homeland without creating much conflict with Arabs, it soon became clear that—with the demise of the Ottoman empire, impending end of European colonial rule, and the rise of Arab nationalism—a conflict over land was likely to feed intergroup conflict. And this intergroup conflict, especially when coupled with the long history of at least moderately unpleasant Arab-Jewish interactions, fed Jew-hatred and made Arabs receptive to the offerings of the European antisemites as well.[21] After Israel achieved independence in 1948, despite whatever tolerance for Jews had existed in some parts of the Muslim world, conditions rapidly became intolerable.[22]

♦ *The rise of Islamism.* The Islamist perspective of the faith had been developing gradually over many years, starting all the way back with the Wahhabi movement in eighteenth-century Arabia.[23] The Salafist approach, which emphasized return to the early days of Islam, brought additional focus on Muhammad's negative interactions with Jews. The Muslim Brotherhood movement, founded in Egypt in 1928 by Hassan al-Banna, grew increasingly anti-Jewish during World War II (in part through its connection to the virulently antisemitic grand mufti). Sayyid Qutb perhaps brought antisemitism to its ideological fruition in his mid-century works; as Qutb's extremist approach was accepted by more and more Muslims, antisemitism spread with it.

♦ *The intensification of Palestinian nationalism.* At first, Arab nationalism was relatively undifferentiated. During the middle of the twentieth century, a unique Palestinian identity began to develop, partly in response to interactions with the Zionists and Israel, partly as a consequence of rejection of Palestinians by other Arabs. Not until the 1960s and 1970s, however, was specific Palestinian nationalism sharply distinguished from other Arab nationalism. From 1948 to 1967, after all, there was no attempt by Egyptians or Jordanians to establish any sort of Palestinian state. But by the mid-1970s, Palestinian nationalism became an acknowledged cause—perhaps *the* cause—not only for Palestinians but for others in the Muslim world as well. This increased focus on the plight of the Palestinians led to increased anger at Israel and a rise in associated antisemitism.

◆ *Political failures in the Arab world.* Following the devastating loss in the 1967 Six-Day War, it became apparent that Arab nationalism, pan-Arabism, and anti-Zionism had not produced intended or expected results. While sources of the failures were many, the most obvious defeat took place at the hands of the Jewish state. Hatred for that state and, by extension, for Jewish people increased, especially as it was far more difficult to attack those who retained power in the Arab world.

◆ *Successes of extremism.* From Khomeini's triumphant return to Iran in 1979 through the beginning of the twenty-first century, extremist Muslims seemed to be winning in ways that eluded their more moderate coreligionists. Hezbollah killed a large number of American troops without serious military repercussions, despite a threat from then-president Ronald Reagan. The secular but extremist PLO gained in prominence, influence, and respectability, in part because of its many terrorist acts. Although American aid helped militant Afghans defeat the Soviets, the victory was widely interpreted as the product of Allah's favor showered upon believers. Finally, al Qaeda's ability to throw the world into disarray was further interpreted as evidence that the tide had begun to turn in favor of those who returned to the "ancient" and "true" ways of Islam. Since the Salafist movement was already anti-Jewish, any stimulus to its growth also meant the growth of Jew-hatred.

In short, the religious tradition and history of Islam offered a firm foundation for the growth of intense Jew-hatred. European antisemites exported voluminous and virulent hostility, which was piled high upon this existing foundation. As the

Arab-Israeli conflict heated up in the twentieth century, conditions were ripe for the transformation of a dispute over land into a race-based and religion-based anti-semitism at levels not seen before in the Muslim world. The simultaneous growth of Islamism fed anti-Jewish fires by reviving all the worst historical and theological precedents, many of which had been relatively weak for centuries. With Israel's military and economic successes, Arab political failures, and the growing central-ity of the Palestinian issue in Muslim consciousness, hostility toward Jews turned from a sideshow into an obsession. Finally, when the most extreme elements in the Muslim world—e.g., the PLO, Hezbollah, Khomeini, Hamas, al Qaeda—appeared to be winning and leading the path to the future, many people marched behind their banners, one of which was the flag of noxious antisemitism.

Dhimmi Winners and Islamic Identity:
A Case of Cognitive Dissonance

The nineteenth and twentieth centuries repeatedly challenged the religious iden-tity and self-esteem of many Muslims around the world—pious believers, espe-cially, but also some Arabs whose primary orientation was ethnic, nationalistic, or pan-Arab. In this context, antisemitism emerged as a by-product of the failure to constructively resolve a host of political, theological, and—at bottom—social psychological challenges.

Unfortunately, none of the many social psychological theories of prejudice and discrimination were developed with an eye toward explaining antisemitism in the Muslim world, and none have been tested with data from Muslim or Arab countries.[24] Some theories, created with other instances of bigotry in mind, appear generally consistent with the facts concerning Muslim antisemitism, but these theories are insufficiently specific to add much to what is already known.

For example, one frequent approach, realistic conflict theory, holds that people often come to dislike members of groups with whom their own group competes for scarce resources.[25] The Palestinians and Israelis want the same land and with the ensuing conflict comes intergroup animosity. However, even in its most refined form, this theory cannot account well for the intensity of anti-Jewish hostility in, say, Pakistan or Iran, where there is no clear conflict with Jews over any scarce resource. The theory also does not explain why Muslim animosities stemming from the Israeli-Palestinian conflict have been more enduring and more virulent than most stemming from disputes over land.[26]

Another approach, social identity theory, rests on the credible assumption that people's identities are connected to their group membership.[27] People are motivated to have a positive social identity so they can feel good about themselves; they like to see their own group thrive and even dominate others. They bask in reflected glory when their group succeeds. But the reverse is also true. The group's misfortunes and failures can weigh heavily on individual group members. To ward off affronts to self-esteem and identity, people may derogate members of other groups, especially (but not exclusively) when those groups are perceived as threats. Sometimes group members engage in vicarious retribution against out-group members, even when they personally have not been harmed at all.[28]

The social identity theory has the advantage of explaining why those Muslims and Arabs who are not in direct competition with Israelis (or Jews) for land would still feel intensely concerned about the conflict and why they might strike out against Jews (and, for that matter, against Americans, Hindus, or anyone else they think, correctly or incorrectly, might threaten their group). As with realistic conflict theory, it is not so much that this theory doesn't apply as that it doesn't add much to what is already understood. One interesting prediction, however, is that if people have "multiple concurrent social identities," they are better protected against threats to any one of these identities and hence less likely to become bigoted against out-groups.[29] Thus, when Muslims think of themselves as members of many groups, only one of which is religiously based, they may be less likely to buy into Jew-hatred.

Still, the bigger questions are, why do Muslims—more than other group—feel that their social identity is so severely threatened, and why do so many direct anger specifically toward the Jews? As shall be seen, a good part of the answer to these questions has to do with Israel—but not because Muslims are responding to Israeli misdeeds and not because such virulent anger is a natural outgrowth of conflicts over land. We need to return once again to history as many Muslims perceive it, this time thinking about the psychological ramifications of perceived events.

Many religions—especially universalizing ones (like Islam, Catholicism, and Mormonism) that actively seek converts—see themselves in competition with other faiths. Sometimes this competition can be fierce, not only in the real world but also in the minds of the faithful. Regardless of what they proclaim in public, believers must often wonder about religious matters for which typical earthly evidence is generally lacking. When all the important and successful people one encounters share in one's outlook, and when there are good times for believers, uncertainties about God and his or her will can be readily set aside. But when times are bad and other viewpoints are well represented, religious identities can be threatened.

Christianity saw itself in deep competition with Judaism, a parent faith whose rules it had partly abandoned in favor of a new vision. One common outlook, replacement theology, held that Christians had replaced Jews as the "chosen people" and that God had no further plans for the Jews. A popular Christian notion—sometimes traced to St. Augustine—was that the Jews should survive but that they should not thrive.[30] Their continued misery could serve as a lesson to Christians of how God treats those who did not accept the Christian viewpoint. Moreover, Jewish suffering served as evidence of Jewish corruption and evil in connection with Jesus; why else would the Jews be so severely punished?

In Islam, both Judaism and Christianity were acknowledged as "peoples of the book" who possessed small bits of religious truth. Yet, for Muslims too, the poor condition of the Jews served—at least informally—to reinforce the notion that God was on board with the Muslims. Real political, military, and religious competition with the Jews—to the extent that there was any—had ended before Muhammad's return in victory to Mecca. Historian Bernard Lewis compared the origins of attitudes toward Jews in Christianity and Islam:

> Jesus was crucified; Muhammad triumphed in his own lifetime and became the head of a state as well as a community. His fight with the Jewish tribes of Medina resulted in their defeat and destruction, not his, and the clash of Judaism and Islam was resolved and ended with his victory. . . . While Christ's dealings with the Jewish priestly establishment in Jerusalem form a central part of the sacred history, Muhammad's conflict with the Jewish tribes of Medina is—or rather was—of minor importance. Of late, there has been a change in this respect.[31]

Hence, while some Jews in early Islamic history were perceived to be treacherous, evil, and dangerous, in Islam the vision of Jews as certainly wrong in their religious beliefs, but also insignificant, emerged. As previously illustrated, there were harsh anti-Jewish passages in the Islamic theological literature that antisemites could summon with great effect.[32] But for more than a millennium, Muslims were big winners, and Jews were big losers.

Jews were not viewed as a threat. Their position as dhimmis confirmed the Muslim sense of superiority. Thus, the Jewish condition under Islam enhanced the Muslim identity and contributed to collective self-esteem. In some ways, the situation resembled the way maintaining American blacks in positions of subservience reinforced whites' egos across the socioeconomic spectrum. There was always someone, some group of people, to look down upon.

But by the middle of the twentieth century, Muslim pride had suffered many blows over a long period.[33] An enumeration and analysis of failures, decline, and backtracking in much of the Muslim and Arab world could fill volumes. Islamic expansion had been the imperialist success story par excellence, but the retreat and demise of the Ottomans along with the rise of European colonialism heralded an era of Islamic weakness.[34]

In many ways, Muslims did not control their own destiny, and their once-great civilization had been superseded. In the Arab world especially, many solutions were proposed, and although some appeared to work for a while, none pointed for long toward a restoration of what had been lost. Arab-nationalist regimes survived, but they did not succeed on a par with states of East Asia. The unification sought by pan-Arabists came to nothing.

As political scientist Barry Rubin explained well in his book *Modern Dictators*, regimes—not only in the Muslim world—have learned to stay in power by using the specter of external enemies.[35] By elevating the battle against Israel to top priority, Arab leaders—whoever they were—could call their people to rally around the flag (which was often a flag of dictatorship). Leaders of sub-par Arab regimes frequently used the Jews and Israel as welcome diversions from their own serious failings.[36] Thus, the Palestine conflict (and by extension Jews and Israel) functioned in the Arab world and in some other parts of the Muslim world as what Bernard Lewis has called a "licensed grievance," the only safe and officially sanctioned public outlet for anger.[37]

Antisemitism in the Muslim world, therefore, is a form of political manipulation that rests on a psychological foundation. According to the social psychological theory of relative deprivation, people feel deprived "relative to what they had in the past or relative to people who have the resources they believe they deserve."[38] The experience of relative deprivation can turn into bigotry if people in a group blame members of another group for their deprivation. In the Arab world especially, feelings of relative deprivation were common at both the individual and group levels. And the sociopolitical system encouraged citizens to attribute both types of suffering to Israel and, not infrequently, to the Jews. The most logical target for aggression stemming from frustration and deprivation would, of course, be the source of the problem. But if it is too costly to attack that source, displacement onto a more readily available target can be acceptable.

Psychologists call this process scapegoating.[39] Social psychologist Peter Glick suggests ideologies that provide a scapegoat can succeed partly because they fulfill needs people have to understand the source of their discontent. Scapegoats can also shield in-group members from blaming themselves and thereby help them to maintain a positive social identity. Good scapegoats have little power to retaliate, are visible enough to be credible, are already disliked, are appropriately stereotyped for their destructive role, and are perceived as a bit of a threat.[40]

In recent decades, anti-Jewish ideologues in the Muslim world have been teaching that Jews are unlikeable, committed to plotting and trickery, and very powerful. Yet, at the same time, despite the ideology, Jews do not pose much real threat to typical Muslims. Most of the time—for many Muslims—it is probably more dangerous to criticize proximal forces such as local religious and governmental leaders than it is to criticize Israel, although there are exceptions to this rule. The United States, too, possesses more power than Israel to protect its interests and hence works only imperfectly as a scapegoat (although—under some circumstances—it will do).

But, all in all, Israel and—better still—the Jews fit the bill exquisitely; judging by the theoretical criteria, they are excellent scapegoats. Moreover, one could utilize all the traditional categories of antisemitism by changing just one word—"Jews" to "Zionists." Sometimes, there was no point in bothering with this change. But it could be helpful for two audiences: the West (where overt antisemitism has been out of style since the end of World War II) and Muslims and Arabs sufficiently imbued with Western values to eschew blatant religious bigotry.[41]

So, simple scapegoating theory explains a lot, but still more is going on. Consider what may have run through many Muslim minds following the defeats of 1948 and 1967. Jews were dhimmis. The matter had been settled long ago. But when Jews, the losers of history, emerged from their dhimmitude to assert national rights, it was more than Muslim pride could bear. There was, to be sure, the anger that frequently resulted from any conflict over scarce resources. But there was much more than that.

Arguments over land can be settled; arguments over identity, pride, and transcendent identity are not so easy to resolve. It was one thing to lose to the massive colonial power of the West. But to lose to Jews required a revision of fundamental thinking about the very theological and political system upon which stood one's social identity. Israel's existence was a violation of the dhimmi system. Reality was not supposed to be that way.[42] Israel's legitimacy was a theological challenge that could not be ignored. Israel's technological and economic achievements further complicated the picture. Early Islamic civilization had been the scientific leader, the creative force in the world. What had gone wrong? The 1956 victory could be explained: Israel had operated in cahoots with the massive imperial powers. But 1948, 1967, and the technological and economic success of Israel could not be fathomed. Some Muslim countries had grown rich from oil, but rewards had not spread far. And, at some level, even this good fortune must not have seemed gratifying in light of Israel's apparent achievements.

The coupling of Arab defeat with prior stereotypes of Jews as inferior created an untenable psychological predicament for many Arabs. The social psychological theory of cognitive dissonance, first formulated in 1957 by Leon Festinger, can help explain this predicament.[43]

When perceptions of reality conflict with deeply held attitudes or beliefs, cognitive dissonance results. This dissonance is unpleasant to experience, and hence people usually want it to end. When the dissonance is related to self-concept and self-worth, few are able to ignore the underlying conflicts. All sorts of uncomfortable inconsistencies may emerge if, for example, a person believes that (1) Jews are religiously ordained to be dhimmis who must always take a backseat to Muslims, (2) a small Jewish state just inflicted a massive military defeat on the combined armies of much larger Arab states, (3) Arabs started the conflicts, and (4) the Jews are being very productive with their land.

To some extent, one can work through these inconsistencies by holding that Jews are, as the religious sources taught, godless, evil, tricky, and, as the imported *Protocols* taught, involved in a massive plot to control the world that has given them power over the United States and other nations. One might also get some relief by maintaining that corrupt leaders betrayed the Muslims. With beliefs such as these, a crumbling yet psychologically important edifice can be buttressed. Such mental manipulations reduce the unpleasant psychological dissonance and restore some tranquility.

The late psychoanalyst Mortimer Ostow explained the situation well:

> The obvious source of current Arab and Muslim resentment against the Jews derives from the establishment of the State of Israel in 1948 on land claimed by the Muslim Arabs. . . . But the Jews also represented a mythic enemy, a principle of cosmic evil. It was only because of that satanic power, the Arabs argued, that they were able to defeat the Arab armies which had come to wipe them out in recent years. Throughout the history of Jewish-Muslim coexistence in Muslim countries, both Jews and Christians were tolerated only as long as they acknowledged the subservient status to which they were assigned, and which they accepted. That the Jew, who, in Muslim eyes, was seen as weak, cowardly and ineffectual, could impose such a quick and definitive military defeat upon the Arab enemy could not be explained except by the theory that the Jews embodied a principle of cosmic evil, a satanic element, whose worldwide conspiracies would some day be disclosed and defeated.[44]

This, then, is the main engine behind contemporary Arab and Muslim antisemitism. It is the deepest reason why the Arab-Israeli conflict has been so difficult to resolve. In a conflict over land, land can be divided. And this isn't a zero-sum game. Peace with Israel would bring huge economic and political dividends to both sides—but relatively more to the Palestinians. The problem is that peace might extract a psychological, and perhaps theological, cost that would be too great to bear. Jews as equals is bad enough. But Jews who prevail in fair competition would be a bad reflection on the faith, the culture, and by extension the self. Ultimately, the real rewards of cooperation and peace should prove greater than the temporary psychological costs. But there is first a high hurdle to leap.

You've Got to Be Taught to Hate and Fear: Socialization for Bigotry

Notwithstanding the influences of history, politics, and depth psychology, there is nothing complicated about the last step in the causal chain describing how many people in Muslim-majority countries become antisemites. It's simply a matter of education and indoctrination—not only the kind one receives in school, but also the sort that comes from every institution in a society, what sociologists and social psychologists call socialization. This is the process through which a society or organization transmits its values to members; it may start during a child's earliest days and continue throughout the lifespan. Although anti-Jewish socialization practices occur much more frequently in some places than in others, they can be found throughout the Muslim world.

Saudi cleric Khaled al-Khlewi is a master of the antisemitic conditioning of children; his approach is not typical, but it is telling. In an "educational" broadcast on the influential Al-Jazeera network in January 2009, he told the previously discussed tale about the Jew who exposed the private parts of the Muslim woman in the marketplace, the same story Egyptian Salafist politician Hazem Sallah Abu Isma'il invoked to justify Jew-hatred. Khlewi then spoke of Muhammad's subsequent banishment of the Qaynuqa Jews, commenting, "This is the only way to deal with them." The cleric further educated his young audience about Muhammad's role in slaughtering many Jews. This, he explained, happened because the Angel Gabriel had appeared and informed the prophet that some Jews were planning to throw a rock at his head. Khlewi went on to tell the children and other viewers that nothing works with the Jews except force. "Memorize the following parable, just like I learned it from others," he told his students. "'Kiss the head of a Jew, and he will deceive you—deceive him, and he will kiss your head.' The Jew is treacherous, disloyal, deceitful, and belligerent by nature." To give examples, he said, "Many U.S. Congressmen are Jews. Most of the media moguls are Jews."

Khlewi's manner in the video seemed warm and loving. No child would suspect that he was a hatemonger. Like any good teacher, Khlewi sought to involve his students. He asked, for example, what slogan pointed to the geographic aspirations of the Jews. When eight-year-old Omar went to the stage to answer Khlewi's question, the cleric greeted him, "Welcome, my dear." He then kissed the boy, asked his name, and when he learned it, said, "Omar? Allah Akbar. They hate Omar and are afraid of him. Omar what? What's your dad's name?" Omar answered, "Mahmoud." Khlewi continued, "And your mom's name?" But then he immediately covered Omar's mouth and said, "No, don't tell us mom's name, there's no need. Right?" Khlewi came across like a friend of the little boy and his family. In contrast to the evil Jew who lewdly exposed the Muslim woman, this teacher acted with excess caution to protect the boy's mother from those who would do her evil.

When Omar said that the Jews' slogan was "From the [Nile] river to the Euphrates," Khlewi congratulated him and explained that this meant the Jews "are motivated by religious considerations, not only by political, economic, or geographic considerations." A bit later Khlewi asked Omar if he liked Jews. The boy said he did not, and Khlewi inquired why. "They wanted to kill the Prophet Muhammad," Omar responded. To this, Khlewi offers a gratified "Well done." When the child added, "Oh God, destroy the Jews," Khlewi again said, "Well done." He concluded by telling Omar about his own son, Abdallah, and suggested that the two boys could play together. He gave Omar a book and some water.[45]

In another 2009 broadcast, radical Egyptian sheikh Salam Abd al-Qawi urged Muslims to teach their children to hate the Jews. He claimed that this was one of the loftiest goals a parent could seek for his or her offspring:

Hating the enemies of Allah is very important. We must teach our children, our youngsters, our brothers, and all the Muslims to hate the accursed Zionist Jews. Why not? They teach their children to hate us. Our hatred of the Jews is based upon our faith. The Koran tells us to hate them, not to love them. . . . We must teach our children to obey Allah, to obey the Prophet Muhammad, and to hate the Jews, the Zionists, and what the Zionists are planning.[46]

Clearly Khlewi and Qawi represent extreme devotion to teaching hatred. But they do not utter their views in a dark room away from the public eye. And one can find many more examples of similar teaching. Recall the previously discussed children's television special about Jews being turned into pigs and apes and cast into the sea.[47] And think of the Mickey Mouse–type Palestinian television character, Farfour, who was killed off by the Jews.[48] And a child on a 2009 Egyptian children's television show asked Allah—without adult rebuke—to torment the Jews "with a disease that has no cure or remedy." Another child repeated the hadith about Judgment Day not coming until the Muslims fight and kill the Jews.[49]

Recall Ayaan Hirsi Ali's early thoughts about Jews being evil *djinns*, spirits that, according to Islamic legend, can sometimes assume human or animal form and exercise supernatural influence over people.[50] Similarly, ex-Muslim Nonie

Darwish remembers the following from her childhood in Gaza and Cairo: "As a child, I was not sure what a Jew was. I had never seen one. All I knew was they were monsters. They wanted to kill Arab children, some said, to drink their blood. I was told never, ever, take candy or fruit from a stranger. It could be a Jew trying to poison me."[51] And Canadian Muslim reformist Irshad Manji recalls being taught at a Muslim school in Canada in the early 1980s that "Jews worship moolah, not Allah, and that their idolatry would pollute [her] piety if [she] hung out with them."[52]

Consider also the 2004 testimony of Muhammad Al-Zurqani, editor of the official newspaper of Egypt's then-governing National Democratic Party. On June 24 and July 1 of that year, Zurqani published a two-part article by Dr. Rif'at Sayyed Ahmad titled "The Lie about the Burning of the Jews." The author wrote:

> This lie [about] the burning of the Jews in the Nazi crematoria has been disseminated throughout the world until our time in order to extort the West and make it easier for the Jews of Europe to hunt [sic] Palestine and establish a state on it, in disregard of the most basic principles of international law and the right of peoples to independent life without occupation. [This lie] was raised [also] so that [the Jews] would receive financial, technological, and economic aid from the West.[53]

When the Middle East Media Research Institute circulated a translation of the articles, more moderate elements in the Egyptian government reacted by distancing themselves from them. In the ensuing flap, Zurqani either left or was fired from his position as editor. A little later, on an Egyptian television program about Ahmad's articles, participants expressed strong support for Holocaust denial. Ex-editor Zurqani joined the discussion by telephone to indicate his agreement with the ideas expressed in the original articles, explaining, "We were educated from childhood that the Holocaust is a big lie."[54] He felt betrayed by his own and apparently had no need to examine whether what he had been taught since childhood was true.

For many in Muslim-majority countries, especially in the Arab world, the lesson that Jews are evil is learned before adolescence. The lesson is, in fact, so well learned that it sometimes works in reverse. Not only are Jews bad, but bad things are also assumed to be Jewish. Thus, rumors circulated during the early days of the 2011 revolt in Libya that Muammar al-Qaddafi was secretly a Jew.[55] More generally, when the 2011 revolts started, some on both sides accused the other of doing the work of the Israelis, the Jews, or the Americans. And when Amina Abaza engaged in animal rights work in the Arab world, those who disapproved denounced her too as a Jew (also as an American and a Freemason).[56] Some Muslims objected to Valentine's Day because they saw it (yes, St. Valentine's Day) as a Jewish product designed to weaken their religious beliefs.[57] In the eyes of quite a few Muslims, Jews are responsible for illegal organ-trafficking.[58] Child rape and child murder are also associated with Jews—who, bizarrely, are said to need the blood for Passover matzo. AIDS, too, comes from the Jews.[59] And so the list of misdeeds associated with the Jews goes on and on.

Undoubtedly, large numbers of Muslims—maybe most—see through a good portion of the nonsense. But it would not be unreasonable to predict that for any unpopular innovation that arises, one would be able to find those who denounce the innovators as Jews. And for many controversies that arise in the Muslim world—political, economic, cultural, or otherwise—one side or both will attempt to discredit their opponents by linking them to Israelis or Jews. That all this happens so often is a measure of the confidence demagogues across the political spectrum have that the terms "Israeli" and "Jewish" have been successfully conditioned to evoke powerful negative responses in the gut.

Partly as a consequence of persecution and partly because of the lure of Israel, only tiny remnants of once-numerous Jewish populations now remain in the Arab countries—or, for that matter, anywhere in the Muslim world. Thus, few people living in Muslim-majority countries can form their impressions of Jews on the basis of personal interactions. And few can use personal experience as a corrective for antisemitic propaganda.

Images of Jews come almost entirely through opinion leaders and the mass media. Gabriel Schoenfeld, a perceptive student of contemporary antisemitism, has documented mass media antisemitism in various Muslim countries, even beyond the Arab world, noting that few voices have uttered even a word of objection. He argues that in the Muslim world, "native antibodies to anti-Semitism are pitifully lacking. . . . What's worse, the disease flows largely from the top, those nominally responsible for maintaining the public health: government officials, educators, opinion-makers, religious authorities and the like."[60]

According to Tufail Ahmad, who conducted a careful but nonquantitative study, the situation in Pakistan—far from the epicenter of the Palestinian-Israeli conflict—has been deteriorating in recent years. In 2011 he wrote:

> By 2010, it could be said that not a week passed . . . without a religious leader, a columnist, or a politician issuing a statement against Israel and the Jewish people, blaming them as well as the United States and India for one or another of the problems facing Pakistan. Although not all criticism of Israel can be described as antisemitic, it does not appear that the Pakistani leaders in their own minds see subtle differences between their hateful ideological sloganeering against the Jews and possibly justified criticism of Israel's policies.[61]

It may well be that large numbers lower down in the social structure in many parts of the Muslim world find the hatred coming from above to be abhorrent. But, if this is so, they are cowed by social pressures to engage in only the most passive form of resistance; that is, refusing to add their own voices to the din.

Of course, the degree of anti-Jewish indoctrination varies greatly in the various Islamic-majority countries and among different segments of the population. It would be useful to have a systematic country-by-country review of such practices, especially with an eye toward identifying hopeful models for replication. But that task unfortunately lies beyond the scope of this book. Still, it is hard to imagine how people in Muslim-majority countries could develop a positive impression of Jews when there is so much socialization for hatred.

Biased Books, Biased Teachers

Perhaps one of the most important ways children are indoctrinated is via the formal educational system. In 2011 Hannah Rosenthal, the U.S. Department of State special envoy to combat and monitor antisemitism, correctly dubbed Saudi Arabia "the epicenter of much anti-Semitic teaching, textbooks, and curriculum development that are exported all over the world."[62] Materials of Saudi origin, sponsored by the government and paid for with oil dollars, have poisoned the minds of countless children in many Muslim-majority countries. Saudi anti-Jewish educational materials even found their way into Muslim schools in Fairfax County, Virginia, according to a 2008 study conducted by the U.S. Commission on International Religious Freedom.[63] And in 2010, the British found similar antisemitic curricular materials being used at more than forty Saudi-sponsored schools and clubs across the United Kingdom; about five thousand youngsters attend the schools.[64]

Back in 2003, a study examined some salient themes in Saudi textbooks: Christians and Jews are denounced as infidels, the West is portrayed as decadent and responsible for suffering in the Muslim world, and terrorism is rejected unless it constitutes jihad and martyrdom.[65] The Saudi materials also teach that the penalty for being gay is death. And finally they say that Jews are wicked, sly, deceptive, and aggressive. Since Israel is not recognized as a state by Saudi Arabia, it cannot be found on maps in these textbooks.

More recently, a 2008 study determined that very little progress had been made since the earlier study—despite American protests and Saudi promises. The later report, for example, found an eighth-grade dictation book including the sentence, "Now it [Palestine] is occupied by Jews, a people of treachery and betrayal." A tenth-grade text dealing with the hadith and Islamic culture listed among the Zionists' methods "attempting to immerse the peoples in vices, and spreading prostitution." A ninth-grade text included a fill-in-the-blank question: "This Prophetic Saying demonstrates one of the Jews' traits, which is _____." The correct answer was "cowardice." Tenth graders were asked to write an essay: "Deduce [from the text] some of the Jews' traits which necessitate caution and avoidance of [any] dealing with them at present."[66] And Palestinian textbooks are worse.[67]

The problems with some Muslim education systems do not stop with the textbooks. In 1998 a group of Palestinian Authority historians gathered together to discuss how they might present the history of the region in way that advanced the struggle against Israel.[68] This meeting took place at a time when the Palestinian Authority was ostensibly Israel's partner in the Oslo peace process. The historians expressed a commitment to using the "past" to reinforce the message that Israel has no right to exist. Thus, Jirar al-Qidwa, a leading historian and later chairman of the PA Public Library, asserted that the Biblical Hebrews were, in fact, Arabs. He said, "They were Arab tribes and among the purest. . . . And believe me, in Allah's name, that my blood has more of the Israelites' blood and the blood of the ancient Hebrews than does the blood of Netanyahu and Sharon."[69] In October 2006 Dr. Hassan Khader claimed on television that the Jews had no ancient historical link to the Western (Wailing) Wall in Jerusalem, widely regarded as one of Judaism's holiest sites. He announced, "The first connection of the Jews to this site began in the sixteenth century. . . . The Jewish connection to this site is a recent connection, not ancient . . . like the roots of the Islamic connection."[70] Of course, reputable historians in the West would not countenance any of these theories.

Dr. Khader Abbas, a psychology professor at Gaza's Al-Aqsa University, announced, "From the moment the [Jewish] child is born, he nurses hatred against others, nurses seclusion, nurses superiority." Abbas offered a theory of antisemitism that blamed the victim. Using the word "Israelis" but from the context meaning Jews, he said, "The Israelis brought it on themselves, I emphasize, brought it on themselves in every society they lived, disasters and massacres. First, they concentrated money in their hands, denying it to others. Second, they spied against the nations where they lived. And the third important and basic aspect: they were condescending. . . . Thus the people of the societies they were in took revenge against them, or tried to punish them."[71]

One does not need to wonder what some college students and scholars-in-training are taking away from these professors' classes—and what might happen in some regions to the career of a student who took it upon himself or herself to reassess prevailing attitudes toward Israel or even Jews. Socialization, after all, continues for intellectuals.

There are many better scholars than Jirar al-Qidwa and Khader Abbas in Muslim-majority countries, but few who are willing to evaluate Israel's case with an open mind, and fewer still who will bend over backward to understand their opponents as they do at, say, Tel Aviv University. But in Western countries, the situation for Muslim and Arab intellectuals is different. They are socialized with an entirely different set of academic values, and some have broken through the mind-set that prevails in some Muslim-majority countries. The previously mentioned impact of multiple concurrent identities comes into play, along with the protections of an open marketplace of ideas. Thus, one finds a fuller range of opinions about Israel and much less overt antisemitism.

Muslim secular writer Irfan Khawaja, who—as previously discussed—believes that the "antisemitic" label is too often applied to critics of Israel, nonetheless concedes that

far too many Arabs and Muslims grow up with the belief that God commands them to side with the Palestinians against the Israelis in that conflict.

Without bothering to acquaint themselves with facts or context, such people come to believe that the history of the dispute consists of nothing but Israeli atrocities against Arabs. In this view of things, the Arabs are nothing but victims, and the Israelis nothing but aggressors; the Arabs are responsible for nothing, and the Israelis are responsible for everything. From such a view, it's easy enough to slide into conspiracy theorizing, and from there to the belief that the Jews are a corrupt and diabolical race, while the Arabs are a noble and pure one. Unfortunately, this view of history has less to do with the pursuit of Palestinian rights than it does with role-playing, and does no one any real good, much less the Palestinians.[72]

Looking at all this, Cardinal Roberto Tucci concludes, "Today in all the Islamic world, in their media, the schools, there is an education of anti-Semitism . . . the worst anti-Semitism that you can imagine after that of the Nazis, or even equivalent to that of the Nazis." Perhaps he engages in overstatement; what we see is not yet equivalent to Nazism but it is, irrefutably, the worst antisemitism since the Nazis.

Further, one can make the case that Muslims are hurting their own children most of all, for a hater is not a good thing for a child to become. As a senator, Hillary Clinton noted that educating children to celebrate hatred and bigotry is a form of child abuse. In 2007, reviewing a report on antisemitism and other incitements to hatred in Palestinian textbooks, she concluded, "We cannot build a peaceful, stable, safe future on such a hate-filled, violent, and radical foundation."[73] She is right.

6

FIGHTING BACK AGAINST BIGOTRY

It is important to call bigotry by its name. In October 2004 a small group of Muslim and non-Muslim intellectuals in Turkey signed a petition, unprecedented in the Muslim-majority world, calling for "zero tolerance for antisemitism."[1] Lamenting an "ever-present and steadily increasing" hostility toward Jews even in that relatively Westernized and secular country, the signers proclaimed their determination "to become informed, to object, to write, to draw, to raise our voice, and to maintain solidarity with all who feel and think likewise."

According to the petition—published in *Birikim*, a tiny leftist monthly journal—Turkey's biggest problem came from its influential Islamist media, "a large segment of which has gone so far as to recklessly praise Adolf Hitler for his 'foresight.'" The petition also noted many "campaigns against so-called 'Sabbetaists' [Muslim Turks], whose Jewish roots are traced and emphasized in a manner reminiscent of the Nazi obsession with creating a 'pure race,' targeting them as the evil-intentioned members of a secret sect which is integral to the 'Jewish plot to dominate the world.'"

These "Sabbetaists" play a central and idiosyncratic role in the mind-set of many Turkish Islamist Jew-haters. Their name comes from Sabbetai Zevi, the seventeenth-century Jew who claimed to be the long-awaited messiah and headed a large but short-lived movement. The messianic flurry ended abruptly when the Ottoman sultan gave him the choice of death or conversion to Islam and Sabbetai Zevi chose Islam. He brought with him a number of followers, known as the *Dönmeh*. Some Islamist writers assign an outsized role to the descendants of these seventeenth-century converts to Islam—who are thought to be secret Jews acting partly in search of revenge.[2]

Most importantly, many Islamists believe that Kemal Ataturk, the father of modern Turkey, was a Dönmeh. Hence, the demise of the Ottoman sultanate, the end of the Islamic caliphate, and the rise of secular Turkey can all be tied, in a sense, to the Dönmeh. A bestselling book by Soner Yalçın, a writer associated with the influential newspaper *Hürriyet*, argued that, in light of the Dönmeh connection, Jews and crypto-Jews deserve blame for much that is evil in modern Turkey. Yalçın's book sold close to 200,000 copies.[3]

According to the *Birikim* petition as well as more recent research, antisemitism in Turkey has assumed many forms and is popular not only among Islamists, but also among ultranationalists and some leftists as well.[4] Thus, Islamists widely believe in *The Protocols of the Elders of Zion*, ultranationalists read *Mein Kampf* for its insights, and leftists frequently talk of Israel as an illegitimate Nazi state—all this in the Muslim country that had the most positive relationship with Israel and the best on-the-ground conditions for its small Jewish community. But now, in the context of increasingly feverish hostility toward Israel, Turkish Jews feel—more than ever—that they must hold their tongues to keep things from getting worse.[5]

Still, as historian Rifat N. Bali has argued, despite unbridled anger against Israel, intense beliefs in secret Jewish plots, and numerous other forms of antagonism toward Jews, few in Turkey admit that they are antisemitic. Islamists, for example, say, "Anti-Semitism is *haram* [forbidden] in our religion. One cannot have enmity against the Jew because of his religion/race. . . . As a matter of fact, we have seen in all parts of the world 'good Jews' who reacted to the murders [committed by] Israel."[6] Similarly, Selçuk Gültaşlı, Washington correspondent of the English-language Islamist periodical *Today's Zaman*, argued, "Being against racism of all sorts is a distinctive characteristic and is an integral part of any Muslim. . . . However, we must never allow the difference between anti-Semitism and anti-Zionism to be blurred."[7] And Turkish leftists, too, believe that they possess immunity to the antisemitic virus by creed and constitution, as all leftists oppose racism and prejudice.

Even so, the *Birikim* petition concluded, "When people cannot make sense of a complex world, they need to create and isolate 'enemy others.' Historically Jews have been, and still are, the target of that 'need.'" Moreover, "this rising tide of antisemitism has been allowed to flow unhindered in the channels of the Islamist as well as the mainstream media, and to settle into Turkish daily life and discourse. It is now second nature to find a 'Jewish finger' under every stone, and to invent various conspiracy theories with 'the Jew' as the villain." Thus, some Turks seem to have found a way to be antisemitic despite their supposed ideological incapacities.

The *Birikim* petition also took on those elements of the liberal and human rights community who ignored the problem or who, "when forced to confront it, merely subsume it under the rubric of discrimination, and ignore its vehemence." Although the mainstream media in Turkey are not obsessed with Jews in the way that the Islamists and the ultranationalists are, the petition explained that many "publications have become vehicles for promoting confusion regarding concepts such as Nazism, fascism, Zionism, the Holocaust, genocide, etc., emptying these of their [true] content and blurring their differences."

The petition further noted, insightfully, "As long as a danger is not properly articulated, it cannot be fought against. On the contrary: Vague words only conceal the evil." Finally, the signers of the petition were on target when they asserted, "The historical specifics of antisemitism, its geographical pervasiveness, and its all-encompassing class, social, and cultural basis deserve to be dealt with as a separate issue."

It is never enough in the case of antisemitism or any other form of bigotry merely to recite formulaic denunciations and condemnations of "racism and prejudice in all its forms." Certainly, opponents of various forms of bigotry and hatred must be consistent and must avoid double standards. Moreover, for obvious moral reasons, no battle against a specific bigotry can be against only that particular bigotry. Alliances among activists are crucial, and morally serious people have an obligation to consider the plights of all who suffer mistreatment. But focusing on one type of bigotry does not imply lack of concern about other types. And, too often, opposition to "all forms of injustice" has been merely a smoke screen used to justify inaction. When, for example, in response to charges of antisemitism, a person claims to oppose "all forms of prejudice," much depends of whether they use this line as a dismissive ploy or follow up with more focused interest and action.

After all, battles must be fought on specific battlefields. At a minimum, generic sentiments of antiracism that fail to provide details and name names reflect the height of intellectual laziness. The world, after all, is a complex place, and little agreement exists about what constitutes unacceptable bigotry. One must always state precisely the forms of expression and behavior that one condemns and establish how one will adjudicate among competing claims in a particular context. Does one, for example, believe that religion-based prejudice should be exempt from condemnation on the grounds that criticism of a particular religion is, in itself, antireligious bigotry? Moreover, one must document as specifically as possible the nature, extent, locus, and implications of the hatred; to fail to expose these specifics is to shield bigotries from countermeasures. Nonspecific, cursory, and dismissive condemnations of prejudice, those that avoid the specifics, can, arguably, be worse than no condemnations at all.

The Turkish signers of the *Birikim* petition handled all these issues boldly and well. Unfortunately, although not unexpectedly, their petition had little impact, and their efforts were largely in vain. Most mainstream media in and out of Turkey ignored the petition altogether; some on the left, predictably, pronounced it guilty of Israel-support and of mislabeling anti-Zionism as antisemitism.[8] So Jew-hatred in Turkey continues to grow.

It will be clear, however, that the struggle against antisemitism in the Muslim world is beginning to succeed when petitions like the one in *Birikim* (with its circulation of around a thousand) appear in the mainstream press of Muslim-majority countries and when they are signed by thousands, tens of thousands, hundreds of thousands, or even millions—and not just by a handful of Don Quixote intellectuals, possibly a fifth of whom were Jewish.[9] Indeed, the petitioners' call for intellectual honesty and zero tolerance is much needed, not only in the Muslim world, but also among the governments, human rights organizations, religious leaders, and intellectuals of the West.

The Varieties of Muslim Anti-Antisemitism

Needless to say, it would be best for Muslims to lead the fight against Jew-hatred in the Muslim world. But, the question is, which Muslims? As has been seen, one cannot assume that just because someone has been dubbed a moderate, progressive, or liberal, he or she will automatically reject Jew-hatred, much less oppose it vocally and publicly.

In a 2009 *Wall Street Journal* article, Amr Bargisi and Sam Tadros, two affiliates of the Egyptian Union of Liberal Youth, claimed to expose "a dirty little secret about [Egypt's] self-described liberal parties: they are, for the most part, virulently anti-Semitic." The authors backed up this contention with examples that have little or nothing to do with the Arab-Israeli conflict. Thus, they reported that Khairi Ramadan, a popular talk show host and columnist for Egypt's largest "liberal" newspaper, speaks of Jewish conspiracies to control the American presidency, Jews avoiding the World Trade Center on 9/11, and Jews bringing down the Lehman Brothers firm by withdrawing $400 billion a couple of weeks before its collapse.[10] Bargisi and Tadros also told of another columnist from the "liberal" Wafd Party's newspaper who was angry at President Obama for insisting in his Cairo speech that the Holocaust was a historical event. More recently, in July 2011 the vice chairman of the Wafd Party declared the Holocaust a "lie" and Anne Frank's memoir a "fake."[11]

According to Bargisi and Tadros, "anti-Semitism remains the glue holding Egypt's disparate political forces together. This is especially true of the so-called liberals, who think they can traffic on their anti-Semitism to gain favor in quarters where they would otherwise be suspect." Bargisi notes elsewhere that although Egypt and Israel are officially at peace, "the Egyptian state and the country's newspapers go out of their way to make a leper of any author who expresses even remote sympathy with Israel."[12]

When asked in 2011 whether the situation regarding antisemitism had improved, Bargisi replied, "I am afraid not, and it will not change unless Western sympathizers get over the idea of one good unified 'opposition' in Egypt."[13] Time will tell whether Jew-hatred in Egypt will increase, decrease, or stay the same in response to political developments. But Bargisi and Tadros's point remains important: one must go beyond labels and listen to what people are actually saying.

Similarly, not all Muslim and Arab condemnations of Jew-hatred are equivalent in sincerity, motivation, accuracy, scope, and impact. Various shades and styles of opposition to antisemitism have emerged—some brave beyond belief, some manipulative and disingenuous. Collectively, there are not many Muslim anti-antisemites, but their messages can be significant. One might identify three overlapping strands of limited opposition to antisemitism along with frontal assaults on anti-Jewish hatred launched by a number of intrepid souls.

One group of restrained anti-antisemites can be classified as "hear no evil, see no evil, speak no evil" progressives. They state publicly, sometimes repeatedly, that antisemitism, like Islamophobia and other prejudices, is wrong. However, they avoid reference to specific instances, understate the dimensions of the problem, and whitewash its religious and cultural sources. Sometimes they speak only in response to the accusations of others outside Islam. Some highlight their opposition to racism "in all its forms," possibly naming antisemitism on a list, possibly not. Sometimes, one hears that Islam, like all religions, is not immune to prejudice and that when prejudice does occur, it is as wrong as when it happens in any other religion. This statement is, of course, correct, but it is vague and incomplete. It is only a starting point from which serious discussion may emerge. Moreover, some critics of antisemitism offer liberal and tolerant readings of classic Islamic sources but downplay the extent to which other, more regressive readings command large followings.

At its worst, this category of opposition to antisemitism can sound more like a public relations campaign for Islam than a genuine antibigotry program. However, often the opposition seems sincere, and when this is the case their words have the potential for constructive impact. "Hear no evil, see no evil, speak no evil" progressives may also be taking additional steps behind the scenes to combat antisemitism. They may be motivated, in part, by a natural and common desire not to speak disrespectfully about their coreligionists and not to air their religion's dirty laundry in public. Moreover, some Muslims in the West, like other Westerners, may lack awareness of the depth and extent of hostility to Jews in some Muslim-majority countries. Finally, opponents of antisemitism may deliberately play down the scope of Jew-hatred in the Muslim world because they believe doing so is good tactics. After all, one may in fact be more effective in winning over believers by drawing attention away from the deeper sources of antagonism toward Jews in Muslim religion and culture. It may—at least sometimes—make sense to emphasize the positive.

A second group of restrained anti-antisemites might be called the "let's keep it respectable" progressives. They speak out against one or perhaps a few of the grossest manifestations of antisemitism, including Holocaust denial, Nazi sympathizing, references to *The Protocols*, or use of "pigs and apes" as a designation for Jews. Their opposition to these instances of Jew-hatred, however, does not lead them to a generally more positive reorientation of thinking about Jews. And although their discontent with extreme or gutter-style manifestations of Jew-hatred may be genuine, something about the perspective calls to mind the famous definition of an antisemite as someone who hates the Jews more than is necessary.[14]

Nonetheless, the prevalence of Holocaust denial seems to disturb quite a few Arab and Muslim intellectuals, and when conferences dedicated to "research" on the matter have been proposed or held, there have been numerous condemnations.[15] Many educated Muslims and Arabs see Holocaust denial as an intellectually indefensible position and are willing to say so publicly. Thus, progressive writer Basem Muhammad Habib denounced the stupidity and moral repugnance of Holocaust denial, noting, "There is no connection at all between the reality of the Holocaust and what has happened in Palestine. These are two different matters that [occurred in different] times and places, and we can assess each of them independently of the other. [Only] then . . . will our judgment be free and grounded in correct values and sincere sentiments."[16] And Aziz Abu Sarah, a Palestinian research associate at George Mason University, also spoke strongly against Holocaust denial, exploring some of his prior reluctance to think about the Nazi murder of European Jewry. He explained poignantly, "Deep down, I think I felt that by acknowledging the victims' pain, I would betray or marginalize my own suffering. Also, some part of me feared that if I sympathized with 'the enemy,' my right to struggle for justice might be taken away. Now I know that this is nonsense: you are stronger when you let your humanity overcome enmity. However, it took me time to learn this lesson."[17] Sarah now works with bereaved Jewish and Palestinian families to promote peace.

But even some anti-Zionists want no part of grossly disreputable Jew-hatred. For example, Sallah 'Issa objected strongly to the exhibition of *The Protocols of the Elders of Zion* as a sacred book of the Jews in the Library of Alexandria, Egypt. He argued:

> The newspapers that highlighted this stupid event [could have] refrained from shaming the library, and giving the Zionists and their allies an opportunity to accuse us of antisemitism and racism. . . . It is not very smart at all to espouse a book such as the 'Protocols of the Elders of Zion,' that attributes to the Jews the honor of being the ones to plan the French Revolution, wave the mottoes of liberty, brotherhood, and equality, spur workers to establish trade unions, support political and ideological pluralism, and stand behind all revolutionary movements throughout history.[18]

Another example of a "let's keep it respectable" opponent of antisemitism is Khaled Al-Hroub, a Palestinian academic and journalist affiliated with Cambridge University. He advised Hamas to amend its antisemitic charter, suggesting that the document's inclusion of blatantly anti-Jewish hadiths and direct quotations from the forged *Protocols* would keep the organization from achieving its goals. In March 2009, with one eye on academic respectability and another on public relations in the West, Hroub wrote, "This may be the best moment to initiate a change in the charter—since Israeli society has collectively slid to the right, while the U.S. administration is interested in openness towards the problems of the region and wants to speak with all the sides." He described the antisemitic charter as a "gift" to Hamas's enemies and focused on the harm done by repetition of anti-Jewish canards that have been discredited in the West. But his position appeared entirely tactical, with moral arguments nowhere in sight.[19]

Regardless of motivation, condemnations of gross manifestations of Jew-hatred are usually constructive and welcome, even when they are badly insufficient. Sometimes sincerity is apparent. Often, it is difficult to tell whether the impetus behind such efforts is rooted in genuine disapproval of antisemitism, a desire to retain a respectable intellectual self-concept, a need to ward off denunciations of the Muslim community by Westerners, or something else.

Some of those who denounce only extreme instances of antisemitism may wish to go further but end up limiting their dissent to what their audience might deem acceptable. An example of this might be the Egyptian writer Hisham Al-Tuhi, who in 2007 denounced the use of "pigs and apes" epithets, claimed many Arabs have Jewish ancestors, and then went on—in the face of much criticism—to wish the Jews remaining in Arab countries a "happy Passover."[20] While this greeting might not amount to much, it symbolically seems to convey a desire to change the general mentality about Jews.

Another group of restrained anti-antisemites, "liberal" Israel-haters, oppose some manifestations of anti-Jewish bigotry but, in the same breath, enthusiastically uphold and defend their intense anger toward the Jewish state. Such opposition usually takes the form of "antisemitism is wrong but. . . ." Thus, when a spike in antisemitic incidents occurred in England during the 2008–2009 Gaza War—and that spike was attributed largely to Muslims and Arabs—some Muslim scholars in the United Kingdom proclaimed their opposition publicly. A petition from important community leaders stated:

> We unreservedly condemn attacks on innocent British citizens and the desecration of all places of worship. The ongoing killing of Palestinian civilians in Gaza by Israeli forces has angered us all. However, this does not, and cannot, justify attacks on our fellow citizens of Jewish faith and background here in Britain. Most Muslims are completely against such behaviour. However, we

call on all Muslims to continue to remain vigilant against attempts to bring our own faith and community into disrepute. British Jews should not be held responsible for the actions of the Israeli government.[21]

Jihad Khazen, a respected Arab journalist, summarizes the "liberal" Israel-hater's creed in the title of his article in the newspaper *Al-Hayat*: "Israel, Not the Jews, Is the Problem."[22] Khazen says Jews are neither better nor worse than other groups.

The question is, can one be an ardent Israel-hater while, at the same time, bearing no ill will toward Jews. The answer, I think, is no. For one thing, as I have argued, the emotional intensity of Arab hostility toward Israel has its roots—to some degree—in a social and psychological inability to tolerate the Jewish emergence from dhimmi status. But, nowadays, antisemitism has become so intertwined with Arab anger toward Israel that it is difficult, if not impossible, to disentangle the two types of rage. A genuinely liberal Israel-hater would have to eschew demonization of Israel and the use of double standards in evaluating its conduct. He or she would be unable to embrace the total delegitimization of Israel without denying Jews the same rights to national identity that all other people are permitted by liberal creed. And if one were to disown demonization, delegitimization, and double standards, one would no longer be a virulent Israel-hater. One might still offer abundant criticism of Israeli policies and stand firmly for Palestinian rights. But one would not be a hater. Moreover, to be a liberal Israel-hater, one would have to wage a battle against Hamas with its bigoted charter, against suicide bombers with their illiberal objectives, and against anti-Jewish socialization practices. Anti-antisemites such as Khazen believe it is necessary to retain Israel as the bogeyman of the Muslim world, but they do not believe that Jews, qua Jews, can be tarnished in the process. Whether this is possible and whether it represents progress seems questionable.[23]

It is hard to know the extent to which "liberal" Israel-haters oppose Jew-hatred out of conviction or in order to lend credibility to their attacks on Israel. The previously discussed British Gaza War petition, for example, stated, "The ongoing killing of Palestinian civilians in Gaza by Israeli forces has angered us all."[24] Thus, this condemnation of anti-Jewish violence (but not antisemitism per se) occurs in the same breath as an attempt to feed anger at Israel and to promote a vision of Israeli soldiers as those who target civilians. Just what impact this statement might have on Jew-hatred in London and the probability that a British jihadi might attack Jews is not known.[25] Also note that the British petition specifically limited its objection to violence against *British* Jews.

The "hear no evil, see no evil, speak no evil" progressives are sending a useful message, even though it is not all that it might be. Even the "let's keep it respectable" progressives and the "liberal" Israel-haters, arguably, reduce the amount of anger and hatred in public affairs. However, if opposition to some forms of hostility to Jews is used to provide cover for other types of unfair treatment, the activity may not amount to a net plus. But when Muslims and Arabs oppose antisemitism mainly to improve relations with the West, this may still be ultimately constructive. So, in a world where beggars can't be choosers, even halfhearted opponents of Jew-hatred are still, on balance, a good thing.

Heroic Opposition to Jew Hatred

Fortunately, some activists of Muslim and Arab origin whose integrity cannot be doubted and who offer fair-minded, insightful, and comprehensive challenges to Jew-hatred have emerged. In short, they say exactly what needs to be said. They acknowledge and publicize the extent to which Jew-hatred has come to dominate Muslim institutions and infect the minds of many Muslim believers. They locate the origins of this hatred in indigenous as well as imported sources. They call religious and political leaders to task for spreading hatred. They demand and defend a tolerant reading of the sacred texts and sometimes find ways to counteract or reinterpret religious sources that have promoted hostility toward Jews and other nonbelievers. They also call for a total rejection of the antisemitic tradition that was imported from Europe.

While not all Muslim progressives have spoken out against antisemitism, those who do nearly always also support political freedom and human rights in other realms. For example, virtually all anti-antisemites support extending and redefining the rights of women in Islam. Although opponents of Jew-hatred offer various perspectives on the Arab-Israeli conflict—some quite critical of Israel and some strongly advocating Palestinian interests—they all reject demonization and dehumanization of Israelis and delegitimization of the Jewish state.

Unequivocal opposition to antisemitism requires moral and physical courage anywhere in the Muslim world but much more so in the Muslim-majority countries of the Middle East. There is, after all, a long history in this region of vilifying, attacking, and sometimes killing those who go too far in supporting reconciliation with the Jews. King Abdullah of Jordan and President Sadat of Egypt come to mind first, but many, many more victims have paid a price for the crime of too much sympathy for the Jews.

Many of those who have spoken loudly against Jew-hatred in the Muslim world report death threats, although because most express numerous controversial opinions, it is sometimes unclear what exactly sparked the threats. Anyone seen by extremists to criticize Islam or the Prophet Muhammad in any way may face danger, even if he or she does not defend the Jews.[26] Still, some critics in the West report that the physical danger has been exaggerated and that mostly they face verbal attacks and ostracism.

When Irfan Khawaja, a clear-thinking opponent of antisemitism and a New Jersey academic who describes himself as "an ex-Muslim of a fairly militant 'new atheist' variety," was asked what issues cause critics the most trouble, he replied:

> There are so many that I don't know how to list or prioritize them. Anything that ties anti-Semitism to the Qur'an or Sunna will land you in hot water. Anything that directly challenges the evidential poverty of favorite conspiracy theories will land you there. Anything that suggests that you no longer identify with "us" (Arabs, Muslims) but identify with "them" (Jews, Zionists) will do it. (Obviously, being very pro-Israel will do it.) Getting paid well to denounce anti-Semitism will do it (whether in monetary terms, or in terms of prestige, adulation, etc.). Direct accusations of individual people will get you in hot water.[27]

It is not surprising, then, that the strongest condemnations, best analyses, and widest range of opinions on Muslim antisemitism have come mainly (but not exclusively) from those living in Western countries. In addition to providing haven from extremist criticism, life in the West offers more opportunities for positive everyday interactions with Jews as well as easier access to balanced media coverage of Jews and Israel.

Most Muslim reformist critics of Jew-hatred value their Muslim identity greatly, although they are frequently denounced as turncoats by extremists, Islamists, and even members of the Muslim mainstream in the West. The reformist critics do not offer a unified position regarding Islam, Jews, the Arab-Israeli conflict, politics, or anything else. They differ greatly in style, social values, and lifestyle. They also do not agree about which sources are most relevant or which types of argumentation are most appropriate. They all, however, speak from a humanistic vision, offering socially constructive, intellectually responsible, and morally honest perspectives.

Professor Khaleel Mohammed teaches religion at San Diego State University. In addition to holding a doctorate in Islamic law from McGill University, he studied in Saudi Arabia at the Imam Muhammad ibn Saud Islamic University. Thus, he is hardly an amateur in matters concerning Islamic law and tradition. Yet Mohammed boldly declared, "Anti-semitism has become an entrenched tenet of Muslim theology, taught to 95 per cent of the religion's adherents in the Islamic world."[28] Despite many verbal attacks from other Muslims—not only Islamists and extremists—Mohammed persists in arguing that the genuine Islamic attitude toward Jews is one of profound respect. He further believes—even more controversially—that, according to the Quran, Israel belongs to the Jews.

Professor Mohammed offered some insight into his motivation when in 2007 he wrote, "I write not only as an academic scholar of religion, but also in my role as a father, troubled by the pervasive anti-Jewish, anti-Western teachings that I know exist in some mosques."[29] In an earlier interview he said:

> Many Muslims stand against me for no other reason than I say that Israel has a right to exist. Overall . . . they are upset that I should give any legitimacy to Israel, assuming that in doing so, I am denying the rights of Palestinians. My answer [is] that I in no way deny that Palestinians have rights. But this is generally not considered by those that criticize my position: because for them, it is either all or nothing.[30]

Fortunately, the America-based Mohammed has reported that people argue against him and denounce him but that he has not been subject to the physical threats that some others have experienced. He explained:

> Whatever problem my fellow Muslims have with my views, they are aware that I am a Muslim. I do not deny my religion, and therefore we can argue. Here at San Diego State University where I teach, the local MSA [Muslim Student Association] attempted to have me disciplined for having accused them of anti-Semitism and homophobia. They did not pursue the issue—an

astute decision for they would have looked very foolish. Their answer was that they too are Semites (the writers of the letter were by the way not even Arabs), and that they could not be homophobic since their neighbors are gays and lesbians![31]

Sheikh Abdul Hadi Palazzi, from the Italian Muslim community, is another tireless opponent of antisemitism.[32] He goes so far as to describe himself as a Muslim Zionist, explaining that he arrived at this position partly by reading sacred Islamic texts. He strongly opposes the Wahhabi form of Islam that the Saudis have been exporting in recent decades and has labored to improve relations between Muslims and Jews. He asks Muslim audiences to recall that Islamic lands, for many years, were a refuge for Jews victimized by discrimination and persecution in Europe.[33] Palazzi wrote: "I really feel that 'silence is complicity,' and cannot but exhort other Muslim scholars to overcome fear and to take a clear and unquestionable stand. . . . Apart from representing a barrier against other similar forms of racial discrimination, a refutation of antisemitism from an Islamic point of view could also be one of the most relevant . . . [contributions] to interfaith dialogue and to cooperation between the different branches of the Abrahamitic family." He further believes that if Islamic scholars look at classical Islamic sources, they will find that these sources do not support "so-called 'Islamic anti-Zionism,' preached by radical groups in Middle East and abroad."[34]

The Canadian writer Irshad Manji agrees with Palazzi and Mohammed on many issues regarding the Jews.[35] However, her approach is more that of a hip Canadian journalist and cultural critic who draws on an idiosyncratic reading of Islam. The *New York Times* once called her "Osama bin Laden's worst nightmare," and Indonesia's *Jakarta Post* listed her as one of three women creating positive change in Islam.[36] She is a lesbian, and that alone earns her enemies in many Islamic circles. Moreover, she does not bring high scholarly Islamic credentials to bear. But Manji argues convincingly—at least to some liberal-minded Westerners—and often employs humor as effectively as Khaleel Mohammed wields Islamic chapter and verse.

Manji obviously interacts frequently with Jews, Christians, and nonbelievers, she respects atheists and agnostics, and she refuses to cede rights to her Muslim religion to those with less progressive, less tolerant, or more mainstream approaches. Clearly, being Muslim is centrally important to her. For a while this brave woman required a bodyguard. But, ultimately, she did away with his services—not wanting to send the message that the only way one could speak truth to Muslims was with an armed man by her side.[37]

Others, including Morad El-Hattab El-Ibrahimi, have proposed Islamic solutions to Muslim antisemitism. Hattab is an influential French Muslim writer on diverse topics whose roots may go back to the fourth caliph of Islam. He acknowledges that "the Qur'an contains about ten [arguably anti-Jewish] verses which need to be looked at in relation to the circumstances of the time." But he ultimately concludes, "The barbaric violence perpetrated against our Jewish brothers and sisters is reprehensible and has nothing to do with our faith." Moreover, he places blames squarely on "misguided jihadists, paltry preachers, and literal-minded Muslims." He claims they are "undermining and ruining our culture, denying the mystical and Sufi heritage and preventing men and women who might have believed in our tradition from turning to it. Then afterwards [they tearfully complain or threaten]: 'They [meaning outsiders] are criticizing Islam, they are insulting religion.'"[38]

German professor Bassam Tibi is another important Muslim fighter against antisemitism. Descending from many generations of leading Islamic scholars in Syria, he served as a visiting professor at the now-defunct Yale Initiative for the Interdisciplinary Study of Antisemitism.[39] Although he claims to know the Quran by heart and is immensely proud of his Islamic heritage, Tibi reports that he is regularly denounced as a tool of the Jews. He advocates a wide-ranging reform of Islam. Yet he notes that while traditional Islam was not free of anti-Jewish content, full-fledged antisemitism is a creation of the modern era. In particular, he believes that Islamists completely subscribe to antisemitism as it was Islamized by the mid-twentieth-century radical Islamist Sayyid Qutb. Moreover, he attributes the lack of conflict resolution in the Middle East to this "Islamization of European antisemitism carried out by the Islamist movement."[40] The "religionization" of the issues has closed the door to negotiation. Yet, it should be noted, Tibi frequently criticizes the Israeli government.

Canadian Tarek Fatah also deserves special attention for the scholarship, guts, and forthrightness he brings to the topic in his provocative 2010 book, *The Jew Is Not My Enemy: Unveiling the Myths That Fuel Muslim Anti-Semitism*. Fatah is a journalist, not a theologian, but he is learned in Islamic matters. Some of his views on the hadith and early biographies of Muhammad as sources of Muslim antisemitic thinking have been covered in earlier chapters. More generally, Fatah shows awareness of the many sources—imported and indigenous, distant and recent—of Muslim hostility to Jews. He has written, "We need to stand up to members of our community who spread hate against the Jew, the atheist, the apostate, the Hindu, and the Christian and then hide behind the Quran. We should not hesitate to say they are hate-mongers and cowards."[41]

Fatah has discussed the origin of his book. On a 2006 trip to Pakistan, he grew appalled by the extensiveness of antisemitic conspiracy theories and decided that he needed to write a book about Islamic Jew-hatred. Yet, after some preliminary research, he heeded his wife's advice and dropped the idea. She told him, "You will end up antagonizing both the Jews as well as the Arabs. . . . This is not your fight and no good will come of it." But, ultimately, Fatah could not abide by this decision when, in November 2008, Pakistani jihadis murdered a rabbi, his pregnant wife, and other members of the local Jewish community in Mumbai. In addition to being horrified by the overall scope of the attack that left 166 dead, he wondered, "Why would a group of Punjabi villagers seek out a Jewish centre in a densely populated part of Mumbai to massacre Jews? It is unlikely they could ever have met a Jew, let alone have a grievance with him, yet they had been brainwashed by their Islamist handlers to the extent that they were willing to die to kill a few Jews. What had the Jews done to Pakistan?" Fired up, he returned to the book project, resolving to "end this cancer before it consumes us Muslims."[42]

Yet Fatah would not go so far as to identify himself as a Muslim Zionist, and in places he is very critical of Israel.[43] But he objects to Israeli deeds and policies without antisemitism and without denying Israel's right to exist. According to Fatah, "For me, a discussion about Muslim-Jewish relations or the Arab-Israeli dispute becomes a non-starter the moment the right of Israel to exist as a Jewish state is challenged. Having said that, I firmly believe Israel, in continuing its occupation of the West Bank, is in serious violation of international law. I am against this occupation not because I am a Muslim, but because I am against the occupation of any people by a foreign country."[44] Unlike many others who oppose the Israeli occupation, Fatah also calls attention to the Saudi occupation of Arabia, Sudan's occupation of Darfur, Morocco's occupation of Western Sahara, and the lack of a homeland for the Kurds because of opposition from Turkey, Iraq, Syria, and Iran. One can, then, disagree with Fatah about Israel, but one cannot easily accuse him of employing the double standards that are the hallmark of the unfair critic. Although many of his specific contentions about the Arab-Israeli conflict remain far from the mainstream pro-Israeli consensus, one has the sense that if most Muslim and Palestinian leaders thought like Tarek Fatah, the Arab-Israeli conflict might be resolved in an afternoon.

While most of the prominent Western anti-antisemites of Muslim origin advance minority Islamic positions, propose some reinterpretation of the faith, or call for a reformation of sorts, some have abandoned Islam altogether. Partly their apostasy may stem from dissatisfaction with treatment of Jews, but usually it is the product of more general discontent. Vocal ex-Muslim opponents of antisemitism include, among others, Ayaan Hirsi Ali, Nonie Darwish, Wafa Sultan, Mark Gabriel, Ibn Warraq, Kamel Al-Najjar, and Irfan Khawaja.[45]

Dr. Kamel Al-Najjar is a British surgeon who is often sharply critical of Muslim practices. Najjar, for example, criticizes some Muslim leaders whom he believes falsely claim that they are open to serious interfaith and intercultural dialogue:

> How can we call for co-existence between religions when the religious scholars of Al-Azhar, Najaf, and Qom say every day that the Bible and the New Testament are falsified, that Christians are polytheists because they worship the Trinity, and that Jews are the descendants of apes and pigs? [When] every Friday, the [Muslim] worshipers call upon Allah to eradicate the Jews, and when the Muslims ridicule the Hindus for worshiping a cow? Who are those who [supposedly] call for [dialogue]? Are they religious scholars who believe in the superiority of Islam?[46]

Some ex-Muslim critics of antisemitism have adopted Christianity; others have become atheists or agnostics. Most have acquired reputations for their strongly unfavorable views of their former faith. Thus, many Muslims and some non-Muslims argue that these critics' outlook on Islam is intemperate, unbalanced, insufficiently precise, angry, or unaware of liberal and reform movements in the faith. In defense of the apostates, however, it should be noted that many are reacting to disturbing personal experiences with the religion, especially once they became individuals seeking to leave the fold.[47] It is also important to remember that one of the hallmarks of freedom in the West has long been tolerance for intemperate intellectual criticism of religion, and some of the greatest intellectual figures did not pull punches when criticizing the faith they had abandoned. Recall, for example, the attitudes of Spinoza, Voltaire, Bertrand Russell, Sigmund Freud, and Karl Marx. Out of this criticism, the West has made many advances.[48]

Ex-Muslims are widely—and perhaps understandably—denounced by many practicing Muslims. Muslim scholars disagree about whether apostasy should be punished by death or whether punishment comes only in the afterlife. But clearly, in the eyes of most Muslims, while people should enter the religion as a matter of free choice, one cannot convert out of Islam. There is also a general sense that public apostasy—for example, leaving and then criticizing the faith—is considerably worse than private apostasy. However, those of us with true progressive values should not dismiss the voices of public apostates. It is, whatever any religion says, a basic human right to make one's own decisions about matters of faith. And while one ought not assume that experiences of converts and nonbelievers are typical, neither should one disregard their perspectives.

Irfan Khawaja has noted that people often regard apostasy as

> a quixotic position to take, and often object to it by claiming that they cannot imagine very many Muslims abandoning their faith. But that objection has always seemed irrelevant to me, and also subtly misinformed. It's misinformed because I think it misses the fact that there are pockets of atheism in the Muslim world that are concealed to view only because the people in those pockets lack the freedom to express themselves. Given the freedom to do so, I suspect that many, many nominal Muslims would [become apostates]. The objection is irrelevant because it doesn't really matter what proportion of the population would apostasize and what proportion wouldn't. What matters (to me) is that apostasy is intellectually justified, that people should have the freedom to engage in it, and that they should feel empowered to do it if they wish. Even if that's 1% of the aggregate, 1% of 1.25 billion people is enough for me.[49]

This is not the place to judge the appropriateness of ex-Muslim writings in general. Neither can we determine whether apostasy represents a legitimate reaction to extremism. But we should accept the apostates' testimony as one source of insight into Muslim antisemitism.

The Central Problem

For those concerned about ending this bigotry, however, it is an inescapable fact that neither the ex-Muslim opponents of antisemitism nor the reformist Muslim opponents of antisemitism have large followings. Herein lies a critical problem. There are, by now, numerous Muslims writers who have strongly condemned anti-semitism in terms that are highly credible and morally admirable. But the most truthful and the most forthright may not be the most useful in changing the at-titudes of mainstream Muslims. The most tolerant and sympathetic toward Jews are the least likely to be influential in Muslim-majority countries and even in mainstream Islamic circles in the West. There is, indeed, an inverse relationship between how strongly one condemns antisemitism and how warmly one will be received in most mainstream circles. And, in Islamist circles, condemnation of antisemitism is nearly always at best a ticket to the door.

Still, it is hard to gauge how much quiet support there is among Muslims in the West and elsewhere for those who condemn antisemitism in strong, specific, clear, and forthright terms. Moreover, there may be a large group that condemns most Jew-hatred but persists in supporting demonization, delegitimization, and double standards regarding Israel.

One Muslim website, Muslimmatters.org, provides some perspective on the extent to which some of the chief opponents of antisemitism are regarded as "fringe" Muslims. A statement on the Web page describes the site as "primarily addressing Muslims residing in the West; MuslimMatters also serves as a reliable source for non-Muslims seeking information about the faith of Islam and glob-al community of Muslims. We strive to: Embody truthfulness and moderation through a commitment to scholarship, creativity, critical thinking, education, and cultural diversity."[50] Writers associated with the website seem to think of them-selves as either mainstream or progressive Muslims.

A well-received article on MuslimMatters.org titled "Tarek Fatah Does NOT Represent Me: Muslims 101 for Media" strongly objected to what it saw as the Western media's tendency to overemphasize reformist Muslims.[51] The article started by asking the reader to imagine a fictional woman: "Reverend Kathy Lis-bon, a leftist, gay & lesbian, ardent pro-choice activist, representing the 10 people of the Protestant Church of Noone was asked about the use of birth-control by Catholics." The writer then asked, "In what capacity would the imaginary Kathy Lisbon, regardless of her claims of Christianity, discuss issues about mainstream

Catholicism (which for the most part rejects pro-choice and homosexuality)?" He concluded:

> If fringe opinions are used, then at least shouldn't mainstream views also be obtained? And wouldn't it be fairer if the views were published in proportion to the views held? So, if 1% held a certain Islamic opinion versus 99% holding an opposite view, shouldn't the space and press devoted to the 1% be close to 1% and not close to 90% as it is now? . . . So, "media": please start doing . . . homework before reporting Muslim opinion. Please STOP picking out any Muslim (by name or claim) to represent the mainstream, everyday Muslim, even if he claims "subject expertise" but is not widely followed by Muslims.

He then elaborated:

> So, I am sick of Tarek Fatah's tirades, the Communications Director of the fringe organization Muslim Canadian Congress. The fact is that most of his positions are outright unIslamic and unrepresenting [*sic*] of the vast majority of Muslims. For instance, his organization endorsed same-sex marriage, campaigned against Islamic family courts, and pretty much came out on the wrong side of every mainstream Muslim opinion. So, WHY, does any of the media give ANY credibility to this tiny group of fringe nut-cases?
>
> While I am at it, let me also tell you who else does NOT represent the vast majority of Muslims.

The author then listed several other reformers and explained his objections. When he got to Irshad Manji, he simply listed her name and wrote, "Do I need to say more?" At the end of the article, there was a link to the "Tarek Fatah Does Not Represent Me" Facebook group.[52]

Like Irfan Khawaja, many other reformers believe that more Muslims agree with them than are willing to say so publicly and loudly. In the introduction to her 2011 book *Allah, Liberty and Love: The Courage to Reconcile Faith and Freedom*, Manji, one of the most radical perhaps and least grounded in Muslim traditional ways, cited a girl, Ayesha, who e-mailed her saying, "Millions think like you but are afraid to go public with their views for fear of persecution." The author further noted that free online translations of her previous book, *The Trouble with Islam*, had been downloaded more than two million times; many who downloaded the work lived in Arab countries and in Iran (where the book was banned).[53] But, still, it is important to recognize the deep unpopularity, even in many Western Muslim circles, of those who reject antisemitism loudly, specifically, and without reservation.

Yet, not all worthwhile criticism of antisemitism comes from those widely, if unfairly, regarded as "fringe" Muslims. The problem is that as leaders get closer to the mainstream, their approaches, however well intentioned, become incomplete and inaccurate:

◆ At the Simon Wiesenthal Center's Museum of Tolerance, King Hussein of Jordan said in 1995—before the Oslo peace process fell apart—"The Christian-Islamic tradition of tolerance and coexistence in mutual respect has happily survived in the Middle East despite the events and attempts that have threatened, even sought, to undermine it. As we consolidate and develop this tradition, we shall now work to revive the equally noble Judeo-Islamic tradition, which also endured for centuries, though it was temporarily overshadowed by the Arab-Israeli conflict. . . . For our part, we shall continue to work for the new dawn when all the children of Abraham and their descendants are living together in the birthplace of their three great monotheistic religions, a life free from fear, a life free from want—a life in peace."[54] A decade later, King Abdullah II of Jordan called for interfaith cooperation—to include Jews—and noted similarities among Islam, Judaism, and Christianity.[55]

◆ A number of years ago, one of President Mubarak's top advisers, Osama El-Baz, wrote a series of constructive newspaper articles systematically attacking several antisemitic positions. From his influential perch, he said Arabs should stop thinking about Jews in terms of conspiracy, stop expressing sympathy for Nazis, and stop using the Star of David in cartoons that criticize Israeli policy and officials. He also said that Muslims should cease making "improper use of the Koran by describing the Jews as the sons of apes and pigs, as it is clear that the words of the Koran on the matter of this metamorphosis do not mean that all the Children of Israel or the Jews were punished with this punishment. . . . Similarly, we do not know for certain whether the transformation was physical or used as a metaphor and an image."[56]

◆ Basharat (Bashy) Tahir Quraishy, a European antiracist activist and promoter of interfaith cooperation, was president of the largest European Union network against racism, one that had over seven hundred member organizations. He wrote, "Since Jewish and Muslim communities are two major victims of [cultural and religious discrimination in Europe], they have a common cause to join forces. I know this is not a traditional logic but in the struggle for a discrimination-free society, we do have a common destiny. It has always been my personal understanding and conviction that without concrete cooperation with Jewish communities in Europe, Muslim groups will have difficulty in tackling Islamophobia. Both Jewish and Muslim people have to grasp the fact that antisemitism and Islamophobia are two sides of the same coin."[57]

◆ Sayyid M. Syeed has also taken a lead in the interfaith movement. He is a former president of the Muslim Students Association and the national director for the Office for Interfaith and Community Alliances for the Islamic Society of North America (ISNA), an umbrella organization with many affiliates all over the United States and Canada. In 2011 Syeed declared, "As Muslims, we must understand that there is absolutely no place for antisemitism in Islam, and we must speak out against all instances of antisemitism, wherever they may occur."[58]

◆ Palestinian leader Salam Fayyad has declared—at least to a Western audience in Colorado—that Jews will be welcome in a future Palestinian state. This contrasts with the more common assertion that despite the general agreement that Palestinian Arabs will remain in Israel as citizens, all Jewish settlers will have to be relocated to Israel. Fayyad said, in response to a question, "Jews, to the extent they choose to stay and live in the state of Palestine, will enjoy those rights and certainly will not enjoy any less rights than Israeli Arabs enjoy now in the state of Israel."[59]

Although they are constructive, these messages have clear limitations. Kings Hussein and Abdullah II, as Jordanian heads of state, offered appropriate, well-intentioned, and broad guidelines, but they were important primarily because of their source. Listeners remained free to interpret their messages in an infinite variety of ways. Judged by their comments to Western audiences, both kings seem progressive. But there has been no effective follow-through with domestic audiences; after all, both Jordanian kings operated in the shadow of the first King Abdullah, who was assassinated because of his overtures to the Jews. Osama El-Baz was an important voice of reason on many issues, yet he was associated with the discredited Mubarak regime. Also, despite his high-level connections, El-Baz was always, as Gabriel Schoenfeld wrote, "a soloist, and a carefully restrained one at that" in his opposition to Jew-hatred the Muslim world.[60] Sayyid Syeed says some of the right things and takes some useful steps, but he is not clear about the roots and extent of antisemitism in the Muslim world or its connection to demonization of Israel. What's more, he has never really taken on, at least publicly, the anti-Jewish and extremist elements in the ISNA.[61] And even though Salam Fayyad has made his Colorado comments into policy proposals, his influence has waned in large part because segments of the Palestinian population regard him as too moderate. The Palestinian Authority, after all, signed a pact of reconciliation in 2011 with the openly antisemitic Hamas.

More generally, no mainstream Muslim leaders really are willing to address the issues identified by Khawaja as likely to land one in hot water. They don't address religious roots, take on people by name, or include any Israel-related attacks under the label of antisemitism. They tend to speak in glittering generalities and, as a result, can be as useful to those who wish to deny the scope and dimensions of the problem as to those who wish to address it. If a mainstream Muslim leader took the problem of antisemitism by its horns, he would in all likelihood encounter difficulty remaining a mainstream Muslim leader.

To some extent, it is the task of well-intentioned and sincere Muslims to figure out how to end Muslim antisemitism. As the Catholic theologians of Vatican Council II came to realize, Jew-hatred constituted as deep a threat to Catholicism as it did to Jews. Similarly, Muslim antisemitism challenges Islam as much as it attacks the Jews. The proper path may involve the mechanisms of orthodox Islamic religious faith. It may require moderate reform, radical reform, abandonment of Islamism, abandonment of political Islam, or—even—abandonment of faith. These are decisions for Muslims to make. It's not right for outsiders to weigh in, and in any case such outside stage management would likely prove counterproductive. But outsiders do have a right to insist that Muslims fix the problem.

It is not clear how to end antisemitism in Muslim and Arab populations while so many in these populations continue to demonize Israel. Still, even if only the non-Israel-related antisemitism issues are addressed initially, changes in attitudes toward the Jewish state might ultimately ensue. Muslims and Arabs will still advocate for Palestinian rights and still criticize Israel; differences arising from group interest and historical experiences will not disappear. But demonization, delegitimization, and double standards will diminish.

The first and most important step is to make the world safe for Muslim critics of antisemitism—physically safe, socially safe, organizationally safe, even academically safe. Many Muslim organizations in the West and in Muslim-majority countries claim, in principle, to oppose anti-Jewish bigotry. They should be held to their word and asked to defend and honor those who speak out forcefully against antisemitism. The policy of treating friends of the Jews as lepers has to end. Then, perhaps more Muslims would be able to offer and hear full-blooded critiques of Muslim antisemitism.

Huge amounts of money are likely to continue to flow to oil-rich countries, including some of the most antisemitic countries on earth. Given the proven value of Jew-hatred in distracting people from real concerns and from failures of the state, it will no doubt remain in the interest of some of these states to use portions of their wealth to foment hostility toward the Jews and Israel—domestically and abroad. None of this bodes well for the future.

But clearly the lead in battling antisemitism in the Muslim world has come from, and will continue to come from, progressive Muslims in the West. The periphery will lead the center. And even in the West, the struggle for justice and tolerance will be difficult. Yet, as Denis MacShane has noted, "An end to antisemitism is the beginning of a rebirth of the Arab peoples and their nations. A defeat for Islamist jihadism and Islamist fundamentalist denial of universal rights is a necessary, if insufficient, condition for Arab democracy to come into being and replace the various forms of authoritarianism in Arab states."[62]

What the Non-Muslim West Can Do

The first thing the West needs to do is to regain its perspective on antisemitism. There are no acceptable excuses for bigotry against the Jews, just as there are no acceptable excuses for bigotry against any other racial, ethnic, or religious group. As Anti-Defamation League leader Abraham Foxman has said, Westerners must "demand honesty from local and national authorities, civic organizations, and members of the news media in confronting words and deeds that embody hatred. Call attacks on Jews and Jewish institutions what they are—acts of antisemitism."[63] Moreover, they must recognize that although in every era Jew-hatred has manifested somewhat differently, contemporary Muslim Jew-hatred shares many continuities with antisemitism from other times and places. This hatred occupies a central position in the worldview of most Islamic extremists, but the virus has also spread far beyond the extremists and into parts of the Muslim mainstream. Consequently, the fight against antisemitism, including its Muslim strain, needs to become a central part of the battle against bigotry. To define the enemy simply as "racism and sexism" is, in this sense, inappropriate because it can lead to the omission of anti-Jewish prejudice.

What's more, opposition to antisemitism cannot focus exclusively on dead antisemites and antisemitism that comes from one's political opponents. Generic antiracist education, thus far, has proved unable to address Jew-hatred in the Muslim world because of its virulence, spread, impact on world affairs, and status as the latest installment of the world's longest and, arguably, deadliest prejudice. Similarly, Holocaust and genocide educational initiatives, although deeply important in their own right, have not proved suitable venues for dealing with contemporary Jew-hatred in the Muslim world. Thus, when Yale terminated YIISA, the only institute in the country that dealt with contemporary antisemitism effectively, it made a serious mistake. The new Yale Program for the Study of Antisemitism, established partly to quell objections to YIISA's closure, may go some distance toward rectifying that error, although—in light of what happened to its predecessor—it might choose to focus on more distant and less controversial forms of Jew-hatred.[64] Nonetheless, we in the West cannot accept toothless, halfhearted approaches to Jew-hatred in the contemporary world. To be sure, the fight against antisemitism should not focus exclusively on Islamic varieties, as one never knows where future danger lurks and vigilance is always wise.

Also, the fight against Holocaust denial is a critical one. President Obama was certainly right when he told the Muslim world, even during his moment of optimistic outreach in Cairo, that

> around the world, the Jewish people were persecuted for centuries, and anti-Semitism in Europe culminated in an unprecedented Holocaust. Tomorrow, I will visit Buchenwald, which was part of a network of camps where Jews were enslaved, tortured, shot and gassed to death by the Third Reich. Six million Jews were killed—more than the entire Jewish population of Israel today. Denying that fact is baseless, it is ignorant, and it is hateful. Threatening

Israel with destruction—or repeating vile stereotypes about Jews—is deeply wrong, and only serves to evoke in the minds of Israelis this most painful of memories while preventing the peace that the people of this region deserve.[65]

But opposing Holocaust denial is only a piece of the puzzle.

The time has come for the West, especially the antiracist left in the West, to decide how serious it really is about fighting bigotry. For one thing, everyone must abandon the "well-honed technique [of defining] anti-Semitism so narrowly as to limit it to the Nazi holocaust and practically nothing else."[66] And people, especially on the left, must stop making excuses for bigotry when it does not come from the usual suspects. They must reject logic like that offered by Peter Wilby, editor of Britain's *New Statesman*. Wilby explained: "Racism against white people is of no consequence because it has no historical resonance. To call somebody a 'white bastard' is just not the same as calling someone a 'black bastard,' with all its connotations of humiliation and enslavement. Given the distribution of power in our world, discrimination by blacks and Asians against white people will almost always be trivial."[67] Even ignoring the fact that antisemitism has quite a bit of historical resonance, Wilby's statement is morally bankrupt nonsense.

The West cannot allow guilt over past imperialism or respect for diverse cultures to become a barrier against the defense of fundamental human rights. Support for freedom of religious expression also cannot become cover for hate associated with religion. Jews, Christians, and Muslims should not be permitted to hide behind antidefamation provisions; there is nothing admirable about tolerating intolerance. Moreover, people cannot allow the desire to get along with others and to resolve conflicts to turn them into enablers of bigotry and defenders of untruth.

Practically, the fight against Jew-hatred starts with careful media monitoring. And results must be publicized. People need to know what is going on around the world, the bad along with the good. One can never avoid doing the homework and merely extrapolate from unrelated contexts. Here, translation and analysis services like those provided by the Middle East Media Research Institute are essential. And if one questions MEMRI's translations or argues—as some have—that the organization highlights a biased sample of articles and broadcasts, then the answer is providing more translation services. The language barrier cannot stand in the way of obtaining critical information about important regions of the world. Unfortunately, academic Middle East studies programs in the West have been sadly lacking.

Interfaith programs can be centrally significant in the battle against antisemitism, but they must be done responsibly. Respect for all well-intentioned believers is a given. Muslims who attend such programs are taking a bold and needed step. Yet the desire for harmony must not become an excuse for ignoring problems and pretending all is well. Well-intentioned Western Jews and Muslims may find it easiest to get along if they agree not to speak of either the Arab-Israeli dispute or antisemitism, and to be sure, small steps may be the best way to start. Reasonable Muslims these days do not face an easy task. Their faith has indeed been under attack from within and without. Concerns about Islamophobia can be real and sincere. And interfaith efforts must always be a two-way street. But the ultimate goal must be truth and honesty all around.

Many organizations have been doing good work in the battle against antisemitism, and it is important to support them. Interfaith efforts can be very helpful. So, too, are movements by political leaders from many countries, which have taken place periodically in order to jump-start the battle against Jew-hatred. The Berlin Declaration of 2004, the London Declaration of 2009, and the Ottawa Protocol of 2010 are all steps in the right direction.[68]

It is also time to restore sense and civility to debates about Israel. Although endless perspectives have been offered on the Arab-Israeli conflict, one rarely hears about the Arabs' inability to tolerate the Jews' emergence from many centuries of dhimmi status. Yet, as I have argued, a key factor is the psychological disconnect between the Jews, historically and theologically, as weak and inferior and the Jews in the contemporary world as competent, successful, and militarily strong. This threat to collective self-esteem, I think, is a core reason why finding a negotiated solution to the conflict has been so hard. And, as Bassam Tibi argues, much of the conflict's intractability stems from the Islamization of antisemitism and the religionization of the conflict itself. Reactions to Israel, then, do not derive principally from Israeli actions.

Regardless of whether this perspective is right, opposition to antisemitism implies no particular position on the Arab-Israeli conflict. The Israeli government, like all governments, is imperfect. In my view, a two-state solution is necessary, and the rights of Palestinians must be respected every bit as much as those of Jews. But the use of demonization, double standards, delegitimization of the Jewish state—whether or not you call it antisemitism—must end. Zionism is not apartheid. Jews are not Nazis. Sharon might have been a bad leader, but he didn't eat babies. One cannot be permitted to revitalize all the old bigotries just by changing the word "Jew" into "Zionist" or "Zionazi."

Moreover, blind pacifism is a problem. As Pierre-André Taguieff explained, "it places aggressor and victim of aggression on the same level—indeed, it accepts or even encourages the former while paralyzing the latter and making a crime of legitimate self-defense."[69] More importantly, in the absence of the Israeli armed forces, little might stand between millions of Jews and a potential bloodbath.

The United Nations and some other human rights organizations must start living up to their principles. They must stop vilifying Israel. Antisemitism or not, it's wrong. And they should place Muslim antisemitism on the human rights agenda where it belongs. False antiracism events—such as those like the Durban conferences that try to make an exception out of antisemitism—do not deserve the participation of responsible nations.

Governments should not relegate antisemitism to a back office; the issue should be raised often by top leaders. And the West needs to stop embracing false moderates. It should demand that those who desire Western support and sympathy issue clear, specific, and frequent condemnations of Jew-hatred in local languages that the antisemites and their fellow travelers can understand. Along these lines, the West should refuse to cooperate with antisemitic organizations. The message should go forth that you cannot be a friend of the democracies and a propagator of racism. There must be zero tolerance.

Above all, zero tolerance requires an end to the socialization for hatred that threatens to embroil future generations in depressingly endless and meaningless conflict. Before the West agrees to deal with Hamas, for example, it must require that the organization reject antisemitism unambiguously—in its charter and everywhere else. And if, as sometimes happens, it becomes necessary to make alliances of convenience—as when the West bonded with Stalin—responsible nations shouldn't fool themselves into thinking they have not been dealing with the devil. They should, above all, remain clear about what their own values are.

Unfortunately, a nuclear-armed Iran brings everyone uncomfortably closer to a worst-case scenario. Indicting leaders who threaten to drop nuclear weapons on Israel for incitement to genocide is not a bad idea. But it may not be enough. If a nuclear Iran is inevitable, the West must then be prepared to contain it by establishing public and precise consequences for particular Iranian steps along the road to nuclear conflict.[70]

As now-deceased former U.S. ambassador Richard Holbrooke explained in reference to Iranian nuclear threats, "Words matter. . . . When people say: 'Don't pay too much attention, they don't mean it'—it reminds me of my grandfather in Hamburg, who read *Mein Kampf*, and he took it for real, but many other people didn't."[71] Thinking more generally about Muslim antisemitism, we don't want to be the generation that wasn't paying attention.

Notes

Chapter 1. A Litmus Test for the West

1. Anti-Defamation League (ADL), *American Muslim Extremists: Fueled by Anti-Semitism* (New York, 2010).
2. Daniel Schwammenthal, "Europe Reimports Jew Hatred," *Wall Street Journal Europe*, January 13, 2009, http://online.wsj.com/article/SB12318003380707 5069.html (accessed June 3, 2011).
3. ADL, *American Muslim Extremists*, 6.
4. Elie Wiesel, "Video Message of Elie Wiesel for the International Iran-Conference 2008," Stop the Bomb, May 2008, http://de.stopthebomb.net/en/sign-now /elie-wiesel.html#c324 (accessed June 2, 2011).
5. See, for example, Michael Slackman, "Mohamed Sayed Tantawi, Top Cleric Dies at 81," *New York Times*, March 10, 2010; "Sheikh Mohammed Sayed Tantawi; Grand Imam of al-Azhar Mosque in Cairo, Sunni Islam's Highest Seat of Learning, Who Championed the Rights of Women," *Times* (London), March 12, 2010; and David Graham, "No Great Sheiks," *Newsweek*, March 12, 2010. But see also Andrew M. Rosemarine, "Sheikh Mohamed Sayyid Tantawi; Controversial Imam Who Preached Tolerance but Spoke Strongly against Judaism," *Independent* (London), March 19, 2010, for an exception.
6. Muhammad Sayyid Tantawi, "Extracts from *The Children of Israel in the Qur'an and the Sunna*," in *The Legacy of Islamic Antisemitism: From Sacred Texts to Solemn History*, ed. Andrew G. Bostom (Amherst, NY: Prometheus, 2008), 391–401 (originally published in Arabic in Cairo, 1986–1987). Excerpts from Tantawi's dissertation, along with some analysis, were published shortly after his death in the Egyptian daily newspaper *Al-Masri Al-Yawn*. See *Egyptian Daily Publishes Antisemitic Dissertation by the Late Al-Azhar Sheikh Tantawi*, Special Dispatch No. 3108 (Washington, DC: Middle East Media Research Institute [MEMRI], July 20, 2010), http://www.memri.org/report/en/0/0/0/0/0/0/4463.htm (accessed July 20, 2010).

7. Quoted in Aluma Solnick, *Based on Koranic Verses, Interpretations and Traditions, Muslim Clerics State: The Jews Are Descendants of Apes, Pigs, and Other Animals*, Special Report No. 11 (Washington, DC: MEMRI, 2002), http://memri.org/bin/articles.cgi?Page=subjects&Area=antisemitism&ID=SR01102 (accessed June 30, 2010). Tantawi's recommendation to stop referring to Jews as "pigs and apes" is discussed in Yigal Carmon, *Harbingers of Change in the Antisemitic Discourse in the Arab World*, Inquiry and Analysis Series No. 135 (Washington, DC: MEMRI, 2003), http://www.memri.org/report/en/0/0/0/0/0/0/854.htm (accessed June 30, 2010).

8. Quoted in *The Meeting between the Sheik of Al-Azhar and the Chief Rabbi of Israel*, Special Report No. 3 (Washington, DC: MEMRI, 1998), http://www.memri.org/report/en/0/0/0/0/0/0/231.htm (accessed June 30, 2010).

9. Slackman, "Mohamed Sayed Tantawi."

10. *Jews Portrayed as Blood Drinkers in Antisemitic Drama Aired on Hamas TV*, Special Dispatch No. 2308 (Washington, DC: MEMRI, 2009), http://www.memri.org/report/en/0/0/0/0/0/51/3237.htm (accessed June 30, 2010).

11. *Statements of Former Hamas Culture Minister 'Atallah Abu Al-Subh on America and Jews*, Special Dispatch No. 3848 (Washington, DC: MEMRI, 2011).

12. *Friday Sermon on Sudan TV: Preacher Abd Al-Jalil Al-Karouri Calls on U.S. 'President Hussein' to Acknowledge That the Jews Carried Out 9/11*, Special Dispatch No. 2460 (Washington, DC: MEMRI, 2009), http://www.memri.org/report/en/0/0/0/0/0/51/3440.htm (accessed June 30, 2010).

13. Muhammad 'Abd Al-Sattar, quoted in *Syrian Deputy Minister of Religious Endowment Muhammad 'Abd Al-Sattar Calls for Jihad and States Jews "Are the Descendants of Apes and Pigs,"* Special Dispatch No. 1217 (Washington, DC: MEMRI, 2006), http://www.memri.org/report/en/0/0/0/0/0/0/1757.htm (accessed June 30, 2010).

14. Muhammad Yusuf al-Qaradawi, quoted in *Sheikh Yousuf Al-Qaradhawi: Allah Imposed Hitler on the Jews to Punish Them—"Allah Willing, the Next Time Will Be at the Hand of the Believers,"* Special Dispatch No. 2224 (Washington, DC: MEMRI, 2009), http://www.memri.org/report/en/print3062.htm (accessed June 30, 2010).

15. Mus'id Anwar, quoted in *Against the Backdrop of Soccer World Cup in South Africa, Egyptian Cleric Mus'id Anwar Blasts Soccer, Other "Harmful Sports," as a Means Prescribed by the Protocols of the Elders of Zion in Order to Rule the World*, Special Dispatch No. 3018 (Washington, DC: MEMRI, 2010), http://www.memri.org/report/en/0/0/0/0/0/51/4355.htm (accessed June 30, 2010).

16. Morad El-Hattab El-Ibrahimi, "The Absurdity of Antisemitism in the Arab World," in *Antisemitism: The Generic Hatred*, ed. Michael Fineberg, Shimon Samuels, and Mark Weitzman (Portland, OR: Valentine Mitchell, 2007), 219. The author usually publishes under the name Morad El-Hattab.

17.   Barry Rubin, "How the PLO 'Adapted' Antisemitism as 'Anti-Zionism'" (lecture, Yale University, New Haven, CT, October 15, 2009), http://vimeo.com /7439044 (accessed April 2012).

18.   See, for example, Denis MacShane, *Globalising Hatred: The New Antisemitism* (London: Weidenfeld and Nicolson, 2008); Fiamma Nirenstein, *Terror: The New Anti-Semitism and the War against the West*, trans. Anne Milano Appel (Hanover, NH: Smith and Kraus, 2005); and Pierre-André Taguieff, *Rising from the Muck: The New Anti-Semitism in Europe*, trans. Patrick Camiller (Chicago: Ivan R. Dee, 2004).

19.   See, for example, Pew Global Attitudes Project, *Islamic Extremism: Common Concern for Muslim and Western Publics* (Washington, DC: Pew Research Center, July 14, 2005), http://pewglobal.org/reports/display.php?ReportID=248 (accessed July 1, 2010).

20.   See Robert F. Worth and Nazila Fathi, "In Iran, President's Deputy Is Stepping Down," *New York Times*, September 19, 2008.

21.   Ayatollah Khomeini, quoted in Efraim Karsh, *Islamic Imperialism: A History*, updated ed. (New Haven, CT: Yale University Press, 2007), 221.

22.   See, for example, Itamar Marcus and Nan Jacques Zilberdik, *No Education about the Holocaust for Palestinian Kids* (Jerusalem: Palestinian Media Watch, 2009), http://palwatch.org/main.aspx?fi=157&doc_id=1292 (accessed April 2012).

23.   Hosni Mubarak, quoted in Ephraim Dowek, *Israeli-Egyptian Relations 1980–2000* (London: Cass, 2001), 120–21.

24.   Quoted in Dennis Ross and David Makovsky, *Myths, Illusions, and Peace: Finding a New Direction for America in the Middle East* (New York: Viking, 2009), 32.

25.   Quoted in Mohamed Ibrahim Kamel, *The Camp David Accords: A Testimony* (New York: KPI/Routledge and Kegan Paul, 1986), 321.

26.   Dan Murphy, "Egypt Revolution Unfinished, Qaradawi Tells Tahrir Masses," *Christian Science Monitor*, February 18, 2011, http://www.csmonitor.com /World/Middle-East/2011/0218/Egypt-revolution-unfinished-Qaradawi -tells-Tahrir-masses (accessed June 2, 2011).

27.   Muhammad Yusuf al-Qaradawi, quoted in Harold Brackman, *"Hitler Put Them in Their Place": Egypt's Muslim Brotherhood's Jihad against Jews, Judaism, and Israel* (Los Angeles: Simon Wiesenthal Center, February 2011), http://www .wiesenthal.com/atf/cf/%7B54d385e6-f1b9-4e9f-8e94-890c3e6dd277%7D /HITLER-PUT-THEM-IN-THEIR-PLACE_BRACKMAN_FINAL.PDF (accessed June 2, 2011).

28.   See, for example, Ethan Bronner, "Dispute Grows as Egyptian Gas Is Still Not Flowing to Israel," *New York Times*, June 2, 2011.

29.   Schwammenthal, "Europe Reimports Jew Hatred."

30.   See Neil J. Kressel, "The Urgent Need to Study Islamic Anti-Semitism," *Chronicle of Higher Education*, March 12, 2004, B14–B15. One notable exception to

the trend is Florette Cohen, Lee Jussim, Kent D. Harber, and Gautam Bhasin, "Modern Anti-Semitism and Anti-Israeli Attitudes," *Journal of Personality and Social Psychology* 97, no. 2 (2009): 290–306—although this study relies on a sample of American college students that limits its generalizability considerably.

31. See, for example, Ruth Wedgwood, "Zionism and Racism, Again: Durban II," *World Affairs* 171, no. 4 (2009): 84–88.

32. ADL, *Attitudes toward Jews in Seven European Countries* (New York, 2009), http://www.adl.org/Public%20ADL%20Anti-Semitism%20Presentation%20 February%202009%20_3_.pdf (accessed July 1, 2010).

33. Robert Wistrich, *Muslim Antisemitism* (Israel: Coordination Forum for Countering Anti-Semitism, 2003), http://www.antisemitism.org.il/eng/articles/7932/ Muslim_Antisemitism_-By_Robert_Wistrich (accessed April 27, 2009).

34. Alan Cowell and Steven Erlanger, "French Police Seize 17 in Raids after Killings in Toulouse," *New York Times*, March 30, 2012.

35. Quoted in Clemens Heni, "German Ideology: Understanding Ahasver, Mammon, and Moloch," *Journal for the Study of Antisemitism* 2, no. 1 (2010): 80–81.

36. Zola's "J'Accuse. . . !," originally published on January 13, 1898, in the newspaper *L'Aurore*, is available in French and English from http://www.chameleon-translations.com/sample-Zola.shtml (accessed July 1, 2010). Among the many good books that have appeared on the Dreyfus case, see Jean-Denis Bredin, *The Affair: The Case of Alfred Dreyfus* (New York: George Braziller, 1986), and more recently, Ruth Harris, *Dreyfus: Politics, Emotion, and the Scandal of the Century* (New York: Metropolitan Books, 2010).

37. ADL, *Anti-Semitism in America* (New York, 2002), http://www.adl.org/anti_ semitism/2002/as_survey.pdf (accessed April 2, 2009). See also ADL, "Poll: Anti-Semitic Attitudes Match Lowest Level Recorded; Targeting of Jews for Violence and Blame Continues," press release, October 29, 2009, http://www .adl.org/PresRele/ASUS_12/5633_12 (accessed June 3, 2011).

38. Bernard Harrison, *The Resurgence of Anti-Semitism: Jews, Israel, and Liberal Opinion* (Lanham, MD: Rowman and Littlefield, 2006), xiii.

39. Charles Small, personal communication with the author, 2010. Many have argued that Yale's closure of YIISA and its replacement with a less controversial institute stemmed in large part from its discomfort with the study of Muslim antisemitism.

40. Yaakov Kirschen, "Antisemitism and the Power of Cartoons" (lecture, Yale University, New Haven, CT, October 14, 2009), vimeo.com/7436478 (accessed April 2012).

41. See, for example, Taguieff, *Rising from the Muck*, 12.

42. See Moshe Zimmermann, *Wilhelm Marr: The Patriarch of Anti-Semitism* (New York: Oxford University Press, 1987). See also Yehuda Bauer, "Problems of Contemporary Anti-Semitism," in *Varieties of Antisemitism: History, Ideology, Discourse,*

ed. Murray Baumgarten, Peter Kenez, and Bruce Thompson (Newark: University of Delaware Press, 2009), 315–27; and Jacob Lassner, "Can Arabs Be Anti-semites?," in *Varieties of Anti-Semitism*, 345–69.

43. For a dated but still useful discussion of the history of the term, see Gotthard Deutsch, "Anti-Semitism," *The Jewish Encyclopedia*, online ed., 2002 (originally published 1901–1906), http://www.jewishencyclopedia.com/viewjsp?artid=16 03&letter=A#4621 (accessed July 1, 2010).

44. Regarding use of this language at the United Nations World Conference Against Racism (Durban I), see ADL, *The Draft Declaration: Unfair Charges of Racism against Israel* (New York, July 5, 2001), http://www.adl.org/durban/draft.asp (accessed July 1, 2010). See also, for example, Ibrahim Nafie, "Israel's Anti-Sem-itism," *Al-Ahram Weekly Online*, November 20–26, 2003, http://weekly.ahram. org.eg/2003/665/op1.htm (accessed July 1, 2010).

45. Léon Poliakov, *The History of Anti-Semitism*, vol. 2, trans. Natalie Gerardi (London: Routledge and Kegan Paul, 1974), vii–viii. See also the fine discussion of these issues in Dina Porat, "The Historiography of Antisemitism in the Shadow of the Holocaust," in *Antisemitism*, 285–300. Poliakov—like Heinrich Graetz and most other early Jewish historians who studied both Christianity and Islam— saw many relatively positive elements in Islam's encounter with the Jews. See, for example, Poliakov, *History of Anti-Semitism*, vol. 2, 46–105.

46. Poliakov, *History of Anti-Semitism*, vol. 2, viii.

47. Porat, "Historiography," 286.

48. Neil J. Kressel, *Bad Faith: The Danger of Religious Extremism* (Amherst, NY: Prometheus, 2007).

49. Fouad Zakariya, quoted in Taguieff, *Rising from the Muck*, 25.

50. See, for example, Rosemary Ruether, *Faith and Fratricide: The Theological Roots of Anti-Semitism* (Minneapolis: Seabury, 1974).

51. Philip A. Cunningham, foreword to *The Anguish of the Jews: Twenty-Three Centuries of Antisemitism*, rev. ed., by Edward H. Flannery (New York: Paulist Press, 2004), xi.

52. Translation from the Ibn Arabi Foundation, http://www.sufiway.org/history/texts/garden_among_the_flames.php (accessed July 1, 2010).

53. Tarek Fatah, *The Jew Is Not My Enemy: Unveiling the Myths That Fuel Muslim Anti-Semitism* (Toronto: McClelland and Stewart, 2010).

54. Cited in ibid., xxiv.

Chapter 2. Evidence

1. S'ad Al-Bawardi, quoted in B. Chernitsky and E. Glass, *Antisemitic Statements and Cartoons in Wake of Gaza War*, Inquiry and Analysis Series Report No. 507 (Washington, DC: MEMRI, March 30, 2009), http://www.memri.org/report/en/0/0/0/0/0/0/3213.htm (accessed July 1, 2010).

2.   Ibid. The Talmud does not have psalms. The reference to "one of the psalms in the Talmud" may, in fact, stem from Psalm 137 in the Bible: "Remember, O Lord, against the children of Edom the day of Jerusalem; Who said: 'Rase it, rase it, even to the foundation thereof.' O daughter of Babylon, that art to be destroyed; Happy shall he be, that repayeth thee as thou hast served us. Happy shall he be, that taketh and dasheth thy little ones against the rock." *The Holy Scriptures* (Philadelphia: Jewish Publication Society of America, 1955), 976.

3.   Chernitsky and Glass, "Antisemitic Statements."

4.   Quoted in *On Hamas TV, Friday Sermon Cites "Protocols of Elders of Zion," Calls to Annihilate the Jews, Compares Jews to Dogs*, Special Dispatch No. 2318 (Washington, DC: MEMRI, April 20, 2009), http://www.memri.org/report/en/0/0/0/0/0/0/51/3247.htm (accessed July 1, 2010).

5.   Emile Alghori, quoted in Taguieff, *Rising from the Muck*, 6.

6.   Lutfi Abd al-Azim, quoted in Efraim Karsh, "Intifada II: The Long Trail of Arab Anti-Semitism," *Commentary* 110, no. 5 (December 2000): 49–53. Karsh also cites prominent Egyptian journalist Anis Mansur, once a confidant of President Anwar Sadat, who stated, "There is no such thing in the world as a Jew and Israeli. Every Jew is an Israeli. No doubt about that." See also Raphael Israeli, "The New Muslim Anti-Semitism: Exploring Novel Avenues of Hatred," *Jewish Political Studies Review* 17, nos. 3–4 (Fall 2005), http://www.jcpa.org/phas/phas-israeli-f05.htm (accessed July 1, 2011).

7.   Hannah Rosenthal, lecture (Yale University, New Haven, CT, April 12, 2010), http://vimeo.com/11081626 (accessed April 25, 2012).

8.   S'ad Al-Bawardi, quoted in Chernitsky and Glass, "Antisemitic Statements."

9.   For one example of this approach, see Joseph V. Montville, "Commentary on 'Mass Hatred in the Muslim and Arab World: The Neglected Problem of Anti-Semitism' by Neil Kressel," *International Journal of Applied Psychoanalytic Studies* 4, no. 3 (2007): 216–20. See also Nadia Ramzy, "Commentary on 'Mass Hatred in the Muslim and Arab World: The Neglected Problem of Anti-Semitism' by Neil Kressel," *International Journal of Applied Psychoanalytic Studies* 4, no. 3 (2007): 191–96.

10.   See Robert S. Wistrich, *A Lethal Obsession: Anti-Semitism from Antiquity to the Global Jihad* (New York: Random House, 2010), 748.

11.   See "Hitler Book Bestseller in Turkey," BBC News, March 18, 2005, http://news.bbc.co.uk/2/hi/europe/4361733.stm (accessed July 1, 2010). See also Wistrich, *Lethal Obsession*, 823–29. For more on the production and distribution of antisemitic literature in the Arab and Muslim world, see Intelligence and Terrorism Information Center, *The Arab Hate Industry* (Ramat HaSharon, Israel: Center for Special Studies, August 2, 2006), http://www.terrorism-info.org.il/malam_multimedia/English/eng_n/html/arab_hate_ind.htm (accessed July 1, 2010).

12. Quoted in *On Hamas TV, Friday Sermon.*

13. See the final chapter of this book for a discussion of some varieties of Muslim and Arab opposition to Jew-hatred.

14. Suhaib Webb, "Does the Qur'an Call Jews Pigs and Apes? And Is It Allowed for Muslims to Do So?" SuhaibWebb.com (blog), April 27, 2008, http://www. suhaibwebb.com/blog/br-suhaib/does-the-quran-call-jews-pigs-and-apes/ (accessed July 1, 2010).

15. "Apes and Pigs?," Ruqaiyyah Waris Maqsood, http://www.ruqaiyyah.karoo.net/ articles/apes.htm (accessed July 1, 2010).

16. *Syrian Deputy Minister of Religious Endowment*, MEMRI Special Dispatch No. 1217.

17. Kressel, *Bad Faith*, 42–49.

18. *Friday Sermons in Saudi Mosques: Review and Analysis*, Special Report No. 10 (Washington, DC: MEMRI, September 26, 2002), http://www.memri.org /report/en/0/0/0/0/0/0/736.htm#II (accessed July 1, 2010).

19. Hassan Nasrallah, quoted in Solnick, *Based on Koranic Verses.*

20. Ibrahim Mahdi, quoted in Irwin Cotler, "The New Anti-Semitism: An Assault on Human Rights," in *Antisemitism*, 28–29.

21. *Saudi Government Official on Bin Laden as a Hero: He Did Not Present a Distorted Picture of Islam to the West, American Jews Are "Brothers of Apes and Pigs,"* Special Dispatch No. 343 (Washington, DC: MEMRI, February 8, 2002), http://www .memri.org/report/en/0/0/0/0/0/51/606.htm (accessed July 1, 2010).

22. The communiqué is quoted in Taguieff, *Rising from the Muck*, 56.

23. See Ishtar, "Antisemitisme Ordinaire en Terre d'Islam: Grippe Porcine et Diabolisation d'Israel," May 8, 2009, http://www.bivouac-id.com/2009/05/08 /antisemitisme-ordinaire-en-terre-dislam-grippe-porcine-et-diabolisation -d%E2%80%99israel/ (accessed July 1, 2010).

24. *Egyptian Cleric Safwat Higazi on Hamas TV: Dispatch Those Sons of Apes and Pigs to the Hellfire—On the Wings of Qassam Rockets*, Special Dispatch No. 2176 (Washington, DC: MEMRI, January 6, 2009), http://www.memri.org/report /en/0/0/0/0/0/51/2997.htm (accessed July 1, 2010).

25. "3-Year-Old Egyptian Basmallah: Jews Are Apes and Pigs," Iqra TV (Saudi Arabia), TV Video Clip #924 (Washington, DC: MEMRI, May 7, 2002), http:// www.memritv.org/clip/en/924.htm (accessed July 13, 2010).

26. *Hizbullah Al-Manar TV's Children's Claymation Special: Jews Turn into Apes and Pigs, Are Annihilated and Cast into the Sea*, Special Dispatch No. 1050 (Washington, DC: MEMRI, December 16, 2005), http://www.memri.org/report /en/0/0/0/0/0/51/1557.htm (accessed July 1, 2010).

27. See Alexandra Frean, "Teacher Accuses Islamic School of Racism," *Times* (London), April 15, 2008, http://www.thetimes.co.uk/tto/education/article1878298 .ece (accessed July 13, 2010).

28. Six discussions of the source material from different perspectives are (1) Solnick, *Based on Koranic Verses*; (2) Maqsood, "Apes and Pigs?"; (3) James M. Arlandson, "Did Allah Transform Jews into Apes and Pigs?" *Answering Islam*, http://www.answering-islam.org/Authors/Arlandson/jew_apes.htm (accessed July 22, 2009); (4) Jamie Glazov, "Symposium: Apes, Pigs and Anti-Semitism," *Front Page Magazine*, April 6, 2007, http://archive.frontpagemag.com/readArticle.aspx?ARTID=26007 (accessed July 22, 2009); (5) Uri Rubin, "Apes, Pigs, and the Islamic Identity," *Israel Oriental Studies* 17 (1997): 89–105; and (6) Ilse Lichtenstadter, "'And Become Ye Accursed Apes,'" *Jerusalem Studies in Arabic and Islam* 14 (1991): 153–75.

29. *Egyptian Religious Endowments Ministry Official: The Pigs Living Today Are Descended from Jews—and Must Be Slaughtered*, Special Dispatch No. 2359 (Washington, DC: MEMRI, May 15, 2009), http://www.memri.org/report/en/0/0/0/0/0/0/51/3300.htm (accessed July 1, 2010).

30. Ibid.

31. Jeffrey Goldberg, "Nizar Rayyan of Hamas on God's Hatred of Jews," *The Atlantic*, January 2, 2009, http://www.theatlantic.com/international/archive/2009/01/nizar-rayyan-of-hamas-on-god-apos-s-hatred-of-jews/9278/ (accessed July 1, 2010).

32. See "Sheik Yousuf Al-Qaradhawi, Recently Barred from the U.K., Reiterates His Position on Suicide Bombings and Declares: Jews Are Not the Offspring of Apes and Pigs," Al-Jazeera TV (Qatar), TV Clip #1691 (Washington, DC: MEMRI, February 15–18, 2008), http://www.memritv.org/clip/en/1691.htm (accessed July 1, 2010).

33. Ibn Ishaq/Ibn Hisham, "The Extermination of the Banu Qurayza," in *Legacy of Islamic Antisemitism*, 277. (Excerpt from Ibn Hisham's ninth-century biography of Muhammad, which was based on Ibn Ishaq's biography; translation from Norman Stillman, *The Jews of Arab Lands: A History and Source Book* [Philadelphia: Jewish Publication Society, 1979].)

34. Ibid., 278.

35. Ibn Ishaq/Ibn Hisham, "Muhammad and the Jews of Khaybar," in *Legacy of Islamic Antisemitism*, 280. See also Ibn Sa'd, "Excerpts from the Sira of Ibn Sa'd," trans. S. Moinul Haq and H. K. Ghazanfar, in *Legacy of Islamic Antisemitism*, 294–95. (Ibn Sa'd wrote another ninth-century biography of Muhammad.)

36. Tarek Fatah theorizes that many of the anti-Jewish stories about Muhammad that originate in the hadiths and the early biographies (*sira*) were fabricated many years after Muhammad's death with the conscious intent of recasting the Jews as the Prophet's main enemies. By creating these stories, the Muslims who were at the time in power were able to rescue the reputations of their own Meccan ancestors who had come relatively late to Muhammad's camp and who, be-

fore that, had fought against him. Similarly, according to Fatah's nonmainstream viewpoint, much, though not all, of the anti-Jewish spin attached to Quranic verses was a later addition. See Fatah, *Jew Is Not My Enemy*, 130–47. We return to Fatah's brave and interesting approach later. See also Mustafa Aykol, *Islam without Extremes: A Muslim Case for Liberty* (New York: Norton, 2011), 57–58. Aykol noted the possibility that the massacre of the Banu Qurayza never took place. He additionally concluded, "Yet even if the mass execution had really happened, as the mainstream view holds, one should note that it took place not as a commandment of the Qur'an but as the result of the customs of the time. . . . And this takes us to a crucial question: Are all things that Muhammad did normative for Muslims? Or do some of them reflect not the everlasting rules and principles of Islam but rather those of the Prophet's time and milieu?" Aykol and Fatah offer interesting and constructive approaches that, at present, would not likely convince many mainstream Muslims. And certainly their views are anathema to the extremists.

37. See Neil J. Kressel, *Mass Hate: The Global Rise of Genocide and Terror*, rev. ed. (Boulder, CO: Westview Press, 2002), 172.
38. Menahem Milson, *Arab and Islamic Anti-Semitism*, Inquiry and Analysis Series Report No. 442 (Washington, DC: MEMRI, May 27, 2008), http://www.memri.org/report/en/print2680.htm (accessed July 1, 2010).
39. Kressel, *Mass Hate*.
40. Jacob Lassner wrote, "A trip to virtually any bookstall in almost any major Arab city will feature the likes of the *Protocols of the Elders of Zion*, together with a host of subtle and not so subtle anti-Jewish missives enriched by anti-Jewish themes of European origin." See Lassner, "Can Arabs Be Antisemites?," 354.
41. See *Al-Shatat: The Syrian-Produced Ramadan 2003 TV Special*, Special Dispatch No. 627 (Washington, DC: MEMRI, December 12, 2003), http://www.memri.org/report/en/0/0/0/0/0/0/1018.htm (accessed July 1, 2010); *Director of Iranian TV Series "Secret of Armageddon" Comments on MEMRI TV's Translation of Series; Confirms "Protocols of Elders of Zion,"* Special Dispatch No. 2108 (Washington, DC: MEMRI, November 9, 2008), http://www.memri.org/report/en/0/0/0/0/0/175/2946.htm (accessed July 1, 2010); *Iranian TV Series Based on the Protocols of the Elders of Zion and the Jewish Control of Hollywood*, Special Dispatch No. 705 (Washington, DC: MEMRI, April 30, 2004), http://www.memri.org/report/en/0/0/0/0/0/80/1119.htm (accessed July 1, 2010).
42. *Sports Commentator on Egyptian TV Turns His Show into Platform for Spreading Antisemitism, Conspiracy Theories, and Anti-Americanism, Features Producer of Notorious 2002 Antisemitic Series "Knight without a Horse,"* Special Dispatch No. 2919 (Washington, DC: MEMRI, April 21, 2010), http://www.memri.org/report/en/0/0/0/0/0/0/4112.htm (accessed July 29, 2010).

43. *Post-Revolutionary Egyptian Al-Tahrir TV Channel Resurrects Controversial 2002 Egyptian Antisemitic TV Series "Horseman without a Horse,"* Special Dispatch No. 4611 (Washington, DC: MEMRI, 2012).

44. See Menahem Milson, *A European Plot on the Arab Stage: The Protocols of the Elders of Zion in the Arab Media,* Inquiry and Analysis Series Report No. 690 (Washington, DC: MEMRI, May 20, 2011), http://www.memri.org/report /en/0/0/0/0/0/177/688.htm (accessed June 6, 2011).

45. For an answer to antisemitic attacks on the Talmud (not necessarily originating in Muslim and Arab countries), see ADL, *The Talmud in Anti-Semitic Polemics* (New York, 2003), http://www.adl.org/presrele/asus_12/the_talmud.pdf (accessed August 10, 2010).

46. Maria Maalouf, quoted in *TV Channel Affiliated with Lebanese Parliamentary Speaker Nabih Beri in Show on Protocols of the Elders of Zion,* Special Dispatch No. 1754 (Washington, DC: MEMRI, October 31, 2007), http://www.memri. org/report/en/0/0/0/0/0/80/2440.htm (accessed July 1, 2010).

47. See Hadassa Ben-Itto, *The Lie That Wouldn't Die: The Protocols of the Elders of Zion* (London: Valentine Mitchell, 2007), and Norman Cohn, *Warrant for Genocide: The Myth of the Jewish World Conspiracy and the Protocols of the Elders of Zion* (New York: Penguin, 1970).

48. One antisemitic website—not connected to Islam or the Arab world—summarizes in modern English the methods outlined in *The Protocols*. See "The Protocols of Zion in Modern English," French Connection, http://www.iamthe witness.com/ (accessed August 2, 2010). Jews are instructed by their leader to
    Place our agents and helpers everywhere
    Take control of the media and use it in propaganda for our plans
    Start fights between different races, classes and religions
    Use bribery, threats and blackmail to get our way
    Use Freemasonic Lodges to attract potential public officials
    Appeal to successful people's egos
    Appoint puppet leaders who can be controlled by blackmail
    Replace royal rule with socialist rule, then communism, then despotism
    Abolish all rights and freedoms, except the right of force by us
    Sacrifice people (including Jews sometimes) when necessary
    Eliminate religion; replace it with science and materialism
    Control the education system to spread deception and destroy intellect
    Rewrite history to our benefit
    Create entertaining distractions
    Corrupt minds with filth and perversion
    Encourage people to spy on one another
    Keep the masses in poverty and perpetual labor
    Take possession of all wealth, property and (especially) gold

Use gold to manipulate the markets, cause depressions etc.

Introduce a progressive tax on wealth

Replace sound investment with speculation

Make long-term interest-bearing loans to governments

Give bad advice to governments and everyone else

49. Richard S. Levy, "The Migration of Discredited Myths: The Wandering Protocols," in *Not Your Father's Antisemitism: Hatred of the Jews in the 21st Century*, ed. Michael Berenbaum (St. Paul, MN: Paragon House, 2008), 170.

50. Ben-Itto, *Lie That Wouldn't Die*, is an excellent, up-to-date introduction to this topic. Reasonable people do not disagree about whether *The Protocols* is a forgery. Some details of the story remain matters for debate, but the sources from which the document was plagiarized have been located. There is also some agreement that the operation was conducted under the direction of the czarist secret police in the late 1890s. The main source of the forgery—the French writer Maurice Joly's 1864 *Dialogues aux Enfers entre Machiavel et Montesquieu* (Dialogues in Hell between Machiavelli and Montesquieu)—was a relatively unknown satire of Napoleon III's rise to power. It was a clever and interesting book that had nothing to do with Jews. Other aspects of *The Protocols* are drawn from the little-known 1868 German novel *Biarritz* by Hermann Goedsche, writing under the pen name of Sir John Retcliffe. A chapter from this work of fiction had even been circulated under the title "In the Jewish Cemetery in Prague" as an antisemitic (nonfiction) pamphlet years before *The Protocols*. When passages from Joly's book are placed side by side with *The Protocols*, the similarities become inescapable. See, for example, Pierre-André Taguieff, *Les Protocoles des Sages de Sion: Faux et Usages d'un Faux* (Paris: Berg International-Fayard, 2004), 427–73. And when Joly's work is combined with the ideas in the chapter from *Biarritz*, one obtains a product very close to the final *Protocols* document. Moreover, in addition to knowing its precise sources, we have considerable historical understanding of how *The Protocols* made its way around the world, usually as part of self-conscious antisemitic campaigns.

51. All quotes from the Hamas Charter are taken from "The Covenant of the Islamic Resistance Movement," The Avalon Project: Documents in Law, History and Diplomacy (New Haven, CT: Yale Law School, August 18, 1988), http://avalon .law.yale.edu/20th_century/hamas.asp (accessed July 20, 2010).

52. Meshaal, quoted in Paul McGeough, "Hamas Comes out of Hiding," *New York Times*, April 13, 2009.

53. Abu Al-Subh, quoted in *On Hamas TV: Hamas Culture Minister Presents Excerpts from Protocols of the Elders of Zion, Claims Jews Trying to Control the World*, Special Dispatch No. 1905 (Washington, DC: MEMRI, April 22, 2008), http:// www.memri.org/report/en/0/0/0/0/0/0/2737.htm (accessed July 22, 2010).

54. *Jewish Holy Books on Display at the Alexandria Library: The Torah and the "Protocols of the Elders of Zion,"* Special Dispatch No. 619 (Washington, DC: MEMRI, December 3, 2003), http://www.memri.org/report/en/0/0/0/0/0/51/1009.htm (accessed July 30, 2010).

55. *Saudi Daily Al-Madina Series: Reality Confirms Authenticity of Protocols of the Elders of Zion,* Special Dispatch No. 1311 (Washington, DC: MEMRI, October 6, 2006), http://www.memri.org/report/en/0/0/0/0/0/51/1897.htm (accessed July 20, 2010).

56. Yossef Bodansky, *Islamic Anti-Semitism as a Political Instrument* (Houston, TX: Freeman Center for Strategic Studies, 1999), 169–70. See also "George Soros," Wikipedia, http://en.wikipedia.org/wiki/George_Soros (accessed August 2, 2010).

57. Ibnu Burdah, "Indonesian Muslims' Perceptions of Jews and Israel," in *Muslim Attitudes to Jews and Israel: The Ambivalences of Rejection, Antagonism, Tolerance, and Cooperation,* ed. Moshe Ma'oz (Portland, OR: Sussex Academic Press, 2010), 234.

58. MacShane, *Globalising Hatred*, 51.

59. See *Egyptian Professor of Hebrew Literature Ibrahim Farid Denounces Endorsement of Antisemitic Myths by Arab Media and Institutions,* Special Dispatch No. 2966 (Washington, DC: MEMRI, May 20, 2010), http://www.memri.org/report/en/0/0/0/0/0/51/4183.htm (accessed August 2, 2010). See also *Editor of Egyptian Weekly Criticizes Arab Embrace of European Anti-Semitism,* Special Dispatch No. 703 (Washington, DC: MEMRI, April 29, 2004), http://www.memri.org/report/en/0/0/0/0/0/51/1117.htm (accessed July 1, 2010).

60. *Saudi Writer: The Myth of the Jews Controlling the World Is Just a Cover for the Arab Failure,* Special Dispatch No. 2809 (Washington, DC: MEMRI, February 16, 2010), http://www.memri.org/report/en/0/0/0/0/0/51/3974.htm (accessed July 30, 2010).

61. *Columns in Jihadist Weekly on Dajjal Caution against Overestimating the "Power of Infidels,"* Special Dispatch No. 3064 (Washington, DC: MEMRI, June 29, 2010), http://www.memri.org/report/en/0/0/0/0/0/0/4411.htm (accessed June 30, 2010).

62. Mahathir Mohamad, "Speech by Prime Minister Mahathir Mohamad of Malaysia to the Tenth Islamic Summit Conference, Putrajaya, Malaysia," ADL, October 16, 2003, http://www.adl.org/Anti_semitism/malaysian.asp (accessed July 10, 2010).

63. Michael Backman, "A Moderate Voice for Islam: Malaysia's Mahathir," *International Herald Tribune*, December 6, 2002.

64. See, for example, Marvin Perry and Frederick M. Schweitzer, *Antisemitism: Myth and Hate from Antiquity to the Present* (New York: Palgrave, 2002), 73–117.

65. ADL, *Unraveling Anti-Semitic 9/11 Conspiracy Theories* (New York, 2003), http://www.adl.org/anti_semitism/9-11conspiracytheories.pdf (accessed August 2, 2010).

66. The 9/11 attacks have given birth to many varieties of conspiratorial thinking, not all of them dealing with Jews and not all of them based in Muslim and Arab countries. See, for example, David Dunbar and Brad Reagan, eds., *Debunking 9/11 Myths: Why Conspiracy Theories Can't Stand Up to the* Facts (New York: Hearst, 2006).

67. See Taguieff, *Les Protocoles des Sages de Sion*, 255. See also Deborah Lipstadt, *Denying the Holocaust: The Growing Assault on Truth and Memory* (New York: Plume, 1993), and Clemens Heni, "Secondary Anti-Semitism: From Hard-Core to Soft-Core Denial of the Shoah," *Jewish Political Studies Review* 20 (Fall 2008), http://www.jcpa.org/JCPA/Templates/ShowPage.asp?DBID=1&LNGID=1&T MID=111&FID=624&PID=0&IID=2675 (accessed August 10, 2010).

68. Abdussalam Treki, quoted in *President of the UN General Assembly Abdussalam Treki*, Special Dispatch No. 2946 (Washington, DC: MEMRI, May 11, 2010), http://www.memri.org/report/en/0/0/0/0/0/0/4149.htm (accessed July 20, 2010).

69. Hamid Esmaili, "Israel Emerges from Auschwitz," IRNA, April 21, 2009, available as *Op-Ed on Official Iranian New Website*, Special Dispatch No. 2321 (Washington, DC: MEMRI, April 21, 2009), http://www.memri.org/report /en/0/0/0/0/0/0/3251.htm (accessed July 20, 2010).

70. DPA, "Iran Launches Cartoon Website Aimed at Questioning the Holocaust," *Haaretz*, August 5, 2010, http://www.haaretz.com/news/international/iran -launches-cartoon-website-aimed-at-questioning-the-holocaust-1.306180 (accessed August 8, 2010).

71. See Solnick, *Based on Koranic Verses*.

72. Samir 'Ubeid, quoted in *Iraqi Researcher Living in Europe on Al-Jazeera TV: Nobel Prize Is Racist*, Special Dispatch No. 1359 (Washington, DC: MEMRI, November 16, 2006), http://www.memri.org/report/en/0/0/0/0/0/0/1945.htm (accessed August 2, 2010).

73. *Cultural Advisor to Iranian Education Ministry and Member of Interfaith Organization Lectures on Iranian TV*, Special Dispatch No. 1101 (Washington, DC: MEMRI, February 24, 2006), http://www.memri.org/report/en/0/0/0/0/0/0/1620 .htm (accessed August 2, 2010). See also "Film Seminar on Iranian TV," Channel 4 (Iran), TV video clip No. 1049 (Washington, DC: MEMRI, February 19, 2006), http://www.memritv.org/clip/en/1049.htm (accessed August 3, 2010). Subsequent quotations are taken from this lecture unless otherwise noted.

74. See, for example, Lisa Beyer, "The Eternal Agitator," *Time* (Classroom), Spring 2005, http://www.time.com/time/classroom/glenspring2005/pg26.html (accessed July 31, 2010).

75. *Islamic Republic of Iran News Network (IRINN TV) on "300,"* Special Dispatch No. 1506 (Washington, DC: MEMRI, March 16, 2007), http://www.memri .org/report/en/0/0/0/0/0/80/2124.htm (accessed August 3, 2010).

76. *Iranian TV: Disney's "Pirates of the Caribbean: Dead Man's Chest" Is a Pawn of the Zionist Lobby to Gain Cultural Control*, Special Dispatch No. 1302 (Washington, DC: MEMRI, September 27, 2006), http://www.memri.org/report /en/0/0/0/0/0/0/0/1888.htm (accessed August 3, 2010).

77. See Neal Gabler, *Walt Disney: The Triumph of the American Imagination* (New York: Knopf, 2006).

78. See, for example, *Massoud Shadjareh of the Islamic Human Rights Commission on Al-Jazeera: By Buying Coca-Cola, Starbucks, and Motorola Products, You Are Giving Money to the Killers of Your Brothers*, Special Dispatch No. 3009 (Washington, DC: MEMRI, June 8, 2009), http://www.memri.org/report /en/0/0/0/0/0/0/0/4344.htm (accessed July 10, 2010); *Iranian TV Report Exposes "Zionist Companies"—Coca Cola, Marlboro, Hugo Boss, McDonalds, Disney, Garnier, Tommy Hilfiger, L'Oreal, & Others; Pepsi = "Pay Each Penny Save Israel,"* Special Dispatch No. 1300 (Washington, DC: MEMRI, September 26, 2006), http://www.memri.org/report/en/0/0/0/0/0/0/0/1886.htm (accessed July 10, 2010).

79. See, for example, Per Ahlmark, "Anti-Semitism and Anti-Americanism: Dangerous Links" (speech, Global Forum against Anti-Semitism, Jerusalem, Israel, October 27, 2004), http://www.ncsj.org/AuxPages/102704GFAA_Ahlmark.shtml (accessed July 31, 2010); Josef Joffe, "Anti-Semitism and Anti-Americanism," interview by Mark O'Keefe, May 5, 2006, Pew Forum, Washington, DC, http:// www.pewforum.org/Politics-and-Elections/Anti-Semitism-and-Anti-Americanism .aspx (accessed December 23, 2009); and Andrei S. Markovits, *Uncouth Nation: Why Europe Dislikes America* (Princeton, NJ: Princeton University Press, 2007), 150.

80. *Egyptian Cleric and Former Islamic Lecturer in the U.S. Hazem Sallah Abu Isma'il on Al-Risala TV*, Special Dispatch No. 1161 (Washington, DC: MEMRI, 2006), http://www.memri.org/report/en/0/0/0/0/0/0/51/1685.htm (accessed April 25, 2012); and *Egyptian Presidential Candidate Tawfiq Okasha: Only 60% of the Jews Are Evil*, Clip No. 3207 (Washington, DC: MEMRI, 2011), http://www.memritv .org/clip_transcript/en/3207.htm (accessed April 25, 2012).

81. See European Union Monitoring Centre on Racism and Xenophobia (EUMC), "Working Definition of Anti-Semitism," European Forum on Anti-Semitism, 2008, http://www.european-forum-on-antisemitism.org/working-definition -of-antisemitism/ (accessed August 10, 2010). See also U.S. Department of State, *Contemporary Global Anti-Semitism: A Report Provided to the United States Congress* (Washington, DC, March 13, 2008), 6–7, http://www.state.gov/g/drl/rls/102406 .htm (accessed August 10, 2010).

82. Chapter 3 returns to the question of when, if ever, hostility toward Israel qualifies as antisemitism.

83. See U.S. Department of State, *Contemporary Global Anti-Semitism*, 6.

84. Ibid., 3.

85. Ibid.
86. For a summary of these studies, see Gunther Jikeli, "Anti-Semitism among Young Muslims in London" (paper presented at the International Study Group on Education and Research on Anti-Semitism, London, December 5, 2009), http://iibsa.org/cms/fileadmin/downloads/london_symposia/Gunther_Jikeli.pdf (accessed July 10, 2010).
87. See Steven K. Baum and Masato Nakazawa, "Anti-Semitism versus Anti-Israel Sentiment," *Journal of Religion and Society* 9 (2007): 1–8, http://moses.creighton.edu/JRS/pdf/2007-31.pdf (accessed August 12, 2010).
88. Diana Muir, "Anti-Semitism and Anti-Zionism: The Link," History News Network, July 21, 2001, http://hnn.us/articles/28503.html (accessed August 1, 2010). See also Edward H. Kaplan and Charles A. Small, "Anti-Israel Sentiment Predicts Anti-Semitism in Europe," *Journal of Conflict Resolution* 50 (2006): 548–61.
89. Cohen et al., "Modern Anti-Semitism," 303.
90. Ibid., 304.
91. See U.S. Department of State, *Contemporary Global Anti-Semitism*, 3, 12. See also Pew Global Attitudes Project, *Unfavorable Views of Jews and Muslims on the Increase in Europe* (Washington, DC: Pew Research Center, September 17, 2008), http://pewglobal.org/files/pdf/262.pdf (accessed July 30, 2010). This report concluded, "While European views towards Jews have become more negative, the deepest anti-Jewish sentiments exist outside of Europe, especially in predominantly Muslim nations. The percentage of Turks, Egyptians, Jordanians, Lebanese and Pakistanis with favorable opinions of Jews is in the single digits."
92. Gil Hoffman, "6 in 10 Palestinians Reject 2-State Solution, Survey Finds," *Jerusalem Post*, July 15, 2011, http://www.jpost.com/DiplomacyAndPolitics/Article.aspx?id=229493 (accessed July 15, 2011).
93. See "Covenant of the Islamic Resistance Movement."
94. Pew Global Attitudes Project, *Islamic Extremism.*
95. Pew Global Attitudes Project, *Little Enthusiasm for Many Muslim Leaders: Mixed Views of Hamas and Hezbollah in Largely Muslim Nations* (Washington, DC: Pew Research Center, 2010), http://pewglobal.org/2010/12/02/muslims-around-the-world-divided-on-hamas-and-hezbollah/ (accessed February 8, 2011). This poll is discussed in more detail later.
96. David Sanger, "Malaysia Talk Attacking Jews Draws Bush Ire," *New York Times*, October 21, 2003.
97. Mark Riley, Tom Allard, and Matthew Moore, "Megawati Applauds Mahathir on Jews," *Sydney Morning Herald*, October 18, 2003.
98. "Malaysian Opposition Leader: 'Jews Must Be Criticized for Causing Problems,'" Berita Minggu, Kuala Lampur, October 19, 2003, translated from the Malay

and available on BBC Summary of World Broadcasts, October 21, 2003, available from LexisNexis Academic http://www.lexisnexis.com/hottopics/lnacademic (accessed April 25, 2012).

99. "Leaders Rally to Defend Dr. Mahathir," *New Straits Times-Management Times*, October 18, 2003.

100. Piers Akerman, "Shades of Hitler in Mahathir's Call for a 'Final Victory' over Jews," *Daily Telegraph* (Australia), January 28, 2010.

101. See, for example, Yahya Abdul Rahman, "Mahathir's Racist Words: Not All Muslims Support the Anti-Semitic Remarks Made by Malaysia's Prime Minister and His Words Will Backfire against Islam," *Gazette* (Montreal), October 22, 2003; Salim Mansur, "Muslims Silent against Hateful Worlds," *Toronto Sun*, February 13, 2010; and *U.S. Liberal Arabic Website Rebuttal to Mahathir's Speech*, Special Dispatch No. 618 (Washington, DC: MEMRI, December 2, 2003), http://www.memri.org/report/en/0/0/0/0/0/0/1008.htm (accessed July 1, 2010).

102. Bill Meyer, "Morocco's King Mohammed VI Challenges Muslim World's Holocaust Denial," *Plain Dealer* (Cleveland), July 25, 2009, http://www.cleveland.com/world/index.ssf/2009/07/moroccos_king_mohammed_vi_chal.html (accessed August 4, 2010).

103. Tlass said, "With the publication of this book, I intended to illuminate some of the secrets of the Jewish religion by [describing] the actions of the Jews, their blind and repugnant fanaticism regarding their belief, and the implementation of the Talmudic precepts compiled in the Diaspora by their rabbis who distorted the principles of the Jewish belief (the religious law of the Prophet Moses), as it is said in the Koran." See *The Damascus Blood Libel (1840) as Told by Syrian Defense Minister Mustafa Tlass*, Inquiry and Analysis Series Report No. 99 (Washington, DC: MEMRI, June 27, 2002), http://www.memri.org/report/en/0/0/0/0/0/0/177/688.htm (accessed July 20, 2010).

104. See the discussion in Paul Berman, *The Flight of the Intellectuals* (Brooklyn, NY: Melville House, 2010), 265–99. See also Nonie Darwish, *Now They Call Me Infidel: Why I Renounced Jihad for America, Israel, and the War on Terror* (New York: Sentinel, 2006); Ayaan Hirsi Ali, *Infidel* (New York: Free Press, 2007); Irshad Manji, *The Trouble with Islam: A Muslim's Call for Reform in Her Faith* (New York: St. Martin's, 2004); and Bassam Tibi, *From Sayyid Qutb to Hamas: The Middle East Conflict and the Islamization of Anti-Semitism*, YIISA Research Working Paper Series (New Haven, CT: Yale University, 2010), http://www.isgap.org/working-paper-bassam-tibi/ (accessed April 1012).

105. Hirsi Ali, *Infidel*, 47.

106. Rachid Kaci, "Antisemitism Is the Legitimate Child of Islamism: The Real Cancer of Islam," in *Antisemitism*, 217.

107. Wafa Sultan, *A God Who Hates: The Courageous Woman Who Inflamed the Muslim World Speaks Out against the Evils of Islam* (New York: St. Martin's, 2009), 194.

Sultan, who now lives in America, strongly criticizes Islam, especially for its treatment of women. Her controversial appearances on Al-Jazeera led her to be included on *Time* magazine's list of the 100 Most Influential People in the World in 2006.

108. Ed Husain, *The Islamist* (New York: Penguin, 2007), 54.

109. Kressel, *Mass Hate*, 213–14.

110. See, for example, David Harris, "Palestinian Education," testimony in U.S. Senate, *Hearing before the Subcommittee on Labor, Health and Human Services, and Education of the Appropriations Committee*, 108th Cong., 1st sess., October 30, 2003, and Steven Stalinsky, "Inside the Saudi Classroom," *National Review*, February 7, 2003, http://www.nationalreview.com/articles/205833/inside-saudi-classroom/steven-stalinsky (accessed June 24, 2004).

111. N. Mozgovaya, "Charge Ahmadinejad with Incitement to Genocide, Say Former U.S., Israeli Envoys to UN," *Haaretz*, September 29, 2008, http://www.haaretz.com/hasen/spages/1023773.html (accessed June 6, 2011).

Chapter 3. The Shame of the Antiracist Community

1. See, for example, Martin Jay, *The Dialectical Imagination: A History of the Frankfurt School and the Institute of Social Research, 1923–1950* (Boston: Little, Brown, 1973).

2. MacShane, *Globalising Hatred*, 6.

3. Manfred Gerstenfeld, "Utrecht University: The Myth of Jewish Cannibalism, Censorship, and Fear of Muslim Intimidation," in *Academics against Israel and the Jews*, 2nd ed., ed. Manfred Gerstenfeld (Jerusalem: Jerusalem Center for Public Affairs, 2008), 236–41.

4. Pieter W. Van Der Horst, "Tying Down Academic Freedom," *Wall Street Journal*, June 30, 2006, http://online.wsj.com/article/SB115163738782295106.html (accessed May 5, 2010).

5. See, for example, David G. Dalin and John F. Rothmann, *Icon of Evil: Hitler's Mufti and the Rise of Radical Islam* (New Brunswick, NJ: Transaction Publishers, 2009); Fatah, *Jew Is Not My Enemy*; and Jeffrey Herf, *Nazi Propaganda for the Arab World* (New Haven, CT: Yale University Press, 2009).

6. See, for example, Wistrich, *Lethal Obsession*, 780–829, and Neil J. Kressel, "Mass Hatred in the Muslim and Arab World: The Neglected Problem of Anti-Semitism," *International Journal of Applied Psychoanalytic Studies* 4, no. 3 (2007): 197–215.

7. See, for example, *Anti-Semitism in the Turkish Media: Part I*, Special Dispatch No. 900 (Washington, DC: MEMRI, April 28, 2005), http://www.memri.org/report/en/0/0/0/0/0/0/51/1365.htm (accessed May 5, 2010), and Wistrich, *Lethal Obsession*, 748, 824–25.

8. Van Der Horst, "Tying Down Academic Freedom."

9. Ibid.

10. Quoted in Annie Karni, "Ahmadinejad Will Speak at Columbia Forum," *New York Sun*, September 20, 2007, http://www.nysun.com/new-york/ahmadinejad -will-speak-at-columbia-forum/63050/ (accessed January 11, 2011).

11. Quoted in Martin Kramer, "Professors of Palestine," *Middle East Quarterly* 9, no. 1 (Winter 2002): 91. Falk's comments originally appeared in an op-ed piece titled "Trusting Khomeini" in the *New York Times* on February 16, 1979.

12. See, for example, Richard Falk, "9/11: More Than Meets the Eye," *Journal* (Edinburgh), November 9, 2008, http://www.journal-online.co.uk/article/5056 -911-more-than-meets-the-eye (accessed January 11, 2011), and Tim Franks, "UN Expert Stands by Nazi Comments," BBC News, April 8, 2008, http:// news.bbc.co.uk/2/hi/middle_east/7335875.stm (accessed January 11, 2011).

13. Aaron Smargon, "Censored: The Politics Behind Silencing Nonie Darwish," *Princeton Tory*, December 2009, http://theprincetontory.com/main/censored -the-politics-behind-silencing-nonie-darwish-2/ (accessed January 11, 2011); Pamela Geller, "Free Speech Silenced at Columbia and Princeton," *Human Events*, November 25, 2009, http://www.humanevents.com/article.php?id=34558 (accessed January 11, 2009); Adam Kissel, "More Unsavory Disinvitations: This Time, Nonie Darwish at Princeton and Columbia," *Fire*, December 10, 2009, http://thefire.org/article/11367.html (accessed January 11, 2011); and Phyllis Chesler, "Princeton, Columbia Cancel Free Speech: Darwish Silenced," *PJ Media*, November 19, 2009, http://pajamasmedia.com/phyllischesler/2009/11/19 /princeton-columbia-cancel-free-speech-darwish-silenced/2/ (accessed January 11, 2011, site discontinued).

14. Darwish, *Now They Call Me Infidel*.

15. See Arabs for Israel, http://www.arabsforisrael.com/ (accessed June 7, 2011). There is also a new group in the U.K. called British Muslims for Israel. See the home page at http://www.britishmuslimsforisrael.com/BMFI/Welcome.html (accessed June 7, 2011).

16. Nonie Darwish, *Cruel and Usual Punishment: The Terrifying Global Implications of Islamic Law* (Nashville, TN: Thomas Nelson, 2008), xiii, xxvi.

17. Darwish, *Now They Call Me Infidel*, 217–41.

18. See Adam Brodsky, "Muslim Groups Still MIA on Terror," *New York Post*, January 19, 2010, http://www.nypost.com/p/news/opinion/opedcolumnists /muslim_groups_still_mia_on_terror_vvzt1Uuffh8xE6tGNUSZsJ (accessed January 11, 2011), and Adam Brodsky, "Dissent Crushed: Why Muslims Rarely Speak Out, Even in U.S.," *New York Post*, November 19, 2006, http://www .nypost.com/p/news/opinion/opedcolumnists/dissent_crushed_why_muslims_ rarely_6vO94x4EqtuLw9dxrrA9EN (accessed January 11, 2011). For more on the predicament of former Muslims, see the informative, though unbalanced, book *Why We Left Islam: Former Muslims Speak Out*, edited by Susan Crimp and Joel Richardson [pseud.] (Los Angeles, WND Books, 2008). The authors do

not convey sufficient sense of diversity within the Islamic world or acknowledge the atypicality of the convert's experiences in the religion. However, the book is one of the few sources that illustrates in detail the human costs often imposed on those who wish to leave Islam, given the severe consequences associated with apostasy in many readings of Islamic law.

19. See Kressel, *Bad Faith*, 139–98.
20. John L. Esposito and Dalia Mogahed, *Who Speaks for Islam? What a Billion Muslims Really Think* (New York: Gallup Press, 2007), 48.
21. "Ex-Muslim's College Speech Disrupted by Arson," *WND*, December 5, 2009, http://wnd.com/?pageId=117985 (accessed January 11, 2011).
22. Nonie Darwish, quoted in Chesler, "Princeton, Columbia Cancel Free Speech."
23. Most of this account of Rabbi Roth's role is based on an interview with her conducted by the author on December 8, 2010.
24. See Chesler, "Princeton, Columbia Cancel Free Speech."
25. See "About Us: Meet the Staff," Center for Jewish Life, Princeton University, http://www.princeton.edu/hillel/about-us/staff/ (accessed January 11, 2011).
26. Sohaib Sultan, "Flaws of the Darwish-ian Approach to Understand Islam," *Princeton Tory*, May 2010, http://theprincetontory.com/main/flaws-of-the-darwish-ian-approach-to-understand-islam/ (accessed January 11, 2011). Sultan called Darwish's March 24, 2010, speech "an hour of distortion against one of the world's great faiths." He faults Darwish for, among other things, (1) not seeking the aid of "a reliable scholar-expert," (2) taking items out of historical and textual context, (3) attributing troubling Jew-hatred in parts of the world to Islamic roots, (4) saying that Islamic law contributes to the unfortunate predicament of minorities in Islamic countries, (5) failing to celebrate Islamic voices for women's rights, (6) arguing that most Muslims have nonprogressive interpretations of jihad, (7) faulting Islam for support of honor killings, and (8) missing the generally benign spirit of the faith. My sense is that Imam Sultan, viewed in the context of contemporary Islam, can be classified as a moderate. Moreover, he is certainly entitled to voice his views about the current state of Islam and its relationship to religious foundations of the faith. Whether his views or those of Nonie Darwish better capture the reality of this relationship, however, is a matter for civil debate, and this is precisely what Imam Sultan attempted to suppress.
27. Jonny Paul, "Leeds U. Cancels Anti-Semitism Event," *Jerusalem Post*, March 17, 2007, and Matthias Kuentzel, "My Experience with the University of Leeds," *Engage*, March 24, 2007, http://www.engageonline.org.uk/blog/article.php?id=937 (accessed January 11, 2011).
28. David Horowitz, "The Anti-Semitic Jihad on Campus: My Night at USC," *Front Page Magazine*, January 15, 2010, http://frontpagemag.com/2010/01/15/the-anti-semitic-jihad-on-campus-my-night-at-usc/ (accessed January 20, 2011). Horowitz also describes similar incidents at various other universities. For a dis-

cussion of efforts to use fabricated evidence to condemn Horowitz before the event, as well as the USC administration's efforts to condemn him afterward, see David Horowitz, "Censorship and Libel at USC," *Front Page Magazine*, January 14, 2010, http://frontpagemag.com/2010/01/14/censorship-and-libel-at-usc-by-david-horowitz/ (accessed January 14, 2011). For the record, Horowitz, who is described by some as anti-Muslim, wrote, "There are good Muslims and bad Muslims, just as there are good Christians and bad ones, good Jews and bad Jews. Most Muslims are like everybody else—they want peace; and are law-abiding. . . . There is a difference between religious institutions and the religion of their individual members. . . . One of my concerns regarding organized Islam is that I don't see a comparable [to Catholicism and Protestantism] readiness to condemn Jew-hatred or the genocidal incitements regularly made by individuals and governments speaking in the name of Islam against the existence of the Jewish state." Forged documents distributed by opponents have Horowitz admitting that he "hates" Muslims and considers them "soulless beasts."

29. Quoted on DVD cover for Yoav Shamir, *Defamation* (New York: First Run Features, 2009), DVD.

30. Leslie Felperin, review of *Defamation*, directed by Yoav Shamir, *Variety*, February 5, 2009, www.variety.com/review/VE1117939586?refcatid=2471 (accessed January 11, 2011).

31. Owen Gleiberman, review of *Defamation*, directed by Yoav Shamir, *Entertainment Weekly*, November 24, 2009, http://www.ew.com/ew/article/0,,20322483,00.html (accessed January 11, 2011).

32. Jennifer Merin, "Defamation Opens in Theaters November 20," About.com, November 16, 2009, http://documentaries.about.com/b/2009/11/16/defamation-opens-in-theaters-november-20.htm (accessed January 11, 2011).

33. Akiva Gottlieb, "Israeli Documentary Challenges Jewish Responses to Anti-Semitism," *Jewish Journal* (Los Angeles), November 17, 2009, http://www.jewishjournal.com/film/article/israeli_documentary_challenges_jewish_responses_to_anti-semitism_20091117/ (accessed January 11, 2011).

34. See DVD cover, Shamir, *Defamation*.

35. Yoav Shamir, "Director's Statement," Defamation website, January 2009, http://www.defamation-thefilm.com/html/director.html (accessed January 11, 2011). Subsequent quotes by Shamir are from this statement.

36. Norman Finkelstein, *The Holocaust Industry: Reflections on the Exploitation of Jewish Suffering*, 2nd ed. (London: Verso, 2003), Norman Finkelstein, *Beyond Chutzpah: On the Misuse of Anti-Semitism and the Abuse of History*, updated ed. (Berkeley: University of California Press, 2008).

37. Attorney and Israel supporter Alan Dershowitz, who has criticized Finkelstein's scholarship, wrote the following concerning Finkelstein's response: "The level of 'academic' discourse on the Middle-East reached a new low—quite a feat

considering some of the old lows—when the notorious Jewish anti-Semite and Holocaust-justice denier Norman Finkelstein wrote a screed suggesting that I be targeted 'for assassination' because of my views on Israel. The obscene article was accompanied by an obscene cartoon drawn by 'Latuff,' a frequent accomplice of Finkelstein. The cartoon portrayed me as masturbating in rapturous joy while viewing images of dead Lebanese civilians on a TV set labeled 'Israel peep show,' with a Jewish Star of David prominently featured." Alan M. Dershowitz, "Norman Finkelstein's Obscenities," *Front Page Magazine*, August 22, 2006, http://archive.frontpagemag.com/readArticle.aspx?ARTID=2952. For arguments challenging the seriousness of Finkelstein's work, see Omer Bartov, "A Tale of Two Holocausts," *New York Times Book Review*, August 6, 2000, and Paul Bogdanor, "The Finkelstein Phenomenon: Reflections on the Exploitation of Anti-Jewish Bigotry," *Judaism* 51, no. 4 (Fall 2002): 504.

38. MEMRI's Antisemitism Documentation Project has provided massive documentation of Jew-hatred in Arab and Islamic communities. Archived material, including translated television clips, is readily available at http://www.memri.org/subject/en/51.htm (accessed January 11, 2011).

39. Although his fast-and-free polemical style makes reasonable answers unlikely, Shamir alludes to some issues that merit serious attention. Does the Holocaust loom too large in Jewish identity? Movies, educational curricula, and the mass media may lead too many in the West—including Jews—to think of the Holocaust when they hear the word "antisemitism." But the Holocaust may not, in fact, provide the best model for what has been occurring in the world of Islam. Moreover, the worst-case scenario for Muslim antisemitism is probably not death camps (although, if Iran uses a nuclear bomb against Israel as Iranian leaders have promised, the results could be equally deadly). Also, if excessive attention is paid to the Holocaust, one wonders why recent surveys find knowledge about Hitler, the Nazis, and the Holocaust abysmally inadequate. Ninety-seven percent of American students know Martin Luther King Jr. delivered the "I Have a Dream" speech, yet one in four cannot even identify Adolf Hitler as Germany's leader in World War II. See Sam Dillon, "History Survey Stumps U.S. Teens," *New York Times*, February 26, 2008, http://www.nytimes.com/2008/02/26/education/27history.html (accessed June 7, 2011).

   Shamir also raises a reasonable question about Jews overstating the significance of antisemitism in Western democracies. Some may be late in trusting the Germans and other Europeans, still bearing a grudge for crimes against the Jewish people before and during the Holocaust. Jews may also have failed to take into adequate account the changes that have occurred in most Christian denominations in recent years. Finally, some Jews may too readily assume that antisemitic motivation lurks behind criticism of Israel. These questions are legitimate, but they must be addressed in different context and on the basis of data and careful argumentation.

40. Ella Taylor, "Exploring the Politics of 'Defamation,'" NPR, November 30, 2009, http://www.npr.org/templates/story/story.php?storyId=120452232 (accessed January 11, 2011).

41. "About Jewcy," Jewcy, 2011, http://www.jewcy.com/about (accessed January 11, 2011).

42. Eli Valley, "Abe Foxworthy," EV Comics, http://www.evcomics.com/2009/05/23/abe-foxworthy/ (accessed January 11, 2011).

43. Eli Valley, "The Incredible Hulk," Jewcy, http://assets.jewcy.com/stories/valley/hulk/hulk-lg.jpg (accessed January 11, 2011).

44. Eli Valley, "What If . . . Batman and Robin Worked in the American Jewish Community?," Jewcy, http://assets.jewcy.com/stories/valley/batman/batman-and-robin-full-size.jpg (accessed January 11, 2011).

45. Eli Valley, "The Shonda!," EV Comics, http://www.evcomics.com/2009/02/07/the-shonda/ (accessed January 11, 2009). See also David Duke, "A Jewish Cartoonist Tells the Naked Truth (to Other Jews) That Non-Jews Wouldn't Dare!," David Duke Official Website, http://www.davidduke.com/general/jews-can-say-to-jewish-audiences-what-gentiles-would-not-dare_7448.html (accessed January 11, 2011).

46. Yaakov Kirschen, *Memetics and the Viral Spread of Anti-Semitism through "Coded Images" in Political Cartoons*, YIISA Working Paper Series (New Haven, CT: Yale University, 2010).

47. José Saramago, quoted in Phyllis Chesler, *The New Anti-Semitism: The Current Crisis and What We Must Do about It* (San Francisco: Jossey-Bass, 2003), 119.

48. See, for example, Gordon Allport, *The Nature of Prejudice* (Reading, MA: Addison-Wesley, 1954), 124; Bernard Hennessy, *Public Opinion*, 5th ed. (Monterey, CA: Brooks/Cole, 1985), 183; Robert S. Erikson and Kent L. Tedin, *American Public Opinion*, 6th ed. (New York: Longman, 2001), 190.

49. Arguably, bigotries against homosexuals, obese people, and women have been around longer.

50. Nirenstein, *Terror*, xii.

51. Chesler, *New Anti-Semitism*, 17. On the reaction to the book, she commented, "I was also attacked non-stop on various left feminist listserv groups about my Zionism—as if it were a Thought Crime, not a reasoned and passionate political position to which I'm entitled. Some Arab and Palestinian feminist professionals in mental health sent a barrage of non-stop anti-Zionist screeds and also threatened to resign from the listserv groups if I continued to oppose such propaganda or to say 'unmentionable' truths." See Jamie Glazov, "Fighting Islam's Gender Apartheid," *Front Page Magazine*, February 24, 2004, http://www.phyllis-chesler.com/480/fighting-islams-gender-apartheid (accessed April 26, 2012).

52. See Nora Gold, "Fighting Anti-Semitism in the Feminist Community" (lecture, Yale University, New Haven, CT, August 25, 2010), and Thyme Siegel, "Sisterhood Was Powerful and Global: Where Did It Go?" (lecture, Yale University, New Haven, CT, August 25, 2010).
53. Berman, *Flight of the Intellectuals*, 157. My account here closely follows Berman's analysis.
54. Ibid., 158.
55. Ibid., 159.
56. Ibid., 127–204.
57. Understandably, the targets of Ramadan's attacks were perturbed. Glucksmann and Lévy defended themselves and accused Ramadan, in essence, of being an antisemite. Yet, even Ian Buruma, a scholar who has shown considerable insight into Muslim extremism, taints Ramadan's targets by associating them with "neoconservative" tendencies, a discrediting label for many progressives. He also calls Glucksmann and Lévy's charges of antisemitism "shrill," "overblown," and harmful. And yet the shoe seems to fit.
58. Nick Cohen, *What's Left? How the Left Lost Its Way* (New York: Harper, 2007), 99–100.
59. Omayma Abdel-Latif, "That Weasel Word," *Al-Ahram Weekly*, April 4–10, 2002, http://weekly.ahram.org.eg/2002/580/cu2.htm (accessed January 11, 2011).
60. Andrew Walker, "Tom Paulin: Poetic Polemicist," BBC News World Edition, November 15, 2002, http://news.bbc.co.uk/2/hi/in_depth/uk/2000/newsmakers/2481623.stm (accessed January 11, 2011), and Tom Gross, "Welcome Voice? Harvard Invites Academic Who Wants Jews 'Shot Dead,'" *National Review*, November 12, 2002, http://old.nationalreview.com/comment/comment-gross111202.asp (January 11, 2011).
61. Quoted in Gross, "Welcome Voice?"
62. Ibid.
63. Lawrence Summers, "Address at Morning Prayers" (lecture, Harvard University, Cambridge, MA, September 17, 2002, http://www.harvard.edu.president/speeches.summers_2002/morningprayers.php. This speech is the source of subsequent quotations by Summers in this section.
64. Judith Butler, "No, It's Not Anti-Semitic," *London Review of Books* 25, no. 16 (August 21, 2003), http://www.lrb.co.uk/v25/n16/print/but102_.html (accessed January 11, 2011). This article is the source of all subsequent quotations by Butler in this section.
65. Edward Alexander, "'No, It's Not Antisemitic': Judith Butler vs. Lawrence Summers," *Judaism* 53, nos. 1–2 (Winter–Spring 2004), http://www.thefreelibrary.com/_/print/PrintArticle.aspx?id=126076039 (accessed January 11, 2011).
66. Fatah, *Jew Is Not My Enemy*, 174.

67. Rebeca Siegel (Siegel-Valdes), "Anti-Zionism Is Anti-Semitism: A Response to Judith Butler," *Bad Subjects* 70 (October 2004), http://bad.eserver.org/issues /2004/70/siegel.html (accessed January 11, 2011). This article is the source of all subsequent quotations by Siegel in this section.

68. Zack Furness, "Anti-Zionism Is NOT Anti-Semitism: Reflections on Palestine and What I've Learned about Being an Editor, a Jew, and a Leftist," *Bad Subjects* 77 (2007), http://bad.eserver.org/issues/2007/77/antizionism.html (accessed January 11, 2011).

69. Brian Klug, "The Myth of the New Anti-Semitism," *Nation*, January 15, 2004, http://www.thenation.com/print/article/myth-new-anti-semitism (January 21, 2011).

70. Ludwig Wittgenstein, quoted in Gideon D. Remba and Brian Klug, "Anti-Semitism: New or Old?," *Nation*, April 12, 2004, http://www.thenation.com/article/ anti-semitism-new-or-old (accessed January 21, 2011).

71. Quoted in Robert Wistrich and Brian Klug, "What Kind of Role Does Anti-Semitism Play in the Middle East Conflict?," letter debate, http://sicsa.huji.ac.il/ klug.html (accessed January 21, 2011). Klug engaged in a letter debate with Israeli historian Robert Wistrich. Klug wrote, "You refer to a 'pervasive cult of hatred and martyrdom in the Muslim world' and you say that anti-Semitism has become 'the opium of the Arab masses.' You also depict 'militant Islam' as if it were an inherently anti-Semitic force that 'will continue to fill the political void.' These phrases conjure up an Arab and Muslim world seething with anti-Jewish bigotry. The truth of the matter, I suggest, is different. On the one hand, fanaticism and bigotry exist on both sides. On the other hand, the vast majority of ordinary Jews and Muslims are more interested in getting on with their lives than with becoming either martyrs or heroes in a religious or national war." Wistrich rightly calls him to task, suggesting that Klug's response "ignores the undeniable mainstream character of Muslim Jew-hatred in the Middle East. . . . Contrary to what you imply, anti-Jewish hatred is no longer primarily driven by classical European, Christian or racist motives. It is Islamists who set the tone with their demonization of America, Israel and the Jews, while the media, the academic, artistic, religious and political elites in the European Union meekly follow suit. . . . Denying the specificity of diverse forms of bigotry does no service to the anti-racist cause; it also ignores the fact that Muslim Arabs are the main perpetrators of anti-Jewish attacks in the EU today. What is also missing in your letter is any serious reckoning with the implications of the fixation on Israel as the prime cause of violence and terrorism in the world—an obsession uncannily reminiscent of the fantasies underlying classical anti-Semitism. The contemporary Islamist and leftist mind-set holds Israel responsible for Arab backwardness and decadence, just as Europe traditionally projected the guilt for its own unresolved crises on the Jewish 'other.'"

72. Miriam Greenspan, "The New Anti-Semitism," *Tikkun*, November/December 2003, http://www.tikkun.org/article.pho/Greenspan-the-new-anti-semitism (accessed January 21, 2011).

73. Unitarian Universalist Association of Congregations, "Toward Peace and Justice in the Middle East," August 24, 2011, http://www.uua.org/statements/state ments/13983.shtml.

74. "Biography of Robert L. Bernstein," Yale Law School, http://www.law.yale.edu /intellectuallife/bernsteinbio.htm (accessed January 24, 2011).

75. Robert L. Bernstein, "Human Rights in the Middle East" (lecture, University of Nebraska–Omaha, November 10, 2010), http://www.ngo-monitor.org/article .php?operation=print&id=3116 (accessed January 24, 2011).

76. Ibid.

77. See Isabel Kershner, "Arsonists Damage and Deface Mosque in West Bank Village," *New York Times*, June 8, 2011.

78. Bernstein, "Human Rights in the Middle East."

79. Irwin Cotler, *Global Anti-Semitism: Assault on Human Rights*, YIISA Working Paper Series (New Haven, CT: Yale University, 2009), 15.

80. Quoted in ibid., 7.

81. Ibid., 15. Here Cotler quotes Gregg J. Rickman, who relies on the working defi- nition of antisemitism formulated by the EUMC. The EUMC is now known as the European Union Agency for Fundamental Rights (FRA).

82. Anne Bayefsky, "UN-Speakable Hypocrisy," *Daily News* (New York), June 2, 2008, www.nydailynews.com/fdcp?1295973714722 (accessed January 24, 2011); Haviv Rettig, "Analysis: How Reform Jews Almost Got Kicked Out of UN," *Jerusalem Post*, June 10, 2008, www.ngo-monitor/article.php?operation=print&id=1960 (accessed January 24, 2011).

83. Bayefsky, "UN-Speakable Hypocrisy."

84. Hamas Charter, quoted in Rettig, "Analysis."

85. David Littman, quoted in Bayefsky, "UN-Speakable Hypocrisy."

86. David Littman, quoted in Rettig, "Analysis."

87. Quoted in Betsy Pilsik, "'Rotten' Remark May Cost Charity," *Washington Times*, June 4, 2008.

88. Bayefsky, "UN-Speakable Hypocrisy."

89. David Littman, quoted in Rettig, "Analysis."

90. Littman also represented another nongovernmental organization, the Associa- tion for World Education. When, on behalf of that organization, he attempted discussing various forms of violence against women and its connection to sharia, he was blocked only seconds into the remarks. Representatives of the Organization of the Islamic Conference—the same group that had chaired Mahathir Mo- hamad's famous antisemitic speech—declared that any mention of Islamic law was an insult to the religion. The president of the Human Rights Council then

determined that no religious questions could be discussed, a decision that effectively confirmed the role of religion as an unassailable shield protecting the very human rights abuses that the council was supposed to be addressing. Littman had to agree to the terms in order to continue speaking about violence against women. See Austin Dacey, "Sensitive Words," *Trouw*, December 3, 2008, http://www.trouw.nl/engels/article1914391.ece/Sensitive_words.html?all=true (accessed January 24, 2011, site discontinued).

91. See, for example, Shimon Samuels, "The Durban Protocols: Globalization of the New Anti-Semitism," in *Antisemitism*, 33–35.

92. "NIF, Other NGOs Endorse Statement Condemning Antisemitism at Durban 2001 Conference and Pledging Not to Oppose Use of UN Fora for Incitement and 'Any Form of Racism, including Antisemitism,'" NGO Monitor, March 24, 2008, http://www.ngo-monitor.org/article.php?viewall=yes&id=1768 (accessed June 6, 2011). See also Gerald M. Steinberg, "The Centrality of NGOs in the Durban Strategy," *Yale Israel Journal*, July 11, 2006, http://spme.net/cgi-bin/articles.cgi?ID=799 (accessed June 6, 2011).

93. See UN Watch, *The United Nations and Anti-Semitism: 2004–2007 Report Card* (Geneva, November 1, 2007), http://www.unwatch.org/site/apps/nl/content2.asp?c=bdKKISNqEmG&b=1330819&ct=4566483 (January 24, 2011).

94. Ben-Itto, *Lie That Wouldn't Die*, 2–3.

95. Quoted in Samuels, "Durban Protocols," 34.

96. Ibid., 34. He continued, "I then waited three minutes and strode back in, because I could not leave them to their victory, or miss the game."

97. UN Watch, *United Nations and Anti-Semitism*. See also Paul Lungen, "Arbour Slammed for Failing to Address Anti-Semitism," *Canadian Jewish News*, November 8, 2007, http://www.unwatch.org/site/apps/nl/content2.asp?c=bdKKISNqEmG&b=1319279&ct=4620555 (accessed June 7, 2011).

98. Richard Falk, quoted in Michael Goldfarb, "A 'Supposed' Serious Person," *Weekly Standard*, January 2, 2009, http://www.weeklystandard.com/weblogs/TWSFP/2009/01/a_supposed_serious_person.asp (accessed June 7, 2011).

99. Melanie Phillips, "The Club of Tyranny's Falked Tongue," *Spectator*, April 8, 2008, http://www.spectator.co.uk/melaniephillips/598596/the-club-of-tyrannys-falked-tongue.thtml (accessed June 7, 2011).

100. Quoted in Kressel, *Bad Faith*, 248–49.

101. See UN Watch, *United Nations and Anti-Semitism*.

102. Pedro A. Sanjuan, *The U.N. Gang: A Memoir of Incompetence, Corruption, Espionage, Anti-Semitism, and Islamic Extremism at the UN Secretariat* (New York: Doubleday, 2005), 8–9, 85.

103. Ibid., 88. Sanjuan also suggested that UN Secretary-General Kurt Waldheim's Nazi past was well known prior to his appointment. He maintains that both

the United States and the Soviet Union permitted his candidacy to succeed because they believed his war criminal past would make him easier to control (pp. 92–93).

104. Esposito and Mogahed, *Who Speaks for Islam?*, xv.

105. Ibid., 69.

106. Robert Satloff, "Just Like Us! Really?," *Weekly Standard* 13, no. 33 (May 12, 2008), http://www.weeklystandard.com/print/Content/Public/Articles/000/000/015/066chpzg.asp?page=3 (January 30, 2011). Satloff wrote, "Amazing as it sounds, according to Esposito and Mogahed, the proper term for a Muslim who hates America, wants to impose Sharia law, supports suicide bombing, and opposes equal rights for women but does not 'completely' justify 9/11 is . . . 'moderate.'"

107. Esposito and Mogahed, *Who Speaks for Islam?*, 154.

108. Satloff, "Just like Us! Really?" Satloff wrote, "Esposito and Mogahed don't utter a word about the vast sea of intolerance in which the radicals operate."

109. Pew Global Attitudes Project, *Islamic Extremism.*

110. Pew Global Attitudes Project, *Little Enthusiasm.*

111. Elham Mane'a, *Yemeni Liberal Criticizes Appointment of Dalia Mogahed as Obama's Advisor on Islam*, Special Dispatch No. 2518 (Washington, DC: MEMRI, September 4, 2009), http://www.memri.org/report/en/0/0/0/0/0/0/3609.htm (accessed February 8, 2011).

112. Kressel, "Urgent Need," B14–B15, and Neil J. Kressel, "Antisemitism in the Muslim and Arab World," *Judaism* 52, nos. 3–4 (Summer/Fall 2003): 227.

113. Ira Brenner and Nadia Ramzy, eds., "Special Issue: Anti-Semitism in Muslim Cultures," *International Journal of Applied Psychoanalytic Studies* 4, no. 3 (2007), and Jeffrey A. Schaler, ed., "Special Issue: Anti-Semitism the World Over in the Twenty-First Century," *Current Psychology* 26, nos. 3–4 (December 2007).

114. See, especially, Cohen et al., "Modern Anti-Semitism," 290–306; Roland Imhoff and Rainer Banse, "Ongoing Victim Suffering Increases Prejudice: The Case of Secondary Anti-Semitism," *Psychological Science* 20, no. 12 (December 2009): 1443–47; Susan A. Andrzejewski, Judith A. Hall, and Elizabeth R. Salib, "Anti-Semitism and the Identification of Jewish Group Membership from Photographs," *Journal of Nonverbal Behavior* 33, no. 1 (March 2009): 47–58, and Edward H. Kaplan and Charles A. Small, "Anti-Israel Sentiment Predicts Anti-Semitism in Europe," *Journal of Conflict Resolution* 50, no. 4 (August 2006): 548–61. Note that a search of the Academic Search Complete database—which also includes journalistic work—turns up more articles that address antisemitism in the Islamic world from a variety of perspectives.

115. Nasar Meer and Tehseen Noorani, "A Sociological Comparison of Anti-Semitism and Anti-Muslim Sentiment in Britain," *Sociological Review* 56, no. 2 (May 2008): 195–219; Efraim Karsh, "The Long Trail of Islamic Anti-Semitism," *Is-*

rael Affairs 12, no. 1 (January 2006): 1–12; and Robert Fine, "Fighting with Phantoms: A Contribution to the Debate on Antisemitism in Europe," *Patterns of Prejudice* 43, no. 5 (December 2009): 459–79.

116. Fatah, *Jew Is Not My Enemy*, 174, 175.

117. Of course, empirical research need not depend on interviews alone. With knowledge of languages, one could study newspapers, books, lectures, prayers, fatwas, etc., even from a base in the United States. Indeed, studying publications may sometimes be even more important than interviewing.

118. See, especially, Martin S. Kramer, *Ivory Towers on Sand: The Failure of Middle Eastern Studies in America* (Washington, DC: Washington Institute for Near East Policy, 2001).

119. Edward Said, *Orientalism* (New York: Vintage, 1979).

120. Martin Kramer, "Columbia University: The Future of Middle Eastern Studies at Stake," in *Academics against Israel and the Jews*, 103.

121. Ibid.

122. Gavin Gross, "Anti-Israeli Activity at the School of Oriental and African Studies: How Jewish Students Started to Fight Back," in *Academics against Israel and the Jews*, 225.

123. Kramer, "Columbia University," 104.

124. "Columbia U. Releases Edward Said Chair Donors: Names Arab Government," Campus Watch.org, March 19, 2004, http://www.campus-watch.org/article /id/1076 (accessed February 9, 2011).

125. Harvard agreed and then found other money to sponsor new faculty appointments in Islamic studies. See Jonathan Jaffit, "Fighting Sheikh Zayed's Funding of Islamic Studies at Harvard Divinity School," in *Academics against Israel and the Jews*, 108–14.

126. Martin Kramer, "Georgetown Yankees in Prince Alwaleed's Court," Sandbox (blog), January 2, 2006, http://www.martinkramer.org/sandbox/2006/01 /georgetown-yankees-in-prince-alwaleeds-court/ (accessed March 9, 2011).

127. Tamar Lewin, "Partnership to Further Global Quest by N.Y.U.," *New York Times*, June 9, 2011.

Chapter 4. The Flawed Logic of Antisemitism Minimization

1. David Matas, *Aftershock: Anti-Zionism and Antisemitism* (Toronto: Dundurn, 2005), 113–14.

2. Ashraf Al-Faqi, quoted in Chernitsky and Glass, *Antisemitic Statements*.

3. 'Abd Al-Rahman Al-Khatib, quoted in ibid. Golovinski may well have played a part in "writing" *The Protocols*, but he was a member of the Russian czar's secret police. Machiavelli may have been referenced because http://www.harvard .edu.president.speeches.summers-2002/morningprayers.php *The Protocols* plagiarized Joly's *Dialogues aux Enfers entre Machiavel et Montesquieu*. This book

presented the ideas of Machiavelli, and consequently many schemes in *The Protocols* seem Machiavellian. Golovinski, Joly, and Machiavelli were all non-Jews. See Ben-Itto, *Lie That Wouldn't Die*, 174–204.

4. See, e.g., Ben Halpern, *The Idea of the Jewish State*, 2nd ed. (Cambridge: Harvard University Press, 1969); Arthur Hertzberg, ed., *The Zionist Idea: A Historical Analysis and Reader* (New York: Macmillan, 1972); and Walter Laqueur, *A History of Zionism: From the French Revolution to the Establishment of the State of Israel* (New York: Schocken, 2003).

5. See Daniel Patrick Moynihan, introduction to *The Anti-Zionist Complex*, by Jacques Givet, trans. Evelyn Abel (Englewood, NJ: SBS Publishing, 1982), ix–xiii. Originally published in Paris, Librairie Plon, 1979.

6. America, after all, has fought wars against regimes in several Muslim countries yet strived energetically, appropriately, and with significant—if imperfect—success to cultivate respect for the people living in those countries.

7. See Kaplan and Small, "Anti-Israel Sentiment," 548–56; Cohen et al., "Modern Anti-Semitism," 302–4; and Baum and Nakazawa, "Anti-Semitism versus Anti-Israel Sentiment," 1–8.

8. George Soros, "On Israel, America and AIPAC," *New York Review of Books*, April 12, 2007, http://www.georgesoros.com/articles-essays/entry/on_israel_america_and_aipac/ (accessed March 30, 2011).

9. Some are listed in Alan Dershowitz, *The Case against Israel's Enemies: Exposing Jimmy Carter and Others Who Stand in the Way of Peace* (Hoboken, NJ: Wiley, 2008), 4.

10. David Hirsh, *Anti-Zionism and Antisemitism: Cosmopolitan Reflections*, YIISA Working Paper No. 1 (New Haven, CT: Yale University, 2007), 139, http://eprints.gold.ac.uk/2061/1/Hirsh_Yale_paper.pdf (accessed April 4, 2012).

11. Chesler, *New Anti-Semitism*, 161–72.

12. Dershowitz, *Case against Israel's Enemies*, 4.

13. See Michele Block, "In Darien Church, Tutu Assails 'Vicious System' of Apartheid," *Hartford Courant*, October 29, 1984, http://www.courant.com/about/hc-archives,0,6611981.htmlstory (accessed March 30, 2011). The Nobel Peace Prize winner has made numerous anti-Jewish remarks during the past quarter-century. See also Alan M. Dershowtiz, "Why the Jews?," *New York Post*, March 5, 2011.

14. Some authors who use "new antisemitism" theory and terminology include the following: Chesler, *New Anti-Semitism*; Abraham H. Foxman, *Never Again? The Threat of the New Anti-Semitism* (San Francisco: HarperSanFrancisco, 2003); Paul Iganski and Barry Kosmin, eds., *A New Antisemitism? Debating Judeophobia in 21st-Century Britain* (London: Profile, 2003); Taguieff, *Rising from the Muck*; Nirenstein, *Terror*; and MacShane, *Globalising Hatred*. Earlier but related use of the phrase can be observed in Arnold Forster and Benjamin Epstein, *The New*

Anti-Semitism (New York: McGraw-Hill, 1974), and Bernard Lewis, *Semites and Anti-Semites: An Inquiry into Conflict and Prejudice* (New York: Norton, 1986), 236–59.

15. Matas, *Aftershock*, 113.

16. Natan Sharansky, "3D Test of Anti-Semitism: Demonization, Double Standards, Delegitimization," *Jewish Political Studies Review* 16 (Fall 2004): 3–4, http://jcpa.org/article/3d-test-of-anti-semitism-demonization-double-standards -delegitimization/.

17. Givet, *Anti-Zionist Complex*, 39.

18. Leon Botstein, contribution to Zionism at 100 Symposium, *New Republic*, September 8–15, 1997.

19. Per Ahlmark, quoted in Manfred Gerstenfeld, "Anti-Israelism and Antisemitism: Common Characteristics and Motifs," in *Not Your Father's Antisemitism*, 333.

20. EUMC), "Working Definition of Antisemitism." Two additional parts of the definition refer to more direct applications of traditional antisemitic practice to the Israeli context: (1) "using the symbols and images associated with classic antisemitism (e.g., claims of Jews killing Jesus or blood libel) to characterize Israel or Israelis" and (2) "holding Jews collectively responsible for actions of the state of Israel."

21. Harrison, *Resurgence of Anti-Semitism*, 3.

22. Josh Kaplan, "Contesting Anti-Semitism: Human Rights, Israel Bashing, and the Making of a Non-Problem," *Anthropological Quarterly* 83, no. 2 (Spring 2010): 429–48.

23. Ami Isseroff, "Arab and Muslim Anti-Zionism and Antisemitism: A Study," Zionism and Israel Pages, 2005, http://www.zionism.netfirms.com/ArabAnti Zionism.htm (accessed August 4, 2010, site discontinued).

24. Joseph Goebbels, *The "Nazi-Sozi": Questions and Answers for National Socialists* (Valley Forge, PA: Landpost Press, 1992), http://www.archive.org/stream /NaziSozi/Nazi-Sozi#page/n0/mode/2up (accessed June 6, 2011).

25. Irfan Khawaja, "Poisoning the Well: The False Equation of Anti-Zionism and Anti-Semitism," History News Network, March 28, 2005, http://hnn.us /articles/10866.html (accessed March 31, 2011).

26. Kaplan, "Contesting Anti-Semitism."

27. Earl Raab, "Antisemitism, Anti-Israelism, Anti-Americanism," *Judaism* 51, no. 4 (Fall 2002): 387, 388.

28. Kressel, "Urgent Need," B14–B15.

29. Stanley J. Morse, letter to the editor, *Chronicle of Higher Education* 50, no. 33 (April 23, 2004): B4.

30. Ramzy, "Commentary," 194. Ramzy's will to believe in an benign Islamic past is evidenced by her reference to the Jewish scholar Maimonides's flight from Christian intolerance in Spain. Maimonides was actually fleeing the Muslim Almohad

persecution, although he did eventually find refuge under a different Muslim regime in Egypt. Ramzy's essay was written in response to Kressel, "Mass Hatred in the Muslim and Arab World," 197–215.

31. Ramzy, "Commentary," 195.

32. Yossi Klein Halevi, keynote address at Understanding Facets of Contemporary Antisemitism conference (Yale University, New Haven, CT, April 3, 2009), lecture attended by author.

33. Freedom House, *A Catalyst for Freedom and Democracy: 2007 Annual Report* (Washington, DC, 2007), http://www.freedomhouse.org/uploads/special_report /89.pdf (accessed March 31, 2011, site discontinued).

34. Dershowitz, *Case against Israel's Enemies*, and Alan Dershowitz, *The Case for Israel* (Hoboken, NJ: Wiley, 2004).

35. Matas, *Aftershock*, 40, 49, 53.

36. *Israeli Arabs Prefer Israel to Palestinian Authority*, Special Dispatch No. 117 (Washington, DC: MEMRI, August 10, 2000), http://www.memri.org/report/en/0/0 /0/0/0/0/358.htm (March 31, 2011).

37. Matas, *Aftershock*, 54.

38. David Hirsh, "Occupation Not Apartheid," *Mail and Guardian* (South Africa), October 3, 2008, http://www.engageonline.org.uk/blog/article.php?id=2139 (accessed March 14, 2011).

39. There is also the matter of the media seeking "man-bite-dog" stories. Examples of once-victimized Jews being abusive seem to fit the bill.

40. Hirsh, *Anti-Zionism and Antisemitism*, 6.

41. Moishe Postone, cited in ibid., 7.

42. Montville, "Commentary," 218.

43. See, for example, Kressel, *Mass Hate*, 214–23, and Kressel, *Bad Faith*, 216–31. The relationship among damaged self-worth, group identity, prejudice, and extremism is more complicated that Montville implies.

44. Uri Avnery, "Muhammad's Sword," *Counterpunch*, September 26, 2006, http:// www.counterpunch.org/avnery09262006.html (accessed March 14, 2011).

45. See, for example, Mark R. Cohen, *Under Crescent and Cross: The Jews in the Middle Ages*, rev. ed. (Princeton, NJ: Princeton University Press, 2008); Mark R. Cohen, "Modern Myths of Muslim Anti-Semitism," in *Muslim Attitudes to Jews and Israel*, 31–47; John L. Esposito, *What Everyone Needs to Know about Islam: Answers to Frequently Asked Questions, from One of America's Leading Experts* (New York: Oxford University Press, 2002), 81; and Reuven Firestone, *An Introduction to Islam for Jews* (Philadelphia: Jewish Publication Society, 2008). Numerous Jewish historians from the past shared a belief in the relative benevolence of Muslim rule through the ages. See, for example, Léon Poliakov, *The History of Anti-Semitism*, vol. 2.

46. Cohen, "Modern Myths," 41.

47. Herf, *Nazi Propaganda*. Herf does not take a strong explicit position on the situation of the Jews in Islamic history, but he argues that contemporary Islamists remain heavily influenced by Nazi efforts to spread their antisemitic doctrine.

48. Lewis, *Semites and Anti-Semites*. Lewis argues that some degree of "normal" prejudice existed in traditional Islam but that what is usually thought of as a full-blown, lethal, obsessive antisemitism was largely a European import.

49. See, for example, Bostom, ed., *Legacy of Islamic Anti-Semitism*; Martin Gilbert, *In Ishmael's House: A History of Jews in Muslim Lands* (New Haven, CT: Yale University Press, 2010); Norman A. Stillman, *The Jews of Arab Lands in Modern Times* (Philadelphia: Jewish Publication Society, 2003); Norman A. Stillman, *Jews of Arab Lands: A History and Source Book* (Philadelphia: Jewish Publication Society, 1979); and Bat Yeor, *Islam and Dhimmitude: Where Civilizations Collide*, trans. Miriam Kochan and David Littman (Madison, NJ: Fairleigh Dickinson University Press, 2002). Similar arguments appear on the Web and in periodicals; for example, Bruce S. Thornton, "Islam without Apologetics," *City Journal*, August 8, 2008, http://www.city-journal.org/2008/bc0808bt.html (accessed July 1, 2010); Robert Spencer, "The Persistent Fiction That Islamic Anti-Semitism Is a Borrowing from Nazism," Jihad Watch, April 21, 2010, http://www.jihadwatch.org/2010/04/the-persistent-fiction-that-islamic-anti-semitism-is-a-borrowing-from-nazism.html (August 10, 2010); and Robert Spencer, "The Persistence of Islamic Anti-Semitism," *Front Page Magazine*, December 8, 2009, http://frontpagemag.com/2009/12/08/the-persistence-of-islamic-anti-semitism-by-robert-spencer/print/ (August 10, 2010).

50. Leon Cohen, "New Books Probe Reality of Muslim Anti-Semitism," *Wisconsin Jewish Chronicle*, July 17, 2008, http://www.jewishchronicle.org/article.php?article_id=10346 (accessed April 13, 2009).

51. Lewis, *Semites and Anti-Semites*, 121.

52. Some Muslims blame Jews for their purported attempts to harm Jesus, but this is much less central to Islamic Jew-hatred than it is to Christian Jew-hatred. (Muslims view Jesus as a prophet, although they deny his divinity, the crucifixion, and hence the Jews' role as Christ-killers.)

53. For an English translation of Qutb's work, see Ronald L. Nettler, *Past Trials and Present Tribulations: A Muslim Fundamentalist's View of the Jews* (New York: Pergamon, 1987).

54. See Dalin and Rothmann, *Icon of Evil*, 81, and Herf, *Nazi Propaganda*.

55. John Hooper, "Pope Finds Jews Not to Blame for Death of Jesus," *Guardian*, March 2, 2011, http://www.guardian.co.uk/world/2011/mar/02/pope-jews-jesus-death-crucifixion (accessed March 31, 2011).

56. Christopher Hitchens, "The New Anti-Semitism?," *Times Literary Supplement*, November 19, 2008, http://www.the-tls.co.uk/tls/public/article758321.ece (accessed April 25, 2012).

57. Gallup Center for Muslim Studies, *Religious Perceptions in America: With an In-Depth Analysis of U.S. Attitudes toward Muslims and Islam* (Abu Dhabi: Gallup, 2009), 5, 15, http://www.abudhabigallupcenter.com/144335/Religious -Perceptions-America.aspx (accessed March 31, 2011, link no longer active).

58. Amir Mizroch, "Poll: 90% of ME Views Jews Unfavorably," *Jerusalem Post*, February 9, 2010, http://www.jpost.com/MiddleEast/Article.aspx?id=168176 (accessed March 31, 2011)

59. Pew Global Attitudes Project, *Muslim Publics Divided on Hamas and Hezbollah* (Washington, DC: Pew Research Center, December 2, 2010), http://pewglobal .org/2010/12/02/muslims-around-the-world-divided-on-hamas-and-hezbollah/ (accessed March 31, 2011).

60. Esposito and Mogahed, *Who Speaks for Islam?*, 49–52, 65–98.

61. See, for example, Kaplan and Small, "Anti-Israel Sentiment"; Cohen et al., "Modern Anti-Semitism"; and Baum and Nakazawa, "Anti-Semitism versus Anti-Israel Sentiment."

62. See, for example, Michael Morris, "EU Whitewashes Muslim Anti-Semitism," *American Thinker*, April 1, 2004, http://www.americanthinker.com/2004/04 /eu_whitewashes_muslim_antisemi.html (March 31, 2011).

63. See, for example, "Leaders Rally to Defend Dr. Mahathir," *New Straits Times-Management Times*, October 18, 2003, http://www.lexisnexis.com/hottopics /Inacademic/? (accessed August 5, 2010).

64. Works by these individuals vary greatly in style, academic quality, religious orientation, and political affiliation, but all have value as testimony to the pervasiveness of anti-Jewish hostility in the Muslim and Arab world. If the authors were brought together, perhaps the only thing they would agree on is the destructiveness of Muslim and Arab antisemitism. See, for example, Tibi, *From Sayyid Qutb to Hamas*; Fatah, *Jew Is Not My Enemy*; Kaci, "Anti-Semitism Is the Legitimate Child of Islamism," 212–17; El-Hattab, "Absurdity of Antisemitism in the Arab World," 218–31; Irfan Khawaja, "The Problem of Muslim Anti-Semitism," *Pakistan Today*, January 10, 2003, http://zionism-israel.com/ ezine/Irfan_Kahwaja_Muslim_Anti-Semitism.htm (accessed April 25, 2012); Hirsi Ali, *Infidel*; Darwish, *Now They Call Me Infidel*; Haras Rafiq, "Haras Rafiq, Director of CENTRI, on Combating Antisemitism and Hate as Part of the Inter-Parliamentary Coalition on Combating Antisemitism 2010 Ottawa Conference," YouTube video, 5:46, posted by "icca2010," November 9, 2010, http://www.youtube.com/watch?v=FXUxzoxCqCQ (accessed March 31, 2011); Mark A. Gabriel, *Islam and the Jews* (Lake Mary, FL: Charisma House, 2003); Amir Taheri, *The Persian Night* (New York: Encounter Books, 2009); Khaleel Mohammed, "Muslim Exegesis, the Hadith and the Jews," *Judaism* 209/210, 53 (Winter–Spring 2004): 3–11; Husain, *The Islamist*, 129; and Manji, *Trouble with Islam*, 15.

65. See Austin Dacey, *The Secular Conscience: Why Belief Belongs in Public Life* (Amherst, NY: Prometheus, 2008), and Marci A. Hamilton, *God vs. the Gavel: Religion and the Rule of Law* (New York: Cambridge University Press, 2005), 3–11.

66. Austin Dacey, "Religious Persecution Wolf in Anti-Defamation Sheep's Clothing," *Religion Dispatches*, March 30, 2009, http://www.religiondispatches.org /dialogs/print/?id=1276 (accessed November 9, 2010).

67. Kramer, *Ivory Towers on Sand*, 27–43.

68. "Diversity: 12th International Conference," Call for Papers, http://ondiversity. com/conference-2012/call-for-papers/ (accessed April 25, 2012).

69. Sumbul Ali-Karamali, *The Muslim Next Door: The Qur'an, the Media, and That Veil Thing* (Ashland, OR: White Cloud Press, 2008).

70. Sumbul Ali-Karamali, "Antisemitism through the Lens of Islamophobia," Muslim Next Door, http://www.muslimnextdoor.com/writings/anti_semitism.html (accessed March 31, 2009).

71. Gallup Center for Muslim Studies, *In U.S., Religious Prejudice Stronger against Muslims* (Washington, DC: Gallup, January 21, 2010), http://www.gallup.com /poll/125312/Religious-Prejudice-Stronger-Against-Muslims.aspx (accessed March 31, 2011).

72. Pew Forum on Religion and Public Life, *Muslims Widely Seen as Facing Discrimination: Views of Religious Similarities and Differences* (Washington, DC: Pew Research Center, 2009), http://pewforum.org/uploadedfiles/Topics/Religious _Affiliation/Muslim/survey0909.pdf (accessed March 31, 2011).

73. ABC News/*Washington Post* Poll, "Most Back Outreach to Muslim Nations, but Suspicion and Unfamiliarity Persist," April 5, 2009, ABC News, http://abcnews .go.com/PollingUnit/story?id=7248471&page=1 (accessed March 31, 2011).

74. B. A. Robinson, "Prejudice of Americans towards Mormons and Evangelicals," ReligiousTolerance.org, May 6, 2007, http://www.religioustolerance.org/evan intol.htm (accessed March 31, 2011).

75. Lydia Saad, "Anti-Muslim Sentiments Fairly Commonplace," Gallup News Service, August 10, 2006, http://www.gallup.com/poll/24073/AntiMuslim -Sentiments-Fairly-Commonplace.aspx (accessed March 31, 2011).

76. Gallup, *Religious Perceptions*, 8.

77. Pew Forum, *Muslims*, 3.

78. Council on American-Islamic Relations (CAIR), *American Public Opinion about Islam and Muslims* (Washington, DC, 2006), 5, http://www.cair.com/PDF/cair surveyanalysis.pdf (accessed March 31, 2011).

79. Pew Forum, *Muslims*, 7.

80. Saad, "Anti-Muslim Sentiments."

81. CAIR, *American Public Opinion*, 4.

82. Saad, "Anti-Muslim Sentiments."

83. Frank Newport, "Complex but Hopeful Pattern of American Attitudes toward

Muslims," Gallup News Service, March 23, 2006, http://www.gallup.com/poll/22021/Complex-Hopeful-Pattern-American-Attitudes-Toward-Muslims.aspx (accessed March 31, 2006).

84. ABC/*Washington Post*, "Most Back Outreach."

85. Gallup, *In U.S.*

86. David Folkenflik, "NPR Ends Williams' Contract after Muslim Remarks," NPR, October 21, 2010, http://www.npr.org/templates/story/story.php?storyId=130712737 (accessed April 2012); "NPR Fires Juan Williams; and Fox News Expands His Role," FoxNews.com, October 21, 2010, http://www.foxnews.com/politics/2010/10/21/npr-fires-juan-williams-oreilly-appearance/ (accessed April 2012).

87. Saad, "Anti-Muslim Sentiments."

88. See, for example, Gallup Center for Muslim Studies, *Muslim Americans: A National Portrait* (Abu Dhabi: Gallup, 2009), http://www.abudhabigallupcenter.com/home.aspx (accessed March 31, 2011).

89. Deborah Lipstadt, quoted in Elaine Durbach, "Prof Sees Mixed Picture on Hatred, Shoa Denial," *New Jersey Jewish News*, September 25, 2008, http://njjewishnews.com/njjn.com/092508/cjProfSeesMixed.html (accessed March 31, 2011).

90. See, for example, Gordon W. Allport, *The Nature of Prejudice*, 25th anniv. ed. (Reading, MA: Addison-Wesley, 1979), 154–55; Debra Nussbaum Cohen, "Survey Finds Jews Less Prejudiced toward Blacks than Most Americans," Jewish Telegraphic Agency, June 16, 1993, http://www.highbeam.com/doc/1P1-2238589.html (accessed March 31, 2011); and Institute for Jewish Policy Research, *Social and Political Attitudes of British Jews: Some Key Findings of the JPR Survey* (London, 1996), http://www.jpr.org.uk/Reports/PJC_Reports/no_1_1996/main.htm (accessed March 31, 2011).

91. Two early sources of this frequent finding are Mark R. Levy and Michael S. Kramer, *The Ethnic Factor* (New York: Simon and Schuster, 1973), 109, and Kathleen Murphy Beatty and Oliver Walter, "Religious Preference and Practice: Reevaluating Their Impact on Political Tolerance," *Public Opinion Quarterly* 48 (1984): 318–29.

92. *American Public Opinion about Islam and Muslims* (Washington, DC: Council on American-Islamic Relations, 2006), http://www.cair.com/PDF/cairsurveyanalysis.pdf (accessed April 25, 2012).

93. Gallup, *Religious Perceptions*, 5, 15.

94. Lydia Saad, "Obama Approval High among Muslims, Jews, and Catholics," Gallup Politics, May 1, 2009, http://www.gallup.com/poll/118120/Obama-Approval-High-Among-Muslims-Jews-Catholics.aspx (accessed March 31, 2011).

95. Quinnipiac University, "New York City Voters Oppose Mosque near Ground Zero," Quinnipiac University Poll, July 1, 2010, http://www.quinnipiac.edu/x1302.xml?ReleaseID=1473 (accessed March 31, 2011).

96. American Jewish Committee, *2009 Annual Survey of American Jewish Opinion* (New York, 2009), http://www.ajc.org/site/c.ijITI2PHKoG/b.5472819/k.D6 D7/2009_Annual_Survey_of_American_Jewish_Opinion.htm (accessed March 31, 2011).

97. Marc B. Shapiro, "Islam and the Halakhah," *Judaism* 42, no. 3 (Summer 1993): 332–43.

98. Robert Wistrich, "Muslim Antisemitism," Coordination Forum for Countering Antisemitism, January 2, 2003, http://www.antisemitism.org.il/article/54004 /muslim-antisemitism-robert-wistrich (accessed April 27, 2009).

99. Intellectuals don't have a great record in recognizing the growth of dangerous antisemitism. As Stephen Norwood documented, colleges and universities were appallingly slow to grasp what was going on in Nazi Germany in the 1930s. They offered an abundance of reasons for their failure to notice what should have been patently obvious about the Nazi regime. See Stephen H. Norwood, *The Third Reich in the Ivory Tower: Complicity and Conflict on American Campuses* (New York: Cambridge University Press, 2011).

100. Leaders in many fields have sought better communications with Muslims. See Helene Cooper, "America Seeks Bonds to Islam, Obama Insists," *New York Times*, April 7, 2009; Andrea Elliott, "White House Quietly Courts Muslims in U.S.," *New York Times*, April 19, 2010; and Laurie Goodstein, "Police in Los Angeles Step Up Efforts to Gain Muslims' Trust," *New York Times*, March 10, 2011.

101. Laurie Goodstein, "Three Clergyman, Three Faiths, One Friendship," *New York Times*, November 24, 2009.

102. See Morris, "EU Whitewashes." Even when antisemitism is unearthed, some—especially in Europe—try hard to deflect blame from the Muslim community, although this may mean assigning it where it does not belong.

103. See Ross and Makovsky, *Myths, Illusions, and Peace*, 238.

104. Janet Doerflinger, "Professors Push Israel to Negotiate with Hamas," *American Thinker*, February 6, 2011, http://www.americanthinker.com/2011/02 /professors_push_israel_to_nego.html (accessed February 8, 2011).

105. Harrison, *Resurgence*, 66.

106. Michael Walzer, "A Conversation with Michael Walzer: The Implications of Contemporary Global Anti-Semitism" (lecture, Yale University, New Haven, CT, January 28, 2010), http://vimeo.com/9207083 (accessed March 31, 2011).

107. Taguieff, *Rising from the Muck*, 74–75.

108. Craig Horowitz, "The Return of Anti-Semitism," *New York*, December 15, 2003, http://nymag.com/nymetro/news/religion/features/n_9622/ (accessed April 12, 2011).

109. Montville, "Commentary," 216.

110. Robert Fine, "Between Opposition and Denial: The Radical Response to Anti-

semitism in Contemporary Europe" (paper presented at YIISA Global Antisemitism Conference, Yale University, New Haven, CT, August 24, 2010).

111. Richard Baehr, "Why Does the Left Hate Israel?," *American Thinker*, January 22, 2004 http://www.americanthinker.com/2004/01/why_does_the_left_hate_israel.html (accessed April 12, 2011).

112. Ernest Sternberg, "The Academic Boycott as Persecution," Scholars for Peace in the Middle East, July 10, 2007, http://spme.net/cgi-bin/articles.cgi?ID=2608 (accessed April 12, 2011), and Ernest Sternberg, "A Revivified Corpse: Left-Fascism in the Twenty-First Century," *Telosscope* (blog), January 7, 2009, http://www.telospress.com/main/index.php?main_page=news_article&article_id=288 (accessed April 12, 2011).

113. Sternberg, "Academic Boycott."

114. Ibid.

115. Baehr, "Why Does the Left Hate Israel?"

116. Robert Fine, "New Antisemitism Theory and Its Critics" (unpublished paper prepared for Racism and Antisemitism Mid-Term Conference, European Sociological Association, Belfast, September 2010). Also see Robert Fine, "Fighting with Phantoms: A Contribution to the Debate on Antisemitism in Europe," *Patterns of Prejudice* 43, no. 5 (2009): 459–79; Andrei Markovits in Manfred Gersteinfeld, "European Anti-Americanism and Anti-Semitism: Similarities and Differences—An Interview with Andrei S. Markovits," *Post-Holocaust and Anti-Semitism* 16 (2004), http://www.jcpa.org/phas/phas-16.htm (accessed April 25, 2012); and Barry Rubin, "The Two Great Hatreds," *Covenant* 1, no. 1 (November 2006), http://www.covenant.idc.ac.il/en/vol1/issue1/rubin.html (accessed April 12, 2011). Andrei Markovits argued, "In Western Europe as well as the United States, left-wing intellectuals began to perceive Israel as America's pit bull after the Six-Day War. Israel became America's tool in the latter's imperialist designs on the Middle East and beyond."

117. David Hirsh and Jane Ashworth, "Antisemitism on the Left," *Progress Magazine*, October 31, 2005, http://www.engageonline.org.uk/blog/article.php?id=88 (accessed April 12, 2011).

118. Perhaps reflecting a similar mentality, leftist Venezuelan president Hugo Chávez declared in 2005, "The World has enough for everybody, but some minorities, the descendants of the same people that crucified Christ, and of those that expelled Bolívar from here and in their own way crucified him . . . have taken control of the riches of the world." Again, in August 2006, Chávez continued his attack on the Jewish state, stating, "Israel criticizes Hitler a lot. So do we. But they have done something similar to what Hitler did, possibly worse, against half the world." Chávez's overt antisemitism is unusual, but not his hostility to Israel. Chávez, quoted in Claudio Lomnitz and Rafael Sanchez, "United by

Hate," *Boston Review*, July/August 2009, http://www.bostonreview,net/BR34.4 /lomnitz_sanchez.php (accessed April 12, 2011).

119. Hirsh and Ashworth, "Anti-Semitism on the Left."

120. See, for example, Taguieff, *Rising from the Muck*, 88–121.

121. Yet, as Simon Wiesenthal put it, "anyone siding with us only as long as we play the part of victim has, in a different way, remained the same old antisemite." Quoted in Michael Fineberg, foreword to *Antisemitism*, xvi.

122. Social psychologists have long conceived of political and social attitudes as a pathway to establishing and reinforcing one's identity. For mainstream Jews, support for Israel may help cement one's Jewish identity; for leftist Jews, opposition to Israel may help to differentiate them from mainstream Jews and establish an identity in the intelligentsia.

123. Baehr, "Why Does the Left Hate Israel?"

124. Fine, "New Antisemitism Theory."

125. Fineberg, foreword to *Antisemitism*, xvi.

Chapter 5. Ancient Roots, Modern Roots

1. Abd Al-Wahhab 'Adas, quoted in *Leading Egyptian Journalist: The Jews Are Behind Every Disaster or Terrorist Act*, Special Dispatch No. 700 (Washington, DC: MEMRI, April 23, 2004), http://www.memri.org/report/en/0/0/0/0/0/0/1114. htm (accessed May 1, 2011). All subsequent quotes by 'Adas come from this article.

2. Allport, *Nature of Prejudice*, 207.

3. Ibid., 208.

4. Hala Sarhan quotes come from an interview in the documentary film *Anti-Semitism in the 21st Century: The Resurgence*, written and directed by Andrew Goldberg (New York: Two Cats Productions, 2006).

5. An excerpt from *Knight without a Horse* is included in ibid. For a plot summary, see ADL, "Plot Summary: 'Horseman without a Horse,'" http://www.adl.org /special_reports/protocols/protocols_plot2.asp (accessed May 12, 2011).

6. Interestingly, as a talk show host a few years later, Sarhan's willingness to play fast and free with the facts got her into hot water; she apparently faked a program about prostitution in Egypt and was found out. For this, apparently 80 percent of the Egyptian viewing public felt her program should be taken off the air—and ultimately it was. However, there was no public outcry against her role in *Knight without a Ho*rse. See "Hala Sarhan Criticized by Her Fans," Al Bawaba Entertainment, October 16, 2007, http://www1.albawaba.com/en/entertainment /hala-sarhan-criticized-her-fans (accessed May 24, 2011).

7. The quotations from Hassan Hamed also come from an interview in the film *Anti-Semitism in the 21st Century*.

8. See Wistrich, *Lethal Obsession*, 793–95.

9. For documentation of the Holocaust, see—among many—Lucy S. Dawidowicz, *The War against the Jews, 1933–1945*, 10th anniv. ed. (New York: Free Press, 1986). For discussion of some attempts to deny the Holocaust, see—among several—Lipstadt, *Denying the Holocaust.*

10. *Iranian Cultural Foundation Mocks Holocaust*, Special Dispatch No. 3795 (Washington, DC: MEMRI, April 29, 2011), http://www.memri.org/report /en/0/0/0/0/0/0/5239.htm (accessed May 24, 2011). See also "Holocaust," http://www.holocartoons.com/english/step.php?id=8 (accessed May 24, 2011).

11. Some of these holes were closed, but there is ample evidence from court testimony, old photographs, and forensic investigations that they existed. There is not a shred of support for the deniers to be found here. See Deborah Lipstadt, Maureen MacLaughlin, and Dan Leshem, "Myth/Fact Sheets: 'Gas Chambers' Could Not Have Been Used for Gassing," Holocaust Denial on Trial, http:// www.hdot.org/en/learning/myth-fact/holes1 (accessed June 6, 2011).

12. "Palestinian Kids: The Jews Killed Arafat," Palestinian Media Watch, November 10, 2009, http://www.palwatch.org/main.aspx?fi=774&fld_id=774&doc_ id=1430 (accessed May 24, 2011).

13. Walid Fitaihi, quoted in Andrea Estes, "Islamic Society Urged to Respond; Group Still Quiet on Anti-Semitism Issue," *Boston Globe*, October 7, 2004.

14. The Islamic Society distanced itself from Dr. Fitaihi's views after they appeared in the *Boston Globe*. The society said, "Dr. Fitaihi has always advised Muslims to show the utmost respect towards Jews and Christians and in this case has insisted that his intent was not to incite hatred. Despite this, we recognize that some of Dr. Fitaihi's writings have been extremely hurtful to our Jewish friends and neighbors. We wish to be as clear as possible in stating that we in no way condone Dr. Fitaihi's words as quoted in recent news reports." Even so, one wonders how the good doctor could have shown "the utmost respect" for Jews, given his views, and why he was permitted to remain on the board of the organization after his views were exposed. See Andrea Estes, "Islamic Group Repudiates Trustee's Anti-Semitic Quotes," *Boston Globe*, October 14, 2004.

15. Hazem Sallah Abu Isma'il, quoted in *Egyptian Cleric and Former Islamic Lecturer in the U.S. Hazem Sallah Abu Isma'il on Al-Risala TV: Lectures on the Jews' Conflicts with Islam's Prophet Muhammad, Stating U.N. Documents Assert "82% of All Attempts to Corrupt Humanity Originate from the Jews,"* Special Dispatch No. 1161 (Washington, DC: MEMRI, May 10, 2006), http://www.memri.org /report/en/0/0/0/0/0/0/1685.htm (accessed May 24, 2011).

16. Kressel, *Mass Hate*, 18–19.

17. See Fatah, *Jew Is Not My Enemy*, 103–29. Fatah wrote, "Whereas Islamists and radical jihadis have had to use some fancy semantic footwork to incorporate anti-semitism into the Quran, there is no such need where the Hadith literature is concerned" (p. 121). See also Haggai Ben-Shammai, "Jew Hatred in the Islamic

Tradition and Koranic Exegesis," in *Legacy of Islamic Antisemitism*, 221–28, and "Quranic Verses," in *Legacy of Islamic Antisemitism*, 209–20.

18.   Fatah, *Jew Is Not My Enemy*, 130–47. Fatah argued, "At the time the *Sira* [i.e., the early Muslim biographies of Muhammad] was being pieced together, the great-grandsons of the pagan Meccans who had fought Muhammad had by now taken over the reins of Islam and were the ruling caliphs. It was in their interest to show their own forefathers as having been victims of Jewish scheming and conspiracy, thus allowing the [ruling] Umayyads to assuage some of the guilt associated with their reputation as kings who had stolen Islam from under the very noses of the Prophet's family" (p. 134).

19.   Lewis, *Semites and Anti-Semites*, 122; Bernard Lewis, *What Went Wrong? Western Impact and Middle Eastern Response* (New York: Oxford, 2002), 3–17; Jacob Lassner, "Can Arabs Be Antisemites? Race, Prejudice, and Political Culture in the Islamic Near East," in *Varieties of Antisemitism*, 345–69; and Cohen, *Under Crescent and Cross*.

20.   See, for example, Herf, *Nazi Propaganda*; Dalin and Rothmann, *Icon of Evil*; and Matthias Kuentzel, *Jihad and Jew-Hatred: Islamism, Nazism and the Roots of 9/11*, trans. Colin Meade (New York: Telos Press, 2009).

21.   See Riaz Hassan, "Interrupting a History of Tolerance: Anti-Semitism and the Arabs," *Asian Journal of Social Science* 37 (2009): 452–62. Hassan focuses exclusively on the impact of Zionism and the Arab-Israeli conflict. He fails to consider any of the other sources of anti-Jewish prejudice discussed in this chapter or to place contemporary developments into the context of traditional Islamic attitudes toward Jews.

22.   Gilbert, *In Ishmael's House*, 237–81.

23.   Tibi, *From Sayyid Qutb to Hamas*, 15.

24.   Bernard E. Whitley Jr. and Mary E. Kite, *The Psychology of Prejudice and Discrimination*, 2nd ed. (Belmont, CA: Wadsworth Cengage Learning, 2010), 26, 256. They wrote, "It is important to recognize that the vast majority of social psychological work in the last century dealing with prejudice and discrimination was conducted in North America; this situation did not change until the late 1970s when Western European psychologists began to gain prominence in the field. This is not to say that stereotyping, prejudice, and discrimination are unique to the United States; even a cursory survey leaves little doubt that these processes are found in all nations" (p. 26). See also Kressel, "Urgent Need."

25.   See John Duckitt, *The Social Psychology of Prejudice* (Westport, CT: Praeger, 1994).

26.   Also, according to realistic conflict theory, one needs to make assumptions about which group is dominant and which subordinate in order to draw more insightful conclusions, yet such assumptions are not so easily made about the Arab-Muslim-Palestinian–Israeli-Jewish conflict.

27. See Henri Tajfel and John C. Turner, "The Social Identity Theory of Intergroup Behavior," in *Psychology of Intergroup Relations*, 2nd ed., ed. S. Worchel and W. G. Austin (Chicago: Nelson-Hall, 1986), 7–27.
28. B. Lickel, N. Miller, D. M. Stenstrom, T. F. Denson, and T. Schmader, "Vicarious Retribution: The Role of Collective Blame in Intergroup Aggression," *Personality and Social Psychology Review* 10 (2006): 372–90.
29. S. Roccas and M. B. Brewer, "Social Identity Complexity," *Personality and Social Psychology Review* 6 (2002): 88–106.
30. See David Van Bjema, "Was Saint Augustine Good for the Jews?," *Time*, December 7, 2008, http://www.time.com/time/nation/article/0,8599,1864878,00.html (accessed May 24, 2011).
31. Lewis, *Semites and Anti-Semites*, 118.
32. See Bostom, ed., *Legacy of Islamic Antisemitism*, for a compilation of several early Islamic sources.
33. See, for example, Fouad Ajami, *Dream Palace of the Arabs: A Generation's Odyssey* (New York: Pantheon, 1998), and David Pryce-Jones, *The Closed Circle: An Interpretation of the Arabs* (New York: HarperPerennial, 1991).
34. Karsh, *Islamic Imperialism*.
35. Barry M. Rubin, *Modern Dictators: Third World Coup Makers, Strongmen, and Populist Tyrants* (New York: McGraw-Hill, 1987).
36. See, for example, Yossef Bodansky, *Islamic Anti-Semitism as a Political Instrument* (Houston, TX: Freeman Center for Strategic Studies, 1999), 3–6.
37. Bernard Lewis, *The Crisis of Islam: Holy War and Unholy Terror* (New York: Modern Library, 2003), 93.
38. See, for example, I. Walker and H. J. Smith, eds., *Relative Deprivation: Specification, Development, and Integration* (New York: Cambridge, 2002), and Whitley and Kite, *Psychology of Prejudice*, 341–51.
39. Allport, *Nature of Prejudice*, 243–60.
40. Peter Glick, "Sacrificial Lambs Dressed in Wolves' Clothing: Envious Prejudice, Ideology, and the Scapegoating of the Jews," in *Understanding Genocide: The Social Psychology of the Holocaust*, ed. L. S. Newman and R. Erber (New York: Oxford, 2002), 113–42.
41. See Barry Rubin, "How the PLO 'Adapted' Antisemitism as 'Anti-Zionism'" (lecture, Yale University, New Haven, CT, October 15, 2009), http://vimeo.com/7439044 (accessed April 24, 2012).
42. Ibid.
43. See Leon Festinger, *A Theory of Cognitive Dissonance* (Evanston, IL: Row, Peterson, 1957), and Joel Cooper, *Cognitive Dissonance: 50 Years of a Classic Theory* (Thousand Oaks, CA: Sage, 2007).
44. Mortimer Ostow, "Commentary on 'Mass Hatred in the Muslim and Arab

World: The Neglected Problem of Anti-Semitism' by Neil Kressel," *International Journal of Applied Psychoanalytic Studies* 4 (2007): 229.

45. Khaled al-Khlewi and Omar, quoted in *Saudi Cleric Khaled Al-Khlewi Teaches Children to Hate Jews* (Washington, DC: MEMRI, January 11, 2009), http://www.memritv.org/clip_transcript/en/2061.htm (accessed May 24, 2011).

46. Salam Abd al-Qawi, quoted in *Egyptian Clerics Encourage Martyrdom in Gaza: "We Must Love Death"; "There Are Black-Eyed Virgins Ready for You"; "We Must Teach Our Children to . . . Hate the Jews,"* Special Dispatch No. 2193 (Washington, DC: MEMRI, January 16, 2009), http://www.memri.org/report/en/0/0/0/0/0/0/3028.htm (accessed May 24, 2011).

47. See *Hizbullah Al-Manar TV's Children's Claymation Special.*

48. See "Hamas' Mickey Mouse Character Is 'Martyred' in the Final Episode of the 'Pioneers of Tomorrow' Children Show on Hamas TV," Video Clip No. 1497 (Washington, DC: MEMRI, June 29, 2007), http://www.memritv.org/clip/en/1497.htm and http://www.memri.org/report/en/0/0/0/0/0/0/2296.htm (accessed May 24, 2011). There were some (disputed) charges that MEMRI's translation of this episode was inaccurate on a few substantial points—although, more generally, MEMRI's translations have been widely respected. Regardless of which translation of the Farfour episode one chooses, the point remains valid that the program prepares Palestinian children for hatred and prejudice. Charges of translation errors are made in "MEMRI and Its Mickey Mouse Translation," Facts on the Ground, May 14, 2007, http://www.factsontheground.co.uk/2007/05/14/memri-and-its-mickey-mouse-translation/ (accessed May 24, 2011).

49. Quoted in "Hate TV," *Daily News* (New York), August 3, 2009.

50. Hirsi Ali, *Infidel*, 47.

51. Darwish, *Now They Call Me Infidel*, 3.

52. Manji, *Trouble with Islam*, 15.

53. Rif'at Sayyed Ahmad, quoted in Alex Grobman and Rafael Medoff, *Holocaust Denial: A Global Survey—2004* (Melrose Park, PA: David S. Wyman Institute for Holocaust Studies, 2004), http://www.wymaninstitute.org/articles/2004-denialreport.php (accessed May 24, 2011).

54. Muhammad Al-Zurqani, quoted in ibid.

55. See "Arab Press Ablaze with Rumors that Mu'ammar Gaddafi Is Secretly a Jew," Translating Jihad, March 1, 2011, http://translating-jihad.blogspot.com/2011/03/arab-press-ablaze-with-rumors-that.html (accessed May 24, 2011).

56. See Robert F. Worth, "Activist Relies on Islam to Fight for Animal Rights," *New York Times*, November 21, 2010, http://www.nytimes.com/2010/11/22/world/africa/22egypt.html (accessed May 24, 2011).

57. Tufail Ahmad, *Pakistan's Jewish Problem*, Inquiry and Analysis Series Report No. 676 (Washington, DC: MEMRI, March 13, 2011), http://www.memri.org/report/en/print5090.htm (accessed May 24, 2011).

58. Sheila Musaji, "Israeli Organ Trafficking, Much Ado about Something," American Muslim, April 8, 2010, http://www.theamericanmuslim.org/tam.php/features/articles/israeli_organ_trafficking_much_ado_about_something/ (accessed May 24, 2010).

59. These last two examples are discussed in Gabriel Schoenfeld, *The Return of Anti-Semitism* (San Francisco: Encounter, 2004), 14–23.

60. Ibid., 141.

61. Ahmad, "Pakistan's Jewish Problem." Ahmad wrote, "There is a small liberal class of political commentators, members of non-governmental organizations, columnists and journalists whose views are limited to mainly English-language media, especially the *Dawn* and *Daily Times* newspapers. However, in Pakistan it is the Urdu-language newspapers and magazines, not the English-language media, which exercise massive influence on mass public opinion" (p. 12).

62. Hannah Rosenthal, "Meeting with Ambassadors from Sweden, Netherlands, Hungary, Lithuania, and Saudi Arabia," *SEAS Monitor*, February/March 2011, http://www.state.gov/documents/organization/161061.pdf (accessed May 24, 2011).

63. William C. Flook, "State Department: Saudis to Scrub Curriculum by School Year Start," *Examiner*, June 13, 2008, http://www.campus-watch.org/article/id/5248 (accessed May 24, 2011).

64. J. J. Sutherland, "Saudi 'Anti-Semitic' Curriculum Taught to Thousands of Students in UK," National Public Radio, November 22, 2010, http://www.wbur.org/npr/131507214/saudi-anti-semitic-curriculum-taught-to-thousands-of-students-in-uk (accessed May 24, 2011), and John F. Burns, "Lessons of Hate at Islamic School Network in Britain," *New York Times*, November 23, 2010.

65. Arnon Groiss, comp., *The West, Christians, and Jews in Saudi Arabian Schoolbooks* (Jerusalem: Center for Monitoring the Impact of Peace, 2003), http://www.ajcarchives.org/main.php?GroupingId=4070 (accessed May 24, 2011).

66. Arnon Groiss, *The West, Christians, Israel and Jews in Saudi Arabian Schoolbooks: A Research Update*, with Ido Mizrahi (Jerusalem: Institute for Monitoring Peace and Cultural Tolerance in School Education, 2008), http://impact-se.org/docs/reports/SA/SA2008.pdf (May 24, 2011).

67. See, for example, American Jewish Committee, "AJC-CMIP Report: Small Progress in Revising Palestinian Textbooks," press release, March 19, 2008, http://www.reuters.com/article/2008/03/19/idUS162747+19-Mar-2008+PRN20080319 (accessed May 24, 2011); Hillary Clinton, "Introduction to Itamar Marcus's Overview of PMW's Report on Palestinian Schoolbooks" (speech, Washington, DC, February 8, 2007), http://palwatch.org/STORAGE/special%20reports/Clinton_Marcus_schoolbooks_report_USSenate.pdf (accessed May 24, 2011), and Itamar Marcus, "Overview of PMW's Report on Palestinian Schoolbooks" (presentation, Washington, DC, February 8, 2007),

http://palwatch.org/STORAGE/special%20reports/Clinton_Marcus_school
books_report_USSenate.pdf (accessed May 24, 2011).

68. See Itamar Marcus and Barbara Crook, "Anti-Semitism among Palestinian Authority Academics," in *Academics against Israel and the Jews*, 242–49.
69. Jirar al-Qidwa, quoted in ibid., 243.
70. Hassan Khader, quoted in ibid., 244.
71. Khader Abbas, quoted in ibid., 245, 247.
72. Khawaja, "Problem of Muslim Anti-Semitism."
73. Clinton, "Introduction."

Chapter 6. Fighting Back against Bigotry

1. *Antisemitism in the Turkish Media (Part II)—Turkish Intellectuals against Anti-Semitism*, Special Dispatch No. 904 (Washington, DC: MEMRI, May 5, 2005), http://www.memri.org/report/en/0/0/0/0/0/0/1371.htm (accessed July 1, 2011). All subsequent references to the petition are taken from this translation.
2. Rifat N. Bali, "Present-Day Anti-Semitism in Turkey," *Post-Holocaust and Anti-Semitism* 84 (August 2009), http://www.jcpa.org/JCPA/Templates/ShowPage.asp?DRIT=3&DBID=1&LNGID=1&TMID=111&FID=624&PID=0&IID=3048&TTL=Present-Day_Anti-Semitism_in_Turkey (accessed July 1, 2011), and Rifat N. Bali, *A Scapegoat for All Seasons: The Donmes or Crypto-Jews of Turkey* (Piscataway, NJ: Gorgias Press, 2010).
3. See Bali, *Scapegoat*.
4. See Bali, "Present-Day Anti-Semitism." See also *Antisemitism in the Turkish Media: Part 1*, Special Dispatch No. 900 (Washington, DC: MEMRI, April 28, 2005), http://www.memri.org/report/en/0/0/0/0/0/0/1365.htm (accessed July 1, 2011).
5. See Rifat N. Bali, "The Slow Disappearance of Turkey's Jewish Community," *Post-Holocaust and Anti-Semitism* 63 (December 2010), http://www.jcpa.org/JCPA/Templates/ShowPage.asp?DRIT=4&DBID=1&LNGID=1&TMID=111&FID=623&PID=0&IID=5617&TTL=The_Slow_Disappearance_of_Turkey%27s_Jewish_Community (accessed July 1, 2011).
6. Bali, "Present-Day Anti-Semitism."
7. Selçuk Gültaşlı, quoted in ibid.
8. Rifat N. Bali, e-mail to author, June 30, 2011.
9. Ibid. Bali was one of the signers of the petition.
10. Amr Bargisi and Samuel Tadros, "Why Are Egypt's 'Liberals' Anti-Semitic?" *Wall Street Journal*, October 28, 2009, http://online.wsj.com/article/SB10001424052748704335904574497143564035718.html (accessed July 1, 2011).
11. Ben Birnbaum, "Egypt Party Leader: Holocaust Is 'a Lie,'" *Washington Times*, July 5, 2011, http://www.washingtontimes.com/news/2011/jul/5/egypt-party-leader-holocaust-is-a-lie/ (accessed July 11, 2011).

12. Amr Bargisi, "Egypt's Jew Haters Deserve Ostracism in the West: More Proof
     the Prejudice Has Nothing to Do with Israel," *Wall Street Journal*, December 1,
     2008, http://online.wsj.com/article/SB122809559103068085.html (accessed
     July 1, 2011). In response, Bargisi suggested, "Perhaps Western institutions
     could adopt a similar practice, refusing to invite to their various functions any
     editors who allow their pages to become Jew-hatred platforms."
13. Amr Bargisi, quoted in David Keyes, "Interview with Amr Bargisi, Egyptian
     Classical Liberal," CyberDissidents.org, January 4, 2011, http://www.cyber
     dissidents.org/bin/content.cgi?ID=509&q=3&s=24 (accessed July 1, 2011).
14. This definition is usually attributed to Hungarian nobleman Joseph Eötvösz.
15. See, for example, *Criticism of Tehran Holocaust Denial Conference in Arab and
     Iranian Media*, Special Dispatch No. 1425 (Washington, DC: MEMRI, Janu-
     ary 15, 2007), http://www.memri.org/report/en/print2010.htm (accessed July
     1, 2011), and Y. Carmon, *Harbingers of Change in the Antisemitic Discourse in
     the Arab World*, Inquiry and Analysis Series Report No. 135 (Washington, DC:
     MEMRI, April 23, 2003), http://www.memri.org/report/en/print854.htm (ac-
     cessed July 1, 2011).
16. *Arab Intellectual: The Holocaust Must Be Remembered by Everybody—for It Target-
     ed the Very Essence of Humanity*, Special Dispatch No. 2322 (Washington, DC:
     MEMRI, April 22, 2009), http://www.memri.org/report/en/0/0/0/0/0/0/3252
     .htm (accessed July 1, 2011).
17. *Palestinian Peace Activist Writes on "Lessons of the Holocaust,"* Special Dispatch
     No. 2398 (Washington, DC: MEMRI, June 11, 2009), http://www.memri.org
     /report/en/0/0/0/0/0/0/3358.htm (accessed July 1, 2011).
18. *Editor of Egyptian Weekly Criticizes Arab Embrace of European Anti-Semitism*, Spe-
     cial Dispatch No. 703 (Washington, DC: MEMRI, April 29, 2004), http://www
     .memri.org/report/en/print1117.htm (accessed July 1, 2011). Some vigorous
     debate in the Arab press centered on the airing of the previously discussed Egyp-
     tian television series *Knight without a Horse*, which was based on *The Protocols*.
     See *Arab Press Debates Antisemitic Egyptian Series "A Knight without a Horse,"*
     Inquiry and Analysis Nos. 109, 113, 114 (Washington, DC: MEMRI, November–
     December 2002), http://www.memri.org/report/en/0/0/0/0/0/0/175/775.htm
     (accessed July 1, 2011).
19. *Palestinian Academic: Hamas Must Amend Its Charter*, Special Dispatch No.
     2266 (Washington, DC: MEMRI, March 2, 2009), http://www.memri.org
     /report/en/0/0/0/0/0/0/115/3175.htm (accessed July 1, 2011).
20. *To the Arab Jews: Happy Passover!* Special Dispatch No. 1556 (Washington, DC:
     MEMRI, April 24, 2007), http://www.memri.org/report/en/0/0/0/0/0/0/2161
     .htm (accessed July 1, 2011).
21. Cited in Dominic Casciani, "Muslims Urge End to Anti-Semitism," BBC News,

January 16, 2009, http://news.bbc.co.uk/2/hi/uk_news/7831897.stm (accessed July 1, 2011).

22. Khazen article, quoted in A. Cooper and Y. Adlerstein, "The Problem in the New Arab Spring," *Jerusalem Post*, April 24, 2011, http://www.jpost.com/Landed Pages/PrintArticle.aspx?id=217683 (accessed July 1, 2011).

23. Ibid.

24. Casciani, "Muslims Urge End."

25. Tariq Ramadan's position on the Jews and antisemitism would take a volume to decipher; indeed several have been written. His intellectual background and familiarity with Western Europe has taught him the intellectual costs associated with overt antisemitism. Thus, he seeks on occasion to cleanse his underlying Islamist ideology of its most obvious and distasteful antisemitic elements, principally when presenting to Western audiences. He tries, as best he can, to sweep under the rug most of the virulent antisemitism associated with his intellectual heroes—grandfather Hassan al-Banna, Sheikh Qaradawi, and others—but he never actually breaks with them on the most critical issues. Some believe that, nonetheless, his ultimate goal is to reform Islamism. Yet, despite his condemnations of the most obscene manifestations of antisemitism, he has himself engaged in a bit of his own Jew-baiting as when he denounced some of the top writers in France for acting out of their Jewishness. Thus, in sum, I see him as a pragmatic and disingenuous anti-antisemite. If his desire to cleanse Islamism of antisemitism were, in fact, genuine, he could do so many more things from his position of prominence. The best discussion of Ramadan's outlook is Berman, *Flight of the Intellectuals*, 293–99 (notwithstanding his unseemly quarrel with Ian Buruma). See also Dexter Van Zile, "Tariq Ramadan Obscures the Truth about Muslim Brotherhood," Committee for Accuracy in Middle East Reporting for America (CAMERA), February 16, 2011, http://www.camera.org/index.asp?x_print=1&x_context=2&x_outlet=35&x_article=1996 (accessed July 1, 2011). But see also Tariq Ramadan, "Muslims against Anti-Semitism," *UN Chronicle*, no. 414 (December 1, 2004).

26. See, for example, Irshad Manji, *Allah, Liberty, and Love: The Courage to Reconcile Faith and Freedom* (New York: Free Press, 2011), 1, and Berman, *Flight of the Intellectuals*, 293–99.

27. Irfan Khawaja, e-mail to author, June 28, 2011. Khawaja added, "This is really a laundry list, though. I don't have an overarching theory about this."

28. Khaleel Mohammed, quoted in Fatah, *Jew Is Not My Enemy*, 103.

29. Khaleel Mohammed, "We Are Our Own Enemies," *Ottawa Citizen*, February 19, 2007, http://communities.canada.com/ottawacitizen/forums/p/7513/52956.aspx (accessed July 1, 2011, site disabled).

30. Khaleel Mohammed, quoted in Jamie Glazov, "The Koran and the Jews," *Front*

Page Magazine, June 3, 2004, http://archive.frontpagemag.com/readArticle
.aspx?ARTID=12825 (accessed July 1, 2011).

31. Ibid.

32. See, for example, Sven Behrisch, "The Zionist Imam," *Jerusalem Post* (Christian ed., July 19, 2010, http://www.jpost.com/ChristianInIsrael/Blogs/Article
.aspx?id=181905. See also Abdul Hadi Palazzi, "Hazim Nada's Deception,"
Daily Targum (Rutgers University), March 23, 2004.

33. Extensive information about Sheikh Palazzi's views was found at the Italian Muslim Assembly website, http://www.amislam.com/. Unfortunately, Palazzi's website is no longer operational. For an overview of his perspective, see Abdul Hadi
Palazzi, "The Islamists Have It Wrong," *Middle East Quarterly* 8, no. 3 (2001):
3–12, http://www.meforum.org/14/the-islamists-have-it-wrong.

34. Abdul Hadi Palazzi, "Anti-Zionism and Antisemitism in the Contemporary Islamic Milieu," Italian Muslim Assembly, http://www.amislam.com/racism.htm
(accessed July 1, 2011, site now disabled).

35. See Manji, *Allah, Liberty, and Love*, and Manji, *Trouble with Islam*. Manji's website is https://www.irshadmanji.com/.

36. Manji, *Allah, Liberty, and Love*, book jacket.

37. Ibid., xix.

38. Hattab, "Absurdity of Anti-Semitism in the Arab World," 224, 225, 229.

39. I initially met Tibi more than thirty years ago at an Israeli-Palestinian conflict
resolution workshop held at Harvard University under the sponsorship of social
psychologist Herbert Kelman.

40. Tibi, *From Sayyid Qutb to Hamas*. See also Bassam Tibi, "The Islamist Islamization
of Antisemitism" (lecture, Yale University, New Haven, CT, August 24, 2010),
http://vimeo.com/20214853 (accessed July 1, 2011).

41. Fatah, *Jew Is Not My Enemy*, 201.

42. Ibid., xix.

43. Ibid., 78–102.

44. Ibid., xvii.

45. See, among others, Sultan, *God Who Hates*; Ibn Warraq (pseudonym), *Why I Am
Not a Muslim* (Amherst, NY: Prometheus, 1995); Mark A. Gabriel, *Islam and the
Jews* (Lake Mary, FL: Charisma House, 2003); Darwish, *Now They Call Me Infidel*; Hirsi Ali, *Infidel*; Irfan Khawaja, "The Problem of Muslim Anti-Semitism,"
Pakistan Today, January 22, 2003, http://www.centerforinquiry.net/isis/articles
_and_books/the_problem_of_muslim_anti_semitism/ (July 1, 2011); and Irfan
Khawaja, "Muslim Anti-Semitism, Zionist Orientalism, and Practical Identity,"
Proteus: A Journal of Ideas 23, no. 2 (Fall 2006): 47–54.

46. Kamel Al-Najjar, cited in *Reformist Writer Dr. Kamel Al-Najjar: "If the Muslims
Are Serious about Presenting the Radiant Face of Islam . . . They Must . . . Acknowledge Their Dark Past,"* Special Dispatch No. 1128 (Washington, DC: MEMRI,

March 29, 2006), http://www.memri.org/report/en/0/0/0/0/0/0/1650.htm (accessed July 1, 2011).

47. See, for example, Crimp and Richardson, eds., *Why We Left.*

48. See, for example, Susan Jacoby, *Freethinkers: A History of American Secularism* (New York: Metropolitan Books, 2004), and Dacey, *Secular Conscience.*

49. Irfan Khawaja, e-mail to author, June 28, 2011.

50. "About," MuslimMatters.org, http://muslimmatters.org/about/ (accessed July 1, 2011).

51. Amad, "Tarek Fatah Does Not Represent Me: Muslims 101 for Media," MuslimMatters.org, January 9, 2008, http://muslimmatters.org/2008/01/09/tarek -fatah-and-does-not-represent-me-muslims-101-for-media/.

52. The article about Fatah appeared prior to the publication of his book on Muslim antisemitism, although he had published other works and had expressed his progressive views on this topic and others previously in various forums. Further evidence of the gap between Fatah's approach and mainstream approaches, even in the West, can be seen in a letter to the editor of the website Torontopedia ostensibly from a non-Muslim who expressed similar views about Fatah: "I have a number of friends who are progressive Muslims. Some are practicing Muslims, some are more secular, most were brought up in Canada and have the typically moderate views that 1.5 or 2nd generation Canadians have. None of them feel that Mr. Fatah's views are representative of them or their faith. There is a Facebook group called 'Tarek Fatah does not represent me' with 738 members. The frustration and outrage from Muslims, that I have contact with, every time they see Mr. Fatah in the media represented as a 'Muslim leader' is palpable. My question to you is: why do you continue to present Mr. Fatah as a progressive Muslim leader? . . . I fail to understand why you would continue to print Mr. Fatah's opinions at the expense of alienating the Muslim community, who from what I understand, think that he is crazy." Karen Sun, "Tarek Fatah Does Not Represent the Muslim Community," letter to the editor, Torontopedia, February 1, 2008, http://www.torontopedia.ca/Tarek_Fatah_does_not_represent_the _Muslim_Community (accessed July 1, 2011).

53. Manji, *Allah, Liberty, and Love*, xvii, xx.

54. King Hussein, "Tribute," in *Antisemitism*, lviii.

55. Neela Banerjee, "Jordan's Leader Calls for Unity among Religions," *New York Times*, February 3, 2006.

56. Osama El-Baz, quoted in Carmon, *Harbingers of Change.*

57. Basharat Tahir Quraishy, "Jewish-Muslim Harmony," in *Antisemitism*, li.

58. Sayyid M. Syeed, "Anti-Semitism Has No Place in Islam," *Forward*, April 1, 2011, http://www.forward.com/articles/136421/ (accessed July 1, 2011).

59. "Fayyad: Jews Can Be Equal Citizens in Palestinian State," Haaretz.com, July 5, 2009, http://www.haaretz.com/news/fayyad-jews-can-be-equal-citizens-in

-palestinian-state-1.279395 (accessed July 1, 2011). See also Daniel Pipes, "Salam Fayyad Says Yes to Jews Living in a Palestinian State," DanielPipes.org (blog), July 5, 2009, http://www.danielpipes.org/blog/2009/07/salam-fayyad-jews-welcome-in-palestinian-state (accessed July 1, 2011).

60. Schoenfeld, *Return of Anti-Semitism*, 142.
61. See, for example, "ISNA's Ties to Terror: Images in Conflict," Investigative Project on Terrorism, November 10, 2003, http://www.investigativeproject.org/1076/isnas-ties-to-terror (accessed July 1, 2011); "ISNA Admits Hamas Ties," *IPT News*, July 25, 2008, http://www.investigativeproject.org/732/isna-admits-hamas-ties (accessed July 1, 2008); "Council on American-Islamic Relations (CAIR): Positions on Israel and Jews," Anti-Defamation League, July 15, 2010, http://www.adl.org/Israel/cair/Positions2.asp (accessed July 1, 2011).
62. MacShane, *Globalising Hatred*, 163.
63. Foxman, *Never Again?*, 277–78.
64. See, among others, Adam Brodsky, "Yale's Anti-Semitism Whitewash," *New York Post*, July 7, 2011, http://www.nypost.com/p/news/opinion/opedcolumnists/yale_anti_semitism_whitewash_8vdiunersgmu8WlueAGyTP (accessed July 11, 2011).
65. Barack Obama, "Remarks by the President on a New Beginning" (speech, Cairo University, Cairo, June 4, 2009), http://www.whitehouse.gov/the_press_office/Remarks-by-the-President-at-Cairo-University-6-04-09/ (accessed July 1, 2011).
66. Schoenfeld, *Return of Anti-Semitism*, 145.
67. Peter Wilby, quoted in Harrison, *Resurgence*, 33.
68. See, for example, Kady O'Malley, "Updated—For the Record: The Full Text of the Ottawa Protocol," Inside Politics Blog, November 10, 2010, http://www.cbc.ca/news/politics/inside-politics-blog/2010/11/for-the-record-the-full-text-of-the-ottawa-protocol.html (accessed July 1, 2011); "The London Declaration on Combating Anti-Semitism," February 2009, http://www.communities.gov.uk/documents/corporate/pdf/1151284.pdf (accessed July 1, 2011); and Organization for Security and Co-Operation in Europe (OSCE), "OSCE 'Berlin Declaration' Sets Out Concrete Measures to Fight Anti-Semitism," press release, April 29, 2004, http://www.osce.org/cio/56259 (accessed July 1, 2011).
69. Taguieff, *Rising from the Muck*, 115.
70. See Ross and Makovsky, *Myths, Illusions, and Peace*, 168–82.
71. Richard Holbrooke, quoted in Natasha Mozgovaya, "Charge Ahmadinejad with Incitement to Genocide, Say Former U.S., Israeli Envoys to UN," Haaretz.com, September 29, 2008, http://www.haaretz.com/news/charge-ahmadinejad-with-incitement-to-genocide-say-former-u-s-israeli-envoys-to-un-1.254451 (accessed July 1, 2011).

Suggestions for Further Reading

1. Martin Gilbert's *In Ishmael's House: A History of Jews in Muslim Lands* (New Haven, CT: Yale University Press, 2010) provides a recent, readable, balanced, and generally impressive historical overview of the treatment of Jews in many parts of the Muslim world.

2. Robert S. Wistrich's massive *A Lethal Obsession: Anti-Semitism from Antiquity to the Global Jihad* (New York: Random House, 2010) is comprehensive, scholarly, and intellectually honest in its willingness to face controversial issues. Marvin Perry and Frederick M. Schweitzer's *Antisemitism: Myth and Hate from Antiquity to the Present* (New York: Palgrave, 2002) is another good historical overview, although it pays less attention to contemporary Islamic Jew-hatred than does Wistrich's book.

3. Tarek Fatah's *The Jew Is Not My Enemy: Unveiling the Myths That Fuel Muslim Anti-Semitism* (Toronto: McClelland and Stewart, 2010) is a brave and morally centered book that also includes some fascinating speculation about Muslim religious history.

4. Andrew Bostom's edited anthology *The Legacy of Islamic Antisemitism: From Sacred Texts to Solemn History* (Amherst, NY: Prometheus, 2008) assembles English translations of critical documents and analyses. I do not always agree with Bostom's assessment of this evidence, but there can be no argument that he has rendered an important service by making hard-to-find documents accessible.

5. Many of Bernard Lewis's books remain critical reading. His *Semites and Anti-Semites: An Inquiry into Conflict and Prejudice* (New York: Norton, 1986) is dated but brilliant.

6. There is still much value in the works of W. Montgomery Watt, especially *Muhammad: The Prophet and Statesman* (London: Oxford University Press, 1961) and *Islamic Political Thought: The Basic Concepts* (Edinburgh: Edinburgh University Press, 1968). H. A. R. Gibb's *Mohammedanism: An Historical Survey* (London: Oxford University Press, 1970) also shows how Islam was perceived

by top scholars in the era before Edward Said's *Orientalism* (New York: Vintage, 1979) and the age of terrorism.

7. Various perspectives on the origins of Western indifference to some form of anti-semitism can be found—sometimes in passing—in Nick Cohen's *What's Left? How the Left Lost Its Way* (New York: Harper, 2007), Paul Berman's *The Flight of the Intellectuals* (Brooklyn, NY: Melville House, 2010), Bernard Harrison's *The Resurgence of Anti-Semitism: Jews, Israel, and Liberal Opinion* (Lanham, MD: Rowman and Littlefield, 2006), Pierre-André Taguieff's *Rising from the Muck: The New Anti-Semitism in Europe* (translated by Patrick Camiller; Chicago: Ivan R. Dee, 2004), Fiamma Nirenstein's *Terror: The New Anti-Semitism and the War against the West* (translated by Anne Milano Appel; Hanover, NH: Smith and Kraus, 2005), Gabriel Schoenfeld's *The Return of Anti-Semitism* (San Francisco: Encounter, 2004), Paul Iganski and Barry Kosmin's anthology *A New Antisemitism? Debating Judeophobia in 21st-Century Britain* (London: Profile, 2003), Denis MacShane's *Globalising Hatred: The New Antisemitism* (London: Weidenfeld and Nicolson, 2008), Phyllis Chesler's *The New Anti-Semitism: The Current Crisis and What We Must Do about It* (San Francisco: Jossey-Bass, 2003), Bruce Bawer's *While Europe Slept: How Radical Islam Is Destroying the West from Within* (New York: Doubleday, 2006), Michael Berenbaum's anthology *Not Your Father's Antisemitism: Hatred of the Jews in the 21st Century* (St. Paul, MN: Paragon House, 2008), Ron Rosenbaum's anthology *Those Who Forget the Past: The Question of Anti-Semitism* (New York: Random House, 2004), and Manfred Gerstenfeld's anthology *Academics against Israel and the Jews* (2nd ed.; Jerusalem: Jerusalem Center for Public Affairs, 2008). These books have not received the attention they deserve.

8. Martin Kramer's *Ivory Towers on Sand: The Failure of Middle Eastern Studies in America* (Washington, DC: Washington Institute for Near East Policy, 2001) remains an essential guide to a discipline in trouble.

9. Efraim Karsh's fascinating *Islamic Imperialism: A History* (updated ed.; New Haven, CT: Yale University Press, 2007) should be read as a corrective to currently prevailing perspectives on Islamic political history.

10. Hadassa Ben-Itto's *The Lie That Wouldn't Die: The Protocols of the Elders of Zion* (London: Vallentine Mitchell, 2005) is perhaps the most lively and up-to-date of several fine histories of *The Protocols*. Unfortunately, it lacks adequate source citations.

11. Ed Husain's *The Islamist: Why I Joined Radical Islam in Britain, What I Saw Inside and Why I Left* (London: Penguin, 2007), Ayaan Hirsi Ali's *Infidel* (New York: Free Press, 2007), and Nonie Darwish's *Now They Call Me Infidel: Why I Renounced Jihad for America, Israel, and the War on Terror* (New York: Sentinel, 2006)—all are brave, gripping, controversial memoirs by former "insiders" that testify to the prevalence of Jew-hatred in parts of the Islamic community. For their efforts, all

three authors have found themselves the targets of considerable scorn and abuse, and also threats of violence.

12. David Matas's *Aftershock: Anti-Zionism and Antisemitism* (Toronto: Dundurn, 2005) and, a quarter century earlier, Jacques Givet's *The Anti-Zionist Complex* (translated by Evelyn Abel; Englewood, NJ: SBS Publishing, 1982) are two interesting attempts to describe the extreme character of Arab hostility toward Zionism and Israel.

13. Jeffrey Herf's *Nazi Propaganda for the Arab World* (New Haven, CT: Yale University Press, 2009) and David G. Dalin and John F. Rothmann's *Icon of Evil: Hitler's Mufti and the Rise of Radical Islam* (New Brunswick, NJ: Transaction Publishers, 2009) each offer controversial theses, but both are important efforts to call attention to ties between Nazism and Islamic antisemitism.

14. No new book has ever supplanted Gordon Allport's masterful *The Nature of Prejudice* (Cambridge, MA: Addison-Wesley, 1979), although readers looking for an account of recent developments in the psychology of bigotry might turn to Bernard E. Whitley Jr. and Mary E. Kite, *The Psychology of Prejudice and Discrimination* (2nd ed.; Belmont, CA: Wadsworth Cengage Learning, 2010).

15. My own *Bad Faith: The Danger of Religious Extremism* (Amherst, NY: Prometheus, 2007) is an attempt to understand the psychological, sociological, historical, and theological sources of extremism in Judaism, Christianity, and Islam.

16. Readers who wish to stay current with the latest anti-Jewish television broadcasts in Muslim countries should consult the Middle East Media Research Institute TV Monitor Project's Antisemitism Documentation Project (http://www.memritv .org/subject/en/64.htm).

But be forewarned. Every single source listed here has been denounced by someone—possibly in the Middle East studies, Far Left, or extremist (or even moderate) Muslim communities—as biased. Thus, regarding Muslim antisemitism, there are no universally acknowledged objective sources. The reader must decide where truth really lies. And he or she must do so without adopting the intellectually lazy, even bankrupt, approach of "splitting the difference."

Index

261

Wafd Party, 183
Al-Wahhab Adas, Abd, 152
Walzer, Michael, 146
war on terrorism, 143–44
Washington Institute for Near East Policy, 89
Webb, Suhaib, 26
Weinstein, Warren, 2
Western countries/leaders
    attitude toward antisemitism by, 10, 13, 57
    attitude toward Muslims in, 134–36
    public's view of Jews in, 37
    role of, 201–6
    wishful thinking of, 145–47
Western media
    Ayatollah Khomeini and, 9
    Sheikh Tantawi and, 3, 26
Whig-Cliosophic Society, 62, 64
Who Speaks for Islam? What a Billion Muslims Really Think (Esposito and Mogahed), 89
Wiesel, Elie, 3
Wilby, Peter, 203
Williams, Juan, 138

Wistrich, Robert, 13, 143, 144
Wittgenstein, Ludwig, 79
World Conference Against Racism, 12
World Union of Progressive Judaism (WUPJ), 84

Yalçin, Soner, 180
Yale Initiative for the Interdisciplinary Study of Anti-Semitism (YIISA), 15, 202
Yunus, Muhammad, 42

Al-Zahhar, Najah, 38
Zakariya, Fouad, 19
al-Zawahiri, Ayman, 27
Zevi, Sabbetai, 179
Zionism/Zionist
    dubious uses of term, 102–3, 113
    impact of, 115, 162
    various definitions of, 102
Zionist-occupied government (ZOG) in Washington, 68, 103
Zola, Émile, 14
Al-Zurqani, Muhammad, 173

About the Author

Neil J. Kressel, who holds a PhD in social psychology from Harvard University, has taught at Harvard, New York University, and elsewhere. Currently, he directs the honors program in the social sciences at William Paterson University. In 2008 he was visiting associate professor at the Yale Initiative for the Interdisciplinary Study of Antisemitism. He is the author of three previously published books, including *Mass Hate: The Global Rise of Genocide and Terror*. He lives in northern New Jersey.